THE POLITICS OF LEFT-WING VIOLENCE IN ITALY, 1969–85

The Politics of Left-Wing Violence in Italy, 1969–85

David Moss
Senior Lecturer in Italian Studies
Griffith University, Brisbane

MACMILLAN

First published 1989

Published by
THE MACMILLAN PRESS LTD
Houndmills, Basingstoke, Hampshire RG21 2XS
and London
Companies and representatives
throughout the world

Typeset by Footnote Graphics,
Warminster, Wilts

Printed in the People's Republic of China

British Library Cataloguing in Publication Data
Moss, David, *1946–*
The politics of left-wing violence in
Italy, 1969–85.
1. Italy. Left-wing political movements.
Violence, 1969–1985
I. Title
322.4
ISBN 0–333–41254–0

To the memory of RFM

List of Plates

The author is grateful to Michele Nazzaro for permission to reproduce these photographs.

List of Tables

List of Abbreviations

ANM   Associazione Nazionale Magistrati
ANPI   Associazione Nazionale Partigiani d'Italia
AO   Avanguardia Operaia
AutOp   Autonomia Operaia
BR   Brigate Rosse
COCORI   Comitati Comunisti Rivoluzionari
CSM   Consiglio Superiore della Magistratura
DC   Democrazia Cristiana
DP   Democrazia Proletaria
DIGOS   Dipartimenti Investigazioni Generali Operazioni
            Speciali
FCC   Formazioni Combattenti Comuniste
GAP   Gruppi Armati Proletari
GR   Guerriglia Rossa
LC   Lotta Continua
MD   Magistratura Democratica
MI   Magistratura Indipendente
MPRO   Movimento Proletario di Resistenza Offensiva
MS   Movimento Studentesco
MSI   Movimento Sociale Italiano
NAP   Nuclei Armati Proletari
PAC   Proletari Armati per il Comunismo
PCI   Partito Comunista Italiano
PdUP   Partito d'Unità Proletaria per il Comunismo
PL   Prima Linea
PLI   Partito Liberale Italiano
PO   Potere Operaio
PR   Partito Radicale
PRI   Partito Repubblicano Italiano
PSDI   Partito Socialista Democratico Italiano
PSIUP   Partito Socialista Italiano di Unità Proletaria
RCA   Reparti Comunisti d'Attacco
SdS   Servizio di Sicurezza
SID   Servizio Informazioni Difesa
SIFAR   Servizio Informazioni Forze Armate
SISDE   Servizio Informazioni e Sicurezza Democratica
SISMI   Servizio Informazioni e Sicurezza Militare

TP	Terzo Potere
UCC	Unità Combattenti Comuniste
UCIGOS	Ufficio Centrale Investigazioni Generali e Operazioni Speciali
UniCost	Unità per la Costituzione

Contents

Preface

I began, very tentatively, to accumulate materials on left-wing violence during the course of a different research project in Italy in 1981. At that time the phenomenon was in a decline that was not evidently irreversible, and I was far from certain that I would be able to make it the topic of a book. The object of enquiry seemed to resist even an approximately adequate initial characterisation. Its symbology and rhetorics were bewilderingly diverse, drawing at the same time on contemporary post-structuralist analyses of information flows and desire and on a Winter Palace view of the concentration of social power. Leaflets might contain references to Foucault's micro-physics of discipline and surveillance: actions such as 'kneecappings' mimicked the hamstringing of livestock as a conventional warning technique used by pastoralists in Italy's rural periphery. Many of the armed groups' accusations against the State echoed views to be found among the political parties and complaints audible in any bar or market-place. Even the extent of participation in left-wing violence seemed to be easy to misdescribe. Its agents were neither exactly a tiny sect wholly divorced from the surrounding society nor a fully-fledged social movement nor, despite the inflated claims of its protagonists, an entire political generation. These problems complicated the evaluative dimensions which are always intertwined with, although not inseparable from, the choice of descriptive terms. When I suggested in a seminar in Turin that there could be no general 'theory of terrorism', I was rebuked for discounting the importance of intellectual unity against violence and ignoring the need for citizens to have a general, even if admittedly not wholly plausible, explanation behind which to mobilise – points to which any social scientist opposed to political violence and with no sympathy for the translation of social critique into the deliberate damage of individuals must be sensitive.

In the light of these difficulties, I therefore owe a special debt to the people who initially encouraged me none the less to try to use some ordinary social science categories of analysis on a far from ordinary phenomenon: Franco Ferraresi, whose own research on right-wing violence provided a particular stimulus and whose generosity, practical help and hospitality have been continuous; Gian Mario Bravo, then Dean of the Faculty of Political Sciences at the

University of Turin, who not only welcomed me to the University but arranged for me to enjoy the facilities of the Luigi Einaudi Foundation; and to Dario di Vico and Ettore Santi who provided insights into the particular problems faced by the trade unions in combating violence in factories. In subsequent years information and materials became easier to obtain, and I was able to spend six months on research between January and June 1984, followed by a shorter period covering the end of 1985 and beginning of 1986: I owe the School of Humanities, Griffith University, particular acknowledgement for having granted me leave and supporting the costs of both trips.

Too many people have helped me in too many different ways for me not to feel that I have quite failed to do justice to their very generous assistance. For granting me interviews and providing access to documents of all kinds I am especially grateful to Drs G. C. Caselli, M. Laudi, A. Spataro and R. Priore; Nerio Diodà and Professor G. Pecorella; Eugenio Cazzaniga, Luisa Morgantini, Norma Mander, Neva Maffii, A. Banfi, A. Malinghero, I. Paolucci, Professor N. Dalla Chiesa and Eugenio Rossi. Marco Barbone enabled me to understand something of the world of armed struggle in Milan. In particular I owe an immense debt to Marcello Gentili who not only freely offered materials which would otherwise have been hard or impossible to obtain but also took great pains to help me understand them better. In addition to the kindness of Michele Nazzaro in making available his extensive collection of photographs I have received further valuable help from Professor Enzo D'Arcangelo, P. Colasuga and C. De Niccolò, Dr. G. Mencucci of the RAI-TV and Tonino Malaschini. Not every piece of information was so easily come by, however. It took me four months of reiterated requests, the support of a friendly mole and a probably decisive confusion – never sufficiently vigorously clarified, I regret to admit – between my surname and that of a fortunately illustrious historian to persuade the Ministry of the Interior to provide me with some exceedingly innocuous statistics on violence. Thanks to the generosity of the School of Humanities Research Committee, I was able to employ two invaluable research assistants: Cecilia Rossi in Italy and Regina Ganter in Australia. Their work made the task of writing an account of continuing Italian political violence from the other side of the world seem rather less bizarre. In Milan, Marino and Maria Luisa Regini facilitated research in countless different and equally essential ways. In Brisbane, Linda Weiss did her level and much-appreciated best to force me to clarify my arguments; and Kate Carey, Bev Wolter and Karen Yarrow have continued to transform my hand-writing into a legible text with accuracy, rapidity and great tolerance for my infinite capacity to have second thoughts. Most important of all, Fiorella Carra provided unstinting support for the entire project and helped me in very many ways to manage the extreme emotions generated by prolonged attention to the details and dimensions of violence.

David Moss
Brisbane

1 Italian 'Terrorism' as Translation

THE DISTINCTIVENESS OF ITALIAN POLITICAL VIOLENCE

Between 1967 and 1970 insurgent political violence began, or re-vived, in four European societies (Spain, Northern Ireland, West Germany and Italy), the USA and Japan. So widespread and variously motivated a recourse to forms of clandestine violence suggested that it might come to play an increasingly significant role in political conflicts in the advanced societies. It was perhaps destined to become a regular method in attempts not just to resolve intractable historical disputes but also to overcome the apparently incendiary combination of social self-consciousness and entrenched power in-equalities which characterised the development of liberal democracy itself. Dire prophecies of a generalised use of violence as a technique of resource-extraction were not slow to appear.

By the late 1980s some of the trajectories initiated two decades ago can be regarded as concluded, others as not even within sight of a conclusion. With hindsight the differences lying beyond the merely ideological references to the distant past or to the transformations of the future can be seen more clearly. As far as the four European cases are concerned, the experiments with political violence can be contextualised and distinguished in several ways: the nature of the objectives, the identities and relations of the actors and their institu-tional opponents, the level and duration of violence, the extent of the response and the amount of knowledge about each instance that is publicly available. First, the ethnic-nationalist objectives of ETA and the IRA, which could be conceded directly by their opponents if they chose to do so, stand in contrast to the 'social revolutionary' goals of Italian and West German groups, which could not. Second, the volume of violence generated in each case differs considerably. Between 1969 and 1977, for example, the deaths from all political violence in Italy amounted to 153, barely 9 per cent of the 1798 deaths in Northern Ireland but substantially above the 22 deaths in West Germany.[1] Third, the areas of armed struggle show quite different patterns of fragmentation. ETA and IRA have dominated the conflicts in their respective societies and each has direct private armed antagonists (GAL, UDF) as well as institutional opposition from State police and armies: in West Germany too the RAF has been the principal component in clandestine left-wing violence. In Italy, however, both left-wing and right-wing violence have co-existed without becoming direct reciprocal targets, and both have been much more divided internally than in the other European cases. Between 1969 and 1980 a total of 597 group signatures (484 of the Left, 113 of the Right), authored actions which still only amounted to one in five of all acts of violence directed against political targets: Italy's best-known left-wing group, the Red Brigades, in fact accounted for only a small minority even of the acts for which responsibility was explicitly claimed. Fourth, the armed groups have very different relationships to other political groups or parties. ETA and the IRA have been flanked by legal political organisations which carry the shared nationalist ideology and win seats in Parliamentary elections: in Italy and West Germany no such contiguous political support has existed. Fifth, the practitioners of violence have been confronted by different degrees of unity among their political opponents. ETA, IRA and the RAF have confronted a restricted set of parties which produce stable governments, allowing political violence to be largely, if never completely, taken out of inter-party conflict. Italy, by contrast, has a notoriously unstable set of governing alliances, ensuring that the issue of 'terrorism' was handled by coalition governments whose constituent parties and political formulae were regularly changing. Sixth, the extent of government responses has been very different in each society and shows little straightforward connection simply with the brute volume of violence. In West Germany, for example, substantial restrictions on civil rights have been introduced which redraw the liberties of publics beyond those directly implicated in violence, while in Italy – despite the far greater damage to people and property – direct repressive reaction has been much more limited. Seventh, Italy alone has seen the end of the trajectory of violence begun in the late 1960s. Berlin, Belfast and the Basque country seemed in 1986 to be as intractably locked into their violence today as they were a decade ago: Italy, despite warnings only a few years old that a by-now endemic terrorism would have to be lived with for the foreseeable future, and notwithstanding the occasional murders since 1983, appears to have been a remarkable success story in eliminating a phenomenon which, at its height in 1978, was generating some seven attacks per day. Indeed the actual process of elimination has created a distinctive problem of closure in Italy where, unlike most other societies in which 'terrorism' has come and gone, its political and judicial authorities have had to invent forms of social reintegration not merely for isolated turncoats but for the majority of (now repentant) former enemies of the State. Finally, the extent of publicly available research and knowledge generated in the four societies on the topic of their domestic political violence varies. At least until the end of 1986 Italy's violence had received far less analytical attention than the other European cases: no extended study either of the phenomenon as a whole or even of a particular aspect had yet appeared under the aegis of public authorities or from the academy.[2] In view of the amount of data available in Italy and the practical interest in learning lessons from the most successful example of the elimination of violence, that particular disparity across the four European cases is surprising – especially since, for example, measures used in Italy to favour collaboration with the State by members of armed groups have been introduced in Spain, and contemplated in West Germany, although without any apparent analysis of the specific contribution they actually made to the ending of political violence in Italy itself.

In this book I shall suggest that those features which make Italy's left-wing violence distinctive are closely connected and can help to explain the most significant features of its profile and trajectory. I shall argue that the heterogeneity of both its practitioners and opponents led to difficulties common to both sets of actors in defining clearly the aims of violence and in achieving consensus on the nature of 'terrorism'. The armed groups were deeply and internally divided over whether violence should be used as a surrogate for, or as a supplement to, non-violent political and social conflicts; and they therefore showed different degrees of willingness to try to place themselves outside, indeed to ignore, ordinary political and social relations. Contrary to the stereotypical image of 'terrorists', very few Italian users of violence were prepared to go wholly underground: so the proper location of the boundary marking the limits of the Italian political community was a matter of continuing dispute. Among their opponents too the difficulties of reaching agreement on the definition, causes and extension of 'terrorism' and therefore on how best to intervene against it inhibited any drastic consensual response at national level. The partly deliberate, partly ineluctable strategy of fragmented and dispersed responses, largely entrusted to non-political institutions at local level, prevented the reactions to violence from confirming the claims by armed groups about the repressive nature of Italian society and thus from providing an additional incentive to recruitment. At the same time, although I do not wish to minimise the specifically restrictive effects provoked by violence, the problems of agreeing on the precise direction and scale of measures to be adopted against it served to preserve most of the basic democratic freedoms won in the period immediately preceding the emergence of armed struggle. Neither the users of violence nor their opponents in fact had, or managed to construct, authoritative centres with the power and authority to define by fiat the issues of 'armed struggle' and 'terrorism' respectively. Indeed, the actual profile of types of violence and responses can itself partly be accounted for by the attempts to create such centres in both the political and armed communities.

The practical problem for participants of defining clearly the nature of what they were involved in creates directly parallel difficulties for any social scientific account with a pretence to objectivity. The issue here is not the much-debated question of the extent to which a sociological description must or should contain an evaluation of the legitimacy of violence but rather how an accurate account can be built on constantly shifting foundations. For researchers must be largely, if not exclusively, reliant on data as they appear in the forms already deliberately shaped by participants. In softer areas of crime or deviance at least some of the ordinary sociological or anthropological methods of creating data (surveys, questionnaires, interviews, ethnographies) have proved to be usable, and the participants' versions are not themselves an integral public aspect of their activities except in special circumstances. Such research techniques are effectively excluded for groups still actively engaged in armed struggle: at any rate there have been no instances in Italy of participant observation or phenomenological appreciation of the politically violent. Furthermore since the versions of participants are themselves strategic features of the conflict, no objective elicitations of motivation and aims are feasible; and journalists have of course paid with their lives for producing accounts at variance with the actors' self-understandings. A similarly impenetrable cover, reinforced by the secrecy imposed by the internal security aspects of 'terrorism', makes it impossible to carry out the kinds of grassroots observation of police classification and description of acts of violence which have been made in some American and European cities on less sensitive issues, and which may permit revisionary understandings of what the official figures for crime signify. Thus, no matter how sophisticated the definition of 'terrorism' that a sociologist constructs, nor which of the 110 definitions recently counted he or she adopts, there is no opportunity to operationalise it to collect first-hand data – dependence on lay constructs is absolute.[3]

To a greater or lesser extent that difficulty characterises all research on clandestine political violence as it is taking place. In the Italian case it is supplemented by a further problem, paradoxically generated by the number of *ex post facto* accounts now available. Usually the practitioners of unsuccessful insurgent violence are killed, receive long prison sentences or at any rate exit from the public arena without revising the motivations and values with which they initially described their commitment to violence. In Italy, however, substantial numbers of former members of armed groups have engaged in systematic public recantations of their pasts, providing continuously revised versions of their general and specific aims, the character of relations in the armed community and the determinants of their own attitudes and behaviour. On one hand, these recantations have led many users of violence to be far harsher on their former selves than even their opponents were at the time of the violence itself. On the other hand, the fact that the most detailed accounts available for the years of armed struggle have been given retrospectively, from beyond conversion to the value of non-violence, leads to an obvious and well-known instability in the evidential basis for the attribution of motives and beliefs to the central actors.[4] The analytical decision to incorporate actors' accounts as a primary source in understanding political violence must accommodate from the outset data consisting of regularly readjusted descriptions of the salient features of past actions and relationships. Precisely that indeterminacy has been one important factor in preventing the emergence of a consensual version of what exactly is to be understood and explained by Italian left-wing 'terrorism'.

Appreciation of the intrinsic methodological problems must, however, lead back to the most distinctive feature of Italian political violence and the primary focus of this study. Unlike members of the IRA or ETA the participants in armed struggle in Italy had no base community of reference united around an identity which transcended the recourse to arms. Catholicism in Belfast and Basque ethnicity in North-east Spain provide symbolic and spatially identifiable communities from which users of violence can emerge and into which they can retreat without destroying the ideological basis for their actions. Violence is merely one method, often minoritarian, for expressing that wider identity. In the Italian case the practice of violence had itself to be made to carry a complete range of social meanings and to provide the basis for political and individual identity. The need to make violence continuously intelligible to its users themselves as well as to their audiences was therefore fundamental and a significant determinant of the evolution of the actual forms it took. Two aspects of the general requirement can be mentioned. First, the ultimate 'revolutionary' goals of left-wing armed struggle were too remote to be brought into any direct relationship with a particular act of violence, a gap made still wider by the impossibility for any political opponents of violence deliberately to concede the desired form of social order. Second, only by achieving a sense for their actions could the practitioners of violence accept themselves as deliverers of harm to others – a determinant of ordinary criminal behaviour recently emphasised by Rock and doubly significant in political crime where there is no immediate personal reward to compensate for the dangers of, and ordinary revulsion against, damaging people.[5] For those reasons alone the processes of the management of meaning should be at the heart of explanations for the development and specific trajectory of political violence and for the patterns of entry to, activity in and exit from the armed community.

The making and unmaking of meanings must be regarded as essentially interactive, carried out through exchanges within the community of armed struggle, between its members and their opponents and among the opponents themselves. Confirmation and disconfirmation of accounts of social and political structure, claims to political identity and the identification of the direct consequences of actions are generated by a wide range of actors responding to specific acts and constrained by situational features. No account or account-producer enjoys a clear interpretive privilege. The convergences on particular meanings offered from different positions in the interactional arena – which includes actors from the major institutions of the factory, politics, the judiciary and the academy as well as the practitioners of violence – have to be regarded as fragile agreements, likely to be overturned as the contributors to the public knowledge of what 'terrorism' is revise their views, disagree over assumptions made plain by rival actors and contest the types of evidence acceptable as a basis for interpretation. This approach to political violence implies that both violence itself and the meaning-conferring responses it elicits must be incorporated in any satisfactory analysis. A study which focuses solely on the armed groups themselves in charting the rise, persistence and decline of political violence without also considering the nature and effects among such groups of the full range of institutional responses must miss the central dynamic, certainly in the Italian case and probably elsewhere. To ignore the interactional aspects on the grounds that terrorists are psychopaths or that there is an ineluctable organisational logic of clandestinity or that violence is the product of the distortions of capitalist development may be a boundary-marking strategy *in medias res*; but it makes the actual evolution of violence and its cultural presuppositions impossible to grasp. It also renders the explanation of the consequences of violence – what reactive measures were not taken as well as those that were – very uneven since specific outcomes may often be better understood as responses to responses rather than as an unmediated reaction to the violence itself. As an analytical framework which can not only incorporate a wide range of account-producers and is also sensitive to the methods and contexts in which determination of the meanings of violence is temporarily secured I have adopted a perspective which identifies the pattern of exchanges as a process of continuing 'translation'.[6]

TRANSLATING VIOLENCE INTO 'TERRORISM' AND 'ARMED STRUGGLE'

As deployed by Callon the term 'translation' refers to the processes through which social actors persuade others of the existence of a problem, enrol them behind a certain version of its solution, provide them with defined roles and mobilise them to collective action or willed inaction. Distinct elements, practices and persons are thus brought into (temporary) alliances through successful persuasion by candidate spokespersons of their own indispensability to the resolution of the problem and ability to represent the interests of allies. In this view power is the effect of successful translation and is highly context-specific. Micro-actors can grow in power where macro-actors can be forced into direct negotiation or confrontation on a particular site and be shown to be weaker or inadequate in some way. Alliances can thus be extended across a range of sites, so that the differences in terms of relative power between micro- and macro-actors, between apparently tiny groups and vast collectivities, are treated less as given than as produced through the outcome of multiple interactions in which the actual shape and outcome of any particular translation sequence is never wholly predictable. Applied to the topic of political violence, the translation perspective suggests analysis of the specific resources that make possible the communication of political messages; the forms of solidarity that are engendered in the relationships of control and use of those resources; the methods by which differently placed opponents find – or fail to find – themselves together on specific issues on particular terrains of conflict; and the consequences for broader patterns of solidarity of those successful or failed alliances and the actions they promote. No internal dynamic for the logic of (clandestine) violence nor an intrinsic capacity to penetrate institutions nor any necessary outcome should be assumed.

Insurgent 'terrorism' can be described as the attempt to translate elementary constitutive units, the acts of violence against persons and property committed by clandestine actors, into recognisably political activities. Violence itself is open to many public and private uses, and serves only as an extremely crude language permanently subject to what Clausewitz called 'friction': its syntax (the type and level of infliction of damage) is very limited, comprehensible mostly to a restricted audience of fellow participants and to the police. In a very few instances violence needs minimal translation. Italy's right-wing bomb massacres, for example, aimed to gain an effect simply by the fact of having been carried out at all, thus demonstrating the need to introduce conservative measures to reduce a generic sense of individual insecurity and social disorder. Most acts of violence intended to have political impact require translation into more flexible language to explain the aims and identities of their authors, to persuade non-members that the use of violence is the only solution to a particular social or political problem, to acquire support and penetrate the realm of ordinary politics.

An essential set of resources therefore consists of the telephone calls, leaflets, banners, video cassettes, political tracts and theoretical treatises which disambiguate the otherwise politically meaningless language of violence. The texts are the means by which the murder of a single individual, for example, can be de-privatised and de-localised, conferring symbolic status on the target by identifying the attribute (responsibility for a particular type of action, occupancy of a specific role) to be treated as the dominant reason for the act. Obviously, the extent of disambiguation needed varies: the murder of an English soldier in Northern Ireland or a Spanish policeman in

Basque country requires less interpretive work than the abstract targets of 'revolutionary' groups. But in all cases where a political message is sought, at least some control over the two communicative media of brute violence and political rhetoric is necessary. In Italy the double emphasis is neatly captured in the term for the violence of the later 1970s – *gli anni di piombo* – *piombo* meaning the lead for both bullets and print.

The activity of translation begins with the users of violence themselves explaining their actions publicly to various audiences. However, although the authors of acts of violence and the texts justifying them are often assumed to be the same individuals, in practice that need not be so; nor may the meanings privately conferred by the actors coincide with the translations offered to external groups. The distribution of meaning-making resources within an armed group may locate control over the two languages in different hands, with the result that particular categories of translators are favoured, reinforcing some types of meaning and suppressing others. Texts attempting to legitimise violent acts publicly cannot be assumed to represent directly the beliefs of the authors of the acts themselves. To treat them as if they do may cause both a potential dynamic of conflict influencing the evolution of the organisation of armed struggle and the differential commitment of participants to be overlooked.

Once the act of violence and its accompanying claim reach the public domain, they have to be translated by a range of external agencies and organisations, each with its own institutional vocabulary in which the locally relevant attributes of the acts and actors have to be described. Since violence is illegal, the police and magistrature are always involved, alongside the government as the guarantor of public order. Other political parties, trade unions and social and occupational categories can be drawn into the processes of translation, either directly because their own members are under attack or indirectly because the communicative resources (lexicons, symbols, myths) which they regard as their own monopoly and central to their public identities have been expropriated by the users of violence to explain their actions. Ensuring the purity of their own political language thus forces threatened groups into public translational activities, especially if the polluting texts circulate widely. Other categories of translators – journalists, lawyers, social scientists – are likely also to join the interpretive exchanges to varying degrees, alongside otherwise dispersed or merely latent groups activated by direct attacks or enrolled behind the public responses of others.

In making their own selective translations of acts of violence into 'terrorism' and in defining the problem, its scale and authors, the opponents of violence have as their primary interpretive resources both the acts themselves and their accompanying justifications. The contents of such texts, however, offer hypotheses which are far from incorrigible. Competing claims may be made for a single action; most groups will not publicly author every action committed (thefts, bank robberies and kidnappings for ransom are rarely acknowledged since known involvement in ordinary crimes threatens the authors' political status); different signatures may mask the responsibilities of a single group; the groups represented by distinct signatures may in fact be coordinated at a level perhaps unknown to most of their own affiliates; and texts may simply be intended to conceal the real reasons for action. Establishing a relationship between the contents of violence and texts is therefore a key methodological aspect of translation which leads towards a public definition of the problem of 'terrorism'. As in the armed community itself, the determination of what is to count as 'armed struggle' and 'terrorism' must be examined as an interpretive product generated in specific institutions and on particular occasions. The achievement of consensus depends on the relationships and translation work among the differently-positioned actors within and between separate domains: the local and non-local consequences of dissension have to be considered in the same framework. Most European societies affected by insurgent violence have in fact used various means of closing down disagreements which rely on the elimination of a public voice for certain kinds of translator or translation. Political violence may be defined as a non-party issue, thus removing it from open disputes among its political opponents; special tribunals without jurors may be created to avoid legal dispute over the precise status and seriousness of politically-motivated violence, to provide a consistent judicial interpretation of 'terrorism' and to prevent public conflicts between lay and professional readings; and governments may prevent the media from discussing 'subversion' at all, prohibit certain items from being made news or encourage press and television to develop their own in-house guidelines on how to translate the issue to general audiences. The particular processes of translation in Italy will be discussed in relation to the most important institutions in the following chapters. As a prelude to illustrating the broad scope of disagreements about 'terrorism' and 'terrorists' in the rest of this introduction, I shall briefly note four relevant general conditions in the Italian case which influence the transformation of violence into a means of political communication: the extents of its support, familiarity, ambiguity and publicity.

Despite the weak legitimacy of the Italian political system and the expressed desire of a majority of citizens for substantial change, the explicitly approved methods of political action stopped well short of violence. In the mid-1970s, for example, when as many as 77.8 per cent of Italians insisted that their political and social systems needed either major reforms or a revolutionary overhaul, only 1.3 per cent approved of the damage to property and 1.5 per cent of attacks on people as modes of political participation. Two years later, as political violence intensified, the proportions had fallen to 1 per cent and 0.8 per cent respectively. Since the numbers supporting the use of violence against people included approval of defensive violence against police in marches and demonstrations, the proportion that accepted the immediate contemporary recourse to violence as a legitimate technique of political communication was miniscule. Even smaller, naturally, was the number of people ready to participate actively: 0.4 per cent in 1975 said that they would be prepared to use violence against people, and 0.3 per cent reported that they had already done so.[7]

Notwithstanding the insignificant extent of active consent to political violence, the majority of adult Italians were nevertheless familiar with the successful use of violence by tiny armed minorities. Indeed the regime changes since the Risorgimento had all been closely associated with violence exercised by a few active combatants surrounded by a largely passive, sometimes hostile, population. The successive creation of liberal, fascist and republican states were linked to such uses of violence which became founding events – the exploits of Garibaldi and the Thousand, the March on Rome, the Resistance. Whatever the actual historical significance of the three episodes in bringing about political transformations, they generated a stock of symbols, myths and political narratives to legitimate the ruling centre and to characterise subversion against it. Indeed in 1970 one in four Italians was old enough to have at least a dim memory of the emergence of Fascism in 1920–2 and one in two of the Resistance years, 1943–5. Events which were merely historical for the members of the armed community in the 1970s, who were deprived of any sense of the complexities and ambiguities of violence even for relatively widely-approved goals, were part of living memory for most adults. A more restricted, but still younger, group was directly acquainted with the campaigns of irredentist violence in the South

Tirol in the early 1960s: although geographically very limited, the number of attacks actually credited Italy with the greatest incidence of 'terrorism' in Europe before the most recent wave of violence began.[8] Moreover, the use of violence by police on the occasion of political and labour demonstrations, resulting in the deaths of 220 civilians and 23 police between 1946 and 1977, must also be accounted part of the general familiarity of violence as a likely component, or a potential outcome, of political activity.[9]

Merely the range of historical examples and direct experiences endowed the communicative use of violence with a further essential ambiguity in addition to its intrinsic imprecisions. Examples of clandestine violence from the past could easily be adduced to render plausible the attribution of the assault after 1969 to widely different points on the political spectrum, whatever narrowly distinctive forms violence was given and no matter how precisely the specific content of the accompanying texts was designed. The past provided ready reference points in the translation manuals of the present. Furthermore, the ambiguity of violence was provided with a public exemplar in the very act which is held to be the inaugural attack of recent 'terrorism': the bomb massacre of Piazza Fontana in Milan on 12 December 1969 which killed 16 and wounded 45 people. With the judicial investigations still unconcluded in 1989, the eight trials have seen simultaneous indictments of the extreme Right, extreme Left and State security services with parallel parliamentary investigations into the extent of involvement of leading members of the Christian Democrat and Social Democrat parties. Although there has been little doubt for many years that the bomb was planted by the extreme Right with the aim of throwing the blame on the Left and halting the working-class mobilisation of the Hot Autumn, the protracted enquiries and succession of contradictory court verdicts – revised, overturned or annulled as the case travelled between different judiciaries – ensured that a periodic reminder of the ambiguity of violence would be issued each time a new attempt definitively to fix responsibilities was made. For left-wing users of violence, therefore, the parallel existence of right-wing attacks on occasionally convergent targets, suggesting possible active collusion and inevitably disturbing the communicative clarity of the shared basic language of damage, was a permanent threat to their ability to deliver unequivocally intelligible political messages. Surveyed in 1982, 42.6 per cent of a national sample asserted that left-wing terrorists were identical to their neo-Fascist counterparts and a further 27.7 per cent claimed that although the question was not entirely clear, a growing amount of evidence indicated direct collusion.[10] As well as making the translational work of left-wing armed groups more difficult, the possibility of tracing responsibilities for violence in several different political directions made accountable a wide range of political actors and forced them into extensive interpretive responses.

That accountability influences the last aspect of the overall context for translation – its publicity. Although the general issue of the relationship between political violence and the media has received considerable attention, analysis has generally over-homogenised the frequently very variegated types and stances of different media, confined its examination of press and television behaviour only to single dramatic episodes rather than their routine reporting over a longer period and restricted its focus to the supposedly dominant concern of armed groups merely to gain a generic publicity.[11] In the Italian case the activities and products of translation received very wide coverage throughout the period, so that the views of individuals and associations were highly visible. Although the editorial policies of the different party and non-party newspapers and weeklies varied, a wide range of heterogeneous primary materials from the protagonists themselves circulated in the public domain – the communiqués of armed groups, documents issued by political parties, interviews with users of violence and their police and judicial opponents, extracts from trial documents (including, in one instance, a disc of the voice test for a telephone call made to the Moro family by a member of the Red Brigades), letters between former members of armed groups and their victims, declarations of innocence or of a continuing conviction in the value of armed struggle – alongside a vast mass of secondary commentaries.

The reasons for what was probably an exceptional degree of openness in the publicity given to translations of violence were several. In the first place, the Left in particular argued that the only truly decisive response to clandestine violence was active public mobilisation in order to display rejection of violent methods even by the social groups addressed as potential allies; and that strategy required at least some information on the beliefs and aims of armed groups as well as explicit counter-versions. A second facilitating factor was the rapid and unregulated expansion of communicative outlets, initially in the left-wing press after 1968 and then more generally in local broadcasting after the breaking of the State's monopoly in 1975–6. By 1979 there were an estimated 80 to 90 regular publications of the extreme Left alongside its 100 to 130 local radio stations although often only those radio stations in major cities (for example Onda Rossa in Rome, Radio Popolare in Milan and Radio Sherwood in Padua) provided full and continuous transmission. A third factor was the lack of any new, formal, regulation of media presentations of political violence. No measures to change the existing legal framework governing the publication of subversive material were taken, although the government did, unsuccessfully, try to move towards establishing a new set of restrictions in 1979 (see below, pp. 145–6). The legality of publishing, say, texts encouraging violence therefore remained bound, on one hand, by the ordinary emphasis of the penal code, not on the content but on the intentions of the reproducers and, on the other, by the general rules against publishing documents which were part of an uncompleted judicial enquiry (*segreto istruttorio*). But the penalties for transgression were in any case quite insufficient to deter editors from publishing documents concerned with political violence, sometimes provided by magistrates themselves, that were thought to be in the public interest or likely to improve sales. Readers were therefore often and immediately provided with materials that should formally have been denied circulation until long after the particular context of their production and intended efficacy had disappeared.

Furthermore, none of the reiterated suggestions to devise a formal code of self-regulation in press treatments of political violence was taken up. The diversity of press ownership, the strongly local or regional bias of most newspapers and the defence of editorial and journalistic autonomy inhibited any coordination over a general approach or the handling of specific acts of violence. The attempt to reach agreement on whether to publish some Red Brigades' documents in 1981, demanded as a condition for the release of a kidnap victim, and to impose a news black-out on all political violence actually resulted in open conflicts among different newspapers, between editors and owners and within single newspaper staff.[12] So far as I am aware, that episode also provided the only occasion on which the general public's views on the desirability of giving publicity to armed group's texts were solicited, even if only through a casual and hardly representative sample. Only a small minority of respondents favoured a news black-out either in general (8 per cent) or on the occasion of a kidnapping (19 per cent), while responses were equally divided over whether newspapers should publish all materials received from armed groups (34 per cent), should publish only unobtrusive summaries (37 per cent), or should not publish them at all (29 per cent). In the event that the authors should demand publication as a condition for restraining them from some act of violence, a bare majority favoured outright refusal.[13] Such as it is, that evidence supports the view that the rejection of any formal policy of constraints on the publicity given to the translation of violence was generally endorsed.

Various types of informal pressure could of course be used to influence the extent and direction of media versions of violence. Magistrates could bring pressure to bear on editors and journalists specialising in the reporting of violence by incriminating them on suspicion of giving help to the groups on which their articles seemed suspiciously well-informed. Journalists could also be prosecuted for refusing to reveal their sources, since professional confidentiality for members of the press was not enshrined in law or anticipated by the Constitution. In December 1980, for example, the four editors of *Corrispondenza Internazionale* were indicted, although acquitted in court, for instigation to commit the crimes specified in an extended BR text that they had published; and in January 1981 two journalists from *L'Espresso* were incriminated for aiding and abetting the same group by accepting and publishing an interview with one of its leaders.[14] The government, too, could and did try to bring pressure on the media to restrict or refuse coverage of political violence and in particular to organise the news-directed filming of trials so as to avoid moments when the defendants were reading out their documents or successfully provoking unseemly court responses. But even in so dramatic a moment as the Moro kidnapping, it found itself unable either to influence easily the reformed RAI (the state broadcasting corporation) or to meet the investigating magistrate's request to prevent media publication of the Red Brigades communiqués or Moro's letters.[15] (Interestingly, in the reverse case, when the kin of a kidnap victim tried to obtain a legal injunction for the publication of Red Brigades' texts by a reluctant press, a Roman magistrate rejected the family's request precisely on the grounds that newspapers could not be compelled to publish manifestly criminal content.[16]) Finally, the most obvious form of pressure was exercised by the armed groups themselves through the two murders, eight woundings and regular public and private threatening of journalists accused of having authored articles especially hostile to individual comrades or to armed struggle in general. The more prominent journalists were offered bodyguards; and for some major newspapers, coverage of aspects of violence became anonymous or agency-based or rotated among different commentators to prevent the singling out of any obvious target.

Although the press served throughout as a remarkably accessible forum for materials connected with political violence, it is none the less possible to identify changes in the especially controversial area of publishing documents directly authored by members of armed left-wing organisations. Between 1970 and 1977 the major national newspapers either reproduced in full or quoted extensively from texts claiming responsibility for attacks, providing a circulation which to a great extent made up for the groups' failure to realise the ambition of creating their own regular journal. Indeed it was not uncommon for even longstanding activists to read texts by fellow group members in the press before being able to obtain their own copies through internal channels. [17]

The first direct attacks on journalists in 1977, coupled with criticism of the media's exceptionally theatrical treatment of the Moro kidnapping in 1978, forced the press to reflect more critically on its own role. Thereafter the publicising of 'terrorist' texts became more selective. Reproduction and quotation were gradually restricted to general theoretical documents, divorced from the justification of any specific action: leaflets accompanying single attacks were ignored or summarised in a sentence, no doubt in part also because the rise in the volume of violence reduced the space available for detailed coverage. The increased selectivity had two consequences. First, it gave privileged access to the authors from a particular milieu in the community of armed struggle, translating for a wide public the accounts developed in a specific niche, with effects on solidarities among participants in violence to be examined in the following chapter. Second, because of the circulation of the most respectable presentations of the ideologies of political violence (i.e. those least contaminated by direct association with attacks), further pressure was placed on legitimate left-wing organisations to engage in public translational work to retain control over the meaning of key terms in their own lexicon. By an interpretive multiplier effect contrasting versions were thus prompted from other political parties. On one hand, the result was to display very clearly the disagreements among the opponents of violence over the nature of the phenomenon they were resisting: on the other hand, those same conflicts ensured that no single consensual identity was conferred externally on the users of violence in such a way that they might collectively recognise a unity transcending their own internal disputes. Although the first, negative, aspects of fragmentation and disunity among the political opponents of violence have generally been emphasised, the unintended positive consequences of that very weakness have not been underlined. The publicity granted to contrasting accounts of violence was itself an important contributory factor to the failure to establish unequivocal meanings and identities around which to ground an enduring community of armed struggle.

DEMARCATING 'TERRORIST' ACTS AND ACTORS

While the difficulties of providing a formal definition of 'terrorism' as a basis for international cooperation are well-known, less attention has been paid to the extent and consequences of domestic disputes over the meaning and content of the phenomenon. For Italy, therefore, the substantive variations in the product of the translation of acts of violence into a unitary political phenomenon can be illustrated by comparing the statistics which chart the scale and evolution of 'terrorism', and by examining the broad identifications of the actors held responsible. The exercise indicates how deeply the disagreements have sunk into the very constitution of the object to be explained, and they show clearly the problems raised for analysts by dependence on data classified and counted by others but not systematised by an authoritative centre.

Counting acts of 'terrorism'

Despite the creation of 'terrorism' as a legal category and the regular use of the term by governments, no formal definition exists in Italy. During the parliamentary debate in 1980 on the conversion of decree law 625/1979 which introduced 'terrorism' into the penal code as an aggravating motivation for all crimes, the government's spokesman refused to incorporate a definition of the term in the law, claiming that its meaning in popular and judicial usage was perfectly clear. Pressed by opposition parties to show that the term would not be used to cover unorthodox forms of non-violent protest, he offered an informal definition which must have realised his challengers' worst fears since it omitted all reference to violence:

> [terrorism] indicates the dissemination among public officials and citizens of political terror: that is, the conviction that from the

proper completion of tasks and the exercise of public and political rights or from the proper fulfilment of public and private duties may derive consequences directly or indirectly damaging.[18]

Moreover, applied to left-wing violence in particular, some of the senior State officials most actively concerned to investigate and repress it have expressed some diffidence about its unqualified description as 'terrorism'. Dalla Chiesa, for example, argued that the term *eversione* ('subversion') provided a better description, since 'terrorism' did not require the cultural background that he identified as present in the Italian case. Likewise his immediate superior in the *carabinieri*, Cappuzzo, maintained that the phenomenon should properly be defined as 'nonterroristic terrorism', since its targets were chosen with great care and the indiscriminate involvement of citizens was always avoided.[19] While it is not surprising to find practitioners of violence refusing the term 'terrorism' as a description of their actions, it is less common to find such diffidence among their direct institutional opponents.

Consistent with its definitional unease, the Italian State has not produced detailed official statistics on terrorism. The very general data used by the Minister of the Interior in his reports to Parliament and described as 'practical data' (*dati operativi*) were not made generally available to the public, and were only brought together in minimal form for diffusion to the press in 1982. Although the various police forces and security services have kept their own statistics, these have rarely been made public and do not in any case represent an official profile of the scale of 'terrorism'. No doubt the absence of useful official data for public reference was responsible for the production of two very much more detailed arrays, one by the Communist Party and the other by researchers at the Cattaneo Institute in Bologna. Although published independently, the three profiles were partially linked since the PCI study relied on Ministry data supplemented from party, judicial and journalistic sources and the Cattaneo researchers acknowledged a major debt to the PCI figures. Although the overall arrays are defined slightly differently – 'political terrorism' (Ministry of the Interior), 'attacks and violence' (PCI) and 'episodes of terrorism' (Cattaneo study) – and they include violence of both Left and Right, the different statistical portraits of the problem that appear in Table 1.1, and the periodisations that they license, are remarkable given the interpenetration of the three data bases. They show in fine-grained detail the absence of any consensual

TABLE 1.1   *Terrorism in Italy 1968–82. Acts and deaths in three statistical arrays*

Year	Total no. of acts of terrorism*			Deaths caused by terrorism		
	Ministry of the Interior[1]	*PCI*[2]	*Cattaneo*[3]	*Ministry of the Interior*	*PCI*	*Cattaneo*
1968	142	–	–	0	–	–
1969	400	439	17	17	21	17
1970	376	554	6	8	11	6
1971	537	832	22	4	6	–
1972	563	776	46	5	10	6
1973	412	648	38	41	11	4
1974	571	786	75	30	33	30
1975	741	467	62	14	21	10
1976	1347	685	116	12	17	12
1977	2194	1806	287	20	23	15
1978	2498	2725	716	36	38	36
1979	2384	2139	805	31	36	31
1980	1275	833	294	132	135	130
1981	862	368	136	27	24	24
1982	628	174	92	27	39	30
Totals	14930†	13232	2712	404	425	351

* These totals do not include the bank raids and other robberies carried out by terrorist groups to finance their activities but not explicitly claimed as political acts.
† Further figures have become available from the Ministry for subsequent years which confirm the rapid decline. 1983: 425 (4 deaths); 1984: 334 (25 deaths); 1985: 288 (12 deaths). The total for the period 1968–85 thus becomes 15977.
SOURCES
1. Ministero degli Interni, Dipartimento di Pubblica Sicurezza, Divisione Pubbliche Relazioni, *Sintesi statistica sul terrorismo e violenza politica dal 1968 al 1982*. The annual figures generally differ slightly from those presented in Parliament by the Minister of the Interior: the total differs considerably from that attributed to the Ministry elsewhere (taken from P. Furlong: 'Political Terrorism in Italy: Responses, Reactions and Immobilism', in J. Lodge (ed.) *Terrorism: A Challenge to the State* (New York: St Martin's Press, 1982) p. 73, Table 3.1). The figure cited by Furlong for the period 1969–78 is lower by 12% (8485 against 9639) than the Ministry's later figure.
2. M. Galleni (ed.), *Rapporto sul terrorismo* (Milan: Rizzoli, 1981) p. 49, Table 1. Data for 1981–2 are taken from Direzione PCI, Sezione Problemi dello Stato: 'Attentati e violenze in Italia nel 1981' (Rome, 1982) and 'Attentati e Violenze in Italia nel 1982' (Rome, 1983).
3. D. della Porta and M. Rossi: 'I terrorismi in Italia tra il 1969 e il 1982', *Cattaneo*, vol. III (1983) no. I, p. 11, Table 5. The table combines figures from Galleni, *Rapporto sul terrorismo*, pp. 277, 287.

translation of acts of violence into acts of terrorism, even for a restricted category such as deaths. In failing to generate a single consistent trajectory, they make extremely problematic any analytical exercise which is based on the straightforward correlation of one array with external factors to produce a reliable macro-level explanation of Italian 'terrorism'.

On at least two points the three arrays agree: that the years 1977–9 saw by far the greatest concentration of violence, accounting for about one-half of all actions between 1969 and 1982, and that the fall in the overall number of 'terrorist' acts since 1980 has been rapid and continuing. They disagree, however, on most other issues: the definition of what is to count as an act of 'terrorism'; the categorisation of specific acts of violence even when an extensive definition is shared; the year when 'terrorism' can be said to have begun; the remarkable variations within the most serious and closely scrutinised sub-category, murder; and the pattern of increases and decreases from year to year.

First, the Cattaneo Institute study used a simple practical definition of terrorism – all actions accompanied by a text claiming responsibility. The actors' own claims to identity were thus incorporated directly into the definition of the phenomenon, giving 'terrorism' an essentially organisational basis and producing a problem of a statistically much-reduced scale with respect to the other two arrays. This definition makes assumptions about the demarcation of actors which will be noted below (pp. 24). However, in cases where the general scope of the definition ought to be much less significant, as in the figures for the number of deaths due to politically-motivated attacks, the three arrays still diverge substantially. In no year is there agreement across the three arrays, and in only six of the fourteen years is there actually a total shared by any two of the three columns: in some years (1972, 1973, 1975, 1982) the disagreement about the volume of deaths attributable to 'terrorism' was considerable. Even for the most striking and arguably most consequential instances of violence, there is little consensus on the boundaries of 'terrorism'.

Second, even when similarly extensive definitions are used, the annual totals are often strikingly different. In every year until 1975 the PCI's figures are larger than the Ministry's, sometimes (for example, 1973) by as much as 57 per cent; and over the whole period 1969–74 they are greater by 41 per cent. From 1975 onwards, with the sole exception of 1978, the direction of variation is reversed, so that when the complete period is considered, the totals of the PCI and Ministry are more closely aligned. One conclusion suggested by this comparison is that, contrary to charges about the responsiveness of the depiction of the size of the problem of 'terrorism' to political massaging, neither the dominant governing party (embodied in this instance in the longstanding Christian Democrat control of the Ministry of the Interior) nor the major opposition party appear consistently to have favoured the categorisation of actors that would have either expanded or diminished the scale of the threat to Italian democracy. The actual pattern of divergence may even have been somewhat paradoxical. The DC might have been expected to favour an especially large threat in the early 1970s, when the party was under substantial direct pressure from Left and Right, in order to insist on the need to maintain the *status quo*: the PCI might have been expected to depict the emergency on as broad a scale as possible in order to justify its own participation in government after 1976. Notwithstanding their interest for the purposes of comparison among translations, however, the differences hardly alter the overall statistical significance of political crime in the total volume of criminal activity. The levels of ordinary crime rose very rapidly in Italy up until mid-decade after which they remained roughly stable, particularly in the categories of serious offences. Numerically the weight of political crime remained very low, compared to the 1 175 774 offences against persons and property recorded in 1972 and the 1 866 270 in 1976; even in the cases of the most serious crimes politically-inspired actions made a very small contribution, amounting to 2 per cent of all murders and manslaughters in the particularly violent year of 1978 and to no more than 4 per cent of all kidnappings for ransom between 1973 and 1981.[20] So, while the differences in counts are significant for the specific purpose of illustrating the fragility of the category 'terrorism', they barely affect the calculation of its very limited overall contribution to total criminal activity.

Third, assuming that in each case the particular definition of 'terrorism' was applied consistently, the divergent patterns of annual variation in the three arrays support different trajectories of violence. The Ministry's figures suggest a continuously escalating violence between 1971 and 1978, followed by an initially slow, then more precipitate, decline to a level in 1982 which nevertheless remained significantly above that of 1969. The PCI profile, in contrast, shows no clear trend for the period 1969–76; but it then indicates a dramatic escalation just at the time of the party's advance towards full governmental responsibilities, followed by an equally sharp drop in 1979 (22 per cent lower than for 1978) immediately that advance was put into reverse. The Cattaneo Institute figures offer yet a third pattern, in which political violence reached its zenith only in 1979, so that the significance of the events of 1978 (the Moro kidnapping and the attack on the 'historic compromise' policy) as a key turning-point, as suggested by both the Ministry and PCI profiles, is much reduced. Because the different sets of statistics tell contrasting stories of increase and regression, no one array can unproblematically be used to chart an incontestable reflection of wider political processes in the evolution of violence.

Lastly, although this difference is not directly visible in Table 1.1, the sources from which the arrays were taken pay very uneven attention to the extent of discrimination among types of violence and attribution of responsibility. The Ministry's compilation does not make any distinctions between acts committed by the Left and the Right, by separate signatures within the Left, by geographical incidence of violence, or according to whether the act was claimed or not: its only detailed disaggregations concern the categories of victim, especially State employees. The PCI study, on which the Cattaneo categories also rest, offers extremely detailed figures along all of those dimensions; indeed the only ones publicly available. While that contrast itself may not be significant, except in so far as it is consistent with the particular sensitivity of the Left to different types of violence and to the need to distance itself publicly from all of them, it does point towards the more general question of where and how to draw the boundaries around the actors to whom 'terrorist' actions are attributed. In any case, through their use of particular classificatory grids, statistical arrays cannot help endorsing or failing to endorse the significance of distinctions to be identified in the phenomenon that they fix.

Boundaries around actors

In a political context already saturated with beliefs about the readiness of actors at all points on the spectrum to make use of violence, its appearance in clandestine form offered great scope for conflict over the definition of its agent. Like witchcraft disputes in small-scale societies, arguments about 'terrorism' drew on a whole field of discourse about collective accountability, direct and indirect responsibilities and the moral nature of individual 'terrorists'. As in cases of witchcraft the disputes especially flourished among interpreters whose own roles and relationships were ambivalent or changing; arguments about the contours of 'terrorism' promoted a boundary-sharpening exercise, intended to clarify the proper principles of local and national order.[21] Publicly-expressed views about the nature of political violence were highly context-dependent and responded flexibly to shifts in the broader patterns of political relationships. In

Chapters 3 and 4 I shall try to relate contrasting translations of 'terrorism' to specific aspects of local conflicts. Here I shall simply sketch the broad field of disputes over the identity of the actors of 'terrorism' in which the positions held in different interpretive communities – political parties, the magistrature, trade unions and social scientists – and identified later in more detail have distributed themselves.

Demarcations of the actors alleged to be responsible for the violence of the 1970s have been offered at various levels. At the broadest level, the dispute has turned on whether Italian political violence, particularly of the Left, should be seen as part of an international conspiracy or as a purely national phenomenon. The suggestion of an international dimension has come in three forms: first, that groups such as the Red Brigades were entirely directed by the security services of a foreign power, the KGB and the CIA naturally appearing as the most favoured puppeteers; second, in a weaker version, that foreign powers were able to use the general cover of an indigenous violence to organise the most significant attacks, which would have ramifications far beyond Italy; and third, that, rather than vertical direction by another state, a horizontal organisation of all Europe's clandestine armed groups, exchanging resources and personnel but maintaining their distinct national objectives, constituted the directing agent. The first version is best-known through the affirmations of Claire Sterling (notably in *The Terror Network*) and right-wing American think-tanks, although it has had some support in Italy. In 1981, for example, the then president of the Republic, Pertini, publicly accused East European powers of playing a significant role in directing violence in Italy. At grass-roots level, too, among the 41 per cent of respondents to the PCI questionnaire survey in 1981–2 who had clear views about where the responsibilities for violence lay, two-thirds (68 per cent) attributed them in equal proportions to the East and to conservative western organisations.[22] The second version has been proposed in the case of Moro's kidnapping and murder but for no other instance, so that the explanatory role given to an alleged international connection for violence which in fact lasted for more than a decade is very restricted. The third version points only to possibly instrumental cooperation among groups which have purely autochthonous origins and reasons for persistence. Published evidence for any of the three versions as serious candidates in accounting for the origins and trajectory of Italian political violence does not exist; and I mention them here to indicate that I shall assume that they have no explanatory role in the rise and decline of left-wing violence.[23]

Assigning Italy's 'terrorism' a purely national status has neverthe-less left two boundary questions controversial. The first concerns the distinction between violence of the Left and of the Right: did they constitute two wholly autonomous areas with independent dynamics or was the nomenclature and lexicon of apparently left-wing groups a mask behind which the extreme Right pursued its conservative goals? The least implausible version has suggested that, while all members of groups with left-wing signatures were not necessarily consciously neo-Fascist, some of the leaders with decision-making power may have been. (An analogous account did away altogether with dis-cussion of the intentions of the actors by defining the phenomenon as 'objectively Fascist'.) The second boundary issue rests on an acknowledgement that left-wing violence was an autonomous phenom-enon but insists on asking whether its apparent internal differences between 'organised' (i.e. claimed and serious) and 'spontaneous' (i.e. unclaimed and less serious) acts of political violence represented a genuine heterogeneity of inspiration and responsibility or were rather to be seen as tactical variations in a single jointly planned and directed strategic attack. Some analysts, indeed, have identified the specificity of Italian violence with respect to other European cases precisely in terms of the novelty of its dual-level assault on the state, giving key diacritic weight to the organisational dimension.[24] Others regard the distinction between text-accompanied and text-unaccompanied acts as fundamental, as used in the Cattaneo Institute statistics, and treat the manifest content of the texts as incorrigible in marking internal distinctions.

A continuing set of disputes about the correct identification of the boundaries of the actors thus marked the entire trajectory of violence. Parallel contests over political identity, scale of aims and the privilege to be given to the language of violence or to the texts in determining the meaning of actions and strategies occurred on both sides. For the practitioners of violence the basic goal of creating a distinctive identity and obtaining generalised recognition for it shaped their actual deployment of violence: the knowledge of the interpretive conflicts among their potential interlocutors was a prim-ary factor entering their own decision-making. Ascribing the choice of particular forms for their actions to the single demand for publicity through clamorous effects (the dominant goal often imputed to clandestine users of violence) is reductive and cannot explain why, given the duration of the phenomenon, so few illustrious figures or major events became targets. With only a few exceptions both left-wing and right-wing groups eschewed 'spectacular' actions of the kind practised in other societies – the occupations of buildings and radio stations, the hijacking of aircraft, the kidnapping of prominent figures and other prolonged actions into which the media themselves could be directly incorporated to dramatise the attack. Among their opponents too, conflicts over the basic identity and goals of the actors they were combating were recurrent in a general way throughout; but they also provided specific causes for dispute in the single domains with institutional responsibilities for defining and managing violence. Viewed over time, however, the different domains were not equally and simultaneously salient in contributing to the public delineation of the problem of 'terrorism'. Two distinct phases can be identified, separated by a caesura in 1980.

In the first phase the dominant interpretive domain was the political arena, with an important adjunct in the factory. The exchanges most significant for establishing the public meanings of violence and actors' identities linked the active members and suppor-ters of armed groups, the political élite and the trade unions, each of which also attempted to mobilise further sections of local or national audiences. The perspective from which the different accounts were provided was essentially exploratory. However confidently the his-torical analogies and logical predictions were delivered, no actor could be sure what the capacities and effects of violence and responses to violence would turn out to be. All participants were in search of the meanings of what they were doing, might be able to do and had in fact done. The vocabulary used by both sides to decide the controversial issues of aims and identities was political, since the primary translators of the public significance of 'terrorism' were the political parties. Their interpretive activity did not cease in 1980 but its salience was diminished on one hand, by the confinement of its most focused discussions behind closed doors in the Parliamentary Commission of Inquiry into the Moro affair and, on the other hand, the emergence of the judicial forum as the constitutive arena for the dissemination of public knowledge of violence.

Until 1980 the difficulties of police and magistrates' judicial investigations, especially in the period after 1975, had largely ex-cluded the judiciary's representatives from contributing directly to the elaboration of 'terrorism'. However, the appearance of the first 'repentant terrorists' (*i pentiti*) willing to provide detailed accounts of the past allowed a dramatic expansion in understanding violence, but mediated through a very different translational process than that of the earlier phase. First, the magistrature replaced the political élite as the principal public translator. Second, the repentant terrorists came from a different milieu in the armed community with respect to the account-givers of the first phase. They therefore offered not merely a mass of factual details about armed struggle but also a different – and hitherto submerged – perspective in which to place them. In effect the organisational idiom of *gesellschaft* replaced the communitarian, *gemeinschaft* orientation in characterising the nature of relationships among participants in violence. Third, that shift was also directly tied to the break between the dominant descriptive language of the two phases. After 1980 'terrorism' was presented in judicial terms, constrained by legal procedures, rules for valid evidence and the penal code. Versions for courtroom consumption thus often differed sharply in their basic emphases from the accounts of the same incidents, causes and relationships provided in the political lexicon of the earlier period or in other contemporary contexts. The extent to which the penal and political accounts and grounds for decision were allowed to overlap, or were necessarily intertwined, itself became a focus of dispute in particular instances: however their displacement in time reduced to a minimum cases of apparently flagrant contamination of institution-specific versions and thus worked against confirmation of the armed groups' major charge that the constitutional pluralism of the Italian State was a mere facade. Finally, since the virtual conclusion of the judicial processing of violence a third phase has been opened, characterised by the search for consensus around yet further vocabularies to describe the past in the light of present demands for reconciliation among former enemies and dominated by still another set of public translators for the different interests. Discursively, therefore, 'terrorism' has become a layered sequence of overlapping but unstable redescriptions.

In diachronic perspective for sociological analysis Italian left-wing 'terrorism' (or, from the opposite side, 'armed struggle') appears as a socio-political phenomenon held together as much by the conflicts of its participants as by their agreements and as the product of very different translating communities working on the elementary acts of violence. Interpretations themselves circulate as elements influencing the direction of violence itself, in so far as they supply an identity and role for a wide range of actors involved. Before examining the process in detail, I shall conclude this introductory chapter by considering the translational activities of the social sciences with regard to Italian violence, since they too must ineluctably be part of the same translating process that they seek to describe.

ITALIAN SOCIAL SCIENCE AND POLITICAL VIOLENCE[25]

Far from any interpretive privilege being accorded to its translations of 'terrorism', Italian sociology has been accused of a range of culpable commissions and omissions directly facilitating the rise and persistence of the phenomenon. Just as in other European societies sociology was frequently accused of partial responsibility for the student movements of 1968–9, so in Italy the charge has been more narrowly referred to left-wing violence. The reverberations of the passage of two early Red Brigades leaders through the then recently-established social science degree at Trento marked out any subsequent connection between violence and sociology as immediately newsworthy. Even in 1984 the Director of the Trento programmes was moved to exculpate his institution and its disciplines by pointing out that no more than 11 (0.5 per cent) of the 2312 people arrested for political violence between 1978 and 1983 had actually studied there.[26] Others have claimed that the intellectual concerns of sociology were inappropriate or evasive in the explanation of a phenomenon created directly through deliberate politico-ideological choice by participants. Worse, because of the discipline's encouragement of a facile and over-sympathetic understanding which depicted individuals in the grip of ineluctable forces, it not only obscured the essentially voluntarist and strategically organised nature of political violence but actually supplied a legitimating motivation for the actors.[27] The suggestion that sociological accounts could simply offer an alibi to the practitioners of violence and thus facilitate their commitment was commonly proclaimed by political parties, especially the PCI. But there is no evidence that in fact any of the terms or concepts used in such commentaries were deployed in self-descriptions: the more popular books by sociologists were read simply to confirm how little even their professional social scientific authors appeared to understand the world of armed struggle.[28] All such charges against sociological versions referred exclusively to accounts of left-wing violence as, until very recently, no analyses at all of neo-Fascist violence have been made.[29]

A contributory factor to the low esteem with which other institutions regarded sociological explanations of 'terrorism' lay in the prolonged difficulty in establishing a research programme with a clear problematic and set of questions. For the reasons given earlier, sociologists had no access to a privileged, professionally created, data base; and it would be foolish to overlook the obstacles to knowledge constituted both by the rules of secrecy applying to information turned up in judicial investigations and by the physical dangers courted by academic researchers gathering data on a population which might well include some of their own students. But in any case the subject matter of political crime was not one likely to receive much analytical consideration in what was, in 1970, a very recently institutionalised discipline. Only 2 of the 234 sociology courses being taught in Italian universities in 1972 dealt with crime and deviance, and they were concerned with broad macro-structural dimensions of criminality rather than the understanding of the kinds of restricted sub-cultures that the promoters of armed struggle were trying to build.[30]

Nor throughout the entire trajectory of violence were specific sociological enquiries initiated individually or much encouraged by the State. Between 1975 and 1983 the National Research Council (CNR) funded seven separate and very heterogeneous investigations to a total of 96 million lire (£42 000): two comparative international studies, two inquiries into the relationship between violence and the marginalisation of youth, the culture of right-wing violence, a statistical profile of terrorism 1969–82, and a comparison of the biographies of terrorists as presented by the media of three European states.[31] Unlike the West German case the public authorities did not sponsor comprehensive social scientific inquiries or make use of academic expertise to analyse the social and cultural worlds of political violence. The only Italian case known to me was the irregular consultation of a university psychiatrist and a philologist during the Moro kidnapping who offered respectively prognostications of the likely development of the Stockholm syndrome between hostage and captors, and observations on the texts' probable authors.[32] Likewise, although the investigating magistrates were often compelled to analyse the evolution, structure and ideology of armed groups, they did not draw on the social sciences for assistance, even although some of their more committed members sometimes found themselves sharing a public platform with academic commentators. Indeed, precisely the absence of scientific studies of Italian political violence was identified by one magistrate as the basic reason for the broad coverage of his own account.[33] The only political party to make use of sociological expertise was the PCI in designing its 1981–2 questionnaire, although the intended full analysis of the responses was, for contingent reasons, never carried out. However, in its role as the dominant party in the Reggio Emilia regional government, the PCI sponsored the first serious collective and publicly-funded research programme on political violence, initiated under the auspices of the Cattaneo Institute in Bologna in 1982. In sum, the left-wing groups gave considerable importance to the institutionally integrated counter-revolutionary functions of the anti-guerrilla technicians of word and image who disseminated hostile versions of their own identity to the public at large; but sociologists in their academic role were hardly among them.

In consequence, and unlike other communities affected by violence, no new forms of solidarity or collective enterprise developed among sociologists until the phenomenon was all but over. Moreover the conviction that it was ultimately more important to respond as a citizen than as an academic meant that many published assessments by sociologists not based on primary research appeared in party and union journals rather than in a disciplinary forum: none of the 16 contributions to sociological interpretations surveyed in 1982, for example, had appeared in a sociological journal.[34] That dispersal certainly added to the difficulties in building up sociological trans-lations to oppose to lay versions as guides to better management of any of the issues connected with violence. It also worked against a systematic examination of the conceptual and operational problems in defining and researching political violence, leaving even recent discussions vulnerable to the charge of methodological naivety in handling the issue of actors' accounts.[35] It has also produced very uneven attention to the different questions posed by the topic.

The overwhelming emphasis has been on the national macro-level dimensions of 'terrorism' and on the question of its origins, the first corresponding to the discipline's general orientation in the 1970s and the second to the appearance of most sociological accounts during the years when the outcomes of armed struggle were by no means certain. With the exception of the proceedings of a conference held at Bologna in 1983 few accounts by sociologists or political scientists have appeared since 1981.[36] 'Terrorism' was therefore externalised as a largely homogeneous object of knowledge, at least for the purposes of analysis, and was accounted for in relation to such socio-economic factors as youth and proletarian 'marginality' created by the distorted patterns of Italian capitalist development or by enduring features of the political system. The most influential versions linked the appearance of political violence either to the exclusionary effects of a 'blocked' polity, incapable of adequate response to the demands carried by the social movements of 1968–9, or to the determination of conservative forces to prevent the Italian Communist Party gaining full legitimacy and increasing its mass support.[37] From the macroperspective most distinctions between types of violence are ignored or remain theoretical: illustrative materials have usually been drawn from the group with the highest national aspirations of its own, the Red Brigades, which nevertheless represented only one component of the armed community. The level at which analysis of the interaction between that community and its political antagonists has been pitched is generally abstract and the discussion has in practice been focused on the issue of the genesis of violence. By identifying putative causal factors in the emergence of 'terrorism', those sociological accounts necessarily move very close, whether deliberately or not, to accusations of direct responsibility against other (usually political) actors in Italian society and thus respond to the charges of sociology's own causal role.

Even on their own terms the validity of the substantive macro-level analyses remains far from secure. The 'blocked polity' thesis, for example, has not specified clear indices of blockage at a structural level or identified its perception as a significant element in actors' beliefs; and an awkward counterfactual question needs to be confronted: 'Why did left-wing political violence *not* develop in France where the mobilisations of 1968 were more extensive, and their closure far more decisively conservative, than the contemporaneous student and worker movements in Italy and West Germany from which the early affiliates of clandestine violence came?' The marginality hypothesis has not resolved a similar definitional problem with its major variables or managed to link the actual geographical and social distribution of economic disadvantage in Italy at all plausibly with the striking regional concentration of political violence and the social status of its recruits. In both approaches too many people in identical social-structural positions are swept into the phenomenon, without the question of the successive filters leading only a very few members of the relevant categories actually into the practice of armed struggle being satisfactorily addressed.

The national approach also leaves three areas of enquiry underexplored. First, the actors' own meanings have been largely omitted from the explanation of violence. The different, and often conflicting, ambitions for the use of violence and the distribution of unequal tolerance for distinct types of damage have not been reinstated into sociological accounts, except when the fact of producing a text to accompany an act of violence is used to define the phenomenon of 'terrorism' itself. Second, the local dimensions of political violence – the significance of violence in a particular context, the internal dynamics of single armed groups, the relations among different groups in single cities – have been obscured by the focus on the national level and meanings of political violence. Third, the full range of consequences, especially in the immediate institutional or geographical sites where violence was concentrated, have been hidden by the near-exclusive emphasis on the most visible legal and political restrictions to Italian democracy. Local consequences should not only be scrutinised as a matter of empirical completeness: they also influence the development of violence itself since its users should be presumed to be sensitive, at least in certain respects, to the effects of the damage they seem to succeed in inflicting within often restricted contexts. The sense that the world yields to and for violence is a critical factor in its expansion and decline especially when there is no surrounding community of membership clearly independent of the faith in violence alone. Each of those three areas of enquiry raises many more issues than can be fully explored here.

At the risk of appearing hopelessly naive, this study also resists the explanation of the rise and trajectory of left-wing violence in terms of a conspiracy to cause or prolong it and therefore rejects the identification of 'terrorism' as a purely dependent variable of the aims of groups remote from the participants to direct the evolution of Italian society. I have chosen to describe the *anni di piombo* as the product of two progressively estranged communities, each riven by conflicts of various kinds and endeavouring to reach or confirm a knowledge of the other from a distance. The analysis is organised sequentially according to the key sites where the meanings of violence are contested and (temporarily) fixed, proceeding from the armed community itelf to the factory, political and judicial domains and attempting to show in each case the contests over the identities of the translators, the ideological and organisational influences in determining their translations, and the consequences of their public diffusion. Because the occasions on which representatives of the armed and political communities come into near-direct confrontation are critical in determining the meanings of violence, space is devoted specifically to the episodes of kidnapping organised by the armed groups and to the – in several respects – *formally* analogous occasions of the trials organised by the State. Both show especially clearly the dynamics of symbolic conflict – the level on which ideologically-inspired violence largely conducts its significant battles with antagonists and thus furnishes key moments in the attempt to construct, and subsequently to demolish, the cultural bases for the practices of armed struggle and identities of its participants.

2 The Trajectory of Armed Struggle

For all participants in left-wing violence the fundamental compelling symbol was 'armed struggle' (*lotta armata*); the immediate goal, the construction of an 'antagonistic community' (*comunità antagonista*) which recognised itself in the practice of violence; the long-term project, the realisation of communism. That much at least could be assented to by all activists, however deeply they were otherwise divided on issues of tactics and strategy, allegiance to particular signatures, and range of political experiences. Whether violence was described as primarily a form of 'armed propaganda' in the language of the Red Brigades or as a moment of self-realisation and demonstration of autonomy from the existing order in the jargon of *Autonomia*, concern with its role in both constructive and destructive dimensions was general. Relations with opponents and enemies will be examined in Chapters 3 and 4: here I shall concentrate exclusively on the formation and internal dynamics of the symbolic community of armed struggle.

The building of a distinctive community around the use of violence entailed the creation of a common language for deploying and interpreting violence as a political tactic, a definition of the community's boundaries, and the establishment of recognised positions of power and the authority within them. First, some consensus had to be reached on the meanings of the varied ways of inflicting damage so that actions could be clearly understood by as wide a range of audiences as possible. A language for describing violence had to be borrowed or invented at various levels of generality: replacing ordinary terms for murder and wounding with less-contaminated euphemisms; identifying the reasons for selection of particular categories of target at a given time; explaining why the use of violence was necessary at all for social transformation.[1] Second, the hierarchy of friends, allies, opponents and enemies had to be mapped out, alongside the delineation of the particular social categories for whom the users of violence claimed to speak. Third, some decision-making apparatus was necessary, accompanied by rules of access and specification of tasks, even if it was only rudimentary and formally favoured the abolition of differences among activists and between alleged representatives and the represented. The trajectory of Italy's left-wing violence was a history of unresolved disputes over those issues, punctuated by unsuccessful attempts to establish the hegemony of particular languages, definitions of the community or organisational frameworks.

Both the existence of the disputes and the failure to resolve them can be traced back, on one hand, to uncertainties over the basic use of violence and, on the other, to the heterogeneity of the activists of armed struggle and the difficulties of building solidarity among them. Ideologically, a fundamental ambiguity over whether violence should properly be considered as merely *one* weapon for the radicalisation of existing conflicts or as *the* historically obligatory replacement of those same ineffective struggles divided the community of armed struggle at all levels. Although single organisations, respectively *Autonomia* and the Red Brigades, have been treated as the clear embodiments of those contrasting views, their actual trajectories show that they were themselves in permanent internal tension over the issue. Thus disputes about the relative importance of local and national audiences and about whether to expand the micro-centres of 'counter-power' and openly institutionalise illegality or to insist on full clandestinity and a concentration on the macro-level of the political arena were perennial. They generated a continuous process of fission and fusion within the community as well as stimulating the emergence of yet further groups intent on combining the two perspectives ('closing the scissors' – *chiudere le forbici* – in their leaders' terms) in a single unified project. Treating individual signatures as embodying ideological homogeneity over the correct role and possibilities for violence is to mistake their major users' aspirations for concrete achievements; and it obscures the significant messages carried by violence against external targets but directed internally both to other components in the community of armed struggle and to other users of same signature. Understanding the profile of left-wing violence is therefore dependent on giving equal analytic importance to internal and external audiences.

If group signatures are not to be treated straightforwardly as indices of the basic social and ideological units of armed struggle, then the divisions within the community of armed struggle have to be accounted for differently. After identifying the very heterogeneous composition of the acts and actors involved in armed struggle, I shall argue that the community can best be seen as stratified into three distinct, successively-formed milieux: the intelligentsia, apparatchiks and locals.[2] Each had its own specific origins and political experiences in extreme-Left politics and controlled one of the necessary resources requiring combination to make any communicative political strategy using violence both possible and meaningful: the ideological languages for public justification; the weapons and explosives for carrying out the actions; and the forms of logistical support and recruitment for group survival. Each milieu was also linked informally to different areas of the surrounding society which provided access to further resources for use in internal conflicts.

The so-called 'terrorist organisations' are therefore best seen as fragile and changing combinations of members of the different milieux, so that their collective trajectories and deployments of violence can be plotted in terms of the different patterns of enrolment and conflict, both internal and external. The milieux remained largely distinct, partly because of their heterogeneous composition, partly because of their tendency to entrench enmities with different categories of outsiders, and partly because the linkages established exclusively by participation in clandestine violence led at most to a community based on what Durkheim called 'negative solidarity' – a social world in which resources remain attached to individuals and even in joint use do not enhance the degree of active consensus among participants.[3] The conditions under which violence was undertaken – secrecy, the obligation to withhold rather than share information (*compartimentazione*), the standard formation of the action-sets to carry out specific attacks from participants who in many cases did not know the target or the scale of violence to be used or the motivation behind the act, and the absence of any positive rewards accruing to individuals – prevented the activities of armed struggle, representing the very diacritic of the community's identity, from creating increasingly firm bases for cooperation. Solidarity rested on the reciprocal knowledge of involvement in illegal activities and on the hope that the shared negativity of antagonism towards a range of enemies would compensate for the failures to strengthen positive internal bonds. Likewise, the languages for rendering violence politically intelligible were derived less from positive innovations than from the revelation, then the attempted valorisation, of the darker side of existing rhetorics and symbols. The combination of negativity and instrumental alliances was captured by the title of an anthology of *Autonomia*'s texts – *The Right to Hatred* – and by an ironic line on the longer-term future of armed groups which circulated among their members: 'We'll make the Revolution and then leave'.[4]

THE PROFILE OF LEFT-WING VIOLENCE: ACTS AND
ACTORS

Acts and victims

Although the parabola of left-wing violence has stretched out over
more than 15 years, touched most parts of Italy and many categories
of victim, the overwhelming majority of serious actions were narrowly
concentrated in place, time and target. That focus gave the overall
phenomenon a kind of predictability and a particular intensity in a
few key institutional and urban locales which served as laboratories
for the use of, and resistance to, violence. Throughout the period
left-wing violence was largely confined to central and northern Italy
and in particular to the four provinces of Rome, Milan, Turin and
Genoa. With the exception of Naples in 1980–2 and isolated episodes
in Calabria and Sardinia, the south remained largely untouched by
left-wing attacks: the bulk of its minority contribution to political
violence (18 per cent of all actions compared to 40 per cent in central
Italy and 42 per cent for the north) came from the Right.[5] Moreover,
as the only overall figures show (Table 2.1), four-fifths of violence
claimed by or attributable to the Left was concentrated into the four
years between 1976 and 1979.

The profile of the content and forms of left-wing violence reveals
the progressive salience of the most serious violence carried out by
groups acknowledging responsibility in documents proclaiming their
motivations and political identities. For most of the period 1970–6
left-wing violence came in the dual form of actions by clandestine
groups (amounting to no more than one-third of the annual total of
actions) and by more or less organised components of the extreme
Left, often in the course of collective mobilisations for demonstrations and protest marches. With the exception of the kidnappings
carried out by the Red Brigades, the actions of both sets of actors
were barely distinguishable. The commonest forms taken were minor
physical attacks on individuals, assaults on party and union offices,
arson and damage of police stations, public buildings and utilities and
shops: the destruction of private cars and municipal buses represented a favourite target throughout the period, accounting for nearly
one in five (17 per cent) of all attacks and reaching as high as two in
five actions in the major centre of Genoa. From 1977 onwards, however, the profile changed. First, the absolute and relative numbers of
more serious deliberate attacks on individuals rose considerably: in

TABLE 2.1 *Left-wing political violence 1970–82*

Year	Actions claimed				Actions not claimed		Totals of claimed and unclaimed actions
	Deaths*	Woundings	Other actions	No. of different signatures for claims†	Actions attributed to extremists	Actions attributed to Left	
1970	–	–	4	1	8	1	13
1971	–	–	6	1	3	17	26
1972	–	–	31	4	18	39	88
1973	–	–	11	2	20	20	51
1974	3	–	29	5	49	65	146
1975	2	5	41	8	76	44	168
1976	8	9	89	24	157	63	326
1977	7	33	204	77	533	216	993
1978	32	38	568	179	480	472	1590
1979	24	43	592	217	380	143	1182
1980	29	18	175	73	41	46	309
1981	12	6	97	48	23	26	164
1982	14	3	54	22	3	11	85
Total	131	155	1901	526‡	1791	1163	5141

* Includes deaths resulting from clashes with police as well as ambushes

† An identical signature appearing in different parts of Italy here counts once only in each year, although it indicates no necessary organisational identity.

‡ Total of different signatures appearing in the period 1970–82.

SOURCES

1970–80, M. Galleni, *Rapporto sul terrorismo* (Milan: Rizzoli, 1981) *passim.*
1981–82, Direzione PCI, Sezione Problemi dello Stato: 'Attentati e violenze in Italia nel 1981' (Rome, 1982); 'Attentati e violenze in Italia nel 1982' (Rome, 1983).

particular deaths moved from 3 per cent of all claimed actions (including woundings) to 25 per cent in 1982. Second, the penumbra of generic left-wing violence shrank equally rapidly, so that actions over specific signatures which had contributed only one-quarter of the volume of violence in 1977 accounted for more than four-fifths by 1982. The two trends were clearly linked. The extreme Left became increasingly reluctant to sponsor public protests that small groups of practitioners of violence were determined to turn into armed confrontations with the police, and the State itself responded to that likelihood by a more rigid control of the public arena, banning marches, refusing to allow them through city centres and insisting that the organisers themselves provide more effective guarantees against the degeneration of peaceful protests into street battles.

The substantial concentration of left-wing violence in time and space was matched by the profile of categories of victims, especially for the most serious attacks (Table 2.2).

Italy's various police forces provided the largest single category of all victims, especially among deaths. Roughly half (27) of their 57 victims were killed in the course of incidental conflicts with armed activists: the remainder were deliberately ambushed as symbolic representatives of the State. An analogous dominance among the victims of deliberate woundings and kidnappings belonged to indus-

TABLE 2.2   *Categories of victims: killings, woundings and kidnappings by left-wing groups 1970–82*

	Deaths	Woundings	Kidnappings*	Total	%
Police forces, CC	57	12	–	69	23
Industrial personnel†	11	66	8	85	28
Politicians	4	21	3	28	9
Prison officers and staff	7	7	–	14	5
Doctors	1	16	–	17	6
Magistrates	7	3	3	13	4
Journalists	2	7	–	9	3
Others	42	23	3	68	22
Totals	131	155	17	303	100

* Excludes unclaimed kidnappings carried out solely for ransom. Three kidnap victims were murdered and one was wounded: they have been included in both relevant columns.
† Managers, supervisory staff, foremen, nightwatchmen, business students.
SOURCES
1970–80, Galleni, *Rapporto sul terrorismo, passim.*
1981–2, Direzione PCI, Sezione Problemi dello Stato: 'Attentati e violenze in Italia nel 1981', pp. 12–14; 'Attentati e violenze in Italia nel 1982', pp. 3–4.

trial managers and factory personnel, drawn primarily from a handful of Italy's major firms. Among the remaining categories under attack politicians, prison personnel (including a number of the doctors, who worked in jails) and magistrates provided the most important continuing targets, with their vulnerability occasionally dramatised by a concentrated assault: three journalists were wounded on successive days in June 1977 and three magistrates were murdered in four days in March 1980. Not included in Table 2.2 but nevertheless to be counted among the victims are the 31 members of armed groups killed in conflicts by the police or by the premature explosion of their bombs or by their own former comrades in revenge for real or alleged collaboration with the State.

Actors

The responsibilities for the 2187 claimed actions were very unevenly distributed among the 526 different signatures recorded for the entire period. As Table 2.3 shows, the majority of signatures were not intended to designate continuing identities and distinctive strategies since they appeared only once.

Similarly three-quarters of the 173 signatures authoring between two and ten actions appeared only in the course of a single year. In those cases the production of a claim document served not only to confuse the police by using different signatures and to suggest a wider range of active involvement in violence than was the case but also to signal generic allegiance to the projects of the more important groups and to acquire a small patrimony of armed achievements in order to negotiate entry to a larger aggregation. At this level the link between signatures and organisational or membership continuity was very

TABLE 2.3   *Acts of violence claimed by left-wing signatures 1970–82*

No. actions	No. signatures	Total no. acts
1	329	329
2–5	146	417
6–10	27	211
11+	24	1230
Totals	526	2187

SOURCES
1970–80, Galleni, *Rapporto sul terrorismo, passim.*
1981–2, Direzione PCI, Sezione Problemi dello Stato: 'Attentati e violenze in Italia nel 1981', pp. 9–10; 'Attentati e violenze in Italia nel 1982' pp. 8–9.

weak. The use of one signature rather than another frequently represented a claim to a meaning-making resource – a claim sometimes bitterly opposed where a particular group found that its attempt to preserve a clear connection between its own name, narrow focus on specific targets and types of violence was being undermined by the local use of the same signature for quite different forms of attack.[6]

At the other end of the scale more than half of all claimed actions were authored by no more than 5 per cent (24) of signatures – a responsibility which was actually even more concentrated since eight signatures should be assimilated to the major groups of which they represented the local emanations and at least a further six should be disaggregated into quite distinct smaller groups which happened to have used the same generic left-wing name. The signatures with a pretence to longevity, activity beyond a single city or region and a concern with organisation and strategy effectively amounted to six, among which the Red Brigades and Front Line (*Prima Linea*: PL) were the most important. The Red Brigades was the only signature to appear every year between 1970 and 1985, covering 32 provinces and authoring 494 actions; PL's lifespan lasted from 1976 until 1982, signing 107 actions distributed across 16 provinces. However, notwithstanding the apparent overall diffusion, more than four-fifths of both groups' attacks were concentrated in the four major centres.

What is known about the number and social characteristics of participants in left-wing clandestine violence (sc., affiliates of the named groups) and the place occupied by violence in their lives? According to government figures, at the end of 1985 a total of 2465 left-wing terrorists were in jail (1175) or had been provisionally released pending trial or definitive sentence (998) or were actively being sought by police (292).[7] Adding to that figure both the unknown number of participants who had already served their full sentences by 1985 and the probably relatively few marginal individuals who remained unidentified would produce a total of between 2700 and 3000. That figure indicates the men and women on whom sufficient evidence could be found to bring them to court. It does not include those who had joined in the 'spontaneous' acts of violence in the course of demonstrations and since the provision of merely logistic support counted in penal terms as group membership, it does not entail that every one of the total participants took a direct part in at least one act of violence. The sociological profile of this population has to be put together, however, from various types and sources of evidence, the very unevenness of which may tend to exaggerate the dominant characteristic of the members of the community of armed struggle – their heterogeneity. None the less, even allowing for that effect, it seems clear that beyond the value attached to the use of violence itself, few structural attributes can be divined which provided the entire community with markers for generalised solidarity.

First, as Table 2.4 indicates, the ages, and therefore the political experiences, of the practitioners of violence varied considerably. Some came from a generation whose political initiation had taken place even before 1968. Apart from the early BR members in Milan (1975) who maintained their activism in jail, half of the defendants in the April 7 trial and one in five BR members in Turin were aged at least 30 by the mid-1970s. Others – notably many of PL's affiliates in Turin – had not even reached secondary school at the time of the Hot Autumn. Although there was some tendency for the members of the Red Brigades to be older than the members of the groups associated with *Autonomia* (PL, *Rosso*-BC and less well-known signatures), the difference appears to have been really marked only in Turin where the generational component was uniquely strong.

In the second place, the armed groups were mainly comprised of men, especially among the older cohorts of members. Men constituted between 63 per cent and 85 per cent of the eight sets of defendants and on average outnumbered women by three to one. That proportion was almost identical to the gender composition recorded for one of the major extra-parliamentary Left groups, *Lotta Continua* (LC), in 1975, suggesting that participation in violence was not a relatively more attractive channel for commitment and activism among women in the largely male-dominated extreme-Left politics.[8] Nor, despite several prominent examples to the contrary, did women have disproportionately greater weight as organisers of violence relative to their overall participation rate. In most cases the majority of female defendants were indicted on less serious charges than men: in the April 7 trial, for example, 8 (67 per cent) of the 12 women had been granted provisional release from custody before the trial opened (a sign of the marginal nature of their involvement) compared with only 12 (20 per cent) of the 59 men. Armed struggle in Italy was not therefore a privileged focus for radical rejections by women of normal patriarchal politics, as has occasionally been suggested for revolutionary or guerilla groups in other societies.

Third, for the overwhelming majority of activists participation in violence was seen as a part-time commitment perfectly compatible with family life and full-time employment. One in three respondents

TABLE 2.4   Ages of defendants in selected trials for left-wing violence: Turin, Milan, Rome

Date of birth	Turin		Milan					Rome	
	PL (1981) %	BR (1981) %	BR (1975) %	BR (1981) %	BR (1981) %	Rosso-BC (1983) %	Minor groups* (1983) %	April 7 (1984) %	BR (1986) %
Pre–1940	1	10	16	1	–	2	5	18	3
1940–5	2	8	32	8	15	5	3	31	6
1946–50	7	21	42	14	41	30	13	37	14
1951–5	27	45	10	42	41	34	25	13	37
Post–1955	63	16	–	34	4	29	54	1	40
Totals	100	100	99	99	101	100	100	100	100
No of defendants	108	38†	31	97	27	87	89	71	174

* Formazioni Combattenti Comuniste (FCC), Reparti Comunisti d'Attacco (RCA), Guerriglia Rossa (GR), XXVIII *marzo*.
† Data on 38 ex 75 defendants only.
SOURCES
Magistrates' *sentenze-ordinanze* of committals for trial. In some cases individuals were charged with membership in more than one group and thus appear in more than one column.

TABLE 2.5   *Occupations of members of armed groups according to two samples (1979, 1984)*

Members arrested between 1 September 1978 and 31 December 1979[1]		
Occupation	*No.*	*%*
University and school teachers	24	12
White-collar workers	28	14
Blue-collar workers	35	18
University students	47	24
Unemployed	11	6
Others	52	26
Total	197	100
Respondents from jail in 1984 survey[2]		
Occupation	*No.*	*%*
University staff, senior management	15	8
Teachers, white-collar workers	53	29
Professionals	35	19
Blue-collar workers	73	41
Unemployed, pensioners	4	2
Total	180	99

SOURCES
1. Testimony of General A. Dalla Chiesa to Parliamentary Commission of Inquiry into the Moro kidnapping (*Commissione Parlamentare d'Inchiesta sulla Strage di Via Fani, sul Sequestro e l'Assassinio di Aldo Moro e sul Terrorismo in Italia* (Rome: Senato della Republica, 1983–6), Doc. XXIII, n. 5, vol. 4, p. 271).
2. *L'Area della Detenzione Politica in Italia*, survey directed by E. D'Arcangelo, Rome, September 1984, p. 12.

in a 1984 survey was married at the time of arrest and one in five had children, so that enrolment in armed groups cannot be seen as a direct reflex of social isolation or of a period of licence between adolescence and the family responsibilities of adulthood.[9] The same survey, confirming more impressionistic evidence, also showed that three-quarters of those arrested had been in full-time work, nearly one-quarter were secondary-school or university students and only 2 per cent were actually unemployed. Table 2.5 shows the range of occupations covered, alongside the not quite comparably classified data from an earlier sample.

Although armed struggle attracted the highly-educated to a disproportionate degree compared to their weight in the overall population (42 per cent of the 1984 sample were graduates or students), it also saw the participation of a wide range of blue- and white-collar workers. The data in Table 2.5 show that economic marginality can be discounted as a source of recruits for violence and that broadly-defined class categories are of little help in explaining the actual social composition of armed groups: the phenomenon brought together people from a wide array of different backgrounds and working experiences.

That heterogeneity is also evident on a more speculative final dimension. Although left-wing violence was largely confined to the cities of central and northern Italy, recruitment was by no means confined to the children of long-standing local residents with family traditions in left-wing political sub-cultures and the Resistance. Although figures on birthplace alone (see Table 2.6) are a very crude and not wholly reliable index, it seems clear that the families of recent migrants to the major conurbations provided a significant minority of participants.

In each of the three major centres of violence the armed groups represented a coalition of local and immigrant activists. But whereas the earliest composition of the Red Brigades in Milan was largely based on immigrants to the city from north and central Italy (notably Reggio Emilia), later groups showed a much higher proportion of members born in the south and islands. In terms of 'ethnic' composition and, as I shall indicate below, the idioms of violence, the two

TABLE 2.6   *Birthplaces of defendants in four trials: Turin, Milan, Rome*

Place of birth	Milan BR (1975)[1] %	Turin PL (1981)[2] %	Milan Autonomia-*based groups (1983)*[2] %	Rome BR (1986)[2] %
City	16	37	30	50
Region	19	9	18	8
North	32	9	12	5
Centre	19	7	10	9
South & islands	10	32	17	21
Elsewhere*	3	5	13	7
Total	99	99	100	100

* Abroad; places I have not been able to identify in Italy.
SOURCES
1. Requisitoria BR, G. Viola, Milan, 1975, reprinted in G. Guiso, A. Bonomi and F. Tommei (eds), *Criminalizzazione della lotta di classe* (Verona: Bertani, 1975) pp. 25–6.
2. Magistrates' *sentenze-ordinanze* of committals for trial.

phases of aggregation to the armed community represented a recapitulation of the two major mobilisations of recent Italian history, the Resistance and 1968–9: the first phase (1970–6) as a pale shadow of the almost exclusively northern conflict with the Fascist regime and German army; the second phase (1976–82) as a re-edition of the alliance between northern craft workers and southern manual labour which generated the Hot Autumn in Turin and Milan. It is almost as if the 1970s set out to replay previous conflicts using the same broad categories of participants but emphasising the kinds of violence which had been largely eschewed or given a minor role at the time – a prolonged collective reassurance through tragic experiment that the non-revolutionary outcomes of the earlier mobilisations had indeed been ineluctable, even when a hitherto-suppressed method of struggle was now made central.

Although the community of armed struggle was otherwise very heterogeneous, almost all its members could show a common origin in the extra-parliamentary Left. Whatever political capital might be made out of the accusations that the totalising world-views of the PCI or radical Catholicism were the direct antechamber to the equally totalising recourse to violence, the immediate point of entry to the armed community was from the extreme-Left groups mostly formed in the late 1960s. The later activists of armed struggle had not in fact been politically socialised at all in the traditional Left which suggests that too much causal weight has been attributed to disillusionment with the PCI's explicitly reformist strategy of the historic compromise. For most practitioners of violence that reformism was taken for granted in their earliest political education. The formation of the three milieux of armed struggle can therefore be understood as the products of developments within the aggregations of the extra-parliamentary Left in the major cities, especially with regard to its relations to national politics, through which violence became gradually disembedded from its original political matrix.

THE THREE MILIEUX AND THEIR RESOURCES

Violence and the extra-parliamentary Left

Illegality and violence were key topoi in the political imagination of Italy's extra-parliamentary Left. Indeed they were sufficiently central to the collectivity's identity, both in theory and practice, to become a natural dimension of political experience for the leaders and activists of the major groups which formed after 1967: *Movimento Studentesco* (MS), *Lotta Continua* (LC), *Potere Operaio* (PO), *Avanguardia Operaia* (AO) and, later, *Autonomia Operaia* (Aut Op). Ideological emphasis on the necessity of violence in revolutionary transformations played a vital diacritic role with regard to the parties of the traditional Left (PCI, PSI), accompanied at a practical level by participation in a wide range of more or less collective illegal activities – road-blocks, sit-ins, occupations of housing and factories, coercion of opponents. Members of the extreme Left played an important, but by no means sole, part in the 83 327 politically-motivated offences recorded for the three years 1969–71; over the decade 1969–79 the police denounced 27 000 affiliates of the different groups for various kinds of illegality.[10]

Politically and experientially, however, violence was more significant as a defensive, rather than aggressive, activity. Resistance to the extreme Right unified the understandings of violence in different contexts: internationally, with the anti-Vietnam movement and – more immediately – preventing Italy following Greece into the belt of authoritarian states in southern Europe between 1967 and 1974; nationally, in resistance to the advance of the neo-Fascist Right through *coup d'état*, violence or electoral success; and locally, in defence against the extreme Right's neighbourhood thuggery towards activists and sympathisers of the Left, which between 1969 and 1974 produced thirteen times as many assaults on left-wing individuals and property (3256 to 251) as the Left carried out against the right.[11]

In their early phase, therefore, every group on the extreme Left was equally concerned, theoretically and practically, with violence and the limits of political activity. All had their rudimentary defence squads (*servizi d'ordine*) assembled to protect them at demonstrations, all compiled and circulated lists of local 'enemies' inside and outside the factory, all chanted truculent slogans and sang beguiling songs which took violence for granted. Of course their activities also extended to many quite different and positive fields which the particular focus here on the darker side of their activities is in no way intended to gainsay.

The diacritic role of violence in the extreme Left's identity – which was probably rhetorically essential to maintaining a space to the left of a parliamentary-based Communist Party – ensured that its leaders and members would find the analysis of 'terrorism' especially awkward. Initially criticism of clandestine violence was mainly levelled at its forms, choices of target and timing. After 1976, as the types and levels of violence expanded, as the extreme Left's own public demonstrations were transformed into occasions of violent conflict by small nuclei of provocateurs and as the groups themselves turned or returned to parliamentary politics, the acceptability of violence in any form became a central issue. The deaths of police and bystanders in violent demonstrations in Rome, Milan and Turin in 1977 and the kidnapping of Moro forced a public clarification of attitudes: the rise of *Autonomia* – an archipelago of heterogeneous collectives, united by active antagonism to all institutions, with open sympathy for the use of the P38 and competing for allegiance in the same social and political catchment area as the surviving extra-parliamentary groups – increased the pressure. Different stances appeared: a continuing refusal to consider 'terrorism' a product of the Left; an attempt to define a legitimately neutral position in the conflict between political and armed communities (*'né con le BR né con lo Stato'*); criticism of violence alongside refusal none the less to exclude its users, described as 'comrades in error', from the wider community of committed revolutionaries. Beyond opposition in the extreme-Left press, and a diminished enthusiasm for organising public demonstrations, lists of suspected participants in armed struggle were circulated in some cities to prevent cooperation at neighbourhood level, to which the armed groups themselves responded by threatening extreme-Left leaders and planning never-actually-executed attacks against particularly hostile local antagonists. The definitional difficulties, coupled with the fragmentation of the extreme Left itself and the guilty knowledge that its own members had not only talked of but actually employed deliberate violence against opponents ensured that the boundary between legal extra-parliamentary politics and armed struggle was never clearly or rigorously drawn during the 1970s. Only in 1980, for example, did the much-reduced extreme Left in Milan organise public demonstrations and conferences against 'terrorism' and thus unambiguously deny a revolutionary identity to the users of violence. However even in 1981 the leaders of the non-violent Radical Party were prepared publicly to address the Red Brigades as *compagni assassini*: killers, yes, but comrades none the less.[12]

At the level of 'terrorist' careers no extra-parliamentary group can claim to have innoculated its activists so effectively against clandestine violence that none joined armed struggle. Nor, on the other hand, did any single group, still less the collectivity as a whole, pass over *en bloc* into an active role in systematic violence. The actual size of the extra-parliamentary Left even in a single city can only be guessed at since the groups rarely issued membership cards or kept individual records, so that the proportion subsequently participating in the armed groups must be equally uncertain. In the case of Milan, for example, one estimate put the number of extreme-Left activists in 1972 at *circa* 8000, which would have been considerably increased by the emergence of *Autonomia*, drawing on a different source of recruits, after 1973: since the number of armed group members in the city was very roughly 500, then the proportion of local post-1968 revolutionaries whose political careers took them beyond at most occasional violence during mass mobilisations stood at no more than 5 per cent.[13] One way of making sociological sense of so restricted a fraction from a broader mass movement is to identify the points at which its constituent cohorts deliberately opted to extend their use of violence, partly in response to shifts in the policy and organisation of the extreme Left itself and partly in response to the extension of national politics into areas formerly their own preserve. The three successive points of fission – 1970–1, 1974–5 and 1977–8 – produced respectively the core elements in the milieux of the intelligentsia, apparatchiks and locals. Correspondingly the global, national and local horizons for violence, which had been united for the extra-parliamentary Left in its resistance to the initial threat from the extreme Right, were split up and passed separately into the political imaginations dominating the three milieux from which the community of armed struggle was formed.

The milieu of the intelligentsia

The category 'intelligentsia' designates the creators and diffusers of the vocabularies of legitimation for armed struggle in Italy. They provided the critical materials for giving violence significance both to its activists and to wider audiences, and the control over public meaning represented the primary resource which distinguished their milieu. By manufacturing and applying a stock of descriptions and explanations for violence, the intelligentsia helped to form the political imaginations of activists and potential recruits, provided the basic materials which members used to judge their 'political growth' (*crescita politica*), and supplied the basic abstract phraseology which could be copied on to the specific leaflets composed by activists to locate particular actions as part of a general strategy. Their primary task was the translation of elements from the texts of Marx and Lenin or from the idiom of the Resistance or from discourses such as needs theory into legitimations of violence appropriate for contemporary Italy. The milieu was built up around open-ended networks of relationships, without clear boundaries and with individual participants being also linked to the domains of legitimate politics and the mass media. Membership could be counted according to the ability and willingness to enter into direct public commentary and debate on the widely-circulated texts which accepted armed struggle as a potentially viable revolutionary strategy, especially the documents over the signatures of the major armed groups. Whether or not members of the intelligentsia were also active organisers of violence is a secondary consideration here, since their role in supplying meanings for others' use could be fulfilled independently of their own direct involvement – a controversial judicial issue, discussed later, for non-Red Brigades affiliates. Far from the milieu being governed by consensus, it was riven by disagreements as its members tacked backwards and forwards between different vocabularies, producing increasingly complex textual *bricolages* as they sought plausible meanings to characterise the practice and potential of violence.

The core-set of its members was largely formed in 1970–1 with a dual focus around the early leaders of the Red Brigades and *Potere Operaio*. Although the two groups offered contrasting versions of the proper role of violence, they were ideologically linked from the start by shared internationalist references for its use. In practice, too, regular meetings between members were encouraged by *Potere Operaio*'s readiness – greater than other extra-parliamentary Left organisations – to host sympathetically the BR communiqués in its publications.[14] The Red Brigades' intelligentsia – mostly university-educated, with some journalistic experience, and having already broken with the PCI – constituted themselves in deliberate opposition to the major groups of the extra-parliamentary Left. Refusing to join organisations which they accused of having come to resemble in miniature the parties of the traditional Left and of being equally incapable of defending 'real' working-class interests, they also declined to engage in 'sterile ideological debate', insisting on the acceptance of armed struggle as the key diacritic of a revolutionary identity, framed initially in the language of the Resistance. However, beginning with the first 'Resolution of the Strategic Direction' in 1975 and accelerating after their authors' definitive arrest in 1976, the minimal ideological productions of the early years, consisting primarily of two short self-interviews in 1971 and 1973, gave way to the composition of steadily more abstract and extended texts. Consistent with the declared aim of making their jail the 'university of armed struggle', the dozen members of the BR intelligentsia authored or contributed significantly to the group's 23 major texts of between 10 and 300 pages, culminating in a 1980 monograph, *L'Ape e il Comunista.*[15] After 1976 the localistic Resistance idiom was jettisoned in favour of a steadily more abstract, generically Marxist language, legitimating violence as a national, state-level political strategy. No doubt that was consistent with the authors' remoteness from social conflicts and with the reappropriation of the Resistance symbology by the parliamentary Left in mid-decade: but it led them into increasing disputes with the other major component of the intelligentsia.

The group initially coagulating around *Potere Operaio* can be traced, indeed traced itself, as a solidary network through the subsequent experiences of *Autonomia* and its major broadsheets and journals: *Rosso* (1973–80), *Autonomia* (1978–82) and *Metropoli* (1979–81).[16] Its dominant members worked in universities and research institutes or came from the professions and can be divided into two groups. One, largely based in Padua and Milan, followed exactly the reverse trajectory of the Red Brigades, moving from *Potere Operaio*'s concern with an insurrection to an insistence on the local contextualisation of violence. The second, primarily concentrated in Rome, sought to yoke together both national and local levels and to combine the legitimating vocabularies in a single unified language. Indeed, as the BR and *Autonomia* terminologies for embedding violence in a political strategy diverged after 1975, so repeated attempts were made to build a unifying discursive position between them. But also as arguments over the range of disputed meanings for armed struggle increased, so the meanings themselves became more remote from the actual contexts in which violence occurred. As the dynamics of textual glossing, commentary and critique among the intelligentsia took root, its members became more concerned with their own internal disputes at the expense of relations with the other milieux.

Towards external audiences, however, the intelligentsia maintained a dominant interpretive position in providing violence with meaning. Their translational role was favoured by several factors. First, the intelligentsia of *Autonomia* controlled the publicly-available journals mentioned earlier through which the texts and issues of armed struggle could be reprinted and discussed and from which the national media could inform themselves and their publics.

Although the Red Brigades did not achieve their aim of creating an independent broadsheet, their ideologues had access to *Controinformazione*, a Milan-based journal beginning publication in 1973 in which the editorial policy was to publish solely theoretical texts.[17] It therefore privileged the general strategic documents authored by the intelligentsia over the more specific, action-based productions of the practitioners of violence themselves; so that not until the final phase after 1980, and even then only after their arrests, did the members of the other milieux get regular public space for their texts, with the appearance of *Il Bollettino del Coordinamento dei Comitati contro la Repressione*.[18]

Second, the intelligentsia's long-standing contacts in the extra-parliamentary and parliamentary Left made its members the natural interlocutors to explain the significance of violence to audiences outside the armed community. *Autonomia*'s intelligentsia provided regular interviews in the national press; and some members played an ambiguous role interpreting the BR intentions during the Moro kidnapping to the leadership of the PSI. The Red Brigades' intelligentsia dominated the space in the political weeklies given to interviews and documents of the group, partly because of the access encouraged by a militancy shared with some journalists in the extra-parliamentary Left, partly because, being in jail, they were accessible in a way that clandestine members were not, and partly because publication in the press of general strategic documents on armed struggle was less morally accountable than giving space to the documents or interviews involving direct practitioners of violence. Furthermore, the intelligentsia's texts were given authoritative status by their public presentation as embodying *the* meaning of violence held by all group members, rather than merely *one* version – a rhetorical device encouraged by the press in justifying its own contribution to the understanding of armed struggle as the provision of facts, not simply as the offer of free publicity for partial accounts and propaganda.[19]

Third, in addition to the strategic documents, the intelligentsia was also responsible for producing organisational schemes to define the correct relationships of members of the group with one another and with outsiders. In the Red Brigades case, for example, the formal charter identified a vertical structure running upwards through 'brigades' (3 to 5 individuals in a particular institution), 'columns' (the basic unit for each city), the 'executive committee' (4 to 5 full-time members responsible for the regular high-level decision-making) and the 'strategic direction' (10 to 15 of the longest-standing members meeting perhaps once a year to check the work of the organisation), traversed by horizontal 'fronts' with logistical and defensive concerns: these distinctions were accompanied by norms of behaviour valid for all members.[20] While such schemes, with which most groups were equipped, are sometimes treated as literally accurate flow charts for all actual decision-making, there is no reason for thinking that they are any more adequate in that respect than the official charters of any formal organisation. Indeed, because the sanctions available to clandestine groups to enforce compliance are more limited than in legal organisations, the schemes are better treated as one type of meaning-making resource. For outsiders they provided an apparently clear guide to a hidden world and were useful in particular to the magistrature in defining responsibilities. By providing a language to redescribe personal and informal relationships in organisational terms, charters contributed to the patterning of those same relations. Indeed, an obvious disparity between the organisational scheme and actual influence concerned the intelligentsia itself. In the Red Brigades its members, once arrested, formally lost their decision-making powers, but in practice they retained considerable overall authority. Among the *Autonomia*-based groups – for example the milieu around the broadsheet *Rosso* in Milan – the intelligentsia formed a largely self-selecting network (*segreteria soggettiva*), exerting influence without official responsibility. The exclusion of the intelligentsia from most formal organisational schemes and its consequent freedom from direct accountability in the groups' own terms has helped to obscure the role played by the vocabularies supplying meanings for violence – less the transparent indicators of the shared ideological preconditions for participating in armed struggle than the key resources continuously in demand and maintained under the control of a specific set of actors.

The apparatchiks

The term 'apparatchiks' indicates the full-time activists and practitioners of violence and is intended to capture their particular concern with the bureaucratic organisation of armed struggle. The specific resources which they controlled were the instruments of serious damage and the signatures making actions comprehensible. Control over especially lethal weaponry such as submachine guns was essential for two purposes: first, to ensure the success of bank robberies and kidnappings through which the milieu could become self-supporting and pay itself salaries (usually the equivalent of £100–150 per month per apparatchik in the late 1970s); second, to perform successfully the murders, woundings and assaults through which the syntax of violence could be extended to carry more discriminating messages within and beyond the armed community. Part-time activists could disarm nightwatchmen of their pistols but they could not make such relatively minor weapons the basis of complex actions likely to involve conflict with the police or armed escorts. The more sophisticated the weaponry, therefore, the wider the range of meanings for the violence it was able to deliver.

Although it is sometimes confidently asserted that those resources have been provided freely by foreign agencies interested in 'destabilising' governments, left-wing groups in Italy were in fact armed and financed through the local activities of the apparatchiks, determined precisely to avoid contamination and obligations by accepting gifts from foreign powers and ordinary criminal organisations. Weapons were acquired from three sources: the initial unearthing of guns used in the Resistance which held primarily symbolic significance; known purchases from Middle Eastern groups in 1978–9, two by *Autonomia* and one by the Red Brigades; and acquisition under false names or by theft from armouries and weapon shops. As far as armed robberies from banks and kidnappings were concerned, only the major episodes have been counted, amounting to 23 cases between 1974 and 1981 yielding between 3 and 736 million lire each and a total of *circa* 3 billion lire (£1.5 million). The five successful kidnappings produced a further 4.5 billion lire (£2.2 million), almost all of which went to the two groups, BR and the *Nuclei Armati Proletari* (NAP).[21] Planning and carrying out the acquisition of these resources probably took up more of the apparatchiks' time than the political violence which they made possible. Indeed control over their use provided the major source of personal power for their owners, since access to scarce weapons and funds was a valuable basis for establishing patron-client networks among groups and individuals committed to armed struggle.

The formation of the apparatchik milieu, which developed largely between 1974 and 1976, was attributable to the loss of political control over a set of solidarities based on violence and to the decline in the need for their defensive use against a traditional external threat. In the four major cities the primary source of the recruitment of apparatchiks was the neighbourhood-level leadership of the extra-parliamentary Left groups and particularly of their defence squads (*servizi d'ordine*).[22] The squads, which were initially assembled only on the occasion of public demonstrations to protect participants against neo-Fascists and the police, were gradually transformed into permanent institutions with a strong sense of exclusive internal comradeship. Membership conferred prestige in the extreme Left's neighbourhood organisation, displayed active political commitment in contrast to enervating and eternal talk and provided substantial training in the use of weapons. The autonomy of the squads from political direction was increased by the shift of their originating parent organisations (LC, AO, *Movimento Studentesco*) towards the parliamentary political arena between 1973 and 1976 and the decisions to participate in elections. The related negotiations between the groups' leaderships within and between the cities where each had its primary stronghold gradually became more significant than the tending of internal relations with their members at neighbourhood level. Fission occurred as the new parliamentary orientation appeared as a betrayal of revolutionary commitment: the exit of disgruntled activists from *Lotta Continua*'s section in Sesto San Giovanni, for example, proved a significant source of apparatchiks in the Milan area. The disintegration of the political casing for the use of violence was further accelerated by the electoral failure of the fragile cartel of extreme Left groups in the elections of 1976, which received only one-quarter of the hoped-for votes, and by the subsequent collapse of the constituent organisations, especially *Lotta Continua* which had been the largest and most open group with the most extensive neighbourhood-level activism and support.

More or less simultaneously came a decline in the external neo-Fascist aggression which had provided the original defensive reason for the squads' existence. Although the capacity of the extreme Right to organise massacres remained undiminished, the level of local everyday aggression reached its peak in 1971 (718 actions) declining steadily to its lowest level for the decade in 1976 (259 actions).[23] The decline was more noticeable in some cities and some neighbourhoods than others. But, significantly, in the cities where the level of neo-Fascist local violence remained highest, the proportion of all acts of political violence which were claimed by clandestine groups remained lowest. In Rome and Milan, for example, where aggression by the extreme Right continued to be significant, the acts of clandestine violence as a proportion of all political violence (both Left and Right) stood at 16 per cent and 18 per cent respectively; in Turin and Genoa, where neo-Fascist activism had virtually disappeared by the mid-

1970s, the proportions reached 33 per cent and 48 per cent.[24] The more open and continuing the need for defence, the less likely it was for the *servizi d'ordine* to transform themselves into clandestine groups for offence, and the more difficult it was for the intelligentsia and apparatchiks of armed struggle to gain local allegiance. By 1976, therefore, tiny nuclei had formed whose members' solidarities and status were constituted around the practice of violence, who had become detached from their former role as local activists under broader political direction and who were in search of an enemy to combat with the forms of political expression they had learned best.

Few apparatchiks matched the stereotypical image of terrorists living in complete clandestinity. The majority were clandestine only in the sense that their adhesion to armed groups was not openly acknowledged: many continued to participate in orthodox forms of extreme-Left politics and were classified in police records as 'extremists' rather than 'terrorists'.[25] Their vade-mecum in this existence was the highly influential text by Giovanni Pesce, *Senza Tregua*, describing the stratagems of clandestine urban violence during the Resistance. When suspicions about their involvement were aroused, some moved to other cities where they could retain their legal identities without being so highly visible to local police. The wholly-clandestine set of apparatchiks, living under false names, was a very small minority of the participants in armed struggle at any one time. In 1976 the Red Brigades were reckoned to have no more than six, increasing to some twenty in 1979; the *Autonomia*-based groups had even fewer, at least until 1980 when confessions and police successes drove larger numbers of activists underground for the (usually short) period before their arrests. In one of the worst years for violence in Milan – 1978 – there were only two wholly-clandestine militants from groups other than the Red Brigades. For obvious reasons activists were very reluctant to go fully underground except when absolutely necessary to avoid arrest. Most entered that secret life thanks to contingent events (for example, the arrival of call-up papers for military service) or by the chance discovery of incriminating evidence; and few have described their existence without emphasising its squalor.[26] But even for those who wished to commit themselves to it, a logistical difficulty presented itself – the availability of a flat to serve as a safe base. Until 1978 apparatchiks had been able to buy dwellings under false names with the purchases often unrecorded for months. But the legal obligation on sellers to register the sale immediately, introduced in 1978 and made retrospective to mid-1977, coupled with systematic police investigation of urban cadasters for non-existent or improbable purchasers' names, forced the armed groups to abandon many of their bases as a precautionary measure. Their members were deprived of a resource hitherto under their autonomous control and were forced into dependence on members who had to remain inactive and above suspicion. That restriction made it very difficult for groups to accommodate new full-time and completely clandestine activists and served to limit the numbers wholly outside ordinary social and political relations.[27]

Reflecting both their apprenticeship in the increasingly hierarchical *servizi d'ordine* and the demands of security in a clandestine life, most apparatchiks were very concerned to maintain the internal and external boundaries of their milieu. Emphasis on formal organisational roles served to provide a sense of renewed cohesion as the members who had belonged to different squads and had now committed themselves full-time to armed struggle were brought together; and it also compensated for the disaggregating effects of individual movement to different cities. Furthermore since some of the earliest apparatchiks had pictured themselves as the controllers of violence as a resource to be placed at the disposal of the working class, the need to ensure at least military efficacy was essential to their supporting role: *Prima Linea*'s founding members described their formation as a 'service structure' for factory-based collectives and as responsive directly to the working-class designation of enemies. Great attention was therefore paid to the visible diacritics of organisations, roles and political identities. Efforts were made to restrict the use of the major group signatures to actions which the apparatchiks had expressly approved or organised. Outsiders were warned off any illicit expropriation so that the public association of specific signatures with distinctive forms of armed intervention could be protected. Part-time affiliates were encouraged to author their actions only with generically 'movement'-oriented names such as 'armed squads' or 'proletarian nuclei' or single slogans, and conflicts occurred when non-members of the milieu made unauthorised use of more specific signatures. Conversely, if a group of part-time activists had carried out an attack regarded as especially successful, apparatchiks would sometimes try to persuade its members to adopt their own higher-level signature to reinforce public perception – especially in the community of armed struggle itself – of the level and efficacy of the violence its users could deploy. Signatures were crucial, and necessarily not easily controlled, elements in determining the meanings of violence and the identities of participants.

Of equal concern to the apparatchiks was the occupation of the designated authority positions associated with each signature. The particular bodies – the 'strategic direction', 'executive committee' and 'fronts' of the Red Brigades, the local and national 'commands' of Front Line, and the 'secretariats' and 'commissions' of minor *Autonomia*-based formations – were shared out among the often never-sufficiently numerous apparatchiks, accrediting them with local status but with the result that the formal divisions of labour enshrined in the organisational charters and the desired barriers to the potentially risky circulation of information were poorly realised in practice. Between 1974 and 1982, for example, a total of only 16 individuals participated at some time in the Red Brigades' 'executive committee' which was formally responsible for approving or initiating and directing the more complex actions. Decisions were in fact often taken without any reference to the group's other apparatchiks or to local affiliates: the most striking example was the kidnapping of Moro which was planned, executed and managed by only a handful of Red Brigades' members, excluding from prior knowledge almost all full-time and casual BR activists even in Rome itself. Likewise, local apparatchiks would ignore or reinterpret proposals coming from their own formal superiors. Moreover, whatever the organisational rules proclaimed, positions of authority were in fact filled by cooptation from above rather than election from below, regulating the flow of new full-time members (*regolari* in BR terminology) and establishing a clear boundary between them and less committed participants (*irregolari*).

In parallel with, indeed partly responsible for, the concentration of official responsibilities went the similarly-restricted readiness to participate directly in the most serious acts of violence. Although several people would usually have collected information on the potential targets and others would provide cover during the attack, the number of apparatchiks actually prepared to use their weapons against unarmed civilian targets was in fact rather small. In Rome, for example, the 32 murders and woundings carried out by the Red Brigades between 1977 and 1981 were the direct responsibility of only 20 men and women. Participants who were ready to accept the wounding of opponents could be found: those who made themselves available to cross what was seen as a major boundary between wounding and murder represented a very small proportion of the total population of the armed community.[28] From the standpoint of each group, therefore, such members and the weapons that, in spite of attempts to designate them as part of a collective patrimony, remained firmly in individual hands constituted a scarce resource. The departure even of a single apparatchik could deprive a group, or local segment of a group, of its capacity to contribute to armed struggle.

Structurally the apparatchiks' contribution to the formation of the community of armed struggle rested on maintaining their position as an obligatory passage point between the intelligentsia and the locals for the circulation of documents and the translation of their general indications into acts of violence likely to meet with support in the immediate context where they were carried out. In establishing the public meanings for their attacks the apparatchiks relied heavily on the intelligentsia whose members were respected as belonging to a senior generation with considerable political experience and the capacity to expound the theoretical necessity for armed struggle. The criteria for the apparatchiks' political education were bound to the knowledge of the intelligentsia's texts, from which fragments were copied or combined in order to compose the leaflets justifying specific attacks. Indeed the apparatchiks reproduced the borrowed contents so effectively in their transient documents that investigators credited them with far more cultural capital than they actually possessed.[29] One Red Brigades' member in Turin reported that the elaboration of the general reasons for justifying specific actions was both difficult and dull, to be avoided wherever possible: in some cases at least the leaflets were not actually written until after the press had carried reactions to the attacks so that materials responding to the responses could be incorporated.[30] Moreover, unlike the intelligentsia, members of the apparatchik milieu had almost no direct contacts or cultural authority in the mass media to ensure publication of their own versions and to give weight to their often much more restricted motivations and ambitions for violence. The press was in any case reluctant to give space to direct first-person accounts, even in semi-disguised form, when they emanated from practitioners of violence who had included journalists among their targets. In 1979, for example, an affiliate of the Milan signature *Proletari Armati per il Comunismo* (PAC) persuaded an activist from a different group to arrange an interview with a schoolfriend who had become a journalist, in order to explain to a wider audience the reasons for the PAC's murder of a jeweller. Although the journalist accepted the meeting, his paper refused to publish the results, thus compelling the act's authors to struggle to produce their own leaflet.[31] In these ways the heterogeneity and fragility of the apparatchik milieu were publicly masked behind an apparently inexorable execution of abstract general legitimations of violence, accrediting the community externally with a stability and unity it did not possess.

The apparatchik milieu was caught among conflicting pressures to confer meanings on the use of the capacity to inflict damage which its members controlled. First, full-time commitment and geographical mobility distanced them from participation in, and knowledge of, local conflicts and made attacks increasingly insensitive to local meanings. Second, the multiplying rival accounts by the intelligentsia, each claiming to identify the vital break points in the Italian economy and polity and expanding the range of targets, supplied violence with a wider range of national-level justifications but at the cost of rendering their actions more evidently arbitrary, not least to the apparatchiks themselves. Violence rapidly became an internal matter of displaying allegiance to particular segments of the intelligentsia: the relationship between texts and actions – between the two languages for converting violence into political action – drifted into self-reference. Third, as the apparatchik milieu expanded after 1976, members identified as primary enemies their own direct antagonists in the police, magistrature and prison staff. Public justification of the increasingly lethal attacks on those non-local categories had necessarily to be framed, however, in terms of their role as symbolic representatives of State power since their true salience as the essentially private opponents of the apparatchik milieu could scarcely be acknowledged. But the recourse to the rhetoric of national-level legitimation did not suffice to prevent accusations by the intelligentsia against the apparatchiks' overriding concern with organisational aspects and with their 'military', but politically inconsequential, targets. The same dynamic also separated them still further from the specific city-based contexts and divided them from the crucial sources of logistic and psychological support in the remaining milieu of the locals.

The locals

The 'locals' consisted mostly of the youngest, part-time, participants in armed struggle. Although a small number had been attached to the Red Brigades since the early 1970s, the milieu was largely formed in 1977–8. They saw their involvement in violence as merely one form of political activity, generating no clear break with their previous or contemporaneous commitments and placing them on the frontier between legal extra-parliamentary groups and the apparatchik milieu. Their political allegiance was given a strongly local referent in their cities or, more narrowly still, their neighbourhoods. While for a period they might be part of the lowest-level and often short-lived micro-aggregates of 5 to 10 individuals – *brigate* (BR), *squadre* and *ronde* (PL) – attached to the major signatures, involvement was seen as, and was, neither irreversible nor primarily organisation-focused. Membership was treated as more or less co-terminous with active participation, lapsed with unavailability and was generally mediated through personal relations with already committed activists. Simultaneous assistance to different groups, sequential passages between them and exit from all participation were therefore options just as commonly chosen as the irrevocable shift into the full-time apparatchik category.[32]

The resources which the locals controlled were: distributing leaflets explaining violence; collecting information on potential targets in their workplaces or neighbourhoods; observing and reporting the local impact of violence; identifying potentially active supporters; storing documents and weapons; and – crucially after 1978 – providing accommodation for permanent activists. Some participated in the actions organised by apparatchiks or formed their own transient action-sets for minor attacks against property targets. Locals moving towards full-time commitment acquired pistols by forcibly disarming policemen or nightwatchmen. Those minor weapons could be used in carrying out 'proletarian expropriations' in supermarkets and for provoking conflicts with the police during demonstrations, thus drawing hitherto non-violent participants into deliberately-staged confrontations with State violence. Finally, not their least important role was simply to meet with apparatchiks and thus to provide them with a penumbra of reassurance and admiration for having dared to demonstrate complete adhesion to widely-shared but weakly-realised convictions.

A specific example of a local's career – which is fairly typical in showing features of that level of participation in Red Brigades' activities – can usefully preface a summary of the formation of the milieu and its relation to the apparatchik level in particular. Recounting her story to the public prosecutor in 1985, Maria ascribed her politicisation, aged 21, in Quarto Oggiaro (Milan) to her reaction to the deaths of Mara Cagol (among the founders of the BR), Claudio Varalli (murdered by neo-Fascists) and Giannino Zibecchi (killed in a police charge during a violent demonstration) in 1975, coupled with the firsthand experience of Milan's major jail during a brief period of employment there. As a participant in the *Autonomia*-based local collectives and the 'proletarian youth' movement of 1976–7 her early activities were to join housing and factory occupations and to help from time to time with the distribution of Red Brigades' leaflets. Developing her contacts with the documents' supplier, she took on a battle-name, 'Luisa', in the autumn of 1977 and considered herself a member of the Red Brigades. However, for the following two years her only involvement consisted of occasional meetings with a local apparatchik, the diffusion of leaflets, one molotov attack on the car of a senior manager in the State office where she worked, the compilation of minimal information on every potential target among her superiors and the provision of lodging now and then for full-time BR members needing cover for a few days. In late 1979 BR apparatchiks wounded two further senior staff in her own office without informing her beforehand even of the plan, a silence maintained also on the occasion of the murder of the agency's director in 1981. In the meantime she participated in ordinary workplace conflicts as a union representative and as an active member of the relevant specialist committee in the local PCI section in which she was also enrolled. As the local BR group seceded from the organisation and subsequently disintegrated after 1980, she was called on to participate in woundings and armed robberies and to try to reorganise the very few, and by then almost completely dispersed, group members. The major series of arrests in Milan in February 1982 forced her underground for a brief period until her capture in November. Condemned to life imprisonment in 1984 for alleged direct complicity in the murder of her office director, she subsequently dissociated herself from armed struggle and made a full confession to the public prosecutor.

Maria's career exemplified the intermittent and part-time involvement of locals in violence, even in such a group as the Red Brigades which has usually been credited with the most tightly integrated structure. In part that pattern was a consequence of the individualised, quasi-clientelistic, linkage of locals to particular apparatchiks. While apparatchiks enjoyed particular prestige in their own milieu from the size of their network of contacts, the dispersed and discontinuous pattern of local enrolment – devised also as a security measure – was very vulnerable to the arrest or transfer to another city of the apparatchik at the centre of the web. But the nature of Maria's participation in the acts of violence ascribed to her by the court illustrates a further general source of instability in local-apparatchik bonds. For once the details collected by locals on the work roles, addresses and routines of a vast range of potential victims had been committed to paper and given to full-time activists, power to determine the use of that information was lost to its compilers. The apparatchiks' eventual attack might be carried out at what, from the point of view of the locals simultaneously engaged in non-violent forms of ordinary legal conflict, might seem a wholly inopportune moment against a then irrelevant target, making the entire action counter-productive. Also, since the information was now stored in a document, it could circulate widely, following the movement of the apparatchiks themselves among the various groups, taking their carefully-preserved archives with them. Thus some 'enemies' could become the simultaneous target of different groups; others would disappear into obscurity. For the locals the tenuous and often apparently arbitrary connections between choice of victims, level and timing of attacks, and intended effect continually undermined the attempt to confer clear political and social meanings on the use of violence.

Apart from illuminating some aspects of the internal organisation of armed struggle, Maria's career also indicates the primary catchment area for the development of the milieu of locals. In the early 1970s the practical interventions of the extra-parliamentary Left were strongly focused on the then largely-unpoliticised terrain of neighbourhood issues, especially schooling, housing and basic welfare amenities. Schools in the major urban areas were drawing in social groups, mostly from recent immigrant families, previously under-represented in post-compulsory education, thus contributing to the formation of denser networks of interpersonal links into the city peripheries for school-based extra-parliamentary Left activists.[33] The scarcity and often atrocious quality of housing there generated a continuing series of occupations of new apartment blocks, often followed by violent confrontations with the police and the owners' armed vigilantes. In addition the general level of public services available in neighbourhoods, often built without detailed planning in hasty response to the internal migrations and increased demands of the post-war years, was low and offered a source of regular conflict with municipal authorities. The local space for extreme Left political activism was, however, compressed from two directions in the years 1975–7. First, its political dimension was largely lost with the turn towards national concerns by the surviving extra-parliamentary groups: no overall strategies continued to link fragmented local initiatives. Second, local-level politics in factories, schools and neighbourhoods were increasingly colonised by parliamentary parties and trade unions who monopolised the new organisms of grass-roots democracy: the factory councils after 1970, the representative councils in schools after 1975 and the neighbourhood councils (*comitati di quartiere*) which were legally formalised in 1977. Symbolic of the extension of control downwards from the centre was the party agreement in Milan and Turin simply to appoint the members of the first councils in proportions exactly reproducing the balance of political power at municipal level rather than to rely on direct local elections. Left-wing parties in particular established a continuing presence there, especially after the municipal councils in all four major cities affected by political violence had been won for the first time by the Left in the local elections of 1975.

The absorption of social issues in the urban periphery into orthodox party and administrative routines effectively expropriated the residual extreme Left from the activities which had grounded its members' 'revolutionary' identities.[34] Some abandoned politics, some (re)joined the parties of the Left, some turned to the explicitly non-violent civil rights' issues advanced by the feminist movement and renascent Radical Party. Others retained a local focus in the micro-aggregations of the *collettivi* and the *circoli del proletariato giovanile* under the umbrella of *Autonomia*, which received a powerful, if short-lived, impetus in some cities with the largely university-based 'movement' of 1977. Participants often provided themselves with material bases of 'counterpower' by occupying decrepit buildings, to be defended against the police and municipal administrations. Most of the locals in armed struggle had, like Maria, been involved in similar occupations: the common experiences and contacts made in the occupied buildings, renamed 'social centres' (*centri sociali*), for example, of Via Bruzzesi, Via Novi and Via Tortona in Milan run through members' autobiographical accounts of the salient moments in their career development towards armed struggle. Such informal aggregations frequently extended their neighbourhood activism into newer issues not then covered by the political parties' agenda, in particular the drug trade and the black economy which were also likely to have directly affected their own friends and acquaintances. As clandestine or semi-clandestine illegal activities themselves defended by the threat of violence, neither drug trafficking nor hidden, and often grossly exploitative, employment was particularly responsive to orthodox legal forms of opposition. It is therefore not difficult to see how retaliatory violence against individuals and property could enter the repertoire of those activists for whom such neighbourhood issues constituted an important residual focus for political commitment.

That incorporation was facilitated by three factors. First, connections to the apparatchik milieu of armed struggle gave the impression of participation in a project which transcended neighbourhood horizons even though the immediate context remained primary for the locals themselves. Quite commonly the grass-roots members of armed groups acknowledged that the sense of wider commitment was a sufficient incentive to establish contacts with apparatchiks without even knowing initially which specific group signature they represented. Adoption of a purely symbolic *nome di battaglia* (their real identity was well known to all immediate fellow-adherents) encouraged perceptions both of belonging to a well-organised project and of standing partly outside contemporary Italian society. Second, the refusal of their original reference group, the extra-parliamentary Left, unambiguously to disconfirm a revolutionary political identity for the users of violence for most of the 1970s inhibited the development of any sense of exclusion from traditional class-oriented politics. Third, the institutionalisation of orthodox politics at neighbourhood level ('*il controllo sul territorio*', in the languages of armed struggle) offered easily recognisable party personnel and policies as an immediate focus of antagonism and a basis for an identity based on negation. The overall result was to form a significant catchment area for the low-level affiliation to political violence in fairly clearly identifiable zones of the urban periphery: Sesto San Giovanni and the Barona in Milan, Madonna di Campagna and Le Vallette in Turin, Centocelle, Cinecittà and Torre Spaccata in Rome were some of the quarters which saw the early acts of clandestine violence and the armed groups' bases and which provided a substantial proportion of those locals who came from recent migrant families (Table 2.6, p. 44).[35]

To summarise: the three milieux represented the heterogeneous, fragilely-linked 'horizontal' strata from which the 'vertical' organisations of armed struggle were assembled. The divisions among participants according to age, city, political experience and levels of ambitions for violence were clearly marked; and the trajectories of the various signatures in the armed community illustrated the continuing internal tensions as the different groups' protagonists sought to enrol others behind distinctive and plausible meanings for the recourse to arms. In addition to the indication of external enemies, therefore, violence was also deployed with a view to establishing a single project of armed struggle behind which the variegated array of participants who accepted violence as a legitimate political technique could unite.

THE ORGANISATIONAL DIMENSION: ITS THREE PHASES

Although the Red Brigades represented only one of the 526 left-wing signatures appearing between 1970 and 1982, the group has all but monopolised both lay and sociological discussions of Italian political violence. In one sense this concentration reproduces the participants' own special attention to the BR as the longest-lived, most widely-diffused, most 'effective' and apparently most ideologically-homogeneous of the armed signatures. While the total of 426 BR members (sc., those sufficiently involved to be indicted for armed insurrection) was roughly equalled by the *circa* 450 members of *Prima Linea*, the BR carried out five times as many actions and four times as many woundings as PL:[36] the distribution of their members and actions across Italy is shown in Table 2.7.

The figures show clearly the extent to which the history of the Red Brigades was very largely played out in the four centres of Milan, Turin, Genoa and Rome which accounted for more than three-quarters of the group's members and murders and four-fifths of all actions.

However the general profile does not capture the Red Brigades' evolution in terms of variations in the rate of recruitment and levels of violence practised nor does it show the changing relative significance of BR actions in the overall volume of left-wing violence. Those dimensions are indicated in Table 2.8.

Imposing a periodization on the overall profile of Red Brigades' violence yields three phases. The first, 1970–6, saw the Red Brigades as the dominant group in a form of armed struggle characterised by relatively few serious attacks, the deaths and woundings largely resulting from unplanned clashes with the police rather than deliber-ate ambush. In the second phase, mid-1976 – mid-1979, the group substantially increased its number of actions and the proportion of attacks on individuals: at the same time, however, it lost its dominant

TABLE 2.7   *Red Brigades' members and actions, 1970–82*

Province/ region	No. members[1]	%	No. murders[2]	No. woundings[2]	Total no. actions[2]	%
Milan	87	20	13	18	87	17
Turin	77	18	10	20	133	27
Genoa	38	9	9	14	77	15
Rome	110	26	22	18	105	21
Veneto	27	6	5	–	9	2
Naples	23	5	5	3	12	2
Tuscany	14	3	–	–	5	1
Marches	12	3	–	–	12	2
Sardinia	10	2	–	–	10	2
Other*	28	7	14	1	49	10
Total	426	99	78	74	499	99

* Includes members who were recruited, and those who were murdered, in jail
SOURCES
1. F. Amato, *Ordinanza di rinvio a giudizio contro Acanfora V + altri*, N.995/81 (Tribunale di Roma: 21 July 1983). E. Pacifici, *Ordinanza di rinvio a giudizio contro Adamoli R. + altri*, N.2255/83A (Tribunale di Roma: 22 January 1985). This column indicates the members whose activities were entirely confined to the particular province or region. Some of the apparatchiks of course participated in actions elsewhere – I have classified them by their primary place of activity. The disparity between these figures for membership and the larger numbers appearing in the trials of the local BR groups is accounted for by the inclusion in the city trials of individuals who had committed minor infractions in support of the group but who were not sufficiently continuously involved to justify a charge of full membership.
2. M. Galleni (ed.), *Rapporto sul terrorismo* (Milan: Rizzoli, 1981) *passim*; Direzione PCI, Sezione Problemi dello Stato: 'Attentati e violenze in Italia nel 1981', p. 10; 'Attentati e violenze in Italia nel 1982', p. 9. Some figures have been modified to take account of more recent revelations on responsibilities.

position to the point at which it was authoring no more than one in ten of all claimed left-wing attacks. Finally, in the third phase from mid-1979 to 1984, the volume of all types of BR violence diminished fairly rapidly while the group nevertheless moved back towards recouping its central position in armed struggle. By 1986 the sporadic acts of residual left-wing violence could all be attributed to one or other faction of the by-then divided group, either retaining the signature of the Red Brigades or identifying itself as the *Unione Comunisti Combattenti*. To a considerable extent the shifts in the nature and levels of violence, and its communicative functions, can be explained in terms of the changing relations both among the milieux assembled under the rubric of the Red Brigades and among the competing signatures in the community of armed struggle. The overall trajectory depicts the failure of participants to find a plausible meaning for its basic symbol, *la lotta armata*. It also shows that the

TABLE 2.8   *Red Brigades' annual recruitment, forms of violence and weight in left-wing clandestine violence, 1970–82***

Year	Recruits[1]	Deaths[2]	Woundings[2]	All actions[2]	Murders/ woundings as % of all actions	BR actions as % of all claimed left-wing actions
1970	–	–	–	4	–	100
1971	32	–	–	6	–	100
1972	4	–	–	28	–	90
1973	1	–	–	7	–	64
1974	10	3	–	25	12	78
1975	10	1	3	30	13	63
1976	33	6	2	53	15	50
1977	48	3	19	56	39	23
1978	57	16	18	106	32	17
1979	38	11	14	65	38	10
1980	14	17	11	61	46	27
1981	5	10	5	31	48	27
1982	?	11	2	27	48	38
Total	252	78	74	499	30	23

* This table is based on information available to me for only 252 of the 426 members. The remaining 176 would be distributed through the period 1978–82.
SOURCES
1. F. Amato, *Ordinanza di rinvio a giudizio contro Acanfora V. + altri*, pp. 2963–8.
2. M. Galleni, *Rapporto sul terrorismo, passim*. Direzione PCI, Sezione Problemi dello Stato: 'Attentati e violenze in Italia nel 1981' pp. 2–3, 10; 'Attentati e violenze in Italia nel 1982', pp. 3–5, 9.

community had begun to dissolve prior both to the police's major investigative successes and to the government's introduction of special provisions to encourage active desertion from the armed groups.

Dominance and failure 1970–6

The first phase of clandestine violence was an all but complete failure for its two protagonists, the Red Brigades and the Armed Proletarian Nuclei (NAP), which together accounted for almost all the claimed actions.[37] Geographically and ideologically the two groups were complementary rather than competitive. The coagulation of the first members around the Red Brigades' signature in 1970 was based on a commune in Milan with links to the Sit-Siemens factory where many of the early actions took place. From 1973 onwards the range of attacks was extended to Turin, but attempts to establish nuclei in Rome in 1971 and 1974, in Genoa and in the Veneto region were all unsuccessful. The group justified its use of violence primarily as the necessary form of resistance by the working class to the assault by its industrial and political enemies but also, on the more positive side, as the adaptation to the Italian context of the then apparently successful revolutionary techniques of the Tupamaros and Viet Cong. The idiom of legitimation for armed struggle drew heavily on the rhetoric and symbols of the Resistance and the preferred categories of recruit excluded those such as students or the unemployed who were not directly part of the world of industrial work.[38] The NAP, by contrast, originated in Naples in 1974 from a scission of the extra-parliamentary group *Lotta Continua*, carried out almost all of its actions in Naples, Rome and Florence and focused them especially on the strata ignored by the BR, the sub-proletariat and prison populations. Despite those basic differences lack of success drove the two groups together so that, having earlier denied any organisational connection, by March 1976 actions were being claimed jointly by both signatures.

The internal organisation of both groups was similar. First, both were extremely small. Despite the continuing high levels of industrial and political mobilisation in the north the Red Brigades' actions received little public support, even from the groups of the extreme Left which mostly condemned the groups' specific actions as 'pro-vocations'; and whatever sympathies they may have earned privately were not translated into new recruits. As Table 2.8 (p. 67) shows, even the successful actions, such as the kidnapping in 1974 of the magistrate Sossi who was notoriously unpopular with the extra-parliamentary Left, failed to add significantly to the Red Brigades' membership. Second, and no doubt partly responsible for the low level of recruitment, the majority of activists became fully clandestine, due to police discovery of a base and individually incriminating evidence in Milan in 1972. Nevertheless the difficulty of retaining or increasing their support encouraged a relaxation of security which led to police infiltration and the arrests of almost all the BR members between 1974 and 1976. Third, the division of labour among the participants in both groups was rudimentary during the first phase of armed struggle. For the BR, although an 'executive committee' had been created, no entrenched distribution of the functions of the intelligentsia, apparatchiks and locals existed. The ideological documents were deliberately perfunctory; direct actions were carried out by all or any members (for example, one member of the 'executive committee', Buonavita, was arrested while trying to steal a car); and the failure to gain recruits, coupled with police successes, ensured that the number of locals was very small. Among the NAP the sense of internal hierarchy was even more relaxed and affiliates expressly encouraged the use of the signature by anyone who was prepared to attack the same targets.

Given the homogeneity of both groups and the limited audiences being addressed, the specifically political violence did not need to be especially elaborate. It consisted mostly of minor acts of property damage and symbolic attacks (bloodless kidnappings) on individuals, thus taking the form of 'armed propaganda' primarily designed to show that deliberate violence for political ends was both thinkable and realisable. The absence of competition between the two groups likewise ensured that neither the ideological content of the texts nor the syntax of violence needed to carry very precise diacritic meanings. Indeed the Red Brigades were more concerned to warn affiliates of the dangers of resorting to the kind of indiscriminate bomb attacks used by right-wing groups, for fear of lending support to doubts about their own left-wing political identity. The two cases between 1970 and 1976 in which the Red Brigades deliberately escalated the level of violence to reach murder both responded primarily to internal factors. The first episode involved the murder of two *Movimento Sociale Italiano* (MSI) officials in a party office in Padua in 1974: the attack was organised by two activists whose attempt to set up a nucleus in the Veneto region had failed and who had been strongly criticised by fellow-members for their lack of success. The level of violence used was therefore intended as a domestic response to the rest of the group whose senior members were nevertheless extremely reluctant to translate it into one of their own actions through a public claim bearing the Red Brigades' signature.[39] Serious violence against outsiders was thus carried out for the first time principally as a means of internal communication.

The other case, which underlined the option for violence to become a method of address by other participants within the armed community, concerned the murder of the magistrate Coco and his two bodyguards in June 1976. Both the choice of victim and nature of the action were directed towards a display of solidarity between the now-imprisoned leading members of the Red Brigades, who were confined to the production of texts, and the few remaining activists still at large. The victim was chosen because he had prevented the release from jail of nine 'political prisoners' in return for Sossi's freedom; and the attack was thus intended to demonstrate the continuing identity of objectives, with the recourse to murder indicating criticism of the BR kidnappers in jail for having freed Sossi unharmed despite their failure to achieve an exchange. At another level, the murder was timed to coincide with the first major trial of those same early members (discussed in Chapter 6) and was designed to prove their assertions that the 'revolution' they represented could not be successfully halted by the use of ordinary judicial processes against participants. The violence deployed by the apparatchiks was therefore used to attempt to translate the claim by the intelligentsia about the meaning and power of armed struggle into a fact. The internal, self-referential relationship between acts and texts became increasingly complicated in the second phase as the competition among different signatures increased and the different milieux from which each single group was composed were forced further apart.

The struggle for hegemony, 1976–9

The lack of initial success of the BR and elimination of the NAP provided considerable organisational and ideological space for the new full-time activists of 1974–6 and the locals of 1977–8. In any case their own political experiences and horizons differed greatly from the traditional Marxist-Leninism and Viet Cong or Tupamaros models which had constituted the referents for the Red Brigades during the first phase. Some, nevertheless, were recruited to the project developed by the BR intelligentsia after 1975 which had come to emphasise the State as the primary focus of antagonism – a sufficiently general target to encompass the different orientation of the growing number of local nuclei across several cities and readily assimilated to the 'regime-party', the DC. Others rejected the particular BR concerns with the State and with the necessary role of a fully clandestine vanguard in constructing an armed party. The localist, situationally-specific role for violence theorised by *Autonomia*'s intelligentsia represented a more appropriate framework for activity and licensed a much looser organisational structure. This was embodied in the signature of *Prima Linea*, created in late 1976 by a group of activists from Milan, Turin and Florence who rejected the Red Brigades' levels of armed intervention, as well as in a multiplicity of *Autonomia*-referenced formations with single-city horizons, resulting in the massive expansion of signatures from 24 in 1976 to 217 in 1979. A simultaneous process of fragmentation within signatures and competition between them, punctuated by more or less coercive attempts to translate all uses of violence into allegiance to a single project, thus marked the second phase.

Under the Red Brigades' signature significant presences were established in Rome and Genoa (1976), Sardinia and Venice (1979) and ultimately Naples (1980), alongside the preservation of the existing nuclei in Milan and Turin. In all the cities, but especially in Rome, apparatchiks and locals were recruited who had closer links to neighbourhood politics than to the group's traditional concern with the factory which remained dominant in Turin and, to a lesser extent, Milan. In Rome, too, the recruitment of locals employed in State or municipal agencies (ministries, hospitals, local government) gave the State itself an extra reality as a direct antagonist.[40] Meanwhile, a further new centre of intervention was created by the intelligentsia in the maximum security jails. Parallel to the wider territorial diffusion and the diversity of the social and occupational location of new militants, the boundaries between the three milieux also became more rigid. First, although the jail walls were by no means impermeable to the passage of documents and decisions, they marked off the intelligentsia clearly from the apparatchiks, unlike in the earlier phase. Second, the internal organisational scheme worked out in 1975–6 by the intelligentsia but not yet in place before their arrests was now made the general orienting charter to manage the growth in city-based nuclei and membership. The distinction between apparatchiks and locals was therefore invested with greater formality, accompanied by the abolition in September 1976 of the specific apparatchik organism devoted to local interventions, the so-called *Fronte di massa*. Significantly it was replaced by a new unit concerned strictly with the police, *carabinieri* and magistrature – the most direct antagonists of the apparatchiks themselves.

Similar boundaries between the different milieux became visible in the non-BR (majority) segment of the armed community. The intelligentsia around the journal *Rosso* in Milan, for example, formed an exclusive élite (*segreteria soggettiva*) relying for authority on its members' local prestige in extra-parliamentary Left politics; PL's apparatchiks nominated one another to positions of authority according to 'political' rather than geographical or sectoral criteria, abandoned the original idea of filling leadership roles through election and distinguished themselves sharply from their affiliated aggregations at 'mass' level (*squadre, ronde*); and the myriad of local action-sets used generic left-wing signatures, refusing any permanent subordinate relationship to full-time activists who were the agents of the better-known groups. As with the Red Brigades, the social and occupational locations of participants were very diverse, multiplying the conflicts between the contexts to which violence was referred for its meaning. The result was to exacerbate the divisions within the armed community more acutely as the links across the milieux became more fragile and the representatives of different signatures competed to attract and retain the scarce resources of reliable personnel, weapons and information on likely targets.

Various stratagems for translating the heterogeneous uses and users of violence into single projects were developed. Apparatchiks exploited their control over weapons to establish their own indispensability to a signature and to attract personal sets of clients among locals who required better armament for public intervention. Competing aggregations were infiltrated clandestinely in the hope of directing their availability for violence towards targets favoured by the infiltrator's group. Peaceful demonstrations could be transformed into violent confrontations with the police so as to render State violence an experiential reality and thus attract new recruits. Most important, however, was the use of increasingly serious violence against more complex targets. Such actions could exercise a direct appeal by showing the authors as more effective in the use of violence than their competitors. Indirectly, they could provoke a level of State response which would compel the minor users of violence to seek the protection and superior resources of the authors. The clearest example of such a strategy was the BR kidnapping and murder of Moro and his police escorts in 1978 when the group also launched its own local-level signature *Movimento proletario di resistenza offensiva* (MPRO) through the adoption of which other aggregations with ambitions to contribute to armed struggle could advertise their client status. As far as the action's internal significance for the armed community itself was concerned, the Red Brigades' objective was to force the elimination of *Autonomia* and minor groups through State repression and to encourage their affiliates to commit themselves to an apparently more successful and organised strategy of violence.

As a continuing programme, too, the profile of types of violence used by the major groups in the different cities suggests a positive correlation between the level of competition among signatures and the scale of violence. In Turin where the Red Brigades authored 40 per cent of all claimed actions, murders and woundings accounted for one-quarter (23 per cent) of their attacks; in Milan where the group's overall contribution to armed struggle fell to 35 per cent, its murders and woundings rose to more than one-third (36 per cent); and in Rome where BR actions amounted to only 17 per cent of all actions, the weight of the most serious attacks stood at two in five (38 per cent). A similar pattern is visible for *Prima Linea*. In Florence the group accounted for nearly one-third (29 per cent) of all left-wing actions and committed no murders or woundings, while in the much more competitive arena of Milan where the group contributed only one in eight actions, its members' selection of levels of violence tipped markedly towards serious attacks on persons (one in five).[41] Between them, the BR and PL accounted for three-quarters of all murders and two-thirds of woundings in the deadly spiral of emulation and rivalry which reduced the significance of the specific motivations behind each action: attacks on direct enemies, solidarity with captured comrades and (especially in the case of PL) revenge for real or imagined damage to group members or the public at large. As the major signatures sought to differentiate themselves in the newly competitive conditions for establishing political identities through violence, the minor formations which aspired to their patronage were also drawn into more serious attacks to show specific support. The murders of the Salerno magistrate Giacumbi and the Milan journalist Tobagi in 1980 were both devised and signed by recently-formed groups so as to attract the attention of the Red Brigades and elicit a direct offer of incorporation.

Whatever the intentions to achieve hegemony and internal solidarity through the increasing use of serious violence might have been, the consequences were entirely negative for the armed groups. First, it divorced the apparatchiks more completely from the locals since murder directed against victims outside any local class or institutional conflicts deprived violence of any possible intelligibility as a tactic in the repertoire of methods furthering immediate struggles. Not only was the allegiance of existing locals forfeited in many cases but recruitment even for the low-level forms of support which characterised their milieu therefore had virtually dried up by 1979. It was further inhibited by the increased mobilisation of the parliamentary and extra-parliamentary Left against violence, so that the new membership of major groups, and especially the Red Brigades, from 1979 onwards was largely accounted for by the redistribution of former activists in now-disbanded minor groups. In some cities open conflict between apparatchiks and locals appeared. In Turin, for example, PL's full-time activists dissolved their local-level *squadre* in early 1979 for having become too 'politically autonomous' and replaced them

with the at least formally revamped *ronde*. Moreover, as the intensi-
fication of police action resulted in the arrest of apparatchiks, so
other members of the milieu were forced to become more mobile and
clandestine, breaking their long-standing ties to locals in their cities
of origin and weakening the sense even of firmly-convinced locals
that their views and small-scale ambitions for violence counted for
much. As the pool of available activists diminished, the increasing
(and widely suspected) infiltration of the local level of the remaining
groups by members of competing aggregations rendered all participants still more uncertain of the meanings of the acts of violence to
which they were invited to contribute.

In the second place, the attempt to use violence to unify the
apparatchik milieu was not only not successful but actually provoked
further internal divisions. On one hand *Prima Linea* refused to
provide the Red Brigades with the requested assistance during the
Moro kidnapping in order to resist the implied display of consensus
for the attack. Yet at the very same time its own activists could not
manage to unite with a minor formation, the *Formazioni Combattenti
Comuniste*, to create a focus of opposition to the Red Brigades'
strategy precisely because of disagreements over the value of actions
such as the kidnapping. On the other hand, both the major groups
were weakened by public scissions in 1979. Among the Red Brigades
the divisions occurred precisely in those cities where the emphasis on
political murder had been greatest. In Rome seven activists left after
prolonged internal conflict over the decision to murder Moro; and in
Milan the local 'W. Alasia column' repudiated the militaristic pro-
pensities of new apparatchiks who had arrived from Rome in mid-
1979 to replace the arrested clandestine activists from the city itself.
Prima Linea underwent a similar split in September 1979 when a
group of full-time activists decided to abandon armed struggle in
favour of exile and declared their defection publicly.

The third consequence of the escalation of violence was to convert
the simple physical division between the intelligentsia in jail and the
apparatchiks outside into major conflicts between members of the
two milieux over the appropriate uses of violence. In the case of the
Red Brigades the disputes began early in the second phase. The
emerging availability for violence on the part of *Autonomia*'s affiliates in 1977, for example, was greeted with enthusiasm by the
intelligentsia as a sign of the general development of class war in
Italy. But from the apparatchik perspective, dominated by local
competition for resources, the area recognisable as *Autonomia* was to

be regarded as essentially antagonistic: they therefore warned the intelligentsia that further public approval of the 1977 'movement' would result in an equally public rupture with themselves.[42] Moreover, the increasing violence used by Red Brigades apparatchiks as a response to diacritic and solidaristic pressures in their own milieu earned them charges of excessive 'militarism' from an intelligentsia accustomed in the first phase to a more flexible 'political' deployment of violence. By autumn 1979 near-complete rupture had been reached, exacerbated by the failure of the apparatchiks' several half-hearted plans to force the release of the intelligentsia from jail either in exchange for Moro or through direct assault on the Asinara maximum security prison in July 1979. Also, as more BR members were arrested, amounting to more than half the total group membership by the end of 1979, the power relations between intelligentsia and apparatchiks were altered. Those newly arrested became members of the elaborate structure of prison 'struggle committees' (*comitati di lotta*) which, although they were in fact solely restricted to members of the group itself rather than genuinely representative even of all political arrestees, were largely under the control of the intelligentsia. Its increased salience allowed core members not merely to play an important arbitrating role among the now rival city-based BR factions but also to establish relations directly with sets of locals, evading the intermediary control of the apparatchiks in the wholly unrealistic hope of recovering at least the unified meanings of the first phase of armed struggle.[43]

Among the *Autonomia*-based groups the particular emphasis given to activism pure and simple entailed a looser link between intelligentsia and full-time activists than was the case for the Red Brigades. None the less members of the two milieux in the major cities came into regular conflict, the apparatchiks accusing the intelligentsia of reluctance to participate in the actions their strategy encouraged and the intelligentsia criticising the apparatchiks' reckless preference for 'military' rather than 'political' uses of violence. In Milan, for example, a so-called 'sergeants' rebellion' against the intelligentsia associated with *Rosso* took place as early as 1976; and in the following year the death of a policeman (Custrà) during one of the many street marches which were deliberately turned violent in that period provoked a quarrel resulting in the departure to form a new group by the activists hitherto linked to the publication. Similar episodes of violence in Rome and Turin also focused as catalysts for scissions as the previously-suppressed uncertainties and disagreements about the practical interpretations of armed struggle and the values which should determine its levels were suddenly forced into the open. The accentuation of the disputes over whether violence should have a local or national reference and the conflicts within and between groups encouraged some participants to work for unification in a single organisation of armed struggle. Pursued first by a loose federation of intelligentsia and activists under the label *Comitati Comunisti Rivoluzionari* (COCORI) and subsequently by some activists associated with the journal *Metropoli*, the strategy demanded the infiltration of the major groups (BR and PL) as well as the hidden direction of the transient neighbourhood action-sets which accepted only local horizons for their violence. Not surprisingly the project simply offered yet another focus for allegiance which was no more stable organisationally than its competitors and which added to participants' doubts about where the boundaries among apparently distinct actors lay. The intentions underlying actions and programmes of violence thus became increasingly opaque. Finally the arrest of leading members from *Autonomia*'s intelligentsia in 1979–80 divided them definitively from the apparatchiks, not only because the supply of public legitimations for violence circulated in the area's major journals was largely cut off but also because of the decision of those arrested to insist, truly or falsely, on their innocence of all active participation in violence.

Thus the struggle between 1976 and 1979 to hold together the three milieux of violence and to translate the activities associated with different signatures into a unified armed community with a single strategy achieved no more than to make plain the extent of ideological and organisational heterogeneity. The arbitrariness of the meanings conferred on any single action therefore became increasingly apparent to participants themselves; and the final phase began with the first public breaches of the solidarity which had linked members of the different groups around the key symbol, now repudiated, of 'armed struggle'.

Disintegration and exit, 1979–84

Although the Red Brigades moved back towards a dominant position after 1979, the reality covered by the group signature and by the community of armed struggle had been irreversibly transformed, and their aspirations towards lasting solidarity destroyed, by the dynamics of the second phase. Thus the considerably increased success rate of police investigations and the impact of the laws of 1980 and 1982 rewarding the abjuration of political violence and collaboration with the State were facilitated by the fact that, to a growing proportion of members of armed groups, the deliberate use of violence had already ceased to have any political meaning – or rather, held only a meaning now seen to be diametrically opposed to its users' intentions. The timing of the most dramatic decline in the volume of violence supports that conclusion since it can be traced with some precision to mid-1979, between the semesters with the highest and lowest incidence of clandestine attacks recorded for any six-month period since 1976. The sharpest fall thus anticipated, rather than followed, the State's most innovative legislative initiatives.[44]

With the rapid disappearance of the minor aggregations and signatures from the area of *Autonomia* the world of armed struggle was definitively cut adrift from the extra-parliamentary Left. Its remaining members were ineluctably drawn towards the Red Brigades which, after the disintegration of *Prima Linea* in 1980, constituted the only group with resources to persist with the conflict. The new recruits brought with them further disagreements on the appropriate uses of violence, thus aggravating the fragmentation of the group and fuelling the contest to establish a reduced hegemony, no longer over the community of armed struggle as a whole but over the Red Brigades' signature itself. Through the greater recourse to murder, wounding and kidnapping (which together rose from one-third to one-half of all BR actions between 1979 and 1982), the different segments sought to mark out their local identities as starkly and publicly as possible and to capture the support of the intelligentsia for their own versions of the proper meaning of armed struggle. Thus the murder of two Milan industrial managers (Briano and Mazzanti) in late 1980 by the local dissidents of the W. Alasia column, the kidnapping of the magistrate responsible for prisons in the Ministry of Justice, D'Urso, by a newly-established faction based in Rome and Naples (the *Fronte delle carceri* led by a criminologist, Senzani), the 'retaliatory' murder of a general (Galvaligi) also concerned with prison security by the rival BR group in Rome – these and other actions were primarily intended as vehicles for internal messages rather than for external consequences. Likewise the four simultaneous and prolonged kidnappings of 1981 (Cirillo, Taliercio, Sandrucci, Peci) were designed to indicate the contrasting primary audiences of the hostile factions based in Naples, Venice, Milan and Rome respectively, with each faction attempting to draw representatives of the categories to which the seizures were addressed into public discussion over the conditions for release of the hostages.[45] None of those actions earned any new recruits to armed struggle; and as their authors were arrested, the conflicts among external apparatchiks were carried into the previously homogeneous prison-based grouping and made increasingly public by the antagonistic declarations of fellow-defendants in trials from 1982 onwards. Finally, any residual allegiance that the armed groups might have earned in the course of industrial conflicts, political scandals and a revived neo-Fascist violence in the early 1980s was forfeited by the use of violence against former members who had chosen publicly to declare the meaningless-ness of armed struggle and turn State's evidence. The murders of Waccher, Soldati, Roberto Peci and Di Rocco between 1980 and 1982 made it clear to participants and observers that violence threatened wavering comrades as well as enemies.

Exit from one group to another, whilst remaining within the armed community, had been possible throughout the period – indeed, in the small *Autonomia*-based aggregations which were mostly short-lived and where 'membership' signified primarily active presence, it was a major characteristic of the participation of both apparatchiks and locals. Exit from the community of armed struggle itself was also acceptable, provided some guarantee was available that the knowl-edge gained through involvement would not be betrayed. Locals could simply remove violence from their repertoire of political activities; apparatchiks who were not fully clandestine – the majority – could attempt to do the same, although the more common course was to escape from the pressures of now-vulnerable former comrades into a clandestine existence elsewhere in Italy or abroad; and members of the intelligentsia withdrew from contributing to the journals and cultural initiatives which accepted or approved armed struggle. But exit accompanied by various degrees of public repudia-tion of the symbols and practices of armed struggle occurred for the first time in 1979. The earliest defectors came from groups no longer active but by late 1980 well-informed apparatchiks from all the major existing organisations had turned State's evidence, with inevitably devastating consequences for the remaining members of the shrink-ing community.[46]

In effect the process of disaffiliation from armed struggle by the three milieux exactly reversed the order of their affiliation. The escalating violence of the years 1976–9 dried up the recruitment of locals and transformed the part-time commitments of existing participants either into exit or into a more active commitment to a particular organisation: the second option was encouraged by the need to escape the consequences of confessions. Next, the apparatchik milieu was greatly reduced, but not completely eliminated, through the information provided by its own defectors in 1980, so that the overall volume of violence continued to fall rapidly. Only in Rome was effective collaboration relatively late in appearing (the first significant confessions were not made until 1982), thus allowing members to protect themselves better than elsewhere and to make the city the primary continuing centre of Red Brigades' activity. Without the linkages provided by locals into existing social conflict, and the arbitrary multiplication of targets to virtually every social category by the intelligentsia, the public appeals from former comrades to renounce violence were received by an already largely-convinced audience. In some cases – as with *Prima Linea* in 1983 – the apparatchiks formally announced in public the dissolution of their organisations although in most cases, including PL, they were merely ratifying a *de facto* extinction. Finally, the earliest proponents of armed struggle, the intelligentsia formed in 1968–70, declared its end. *Autonomia*'s journals had already closed or appeared very irregularly after 1981; their collaborators in jail moved first towards a rejection of 'terrorism' and then, more ambiguously, of 'armed struggle'; and links with the residual members of the movement were publicly severed. Closure, symbolic and practical, was assured by the April 7 trial in Rome in 1983–4. More or less contemporaneously the Red Brigades' intelligentsia followed suit. In late 1982 its most influential member announced the end of the BR organisation and its projects, without, however, rejecting the conceptualisation of social conflicts as 'war' or the recourse to future – unspecified – guerilla tactics.[47] The collapse of the milieu's solidarity was publicly indicated by the decision of some leading members to adopt the symbolically non-violent tactic of a hunger strike in December 1983 to improve the conditions of detainees in the maximum security prisons. The attempt to negotiate directly with the State's representatives rather than coerce them through violence was widely regarded as signifying the general rejection of armed struggle.

Despite the complete dispersal of the resources which, in fragile combination, had made armed struggle possible, three residual groups of former participants refused in any way to dissociate themselves from their erstwhile solidarities, to acknowledge the State's legitimacy or to renounce violence. One group was in jail where 444 detainees, equivalent to roughly one in seven of the total membership of the armed community, were still describing themselves as 'political prisoners' at the end of 1984.[48] A second group, with a more recently estimated 212 members, had fled abroad. Most (165) had taken refuge in France where the government was extremely reluctant to grant the Italian requests for the extradition of alleged members of armed groups or even of individuals convicted *in absentia* of serious crimes.[49] The majority of that semi-clandestine community had long renounced the practices and ideologies of armed struggle, and its leading members have regularly but unsuccessfully proposed some form of amnesty or extra-judicial recognition of their disaffiliation which would enable them to return to Italy. It is likely, however, that a few members have kept contact with the clandestine nuclei in Italy, reckoned at some 80 members in 1986, who have constituted the third group of surviving participants.

These residual, wholly clandestine, activists, now reaggregated into two factions (the *Partito Comunista Combattente* and the *Unione Comunisti Combattenti*), have compensated for the loss of all Italian referents for violence by accentuating the international dimensions of their actions. The three murders, two woundings and one kidnapping between 1982 and 1986, standing out against a minimal background of minor local property damage, have included two American generals and a close collaborator of the Minister of Defence: the attacks represented an attempt to provide violence with meaning as a form of opposition to US involvement in Mediterranean and European affairs and to show solidarity with Middle Eastern groups. Their authors' principal reference group, and probably major source of collaborators, has become the range of European and Middle Eastern organisations, some of which have used Italy itself to carry out such attacks as the massacre at Fiumicino airport in December 1985. Attacks on individuals (Giugni, Tarantelli, Da Empoli) linked to domestic issues of wage indexation and unemployment drew strong criticism even from former activists who had not entirely repudiated either their own pasts or the potential role of violence in social transformation. The search for a plausible translation of violence into the international political domain will probably continue to generate isolated attacks. But their very divorce from specifically Italian issues shows that the effort which began in 1970 to build a local community around the languages and values of 'armed struggle' and to make violence a diacritic of individual revolutionary identity is exhausted.

3 Violence in a Local Context: The Factory

Among the institutions selected as targets by armed groups the factory had a special place. Most obviously, the longevity and volume of the attacks on industrial personnel and property were greater than for any other institution. Between the first episodes of sabotage carried out by the Red Brigades at the Pirelli factory outside Milan in 1970 and the murder of the manager of the Montedison plant at Porto Marghera, Taliercio, in 1981, the damage to machinery and products was considerable and the victims (managers, cadres, unionists) constituted the largest single category of civilians attacked (Table 2.2 above, p. 38). Most recently the wounding and murder of two academics closely involved in industrial relations (Giugni, Tarantelli) in 1983 and 1985 respectively showed a continuing, if more distant, attention to the same arena.

The significance of the attacks was redoubled by the place that their primary locales – the large factories of North Italy, especially the giant plant at Fiat Mirafiori in Turin – have long enjoyed in Italy's collective political imagination. Whether as the determinant sites of class struggle and revolutionary transformation in the strong *operaista* tradition in the Italian Left, or simply as the visible premonitors of general changes in the balance of economic and political power, they have been seen as social laboratories where, writ small, the basic power dimensions of Italian society can be tested and the future discerned. In the case of violence, the concentrated presence of the primary referents of the armed groups' actions (the industrial working class), the traditional organisations claiming to represent that class's local and national interests (the trade unions) and the most popular embodiment of the power élite (the *padronato*) combined to give the experiment of using violence as a method of pursuing conflicts a special practical and theoretical salience. Because the factory offered a more focused arena than the other more dispersed sites of violence, its symbolic power to suggest the possibilities and limitations of armed struggle were correspondingly greater. Likewise, in miniature on the shopfloor, evidence could be sought to support or refute views about the genesis and conditions of reproduction of clandestine violence which elsewhere depended on too diffuse or intermittent an array of attacks to prompt any *in situ* verification.

In part because of that very visibility, the factory also saw an extensive attempt to mobilise a civilian population in active opposition to violence. Orchestrated primarily by the trade unions, the effort to enrol workforces against 'terrorism' generated an increasingly elaborate version of the nature of the problem and the means necessary to its elimination. Through analysis of the responses, interpretive and practical, an essential local dimension to the Italian management of political violence can be restored. Furthermore, given the stress frequently laid on the need to involve civilian populations as a means of overcoming the common difficulties encountered in police investigation and of eliminating the indifference which may be as valuable as active support to the micro-organisations of violence, the Italian instance may provide some materials for more general reflection. For the difficulties, successes and consequences of the attempt to transform mere indifference to the projects of the armed groups into active public rejection reveal some of the paradoxes of communicative interaction which make mobilisation less straightforward a task than it might appear. I shall therefore first describe the nature and general context of the attack itself and then consider at some length how meanings for that violence were conferred, disseminated and disputed among its opponents.

POWER AND IDENTITY IN SHOPFLOOR STRUGGLE

Factory-directed violence took two major forms: widely-diffused sabotage and damage carried out both inside industrial plants and against retail outlets for their products, and a much more narrowly-focused campaign against particular categories of personnel in a few major enterprises. The overall profile (Table 3.1) illustrates the geographical concentration in Milan and Turin of damage to persons in contrast to the much wider spread of damage to property.

Most acts of clandestine sabotage and 21 of the attacks on individuals (principally woundings) were the work of the transient action-sets of locals, largely associated with *Autonomia Operaia*. They were too scattered to have any major non-economic consequences in a single firm or plant and were primarily intended to express generic anti-capitalist sentiments, protest against the exploitative conditions of local black economies or punish specific

TABLE 3.1   *Attacks on industrial personnel, plants and retail outlets: Turin, Milan, Genoa and Rome 1969–82**

	Victims			Damage to Property†		
Provinces	Deaths	Woundings	Kidnappings	A Factories and public utilities	B Retail outlets	A + B as % all attacks on property
Turin	3	32	2	65	89	22%
Milan	3	19	4	92	186	27%
Genoa	1	6	1	11	5	12%
Rome	1	2	–	152	434	23%
Others	3	7	1‡	266	431	31%
Total	11	66	8	586	1145	22%

* Figures for victims include attacks by left-wing groups only; property figures include both left and right-wing attacks, the overwhelming majority being carried out by the Left.
† Figures available for 1981–2 do not disaggregate by provinces the overall totals for attacks on factories and commercial outlets (253 & 87). The overall number of attacks on all property, by provinces, in 1981–2 were: Turin 7 & 0; Milan 23 & 13; Genoa 7 & 0; Rome 109 & 52; others 107 & 22.
‡ The victim (Taliercio) was murdered. In all other kidnapping cases the victims were released.
SOURCES
1970–80, M. Galleni (ed.), *Rapporto sul terrorismo* (Milan: Rizzoli, 1981) *passim*.
1981–2, Direzione PCI, Sezione Problemi dello Stato: 'Attentati e violenze in Italia nel 1981' and 'Attentati e violenze in Italia nel 1982'.

individuals for alleged acts of discrimination or damage against members of the workforce. Their authors commonly referred their actions to the ideology of 'the rejection of work' and the theory of needs, purveyed by *Autonomia*'s intelligentsia: the meaning for such actions was therefore achieved in the moment of transgression itself.[1] The carefully managed impression of random, 'spontaneous' violence was also designed to provide an alternative, or perhaps in some cases a complement, to the other, strategically more significant, form of violence.

This second form picked out a restricted band of targets in Italy's best-known industrial enterprises, accompanying the attacks on individuals with regular propaganda for armed struggle through the diffusion of leaflets, display of banners and occasionally the use of tape-recorded messages. Almost all the firms affected were located in the north: the Fiat plants in Turin; Alfa-Romeo Arese and Sit-Siemens (later Italtel) in Milan; Breda, Falck and Marelli at Sesto San Giovanni; Italsider and Ansaldo outside Genoa; and the Montedison petrochemical plant at Porto Marghera. The two firms under the most severe attack were the twin symbols of private and State capitalism in Italy – Fiat and Alfa Romeo – which together accounted for 34 of the 85 attacks on persons, largely concentrated into the years 1977–81 but accompanied by lesser violence and acts of sabotage throughout the decade.[2] Four-fifths (29) of the serious attacks were the responsibility of the two major groups, the Red Brigades and Front Line: the role of the BR was, however, clearly dominant, not simply because the volume of the group's violence was three times larger (48 victims as opposed to PL's 16, 10 of whom were wounded in a single incursion into a business school in Turin in late 1979) but because, by establishing a minimal but continuing presence within the two firms, directing violence against a single set of targets and producing ideological justifications of their attacks, only the members of the Red Brigades seriously attempted to build up an identity in factory politics. Most of the specific evidence in this chapter will therefore come from the violence associated with that one group at Fiat and Alfa-Romeo Arese.

Presence, victims and the language of justification represented the three foci of the Red Brigades' challenge. First, the simple fact of showing that the group could count on active supporters (locals) within the factories was a threat to workplace order. The number of locals present at any one time was never large. In 1981 20 former Fiat workers were tried for BR membership, 14 being convicted, to whom should be added a further half-dozen from the early years of the 1970s: the overall numbers at Alfa-Romeo were comparable, with no more than 5 affiliates employed at any one time. The tasks of the locals (the *irregolari* who formed the workplace *brigate*) were to distribute material clandestinely, acquire the information needed to allow the BR to compile detailed analysis of employer strategies, provide details to apparatchiks on likely victims and report on the shopfloor reaction to attacks. Despite their minimal quantitative presence, amounting to less than 0.1 per cent of the total workforces, its concentration gave it much greater symbolic significance. For the regular appearance of BR material and the selection of victims in particular workshops (for example, the *presse* section at Mirafiori) suggested a possibly broader area of consensus than the mere membership indicated. Furthermore, the revelation that at least some of the arrested BR members had been elected as shopfloor representatives by their workmates, received union sponsorship and – in a very few cases – had reached more responsible positions in the factory councils and union organisations was an obvious potential source of public contamination for the unions.[3]

As far as the choice of victims was concerned, the Red Brigades intended not to provoke terror through unpredictable attacks but to concentrate their assault on highly specific categories. Until 1976 the group was primarily intent on combating the neo-Fascist presence on the shopfloor and on attempting to establish its own role as the most effective, armed, defender of working-class interests against that threat. BR targets were either known extreme Right activists or staff from personnel offices who were believed to be personally sympathetic to the Right or to have collaborated in recruiting its supporters and giving them space to harass the Left. The five symbolic kidnappings carried out between 1972 and 1975 were used to extract information from the victims on the network of contacts between management and the Right, and the transcripts of the 'confessions' were widely circulated to inform the workforce more precisely about strategies of shopfloor control.[4] After 1976 the attack on management cadres (*quadri*) was accentuated. The victims, who were 'kneecapped', were almost exclusively drawn from the categories which had direct supervisory functions over the workforce: foremen, security staff, workshop supervisors, technical staff responsible for production schedules, middle management from personnel offices, full-time negotiators with plant unions. The cadres were especially apt symbolic and specific victims. On one hand, their members represented the factory power structure, 'the capitalist command in the enterprise'; on the other hand, their jobs were certain to bring them routinely into conflict with groups of workers or individuals likely to bear direct grudges. The Red Brigades were also careful not to forfeit the potential sympathy of disgruntled workers by escalating their violence above the level of wounding: the only exceptions were an intended kneecapping in 1978 which went wrong (Coggiola) and the murders in 1980–1 (Gori, Briano, Mazzanti, Taliercio) which were designed to publicise the local presence of the newly-autonomous BR factions rather than to exploit any existing workforce sympathies.

The third dimension of the BR challenge came in the claims made about their own origins and actions. By tying the birth of armed struggle to 'the most advanced sections of the working class at the Pirelli factory in 1970', the group identified clandestine violence as an extension of, rather than a rupture with, ordinary shopfloor class conflict.[5] That claim made violence contiguous to legal struggles and an endogenous factory product. Furthermore, underlying the many specific justifications for attack on individual victims, certain themes recurred: that violence was the most effective way of defending class interests in general; that it could help to protect the particular interests of workers who were the victims of industrial restructuring, especially the groups temporarily laid off under the provisions of the Wage Guarantee Fund (*i cassintegrati*); that the attack on supervisors could increase the general shopfloor power of workers; and that violence was the most appropriate, and only effective, response for the culpable negligence of employers resulting in fatal industrial injuries (*omicidi bianchi*).[6] Moreover in the final phase of armed struggle a direct form of challenge by contamination appeared. Until 1979 the Red Brigades and other groups had been strongly critical of the 'reformist' trade unions and their factory representatives, although confining the scope of hostility to verbal denunciation, threats to individuals and occasional damage to property. Thereafter, attempting to profit from the unions' own difficulties in the late 1970s, the Red Brigades in particular adopted union slogans, language and demands in the continuing search to legitimise their actions. Although the rapid decline of violence both inside and outside the factory after 1980 ensured that the contamination was short-lived, the marriage of violence and feasible local objectives in a form of 'armed unionism' caused considerable worry to the union leadership, especially in Milan.[7]

To understand why the Red Brigades' actions, and accounts of their actions, were seen to represent a serious threat in at least some of the major enterprises affected, some aspects of power on the shopfloor in the aftermath of the Hot Autumn must be identified. Why the grass-roots union activists should have seen the need to elaborate a version of violence at all, why they adopted the particular version that they did, and why they committed themselves to extensive mobilisation against the perceived threat represented by the Red Brigades can best be appreciated by showing how the recourse to organised factory-directed violence probed the consequences of the structural changes in internal and external relations of shopfloor actors after 1969.[8]

In seeking to establish a local identity for their projects, the Red Brigades in effect joined an array of other actors entering the factory for the first time. Certainly in the large firms where the mass mobilisation of the Hot Autumn had been greatest the traditional boundaries around the enterprise, on which the power of an often despotic managerial regime had rested, were at least radically weakened. The trade unions established themselves on the shopfloor for the first time, partly in their own right and partly by recognising as their grass-roots representatives the delegates elected to the new factory councils. Political parties, especially of the Left, were able to set up or extend their plant-level network of organisations: in the largest factories in the province of Turin, for example, the PCI increased its workplace membership by six times, and the number of its factory sections by four times, between 1969 and 1978.[9] The groups of the extreme Left, too, were able to maintain a very small, discontinuous but never completely extinguished presence in most large northern factories, initially under the wing of *Lotta Continua* or *Avanguardia Operaia* and subsequently with links to *Autonomia*. The establishment of the '150 hours' educational and training courses for workers also allowed some protagonists of the extra-parliamentary Left a sustained contact as teachers with students from local factories, especially in Milan and its hinterland. From a largely segregated domain under varyingly strict managerial authority the factory came to be permeated by a range of actors with interests far beyond its walls, multiplying both the number of foci for workforce allegiance and the external influences on factory-level conflicts.

Relationships on the shopfloor itself were also transformed. The traditional prerogatives of management were limited with the introduction of the Workers' Statute (1970) which not only granted individual rights of industrial citizenship to the workforce and provided unions with formal plant-level recognition but also outlawed some techniques of control (for example, the vetting of political opinions) hitherto favoured by employers. At the same time the factory councils, created initially as informal replacements for the generally rather well-domesticated internal commissions, gradually achieved wider recognition from unions and management as the forum for worker representation. However, a key dimension of the post-1969 transformation was precisely its relatively fragile institutionalisation. No collaborative plant-level bodies involving representatives of managements and workforces were set up; the internal organisation and shopfloor powers of the factory councils were not given a legal codification but were established as the (potentially reversible) *de facto* outcome of local bargaining; and few formal rules governed the methods of conflict regarded as legitimate by the various actors. The provision in the Italian Constitution for the regulation of strikes remained unutilised, and no factory-based union agreed to establish a code of self-regulation for dispute management. Under article 28 of the Workers' Statute employers were prohibited from indulging in 'anti-union' behaviour: but what counted as an example of such an activity, as well as the limits of acceptable tactics adopted by unions and workforces, had generally to be decided by the external authorities of the courts and the ordinary penal code.

The combination of new actors and new, somewhat indeterminate relations amongst them ensured a continuing high level of conflict as the respective limits of power and responsibility were explored and negotiated. But while the post-1969 numbers of disputes, workers involved and days lost in strikes did not begin to show a clear decline until after 1980, the peak years 1974–5 represented a convenient watershed between periods of rather different kinds of conflict. Until 1974 mobilisation at the workplace saw a broad alignment of trade unions, factory councils and workforces, as the successes of the Hot Autumn were translated into improvements not merely in wages, culminating in the wage-indexation agreement of 1975, but in a whole range of working conditions. In the first phase, therefore, the factory councils came to establish a dual system of shopfloor power, in some cases with their delegates virtually expropriating the tasks of the lowest levels of the managerial hierarchy and almost everywhere existing in uneasy tension across the increasingly poorly-defined boundaries marking the rights and duties of representatives of the two systems.

After 1974, however, largely in response to the recession which saw the doubling of the inflation rate and unemployment by 1977, the previous alliance between trade unions, factory councils and workforce began to dissolve. The union leadership turned towards the political arena to win resources which were no longer so easily available through market pressure: the forms of union-sponsored strikes therefore tended to replace the small-scale pragmatic mobilisations directed at employers with large-scale symbolic manifestations of union enrolment-power intended to impress political interlocutors remote from the enterprise by displays of what has been called 'image unionism'.[10] The generality of the objectives also served not to aggravate the re-emerging tensions between the three major confederations (CGIL, CISL and UIL) as the unification process of the early 1970s ran out of steam and as long-standing political differences were rekindled by the desire to encourage or resist the PCI's move towards government after 1976. Moreover, as the attempt to find political interlocutors became more important for the unions, the most significant loci of internal decision-making moved away from the factory, thus recentralising some of the authority which had been widely dispersed in the aftermath of the

Hot Autumn. That process opened up various fissures in the linkages between union and workforce which passed through the factory councils. On one hand, the more significant delegates to the councils, especially the restricted group appointed to their executive committees, responded with greater sensitivity to extra-factory union concerns rather than to the specific sets of workers responsible for their election. On the other hand, as the councils found it increasingly difficult to act as centres of aggregation for shopfloor demands, higher levels of micro-conflict were fostered, particularly by the more activist delegates whose socialisation into shopfloor struggle had come in the earlier period of mass mobilisation with its objectives of consolidating the new workplace power structure. Prolonged into the late 1970s, in a quite different economic climate, such conflicts tended to fragment workforces, weakening further the mobilising capacity of the unions and making the task of convincing management of their ability to guarantee shopfloor order more difficult for factory councils. Under those centrifugal pressures disadvantaged micro-groups might begin to tolerate the passage from defensive use of coercion on picket lines, against blacklegs or in response to management prevarication to the active deployment of violence as a supplement to ordinary methods of pursuing limited demands.

Each actor in the factory's fragile network of fluctuating and ambiguous relationships was threatened by the introduction of systematic violence. Obviously, sabotage and attacks on personnel damaged employers economically and its victims physically, and they disrupted the hierarchy of workplace control. Less directly but, from its leaders' viewpoint, no less seriously, the newly-established union position was also put at risk in various ways. First, the continued existence of Red Brigades' nuclei in certain workshops weakened the union claim to guarantee local order, undermining its role in the shopfloor parallel power structure and permitting the recuperation of managerial authority. Alternatively, the same BR presence might provoke allegations that the unions were in fact prepared to tolerate violence – accusations which drew additional force from the evident alignment of the supervisory cadres as the targets of armed groups and as the immediate opponents of the extension of union power on the shopfloor. As a result management would be less ready to treat the official workforce representatives as fully legitimate interlocutors in consultative processes, thereby indirectly strengthening the armed groups' claims that the unions were effectively incapable of defending workers' interests. Further, if the Red Brigades could plausibly claim to have achieved by violence some of the objectives which could only be obtained by the unions after costly mobilisations and foregone pay, then the free-rider temptation among the workforce to accept the violence of an armed minority might increase – and that would encourage further BR recruitment and activity. Beyond plant level, too, any evident diminution in the capacities for mass mobilisation after 1976 would weaken the unions in their search for a political role and resources. An inability to display clear public solidarity between representatives and represented would handicap the ability of the union leadership to present itself as the essential deliverer of shopfloor allegiance and industrial peace. Its role as essential translators between industrial and political actors might be reduced, even abrogated.

Clandestine factory-directed violence also called into question the unions' acceptance, whether by choice or necessity, of high levels of workplace conflict. It invited speculation on the validity of the Red Brigades' claims that their methods were no more than an extension of the violence which had been a long-standing component of Italian industrial relations and which – in the form of intimidation of white-collar workers, supervisors and blacklegs – was an embarassing but undeniable component of shopfloor power.[11] Even if so direct a connection was rejected, the possibility remained open that the continuous mobilisation for strikes and conflict might be sustaining an endogenous factory culture of radical antagonism to management which could hardly fail to provide the users of clandestine violence at least with covert support, if not with much direct recruitment. Union resistance to clear procedures and regulations for industrial conflict increased the likelihood that its organisations would be held to account by management for a violence acknowledged perhaps as unintended and undesired but nevertheless portrayed as an objectively ineluctable consequence of workforce combativeness.

The extent to which violence impinged on the strategies and relationships of actors in different factories depended partly on its volume and partly on how weakly those relations were institutionalised. The two major targets, Fiat Mirafiori (with its huge workforce of 63 000) and Alfa-Romeo Arese (22 000), were also among the most conflictual arenas in Italian industry throughout the 1970s. At Mirafiori the rapid dismantling of the notoriously repressive post-war managerial regime led its successors to describe the factory as 'ungovernable' by 1974; by 1979 levels of shopfloor conflict had reached an annual total of 227 unofficial strikes and a loss of 13 million working hours, ggravated by considerable absenteeism.[12] Disputes at Alfa-Romeo were also numerous, and both factories saw episodes of prolonged conflict when wage contracts were being renegotiated and when management sought to respond to the crisis in the automobile industry. At Fiat the strategies of technological innovation and the relocation of production elsewhere in Italy and abroad led to the loss of Mirafiori's centrality both in the firm and in the automobile sector of the Italian economy. Ironically, therefore, the plant was losing its symbolic status as a terrain for social experiments at the very time when the Red Brigades were making it their primary focus of assault.[13] At both Mirafiori and Alfa-Romeo the introduction of new technology not only threatened unemployment but taken in conjunction with union pressure, contributed further to the undermining of the role of the supervisory staff, *i capi*, on the shopfloor. Although of course overall control over the enterprises was never in doubt, the increasingly ambivalent power structures on the shopfloor were built around poorly defined and strongly contested authority roles.

In other cultures and at other times just such an indeterminacy has generated a witch-dominated cosmos, with accusations of witchcraft appearing both as symptoms of ambivalence and attempts at clarification.[14] In the cases of Fiat and Alfa-Romeo an analogous function was performed by accounts of 'terrorism' and the definitions, descriptions and proposals to eliminate violence from the factory. As the different actors were driven to formulate public versions of the threats represented by the armed groups, they also necessarily produced more or less explicit accounts of proper shopfloor order and the distribution of rights and duties needed to guarantee it. Such versions of local social structure of course transcended the specific issue of 'terrorism'; and precisely because of their genesis in an ambivalent power domain, they were necessarily read as moves in the continuing struggle to define and preserve or alter relationships within it. They therefore provided occasions for internal conflict quite as much as they provided a source of unity against an external challenge.

PROBLEMATISATION: 'MY ENEMY'S ENEMY IS NOT MY FRIEND'

Whose problem?

The significance of the production of accounts of violence as acts in local power contests was underlined by the fact that they were generated *in situ*, and not simply retailed from elsewhere, by the factory level of union organisation. That the national trade union confederations found the issue of 'terrorism' difficult to analyse especially in public, was acknowledged by their own research staff.[1] Although the provincial and national levels of union organisation denounced left-wing clandestine violence and organised mass mobil isations, they produced no extended analyses of the phenomenon either collectively or as individual confederations. That absence was made more conspicuous by contrast with the compilation of dossiers on neo-Fascist violence in the early 1970s by unions in Piedmont and Lombardy.

A major obstacle to a detailed joint version from the three con federations (CGIL, CISL and UIL) was the set of substantial disagreements between the two major components, CGIL and CISL over the boundaries of the phenomenon and how it should best be handled. The divergences broadly reproduced the characteristically different approaches to the relationship between the factory and other social and political institutions. The CGIL tended to favour a 'global' perspective in which events in and policies towards factory conflicts were closely tied to left-wing political strategies, while the CISL generally preferred a 'localistic' set of interpretations and decisions, treating each shopfloor as an autonomous domain and as only loosely coupled with factories elsewhere and with the political arena. The broad contrast was accentuated at the time of maximum left-wing violence in the later 1970s as the advance of the PCI towards power drew the Communist-dominated CGIL into still closer align ment of national/local and political/economic strategies, issuing most clearly in the EUR line of early 1978 and in a general effort to win legitimation from State institutions.[16] As far as the issue of 'terror ism' was concerned, the CGIL-affiliated unions were 'lumpers' supporting a universalist, inclusive approach to the phenomenon insisting on a simple dichotomy between 'terrorists' and 'non terrorists' and accepting the decisions of State agencies (for example the arrest of a union activist ordered by a magistrate) as a sufficient basis for its own internal actions. The CISL members, on the other hand, were 'splitters', arguing against formal definitions and descrip tions, conceding substantial space to local management of the various forms of violence and reluctant to grant priority to external constraints and decisions as limits on their own freedom of action to handle particular issues. The contrast can perhaps best be illustrated through the concrete example of an allegedly 'terrorist' related incident which took place at Alfa-Romeo in December 1979.[17]

The case began with a banal episode of heated verbal exchanges and a scuffle between four workers, one of whom belonged to a micro-collective associated with *Autonomia Operaia*, and two white-collar employees. The 'violence' appears to have been unpremeditated and very short-lived. For a local FIOM-CGIL representative the incident exemplified the clear alignment of *Autonomia* with the clandestine armed groups for whom, it was claimed, the *Autonomia*-linked collectives were scarcely more than the legal agent on the shopfloor: his transmission of an account in that sense to external union levels resulted in newspaper headlines on the general disorder created at Alfa-Romeo by the violence of *Autonomia*, opposed only by the courageous factory council. In response to the public descriptions of the ungovernability of the factory, two FIM-CISL members of the factory council executive carried out their own internal enquiry, relocating the basic features of the event in their local context and denying that they could possibly license a general picture of disorder. In any case the FIM-CISL saw *Autonomia*, not as a strategic component of left-wing organised violence based on clear political antagonism to the parties and trade unions of the traditional Left but as a distorted expression of the aspirations of the marginal social strata produced by an economic crisis; and the union therefore tended to draw a radical distinction between *Autonomia* and such groups as the Red Brigades in spite of their convergent concerns with violence.[18] The FIM-CISL investigation was explicitly motivated as the natural product of the factory council's role in ensuring shopfloor order and handling any breaches; and the union tried, unsuccessfully, to persuade management that the episode could be dealt with internally rather than by recourse to law. This otherwise insignificant example illustrates the preferred interpretive strategies of CGIL and CISL and how the difficulties in reaching agreement on where the boundary around the phenomenon of 'terrorism' should be drawn and who should have the primary responsibility for eliminating violence were likely to frustrate any very elaborate joint analysis.

Even the individual confederations offered no developed accounts of 'terrorism' for either internal use or external consumption. In part, no doubt, that sprang from a desire not to confront publicly an issue on which any adequately detailed debate was likely to undermine the increasingly fragile unity of the confederations, but other factors were also relevant. In 1980 the CISL's research institute, CESOS, began a research project on left-wing violence intended precisely to supply the union with the resource of a general interpretation of the phenomenon, covering other domains besides the factory and usable by its local representatives. However, after the analysis and publication of a survey of the approaches to left-wing 'terrorism' then available,[19] the project was quietly shelved, for two reasons. First, the collection of data at shopfloor level adequate to support an accurate description of local violence was considered too risky for informants. Second, despite the personal dangers, information might none the less have been provided on condition that the results of analysis were directed to the immediate practical task of actually eliminating violence rather than a purely theoretical understanding. Meeting that demand, however, posed the difficult question for the union of how far its own role in the factory could or should be to act as a surrogate police force: at this point the difference between ensuring a valid grounding for analysis and carrying out a criminal investigation almost ceased to exist. The CESOS case thus helps to show why even single external unions found it difficult to go beyond a generalised denunciation of violence. It also points up the issue of the constraints on the content and direction of accounts of the problem, once the task of supplying versions had effectively been turned over to the union structures in the plants themselves – at Fiat Mirafiori the factory councils and the V *Lega* of the FLM, at Alfa-Romeo the factory council.

The climate of intimidation was certainly one such constraint, choking off the flow of necessary information. But, at the other extreme, any union account which appeared to be very well-grounded risked the accusation of its authors' complicity with the phenomenon. To assert a factual basis for a description of the extent of the phenomenon, types of workers involved and methods of recruitment and action would lead straight to the conclusion that access to that information could only be obtained through the maintenance of relations with known practitioners of violence and therefore relied on tacit tolerance of their activities. Paradoxically, the union was equally vulnerable whether it claimed to know too much or too little. Further constraints applied to critical discussion of the ideological analyses and claims of armed groups in the factory. Any direct engagement with those versions of factory reality risked two consequences. In the first place, it would give their authors the status of quasi-legitimate interlocutors of the unions in a debate – even if conducted at a distance through the circulation of documents

- about the nature of factory power and organisation. The public impression of maintaining relationships and thinking the BR documents sufficiently plausible to be worth taking seriously would inevitably be conveyed. In the second place, any detailed exegesis of such texts designed to display their falsity or absurdity would certainly circulate the armed groups' ideas to a much wider audience than the BR authors could reach through their own ramshackle distribution system for leaflets. Moreover, in so far as the unions intended to convince and convert workers potentially sympathetic to armed struggle and perhaps already marginally involved to the extent of having access to the groups' documents, less than faithful rendering of the actual analyses would be counter-productive. For potential recruits and supporters would only be reassured that the Red Brigades' analyses were indeed too embarrassingly accurate to receive honest treatment by unions frightened of their true depiction of the factory and the union position itself. Thus, compelled to provide a public translation of the assault on the factory in order to preserve their own position, the local-level unions were also powerfully constrained in the work of shaping their versions. Their specific resolution of the various interpretive dilemmas was itself a causal factor in eliciting responses from the other actors present.

"Left-wing" terrorism' as a symbolic anomaly

The cognitive status of the versions devised by the local FLM and factory councils can be characterised as 'symbolic knowledge' – their contents fell between semantic knowledge about categories (the definition of 'terrorism') and encyclopaedic knowledge about the world (a detailed empirical report on factory violence).[20] The major *topoi* of symbolic knowledge are intended as foci for public discussion, sensitising devices around which statements can be aggregated without too much concern for logical consistency, since one of the primary aims of its elaboration is to define the identity of the author rather than state truths about the world. Symbolic knowledge, Sperber has argued, is knowledge about statements and actions 'placed in quotation marks', a characterisation intended to mark the difference between the capture of a butterfly in a mime show and in the real world. From the union standpoint the actions and utterances of left-wing armed groups were citations which, despite the apparent similarity of language and targets, were in fact as different from their own activities as the gestures of a mime artist from the pursuits of a professional lepidopterist. The distinction was literally marked in union accounts by the decision, after heated internal argument, to place the actual term 'left-wing' in quotation marks when coupling it with 'terrorism'.[21] The contents of the union versions were therefore simultaneously designed to establish as the central feature their authors' identity *vis-à-vis* violence and to define the nature of the descriptions and actions made by the armed groups. They detached the unions' account from direct verification by excising the problem of 'terrorism' from the shopfloor and thus from the constraints of local empirical evidence. That excision permitted a wide range of more or less contradictory views to be held about the phenomenon among union members. It also facilitated the diffusion of so apparently counter-intuitive a claim that the self-proclaimed enemies (the armed groups) of the unions' own major antagonist (the capitalist *padron ato*) did not represent the logical allies of the unions but another more insidious enemy.

That position was only reached gradually, however. Initially, from the first appearance of the Red Brigades at Mirafiori in 1972 until the systematic 'kneecapping' of cadres began in 1977, the local FLM treated the group's actions publicly simply as a 'provocation' designed to embarrass the unions – an extension in more subtle form of the familiar array of managerially-sponsored uses of violence against the workforce from the days, when ' "terrorism" meant the gang of thugs organised by the CISNAL who attacked you outside the factory gates while you were distributing leaflets'.[22] Who could tell how red the 'Red' Brigades really were? Left-wing language could be used by anyone, and the only sure results of clandestine attacks were to disrupt union negotiations with management and to ensure the lay-off of workers while the damage caused by sabotage was repaired. In any case until mid-decade the levels of union mobilisation and success remained high so that the issue was given little more than ritual attention.

From late 1977 onwards, however, that stance grew increasingly weak. The utter implausibility of supposing that Fiat and Alfa managements had now turned to the regular wounding of their own staff and the subverting of the control hierarchy on the shopfloor was matched by the failure to produce any evidence that the Red Brigades or the increasing numbers of left-wing signatures had any connection with the extreme Right. Furthermore the appearance of steadily more elaborate left-wing texts by the BR intelligentsia partially reproduced in the leaflets claiming responsibility for factory directed attacks, made any easy assimilation to supposed neo-Fascist predecessors very hard, especially since the 'movement' of 1977 had shown clearly the existence of extra-parliamentary Left groups favourable to violence. The product of the interpretive shift was ' "left-wing" terrorism', a label now acknowledging at least its authors' mimetic resemblance to the Left but incorporating also the term signifying traditional recourse to systematic violence of the Right. The phenomenon thus became a monstrous anomaly, standing outside the normal coordinates for assigning political identity, a hybrid reflecting the confusion or bad faith of its activists – a problem whose public conceptualisation in terms of the inversion and juxta-position of the proper categories of political analysis and action contrastively reinforced that same structure of categories which underlay the self-understanding of trade unions and their relations with the working class. From the delineation of the cognitive anomaly in the problem of left-wing violence it was only a short step to its excision from the physical location of the shopfloor, denying any continuity between its methods and the forms of working-class struggle and relegating the significant factors in its genesis to the external environment.

Distilling the accounts of 'terrorism' given by FLM and factory council activists at Fiat and Alfa between 1978 and 1980 reveals the various means of translating the problem outside the workplace.[23] First, terrorist violence was distinguished from the acknowledged occasional excesses of workers primarily by virtue of its clandestinity: 'terrorism is the exact opposite of union struggle – it is clandestinity, cowardly ambushes, contempt for democracy, while our union actions are conducted in the light of day ... There is no continuity between mass struggles, even when they are tough and coercive (*forzanti*), and terrorism, just as explosions of workers' anger have to be distinguished from mafia-like intimidations and violent, organised, *squadrismo* inside and outside the factory'.[24] Second, since there was a radical break between the two forms of violence, 'terrorism' was not generated or encouraged by the existence or intensity of ordinary shopfloor struggle. It was not the reflex product of social or economic crisis nor of any oppressive and alienating labour process: terrorists were not the witting or unwitting representatives of worker interests or marginal strata denied sufficient voice. Rather, they were the deliberate creation of a political strategy formed outside the factory and infiltrated into the workforce and, on occasion, into the unions' own organisations. Terrorist groups were thus accredited as actors, given sharp boundaries and an origin outside the factory – that is, outside the union's own primary responsibility for management of the problem.

In the third place, according to the FLM, the fundamental ideological difference between the union movement and the armed groups lay in their radically-opposed conceptions of the Italian State: a pure apparatus of unmodifiable domination (the view attributed to the BR) as against the open-ended historical conquest of the working class since the Resistance (the union perspective). Concentrating on that abstract level of analysis enabled the unions to underline their own allegiance to the Republic and to evade discussion of the claims about the reality of Fiat advanced by the BR apparatchiks actually responsible for the attacks in favour of a critique of the theoretical assertions of the intelligentsia. The specifically local meanings proposed for factory violence were thus filtered out of the textual exchanges and direct address to particular issues raised by the armed activists was refused. Thus the CISL proposal in July 1981 to obtain the signatures of the entire Alfa-Romeo workforce to a petition asking the BR kidnappers of one of the firm's managers, Sandrucci, for his release was rejected. Not only was the risk of failing to gain the workers' total adhesion, and therefore encouraging the BR to believe they might have support for their limited use of violence, too great; but the initiative would also grant the group the status of interlocutors of the factory council. The union strategy of refusing to contribute to the apparatchiks' search for meaning by confining all discussion of consequences to the remoter State level rather than the immediate context helped to deprive violence of any local meaning for its direct practitioners concerned with their short-term, factory-specific impact. The ineluctable cost, however, was the ignoring of the accounts of the local actors who felt they had indeed borne real immediate consequences but whose experiences and identities simply found no place in the union version. Finally, the problem posed by the arrested members of armed groups who had been workers and shopfloor delegates was managed by singling out for public consumption the elements in their careers which could extract them from any legitimate membership of the authentic working-class community in the factory. Some, like the original BR nucleus at the Sit-Siemens factory in Milan, were traced back to the allegedly politically-suspect petty-bourgeois stratum of white-collar workers; others had worked too briefly in factories to deserve the descriptor 'workers'; and yet others were remembered for having changed their attitudes towards violence as a consequence not of their factory experiences but of some external event such as arrest during a demonstration. For those members who had served as delegates their relations to their shopfloor electors were rendered dubious: either they had not been elected but co-opted, or they had only filled in for another delegate who had resigned, or, where straightforward election could not be denied, it had allegedly been achieved only in the least politicised, most alienated workshops after many unsuccessful attempts elsewhere.[25]

As those elements were added and elaborated between 1977 and 1980, the union translation of 'terrorism' into a direct enemy of the working class took shape. Clandestine violence revealed itself as neither a neo-Fascist plot nor an unwanted, but not fatally disruptive, ally but as an explicit antagonist of the union movement. It was not therefore sufficient merely to ignore it and assume that by improving the success rate in union conflicts with management, the problem of infiltration into the factory could be resolved as a by-product of more effective routine actions. The problem of ' "left-wing" terrorism' became the problem of mobilising the workforce to meet the threat represented by violence as actively and visibly as possible. The only difficulty was – mobilisation to do what? What efficacious methods were available to a civilian population, without formal investigative powers or sanctions, confronted by a numerically tiny and clandestinely-organised phenomenon which its union representatives had characterised as an anomaly originating outside its own field of action?

MOBILISATION: THE SCOPE OF SOLIDARITY

The unions' active responses to violence took two directions: the purification of their own role as legitimate speakers on 'terrorism', validated externally through acceptance of the unions' account by representatives of other institutions; and the demonstration that the workforces they represented did indeed share their own diagnosis of, and prescription for, the problem of violence. In the first case their own structures had to be protected against contamination and relevant categories of interlocutors shown to accredit union views on the State; in the second case the local union leaders had to make publicly clear that, far from constituting an audience receptive to the armed groups' claim to be bearers of its class interests, the workforce positively rejected that spurious enrolment. On both fronts the unions sought to move from merely *ex post facto* mobilisation following an act of violence towards the adoption of preventive measures. They wished to transform passive into active negation, to convert the absence of any desire to support armed groups among the overwhelming majority of the workforce into the positive and explicit rejection of the use of violence – a type of task which, as Elster has pointed out, is always prone to generate paradoxical and counter-productive messages.[26] Some of the intrinsic difficulties with this project were indeed visible in the outcome of the unions' efforts, aggravated in particular at Fiat by the specific characteristics of the union–workforce relationship.

To eliminate any sense of pollution attaching to their own organisations, several union leaders proposed that the membership of anyone arrested for involvement in violence should be automatically suspended and then converted into full reintegration or expulsion once the judicial investigations had reached a conclusion. The proposal, sponsored by the CGIL, was only belatedly adopted as a general rule in 1981 after prolonged opposition from the CISL. The contrast was predictable from the two confederations' more general differences; the CGIL was prepared to show its trust in State institutions' decisions, while the CSIL – mindful of the long-standing use of those same institutions to assist employers by harassing union activists – intended to retain its discretionary power to evaluate the charges against members in the light of their local biographies and reputations.[27] In general, where the CGIL and PCI were strongest, the display of inter-institutional trust received the most attention. Thus the unions at Fiat organised factory assemblies and public conferences at which guest speakers from the police, magistrature and prison staff endorsed the union account of left-wing violence, acted as symbols of groups within the State working for its transformation and offered a concrete representation of institutional co-ordination. At Alfa-Romeo by contrast, and in Milan more generally, the unions paid far less attention to those issues: the magistrates involved in investigating terrorism were rarely invited to attend union-sponsored meetings, and the only external contributor to the single conference on terrorism organised by the city's unions was a journalist.[28]

More controversial, and never in fact implemented, were the proposals designed to prevent the previous problem from arising at all: first, that all elected delegates to the factory council should sign a document explicitly rejecting violence as a condition for their receiving union accreditation as shopfloor representatives; second, that the procedures for the election of delegates be changed so as to narrow the possibilities of candidature (effectively, to include only the names of workers approved in advance by the unions) and ensure that no one could secure election through intimidation – which was just about possible in a small constituency of 50 to 200 workers. Both proposals were variously criticised as ineffective, as likely to lead to exactly the loss of shopfloor solidarity on which the armed groups themselves counted to establish their place in the factory and as a fundamental contravention of the openness of the council's original design. The signature of a declaration against violence was, however, made an issue in the specific case of arrested union members who protested their innocence and wished to avail themselves of the legal defence provided by their union (as, for example, in the case of the Fiat 61, discussed below, pp. 107–11). But it was widely seen as introducing an index of mistrust – or at least an over-formalisation of relations – among participants in a labour movement whose strength lay precisely in its class solidarities, transcending the narrow associational concerns of members alone. Disagreements within and between the unions therefore prevented any responses which, because they entailed consequences for relationships beyond the handling of violence alone, might appear to support the armed groups' contentions about the undemocratic suppression or shaping of workforce opinions by the trade union bureaucracy. No unequivocal message about the seriousness and potential effects of violence therefore reached its practitioners to provide a clear sense for their experiments.

The major union response was to use the traditional collective resource of the workforce, the strike, to show solidarity with the victims of violence and rejection of such methods of political conflict. Successful mobilisations would also verify the clear acceptance of the union version of 'terrorism' as the enemy of the working class. However, the extension of strike use to serve as a communicative device through which to oppose clandestine violence generated difficulties of its own. One kind was formal. Since strikes could only be called after acts of violence had taken place, they ran the obvious risk of appearing first inefficacious, then merely a meaningless ritual for participants. By 1981 one in four (22.5 per cent) blue-collar workers and two in five (41.6 per cent) white-collar workers in Milan's major factories, including Alfa-Romeo, considered strikes useless in the elimination of violence.[29] Moreover, calling a strike in response to an act of violence actually created a direct ground for confrontation between unions and armed groups. Because the quite heterogeneous reasons for non-participation were publicly indistinguishable, the unions had no way of preventing a poor turnout from being widely interpreted as a vote of support either for the specific attack or for armed struggle in general. Since the Red Brigades in particular were known to be extremely attentive to workplace responses, strikes were in perennial danger of transmitting exactly the wrong messages to all external audiences by translating indifference to violence into an index of positive acceptance.[30] Those ambiguities were exacerbated by the second set of problems, the substantive characteristics of the workforce and its relations with the unions in the most transparent laboratory for violence, Fiat Mirafiori.

Organisationally the conditions for mass mobilisation at Mirafiori were unpromising. The unionisation rate (30 per cent) was low, inferior to the overall company rate (38 per cent) and well below the engineering industry as a whole (52 per cent); and while the party most closely connected with the factory, the PCI, had increased its presence substantially after 1968, membership in its Mirafiori cells amounted to a mere 2 per cent of the workforce. The only compensating factor for the fragility of the organisational network was the overwhelming allegiance (83 per cent) of union members to the unitary FLM in contrast to their dispersal among the separate confederations as at Alfa-Romeo.[31] Furthermore the workforce turnover rate was high, running at one worker in eight for the period 1978–80, and commitment to the plant was low: a survey taken in 1980 revealed that one worker in two had contemplated leaving and would do so if a comparably secure job elsewhere became available.[32] Those structural features were hardly conducive to effective mobilisation around general issues, especially when accompanied by specific dissent from the FLM's stance on left-wing violence.

Consistent with the substantially instrumental view towards work and the economic difficulties of the late 1970s, combating terrorism was seen by the Mirafiori workforce as a low priority for union resources – certainly less important than securing the reduction of tax evasion by other social groups, increasing workers' wages and protecting jobs.[33] No doubt the lack of urgency was partly attributable to the belief held by the majority of the workforce (53 per cent) that the optimum strategy for eliminating violence was by making the police more efficient and the penalties more severe: the importance given by the workforce to mass mobilisation under union leadership was actually greater in Taranto, which had seen almost no violence, than in Turin.[34] No doubt, too, the very success with which the union managed to excise the genesis of, and responsibilities for, 'terrorism' from the factory had the ironic consequence of making the problem more remote for the workforce and therefore less significant as a focus of attention.

However the doubts about the union's role in the issue must also be attributed to the positive rejection of its version of violence. At Mirafiori one in six respondents to a 1980 questionnaire explicitly disagreed with a statement summarising the FLM's account, rising as high as one in four in one of the two divisions which had been specifically selected for attacks by the Red Brigades.[35] From the FLM's commentary on those responses, it seems clear that the union's redrawing of socio-political boundaries so as to present workers, management and employers as part of a single community faced with a common external threat was hard to accept. For the sense of a united community whose several components owed each other reciprocal solidarity against violence had to surmount both class and 'ethnic' divisions at Fiat. On one hand, a substantial component of the workforce (26 per cent) rejected collaboration in general with employers on the grounds that their interests were irrevocably opposed:[36] the State, in whose defence the FLM wished to mobilise the workforce, continued to be seen as the essential guarantor of *padronato* power and class inequality. On the other hand, and more difficult to assess in terms of its implications for solidarity, the occupational stratification between the main category of victims of violence, the cadres, and the majority of the manual workforce could be more or less superimposed on a division between native Piedmontese and immigrant southern workers. Most unskilled (75 per cent) and semi-skilled (63 per cent) workers at Fiat had been born outside Turin, largely in the south: but most workshop supervisors (76 per cent) and cadres had been born in the city itself.[37] The same 'ethnic' distinction has become part of Turin's social structure, where Piedmontese families have shown considerably greater inter-generational mobility than southern immigrants. Given that the divisions are often explicitly given general significance by Fiat workers themselves, it is probably safe to suggest that they made large-scale mobilisation to show solidarity across class and workplace boundaries still more difficult.[38]

As a result of those factors the participation rate in strikes at Fiat was often low and always unpredictable, much more so than in the other factories affected by violence. Indeed it was the failure of the one-hour strike in November 1977 against the attack on the deputy editor of the Fiat-controlled *La Stampa*, Casalegno, showing a reluctant participation of between 15 to 60 per cent in the various Mirafiori workshops, that had initially raised public doubt about workforce attitudes to violence when used against someone who could be considered a class enemy.[39] Despite a massive organisational effort through shopfloor assemblies called by the union, mobilisation was still uncertain by the end of 1979: on the occasion of PL's assault on a Turin business school in December participation in the one-hour protest strike reached levels of only between 14 to 34 per cent in the Mirafiori workshops and 3 to 72 per cent at Rivalta.[40] Awareness that the repeated recourse to strikes in response to increasing levels of violence in 1978–9 was steadily depriving them of significance for participants therefore forced the unions to examine more active ways of guaranteeing shopfloor order and eliminating the presence of armed groups.

At Fiat the major initiative came embedded in a questionnaire (*documento-inchiesta*) distributed in early 1980 and designed as both a consciousness-raising exercise for workers and a means through which the unions could obtain a clearer understanding of shopfloor views on violence. The knowledge generated was not encouraging, though hardly unpredictable. The response rate was very low (2.5 per cent at Mirafiori); the responses were compiled individually rather than, as the union had encouraged, collectively by work teams; one-third of respondents saw the State as responsible for violence rather than as the institutional framework of democracy to be defended; a further one-third saw the phenomenon as the unmediated product of economic crisis, *contra* the union emphasis on its deliberately political character; only one in seven believed that terrorism's threat to the working class was sufficiently widely appreciated; and three-quarters reckoned that the workforce was essentially indifferent to the whole issue.[41] But the most controversial issue, which nearly prevented the questionnaire being launched at all, lay in the inclusion of an invitation to provide details on episodes or fellow-workers apparently connected with clandestine violence. Although an informal network of such information exchanges had linked the different unions and had also been created in certain places between political parties and the police, the unions were in effect seeking acceptance from the workforce for a formal recognition of two propositions: first, that the boundaries of the factory did not represent the overriding moral community for any worker and, second, that the union should assume an active policing role on the shopfloor. Not surprisingly, given the range of opinions on the characteristics and relations of factory, State and left-wing violence, the unions and workforces were each deeply divided on the acceptability of both proposals.

In addition to the conflicts over first principles, the debate was shadowed by two practical considerations. First, in all but three cases the woundings and murders of factory personnel had occurred outside the workplace itself, usually near the victims' homes. Members of the workforce could therefore rarely testify against any of the armed groups' apparatchiks over a clear-cut episode of direct violence. At most they could witness minor propaganda activities by locals whose actual relationship to an armed organisation might be suspected but not known with certainty. Second, the murder of Guido Rossa – a factory council delegate from Italsider (Genoa) killed by the Red Brigades in January 1979 for having denounced and testified in court against a fellow-worker observed distributing BR material – suggested that although valid legal procedures demanded public testimony, police protection for witnesses prepared to confirm their evidence in open court could not be guaranteed. Moreover unequivocal solidarity from the factory council could not itself be taken for granted, for Rossa's individual stance had been refused translation into a collective action by the local unions.[42] In many factories the dilemma mentioned above with regard to the delegates' signing of a union declaration against violence reappeared – whether the very workforce–union solidarity required to pursue conflict effectively, discredit BR claims to representative status and mobilise the working class against armed struggle would actually be weakened by increasing the sense of mutual surveillance, especially of the more combative shopfloor activists. In practice the formal questionnaire response at Fiat to the controversial invitation was ineffective. Only one in six respondents admitted to having seen traces of terrorist activity in the factory but mentioned only leaflets and slogans on walls: perhaps significantly the highest levels of ignorance and refusal to respond to the invitation occurred in the one section (*presse*) where the Red Brigades' minimal presence at Mirafiori was continuous.[43] Although it remained publicly unformalised, the unions' *tacit* support for individual collaboration with the police was nevertheless certainly influential; and in at least one of the three cases where a wounding had actually taken place in the factory itself, at

Alfa-Romeo in 1981, workforce witnesses came forward to identify those responsible, in spite of public intimidation.

At the collective level the Rossa case had one sequel which anticipates the following section. In 1983, at the trial of the BR members responsible for the attack, the trade unions and the Italsider factory council applied to the court for the legal status of civil plaintiff (*parte civile*) alongside the prosecution. Their grounds were the direct damage inflicted on their organisations by Rossa's murder. In effect they were inviting the court to validate the union version that left-wing violence was directed primarily against the working class and its representative institutions which could therefore legitimately receive the special protection of the law. The union application carried a demand for external recognition both of its belated wish to identify its own collective position with Rossa and of the validity of its conceptualisation of the nature and targets of the armed groups. In securing acceptance of their claims from the only general adjudicating institution, the unions would have been able to recoup some of the ground lost in failing to obtain clear public support from their workforces on the issue of strikes, questionnaires and denunciation of suspected users of violence. In the event, however, the Genoa court rejected the union request, with the argument that while the union movement's rejection of violence was uncontestable, it could not legitimately claim to represent any more significant a target than the many other institutions whose personnel and property had been attacked. In refusing a form of legal validation for the union version of violence, the court was in fact following the example of a much more significant case – the challenge to the FLM's description of the nature of violence on the Fiat shopfloor mounted by the company itself in 1979.

CONTESTATION: VICTIMS' VERSIONS

The more strongly the unions at Fiat and Alfa emphasised the attack on the working class as the armed groups' primary objective, the more completely the position of the immediate victims – factory owners, senior management, lower-level cadres – was overshadowed. Extracting the factors determining the origin and reproduction of violence from the shopfloor context avoided open discussion of local consequences and the vexed issues of the bases for inter-class solidarity. Like the national levels of the trade union organisations, neither the employers nor managerial staff provided a united public analysis of violence or made a collective response. The problems raised by violence were discussed privately between employers and governments but no public statements insisting on general remedial measures or specific laws were issued. Employers did not take on a distinctive translational role; and so far as I am aware, the four-hour national strike called by the two managers' associations (CIDA, FNDAI) to protest against the murder of the senior executive (Taliercio) at the Montedison plant in Porto Marghera in July 1981 was the sole example of the category's general mobilisation. The reactions to the problem of violence were therefore negotiated locally, at firm or plant level. In private firms in particular arrangements to guarantee the security of property and personnel were improved; and owners generally refused the suggestion of workers' own vigilante patrols – their own rights and responsibility to ensure shopfloor order were not to be ceded to the factory councils, with the accompanying implication of expanded workforce power. The Fiat management, for example, rejected an offer by the factory council to provide assistance with plant security after the first major act of sabotage in 1976. But the local union version of 'terrorism' could also be actively contested and the boundaries of the problem redrawn, to recover dimensions ignored or cursorily treated. The two most significant public challenges took place at Fiat where the levels of violence and conflict were highest and the union account most developed: the so-called 'Fiat 61' case and the subsequent 'march of the 40 000'.

The Fiat 61[44]

The Fiat management's challenge to the FLM's excision of 'terrorism' from the shopfloor was mounted in October 1979, following a summer of prolonged conflict over the triennial labour contract (including brief blockages of access to Turin by road and air) and the murder of a senior executive in September. On 9 October Fiat sent out identical letters of suspension pending dismissal to 61 workers at Mirafiori, Rivalta and Chivasso, accusing them of failure to observe basic minimal principles of cooperative behaviour at work. The same afternoon Fiat's press office distributed to journalists a dossier on terrorism in its factories, prefaced by an explicit connection between the climate and episodes of violence on an ungovernable shopfloor and the clandestine attacks on the firm's personnel. The following day the company announced that it was suspending all further recruitment until order was restored to the factory and the procedures for taking on workers – which prevented employers selecting their workforce according to political opinion, past experience, age, sex or any other irrelevant criterion – had been scrutinised for their contribution to the creation of disorder.

These measures defined the nature of the challenge and the terrain for its resolution. First, against the union accounts, Fiat explicitly re-translated 'terrorism' back onto the shopfloor. Second, by making the grounds for dismissal identical, and identically vague, management created its own counterfigure of a 'terrorist', a symbolic type which neither had clear positive attributes nor was identifiable through specific actions. Third, by deliberately flouting the legal procedures for dismissing workers, Fiat ensured that the conflict between its own and the union versions of violence would be adjudicated in the courts, with their particular forms of description, rules for assessing evidence and attendant publicity. Attempts to prevent the translation of the conflict into the legal context were immediate failures. Despite pressure from most political parties during the instant parliamentary debate, the government refused to try to mediate in the dispute; a meeting between trade unions and management achieved nothing; and the relative failure of strikes called in protest at Fiat by the FLM on 10, 13 and 23 October showed that no effective pressure by shopfloor action could be put on management to rescind its decisions. A survey taken just after the conclusion of the dispute indicated that two-thirds (61 per cent) of Fiat workers regarded the dismissals either with indifference or as a legitimate attempt by management to get rid of supporters of violence and warn the workshy.[45]

To conduct a defence of their version in the courts was unwelcome to unions. Submitting to judicial arbitration issues on the legitimacy of forms of struggle at the workplace, on which the examination of the record of the 61 could be predicted to turn, was to accept legal intervention into an arena hitherto governed by local-level plant bargaining and *de facto* balances of power. Any requirement to define, publicly and formally, the types of workplace conflict that unions were ready to sponsor would provoke disagreements about whether any such definition could be given without simultaneously appearing to tie the workforce's hands in cases of employer prevarication. Legal intervention would necessarily focus on the formal dimensions of decontextualised behaviour: the unions, especially the CISL, preferred to examine questions of justification of disputes, and the actions they elicited, in their immediate, micro-historical environment. In the case of the 61, identified by management as 'terrorists', the FLM would specifically have to concede that its own version of violence was not privileged: other actors could challenge its claims both to know the nature of 'routine' factory violence and its total disconnection from clandestine armed struggle and to be able to act as a guarantor of shopfloor order. Finally of course the nature of its own version and the significance of its key distinctions could not easily resist shifts in meaning as they were reinterpreted into legal vocabularies and diffused to audiences well beyond the shopfloor. The central focus of the conflict, therefore, was the symbolic status of the 61 dismissed workers. Fiat management used them to link forms of violence inside and outside the factory: the FLM had the more difficult task of seeking to keep them wholly outside the workplace context.[46] Like the symbolic kidnappings analysed in Chapter 4, the conflict had a tripartite ritual structure: the separation of the workers from the factory by dismissal, the liminal phase in which debate over their identity took place in the unfamiliar language of the Turin court, and their eventual (re)incorporation into the roles assigned by Fiat or the FLM through the judicial sentence.

In presenting the 61 as symbols of shopfloor activists victimised by the company, the FLM's first move was to detach them from their enrolment by Fiat as emblems of factory violence. As the price for the union's legal assistance in their defence the 61 were required to sign a declaration recognising that violence and intimidation were against the values and traditions of the union movement. The demand immediately provoked divisions among the 61, the different components of the FLM and their legal advisors: it appeared that the FLM was itself demanding precisely the kind of decontextualised assessment of the meaning of violence that was the source of its own unhappiness with the legal process and all formalistic descriptions. The public disagreements and their eventual outcome – ten of the 61 refusing to sign and choosing other lawyers, the remainder signing reluctantly but simultaneously distancing themselves from the contemporary values of the union which they saw as displayed in the then-current 'collaborationist' stance embodied in the EUR line – clearly weakened the FLM's ability to sustain a single identity for the dismissed workers as victims of management. The more divided the 61 became, the less effectively they served as a collective symbol for the union and the greater the likelihood that discussion of their individual cases would thus be re-embedded in the factory. That path offered, as management indeed hoped, the additional chance of embarrassing the union for having acknowledged the responsibility to defend individuals whose actions could be shown in court to be illegitimate or illegal.

In seeking to preserve its radical distinction between endogenous factory conflicts and exogenous 'terrorism', the FLM's primary strategy was to challenge the processes by which management had transformed the 61 into symbolic types and to avoid engaging in discussion of their actual role in any workplace disputes or strikes. By obtaining a legal judgment that the Fiat management's action was neither in intention nor outcome a contribution to the knowledge and elimination of 'terrorism' but a transparent attack on itself, the FLM could preserve the status of its own account of violence. Its own form of symbolic knowledge could be maintained without being brought to the bar of empirical verification in the factory careers of the 61. The first move, therefore, was to get the workers reinstated simply on the technical grounds that the management had flagrantly breached ordinary dismissal procedures. Immediate success on that count was however made hollow by a second collective sacking of the same workers, this time according to the appropriate rules. The FLM was thus compelled to bind the workers more closely to its own identity by invoking article 28 of the Workers' Statute and charging Fiat with anti-union behaviour throughout the events of 9 and 10 of October: obvious indifference to the specific responsibilities of the 61, deliberate orienting of the mass media towards a connection between union-tolerated factory ungovernability and 'terrorism', and casting public doubt on the procedures for taking on workers in which the unions had major institutional responsibilities. Reparation was sought on each count, yet without demanding, crucially, the direct reinstatement of the workers. The FLM aimed to preserve their single symbolic status by excluding their individual biographies and fates from the collective trial, deferring the discussion of their probably very different positions into 61 separate cases for reintegration.

Relieved of the need to defend the specific dismissals of each of the 61 workers, Fiat management joined conflict with the unions at the symbolic level. It was able to concentrate on reinforcing the description of an ungovernable workforce for which the 61 could stand as symbolic representatives, and its eventual success was attributable both to the undermining of the credibility of the FLM to define shopfloor order and to the supplying of an alternative local version of greater plausibility. First, questioned on its general attitudes to forms of shopfloor struggle (coercive picketing, potentially violent marches (*cortei duri, le spazzolate degli uffici*) inside Mirafiori), the union's open reluctance to offer any decontextualised answers necessarily made it appear evasive. The impression was easily given not merely that illegitimate forms of violent or intimidatory conflict occurred at Fiat but that the union was not in principle opposed to them. The claim to describe authoritatively the state of shopfloor order and its absolute separation from clandestine violence was therefore seriously weakened by the clear implication that the criteria for the determination of the meaning of violent actions remained internal to the unions. Their further claim to be acting in the general interest and opposing violence was hardly strengthened by the apparent difficulty in acknowledging the overriding status of the framework of national interest, the law, to define the limits of workplace behaviour. Second, the Fiat management ensured an alternative version of shopfloor order by calling on testimony from the direct victims of clandestine violence – the intermediate cadres. The impossibility for the FLM of effectively contesting the experiences of a category its own version of violence had substantially ignored, uttered publicly and collectively for the first time, allowed the grounds on which management had claimed to be acting to pass virtually unchallenged. The description by the cadres of the breakdown of the managerial power structure having been validated, the legitimacy of Fiat management's responses in early October followed. In the judge's decision, the dismissal of the 61 was construed as the positive initiation of a return to local order rather than a deliberate generalised attempt to weaken union authority. The FLM case against Fiat was therefore rejected in January 1980, decisively enough for the union not to appeal.[47] The failure to obtain validation in court for its version of 'terrorism', entangled in the issues raised by management, had further damaging consequences later in the year, although from an almost entirely unexpected source.

The march of the 40 000

Several commentators on the FLM's defeat in court prophesied a worsening of clandestine violence at Fiat as a result of the decision. Several reasons were adduced: that the Fiat management's victory necessarily weakened the union as a focus for shopfloor allegiance and control; that by including openly combative workers among the 61, Fiat had indirectly encouraged the belief that the forms of resistance to management could best be carried on clandestinely; and that the case had credited the armed groups in the factory with a status that the younger, more disaffected workers might come to see as representative.[48] However, none of these fears was realised, despite additional, exceptionally favourable circumstances. For in June 1980 management's decision to reduce the Fiat workforce led in September to the threat to dismiss 14 469 workers (subsequently transformed into the temporary laying-off of 23 000) and to a 35-day strike closing down most production in Turin and encouraging the PCI's leader, Berlinguer, to announce his party's support for strong workforce resistance, including occupation of the factory, in the event of Fiat carrying out the sackings. Moreover in late 1980 the BR intelligentsia explicitly encouraged the group's remaining members to return to the original terrain of armed struggle and make the factory their primary focus of attack. While in Milan and the Veneto region that call was heeded, the very few BR members in Turin who had escaped arrest after Peci's confessions were not able to utilise the prolonged conflicts at Fiat to re-present the group as a focus of workplace allegiance and intervention. The consequences of the Fiat 61 case, therefore, did not lie in any advantage for the users of violence. But they can be identified, I believe, in contributing to the effects of violence itself in establishing a new public identity for its primary categories of factory victims.

The critical symbolic event in that process was the so-called 'march of the 40 000' through the centre of Turin on 14 October 1980, which followed a much smaller demonstration (600 to 800 participants) at Fiat's Rivalta plant on 9 October.[49] Both marches were organised by the coordinating committee of intermediate cadres at Fiat, founded in 1974, able to attract only 800 to an internal meeting in 1977 but assembling 8000 for its first public demonstration outside the factory in the October march of 1980. The general focus for the mobilisation was opposition to the intransigent union stance in the strike then in its thirty-fifth day at Fiat and the demand to be able to return to work through the picket lines. But the specific issue which united the cadres and which accounted for their enrolment of four times as many participants as themselves from other categories (Fiat manual and non-manual workers, shopkeepers and ordinary citizens) was opposition to violence – the constant refrain in the leaflets distributed to the marchers, the placards carried, the petitions delivered to the municipal authorities and the interviews of their leaders. The problem of 'terrorism' was here construed as violence in all its forms – the use of coercion on picket lines, the routine threats and attacks against supervisory staff, the clandestine activities of armed groups and their factory sympathisers. Redrawing publicly the boundaries of 'terrorism' in that way assigned direct responsibilities of omission and commission to the unions whose claim to be the primary object of attack was thereby rejected.[50] As an immediate consequence the march secured the end of the strike and a return to work at Fiat plants – which were however to lose between 19 per cent (Mirafiori) and 25 per cent (Rivalta) of their workforces over the following three years. Over a longer period the Turin march had significant positive consequences for its organisers both at local and national levels. At Fiat itself the cadres secured recognition from management as a separate negotiating group with rights to increased pay: at national level the general issue of the legal status of the cadres was highlighted by the events in Turin and was eventually resolved in 1985 by their recognition in the civil code as a distinctive category of employees.

For the cadres at Fiat the general fate of isolation and division inherent in the status of potential or actual victims of violence therefore requires qualification.[51] Although the clandestine attacks affected no more than two dozen among the *circa* 18 000 cadres at Fiat, they provided a means by which a very heterogeneous category, ranging from factory foremen up to middle management, could secure a clear focus of identity in terms comprehensible to social groups outside the factory. By showing that the common daily experiences of the *capi* were part of a wider problem, the cadres were able to enrol public support behind their own account and to demonstrate the existence of an audience receptive to a version of a general interest distinct from that of the unions. The creation of their status as speakers for local and wider groups came in two stages. As the first step, the concentration of the Red Brigades' attack provided at least a clear passive identity for a group in the factory hierarchy whose role was otherwise seriously threatened. The expansion of shopfloor control by delegates and factory councils, the disruptive effects of rapid technological change on their authority and the erosion of wage differentials between 1975 and 1980 help to explain why the cadres' associations, although founded earlier in the decade, nevertheless found it impossible to organise collective actions to defend their previously distinctive role in the factory power structure. The Red Brigades' attack paradoxically provided the cadres at Fiat with the symbolic basis for a collective identity that the structural features of their location were in fact causing them to lose.

That passive role was, however, transformed into an active speaker's role by the second step of the Fiat 61 case. The public rejection of the union's attempt to separate sharply all factory violence from external political 'terrorism' left space for an alternative version grounded in shopfloor experience. Moreover, their own accounts did not have to confront the difficulties faced by the unions in defining the phenomenon of 'terrorism' or in avoiding the apparent reliance either on ignorance or complicity as the basis for their descriptions. Furthermore, the cadres' accounts had been given a specific warrant by management and judge during the court hearings in the case between Fiat and the FLM: indeed one influential interview with a foreman from Mirafiori containing details of the climate of violence had been circulated very widely by Fiat to firms and schools. [52] Until that point the cadres had been merely subordinate to the dispute between the major actors, although their detailed evidence had been essential to the success of management's description of shopfloor disorder. The union-sponsored strike of September-October 1980 offered the first opportunity to use their version of 'terrorism' in defence of their own interests: it was the means by which the cadres, as well as substantial numbers of manual and non-manual workers in the company, publicly dissociated themselves from their previous apparent consent to union activists. The FLM and factory council had translated the problem of violence outside the context of its actual appearance, conducting their interpretations on the basis of the intelligentsia's analyses and treating the victims as symbols: the cadres re-localised the issue, refusing to be considered either by the Red Brigades or (of course with quite different objectives) by the FLM as embodiments of abstract functions in the capitalist division of labour.

Analysis of the use and management of violence in Italy's largest factories shows how even among the audiences closest to the actions themselves, its threat was insufficient to generate lasting solidarities for resistance. The conflicting understandings of the boundaries and primary targets of armed groups were built up into versions assigning roles to relevant factory actors – workforce, unions, cadres and employers – which were themselves sources of conflict as the different representatives refused to accept enrolment in the associated obligations and responsibilities. The Fiat case in particular offers a good example of how local interpretations of violence constitute a factor in the evolution of the phenomenon itself and may have their own independent consequences. It also indicates how the apparent weakness of the opponents of the armed groups in failing to agree on a clear meaning for violence had the unintentionally beneficial result of preventing the formation of a single identity to unify its heterogeneous practitioners.

4 Maintaining the Political Frontier

Compared with the factory, the political domain offered a vastly more complex and visible arena for violence and response. Unlike trade unions and employers, the role of the political élites as guarantors of public order gave them no opportunity to externalise the problem of 'terrorism'. Without the possibility of escape from the communicative field created by acts of 'armed propaganda' and diffuse violence, their actions and inactions served to indicate their perception of the seriousness of the attacks as well as to put in place legal and administrative measures to contain and eliminate them. Not all responses were public, of course: the use of infiltrators into the armed groups, techniques of police investigation and informal political pressure on the media, for example, depended on their invisibility for success. But, in the development of ideologically-based violence in search of unified meanings for armed struggle, the symbolic dimension of public responses carried a special importance.

The metaphor of a challenge has often been used to characterise the exchanges between armed groups and their political opponents.[1] That particular type of interaction provides a useful way of identifying both the formal features and the substantive issues that participants had to confront in the specific context of Italian politics after 1970. In his subtle anthropological analysis of the logic of challenge and riposte, Bourdieu emphasises the central concern with the management of meaning in the decisions on whether, when and how to respond to an act of aggression.[2] The nature of the act remains essentially indeterminate until its addressee decides whether it has come from a person sufficiently equal (honourable) to be counted as possessing the authority to issue a serious challenge or merely from a presumptuous inferior whose rash pretensions can be ignored. If the challenge is accepted, further clarifications of its meaning are provided by decisions over when (how long before a delay in response is transformed from the prerogative of superiority into a sign of pusillanimity?) and how seriously (mere equivalence to the original act or a full-scale show of force?) to respond. In Bourdieu's analysis, which extends Mauss' study of gifts and exchange, each actual challenge is therefore built on a history of interaction and mutual nowledge at the same time as it represents a dramatic confrontation n which the public social identities of the participants are clarified, einforced or transformed. The meaning of each act is perpetually leferred: every response, and response to that response, can trans- orm it retrospectively.

In the case of Italian political violence the double temporality nherent in the process of challenge can be identified in the prolonged liffuse assaults against people and property and their punctuation by he focused confrontations between political and armed communities n the five kidnappings of magistrates and politicians between 1974 nd 1981. But in other respects the interactional model needs to be 1ade more complex. First, unlike the conventions of the challenge vhich must be known to participants and audience, the rules overning the political responses to clandestine violence had to be 1ade up and legitimated in the course of the attack itself. Conveying uthoritative messages about violence was, however, particularly lifficult for the dominant actors in a political community whose nstitutional and symbolic centre was itself polluted by violence as vell as faced with loss of both internal coherence and links to its own >eriphery during the 1970s. Second, in contrast to the formally dyadic 10del of a challenge, neither challenger nor respondent were single, ınified actors. The community of armed struggle was deeply divided bout the appropriate levels and objectives of violence and became >rogressively centreless during the years of most intensive attacks. Its >pponents were similarly divided. Between 1970 and 1984 no fewer han 18 governments, embodying 9 different combinations of parties, ad the political responsibility for responding to violence. The range >f understandings of 'terrorism' among ideologically very diverse >arties and the state of relations among them, as well as their links to he State apparati responsible for repression, must count as impor- ant factors in explaining why the responses to violence took the orms that they did. Parties may also show divisions between their ocal and national levels, with different appreciation of the issues lepending on the distance from the context in which violence occurs. \ttention to the party-political dimension of response is often ınderplayed in the general discussions of terror-management which lraw heavily on the experience of those western societies, especially 3ritain and the USA, where the issue has been largely withdrawn rom inter-party conflict.[3]

A third complicating element is the role of the audience, whose >resence and judgement in ordinary challenges are fundamental to the assessment of the actors' social nature. But in the Italian case the legitimacy of any such neutral position was itself controversial. Some participants, especially the PCI, wished to deprive the challenge itself of any meaning by abolishing the status of spectator: intellectuals and members of the extra-parliamentary Left who declared themselves on the side neither of the present State nor of the Red Brigades at the time of Moro's kidnapping were strongly criticised. Others aimed at the same result from the opposite direction, by inviting everyone except the police and magistrature to ignore the actions of armed groups, depriving their authors of an audience, in the extreme case by a black-out on all media information. Further complexities were raised by the need to address quite different audiences simultaneously.

The final issue concerns the process of reciprocal establishment of identity between challenger and challenged. Both the armed groups and the political parties were engaged in a challenge in which their opponents were presented not merely as inferiors or superiors but as fundamentally illegitimate. Yet the structure of a challenge logically requires that antagonists be credited with at least sufficient legitimacy to empower them to confer meaning, recognition and identity through their responses. Thus amongst their objectives the Red Brigades sought to demonstrate their power over a party, the DC which they proclaimed to be illegitimate and for whose responses they should therefore have had scant concern; but in practice nevertheless, the DC's reactions provided a key source of meaning for the political dimension of BR actions. The political parties were also required to make responses of a sufficiently focused and public kind to reassure other members of the political community. They had to do so without either conferring any quasi-legitimate political status on the authors of violence or supplying a general identity which might help to unify the competing armed groups and thus contribute involuntarily, to the achievement of hegemony aspired to by the BR or the intelligentsia associated with *Metropoli*. To use a different metaphor, the objective of the political parties was to prevent the transformation of the frontier between themselves and the armed community into a clear boundary. Preservation of distance between the antagonists across a terrain managed by the non-political agencies of police and judiciary prevented armed groups obtaining explicit recognition by political actors and achieving a direct symbolic equivalence between their own capacity to carry out attacks and political party defeats.

This chapter therefore examines aspects of the interactional man ςement of violence in the political domain. I shall deal in turn with ιe nature of the attack and of the polity which was its target, ιalysing in particular how the weakness of the centre and the gap ςtween the local and national levels of the political community ςrved to inhibit the translation of violence into a problem requiring verriding attention and definition from the centre. Two dimensions f response will be considered – attempts, first, to strengthen the ςmmunity while preserving local/national divisions and, second, to ιddress the problem of 'terrorism' without addressing 'terrorists' and ιnferring on them a form of political recognition. Finally, I shall ιalyse the management and consequences of the focused kidnap-ings in which the BR endeavoured to transform the notional, ιdirect confrontation of ordinary violence into a real, direct confron-ιtion – to reach across the frontier in a particularly dramatic attack. ιmongst these episodes by far the most significant was the Moro case ιhich has subsequently served as a condensed symbol for exegesis in ςtermining the nature of the entire decade and a half of armed ιruggle. It provided the political élite with the major materials for its wn quasi-judicial re-evaluation of the past, through which partici-ιants have sought retrospectively to identify the underlying objec-ςves of the challenge. As I show in the final section, no such closure ιas been possible: the 'problem of terrorism' has eluded any con-ςnsual political formulation.

ιTTACKING THE HEART OF THE STATE

¹he attack

'rom the standpoint of the political parties, clandestine political ιolence had both public and private dimensions. On one hand, the ιrmed groups' activities simply added a further element to existing ιriminality and its threat to public order for which the electorate ιight call its government to account. The first half of the 1970s was in ιny case a boom period for ordinary crime. The annual murder rate ιoubled between 1972 and 1976, the number of serious armed ιobberies reached its high point in 1976, and the highly publicised ιrime of kidnapping for ransom, hitherto largely confined to the rural ςriphery, increased from 8 cases in 1972 to 75 in 1977.[4] Thefts, bank ιobberies and kidnappings by political groups made only a small and ςnerally indistinguishable contribution to the increasing levels of perceived insecurity in the first half of the decade demandir response by the government. After 1976, however, while the volum of ordinary crime remained more or less stable, the dramatic increa in political violence ensured that it would be picked out more clear as an aspect of public concern.

The private dimension of the armed groups' assault was directe specifically against the personnel and property of political partie themselves. Table 4.1 shows the volume and geographical distribu tion of all attacks on the different parties: although the responsibi ities of Left and Right for property damage are not distinguished i the available figures, we can safely assume that the Christia Democrat (DC), neo-Fascist (MSI), Liberal (PLI), Republican (PR and Social Democrat (PSDI) parties were primarily targets of th Left, the Communist (PCI) and Socialist (PSI) parties victims of th Right.

The left-wing parties were the main victims of damage to propert which included acts of minor vandalism, assaults carried out in th course of demonstrations and marches and the use of explosive Apart from its exceptional concentration in Rome which alon accounted for one-third of all acts of damage to political property, th attack was widely distributed across most provincial capitals in nort and central Italy. The periodisation of the assault on the two majo parties shows one significant difference: while damage to the PCI wa evenly distributed throughout the period, varying between 26 and 9 episodes annually, the attack on the DC was much more narrowl focused and its impact therefore heightened. Four-fifths of th attacks on the party came in the years 1977–9: in Rome damage t party offices somewhere in the city was then running at roughly on episode per fortnight, creating a particularly acute sense of bein under siege for its local-level functionaries and activists.

With only four exceptions, the human targets – wounded (21 kidnapped (3) or murdered (4) – were drawn from the DC. Th exceptions were either murdered in direct retaliation (one of the tw MSI victims) or were attacked for particular local activities rathe than as generalised symbols of their party (the two PCI victims): th other major parties remained unscathed by the left-wing groups unt the isolated murder of the former PRI mayor of Florence in 1985. All but one (Moro) of the DC victims belonged to the category c lower-level party cadres, more or less equivalent in position to th primary targets in the factory. Since they too carried a dual identity a symbols of the party and as well-known opponents of the Left i

TABLE 4.1 Damage to political property and personnel 1969–82

Party	Rome		Milan		Turin		Genoa		Naples		Other		Total	
	Property	People	Property	People	Property	People	Property	People	Property	People	Property	People	Property	People
DC	150	4	39	5	24	3	9	5	20	4	223	1	465	22
PCI	220	–	79	–	34	–	5	1	74	1	325	–	737	2
PSI	32	1	19	1	3	–	–	–	6	–	58	–	118	–
MSI	108	1	9	1	4	–	–	–	5	–	67	–	193	2
PSDI-PRI PLI-PDUP	51	–	29	–	18	–	–	–	4	–	122	–	224	–
Total	561	5	175	6	83	3	14	6	109	5	795	1	1737	26*

* This figure differs slightly from Table 2.2 since here the kidnap victims also murdered or wounded are counted only once.

SOURCES

1969–80: M. Galleni (ed.) *Rapporto sul terrorismo* (Milan: Rizzoli, 1981) pp. 104–5, Tables 52, 53.

1981–2: Direzione PCI, Sezione Problemi dello Stato: 'Attentati e violenze in Italia nel 1981' (Rome, 1982) p. 8, 'Attentati e violenze in Italia nel 1982' (Rome, 1983) p. 7.

neighbourhood or municipal politics, they were ideal vehicles ‹
meaning simultaneously for the abstract schemes of the intelligents‹
and for the pragmatic interventions of locals. The attacks began in 197
in Milan and, like the damage to property, were mostly concentrated
the years 1977–9. Until 1980 they were entirely confined to the fo‹
major urban centres of political violence: the four actions in Naples too
place in 1980–1 as an attempt to penetrate the hitherto largely immur
south and to profit from what was perceived as the social disaggregatic
of Naples, particularly in the aftermath of the 1980 earthquake. Finall
responsibility for the attacks was even more markedly concentrate
than in the case of factory personnel. The Red Brigades claimed 2
of the 26 attacks, including all cases of damage to DC politicians. The
were in fact the only signature to translate their antagonism to th
existing political system into a strategy of direct attack on i‹
representatives, and they therefore constituted the specific beare‹
of the most serious private challenge to political parties.

   The Red Brigades' attention to the political arena, and the DC i
particular, was long-standing and distinctive among armed group‹
From 1971 onwards leaflets and actions proclaiming the group's vie‹
were frequently timed to coincide with national political events an
to make use of key symbolic dates: the kidnapping of Sossi on 1
April (the date of the elections in 1948 establishing the DC in powe
before the 1974 divorce referendum, the assault on the DC offices i
central Rome during the 1979 election campaign, the kidnapping ‹
D'Urso on 12 December (the anniversary of the Piazza Fontar
bomb of 1969) and so on. Identification of the DC as the prima‹
antagonist was heralded by the first attack on one of its collater‹
organisations in January 1973 and developed in the series of elabo‹
ate texts by the intelligentsia from 1974 onwards. Treated initially ‹
a contemporary variant of Fascism 'in a white shirt', the party can‹
to assume the central role in the Red Brigades' political scenar‹
which depicted Italy as a 'multinational imperialist state' (SIM
organised around a counter-revolution embodied in the DC whos
personnel mediated the project's national and international dimer
sions. The DC became the symbol of the substantive identity ‹
party, government and State. The equal significance given to th
incorporation of police and magistrature in the alleged grand desig
was highlighted by the kidnapping of a magistrate in 1974, th
creation of a specific component, the *Fronte della controrivoluzion‹*
of the BR apparatus in 1976 to monitor the activities of polic‹
carabinieri and magistrates, and their increasing selection as victin‹

Table 2.2). The major left-wing party, the PCI, received little analytic or active attention in BR texts. The early intelligentsia had taken for granted the party's long-standing reformism so that the policy of the historic compromise, regarded simply as the continuing acceptance of subordination to the DC, was in no sense a sudden or unexpected betrayal of revolutionary hopes; and they had announced from an early stage that they did not intend to spend time criticising the PCI strategy.[6] Other parties were wholly ignored, although the PSI received some attention (including the attempted murder of a senior economic adviser in 1986) after Craxi became prime minister in 1983.

The Red Brigades' attention to the activities, symbols and rhetoric of the political arena was not shared by the rest of the community of armed struggle. The *Autonomia*-based groups were largely concerned with local issues and with the progressive extension of the scope of illegality to protect aggregations of 'counterpower'; and they were therefore reluctant to confront the State or political parties at levels of direct violence which they regarded as suicidal. Gradual occupation and extension of the frontier zone between political and armed communities was the strategy most consonant with the locals' ambitions for violence. Moreover, if they had a direct political antagonist, it was likely to be the PCI, again not because of its reneging on revolution or its insufficiently serious parliamentary opposition to the DC regime but because the party became the dominant component in the governing coalitions in all five major centres of political violence after 1975. Dissent from the Red Brigades' concern with the DC was especially strongly publicised by *Autonomia*'s intelligentsia who were far more concerned with the general significance of the trends in party politics in the mid-1970s than the group which claimed to be most attentive to the political domain. Among the apparatchiks in the *Autonomia*-oriented groups, too, the sequence of BR attacks on local-level DC cadres was read as an indication of the failure of political imagination, a sign of archaism and strategic weakness with no productive consequences.[7] Even in cases of obviously successful infliction of damage, the specifically political dimension of BR violence was therefore unlikely to function as an aggregating device for the other groups. That was shown most clearly by their reluctance to help the Red Brigades during the Moro kidnapping and their refusal to increase attacks so as to distract the police and indirectly to accredit the message that the seizure of Moro should be considered as the central consensual moment of a general assault. Some of *Autonomia*'s leaders were also publicly, if no absolutely unequivocally, critical of the Red Brigades' decision t raise the level of violence.

The proclaimed objectives of the BR assault on the DC and th State were three: revelation, disarticulation and destruction, with th last belonging to the 'civil war' planned to follow the phase of 'arme propaganda' but never achieved. Actions were intended to unmas the hidden structures binding parties and the State together as th local agents of international imperialism and the bases of a tenden tially absolute class domination. That project was therefore to b disarticulated by setting off conflicts within and between the politica parties, State apparati and citizens. Endlessly reiterated as a goal 'disarticulation' was sufficiently indeterminate an event to allo (temporary) aggravation of almost any minor, normal, conflict t count as a success, from a dispute between different sections of th judiciary down to the resignation of police officers or suspension of magistrate.[8] Successful disarticulation would show that violence wa not only possible but efficacious, that it could be translated into rea consequences within the political arena rather than merely constitut a symbolic signal of antagonism.

The direction of violence towards the political community there fore had three distinct addressees: the population, disquieted by th threat to public order and perhaps autonomously mobilisable i support of the armed groups or of a strong reaction; the Stat apparati, especially the police who were the most direct antagonist and victims; and the political parties themselves, especially the DC - more narrowly its local cadres - with the institutional obligation t provide responses. The combination of diffuse local violence and th 'attack on the heart of the State', as the Red Brigades described thei strategy, threatened always to provoke conflict among the thre major individuated groups. Symbolically, in each single attack, th BR claims to unmask and divide were no more than hypothese verifiable in the responses they provoked. Opponents were therefor compelled to shape their responses to exclude two potentiall embarrassing, and perhaps consequential, interpretive outcomes: o one hand, to prevent what were actually the short-lived *products* o acts of violence from being read as confirmatory evidence of th underlying political reality postulated by the Red Brigades; on th other hand, to demonstrate that the ordinary disputes characteristi of a pluralist polity were not themselves significantly influenced b deliberate insertion of violence into them and so could not stand a evidence for the powers of violence to translate issues into the political arena.

At a more abstract level the contest concerned the meaning and alignment of two sets of distinctions; politics/violence and public/private. The political parties aimed to present themselves as the unpolluted speakers for a public interest which transcended ideological differences, simultaneously evading charges that they might be prepared to use violence for their own private advantage and ensuring that armed struggle remained merely a private battle against its non-political direct antagonists, the police. The pairs of distinctions would thus be neatly isomorphic. The Red Brigades' aim was to shift the boundaries of politics to include violence, presenting themselves as the representatives of wider collectivities and attempting to display their opponents as dominated by partial or private concerns. However, because the Red Brigades constituted only one signature in the armed community, the group also laid itself open to the accusation that its distinctive level of assault on the DC was itself motivated by the search for purely private advantage at the expense of violent competitors. The *Autonomia*-oriented groups in fact alleged that the increase in the seriousness of the violence used against political targets was designed less to destroy the DC's regime than to establish the Red Brigades as the effective centre of the community of armed struggle – by extracting some kind of recognition from the DC or by provoking the State into eliminating less well-organised violence (and thus propelling its authors into the Red Brigades). The Red Brigades had themselves to contend with maintaining the public/private distinction, exactly as their major target, the DC, had to meet other parties' suspicions that it might be willing to use its victimage as a means of reinforcing or re-establishing its own position at the political centre.

Clarifying the results of these challenges was made more complicated by two further aspects of Italian politics in the 1970s. First, their sequences cut across the persisting conflicts among the political parties over precisely the same sets of distinctions, with the result that issues beginning as responses to violence were rapidly translated into more general debates and divisions, tending to absorb and obscure the specific effects of violence. Second, the conflicts were progressively accompanied by a decline in any central political authority to fix an interpretive closure for the meanings of their outcomes, in a way which closely paralleled the decline of the hegemony of the Red Brigades in the community of armed struggle itself, especially after

1976. The pattern of interaction became more complex as the primary antagonists from the increasingly acephalous armed and political communities struggled simultaneously to communicate the location of the frontier between each other and to establish their own positions as authoritative representatives within their respective communities.

A State with a heart?

In depicting the national community as coming more firmly under the centralised control of the DC with the complicity of the PCI, the Red Brigades were largely inverting the actual political trends between 1970 and 1984. In several respects the symbolic and institutional centre from which the challenge of violence had to be met became itself less clearly separated from violence, while its internal coherence was weakened and its links to the wider society slackened. Rather than acting as the guardians of a well-defined set of institutional arrangements and core values, the political élites were forced into the task of creating the public sense of such arrangements.

The key symbol of the political community was the Constitution of 1948, which provided the most succinct charter for the rejection of violence and the limits for measures to defend the polity. Although as a symbol the Constitution was interpreted somewhat differently in the rhetoric of the various parties, it was tied closely to anti-Fascism and the Resistance and thus to a period of violence which had included terrorism. The founding act of the post-war democratic order, however, provided symbols and rhetorics not just for the political parties but for the armed groups. For the parties the Resistance represented a period of national collaboration which successfully overturned Fascism in favour of democracy, while for the extra-parliamentary Left and the armed community it was largely a failed social and political revolution aborted primarily by that collaboration. Resistance texts, heroes and weapons provided some of the conceptual and material resources for armed struggle especially in its first phase. Somewhat paradoxically, therefore, both the attack on and defence of the Republic was conducted with reference to the same polysemic symbol. Moreover, the status of the Constitution as a sacred symbol itself changed in the course of the 1970s. While its value went largely unquestioned as long as its substantive institutional provisions remained unfulfilled, their implementation by mid-decade allowed more open interpretations of the charter of political order, including suggestions for fundamental reforms.[9] Disagreements therefore became increasingly possible about the proper reading of the obligations imposed by the Constitution in response to violence: its role as a univocal symbol of a unified political community was inevitably weakened, extending the scope of negotiation at the expense of an unproblematic presentation of a taken-for-granted order. The Constitution became less powerful as a symbol for the rhetorical closure of debate.

The central political institution of the Republic, Parliament, was also seen as standing in an ambivalent relation to violence. First, it included parties at all points on the spectrum which were widely believed to be openly or clandestinely linked to the ideologies and practices of violence. In 1967 only one in seven (16 per cent) electors would assert that the PCI was against violence; and although that proportion rose to nearly one in two (43 per cent) in 1976 and to a bare majority (53 per cent) by 1979, a substantial segment of the electorate remained dubious about the guarantees against violence to be given by Italy's second largest party. On the Right the links between the neo-Fascist MSI and violence were thought to be so clearly established that the majority (57 per cent) in a 1976 survey supported the party's abolition by law. More surprisingly, the earlier consensus that at least the DC was opposed to violence weakened substantially between 1967 and 1974 when the proportion of the electorate ready to state unequivocally that the party rejected violence fell from 72 per cent to 58 per cent.[10] The entry into Parliament of former extra-parliamentary Left groups in 1976 cannot have strengthened the sense of a clear division between armed and political communities.

Furthermore a series of alleged involvements of parliamentarians in episodes or with individuals linked to political violence offered repeated scope for speculation on the relations between the centre and its antagonists. Not until 1982 were three ministers from the DC and PSDI acquitted by Parliament itself of all involvement in the aftermath of the Piazza Fontana bomb massacre. The DC Prime Minister (Cossiga) narrowly escaped impeachment in 1980 on the charge of having informed a senior party colleague (Donat-Cattin) of an imminent arrest warrant for his son – an episode which revealed the ease of access of the then deputy-secretary of the DC to a man who turned out shortly afterwards to be a leading figure in *Prima Linea*.[11] Several examples concerned the PSI: its leaders (Craxi, Signorile, Landolfi) had contacts during the Moro kidnapping with members of *Autonomia*'s intelligentsia (Piperno, Pace), both of whom were subsequently convicted for participation in armed struggle; its former secretary (Mancini) was investigated by a parliamentary committee after allegations of having procured funds for a then suspect research institution (CERPET); and a Calabrian Senator (Pittella) was indicted for membership of the Red Brigades for having treated a wounded group member in his clinic and tried to negotiate the kidnapping of a local party rival in recompense. Finally the Radical Party was prepared to project the videotaped interrogation of a kidnap victim in the parliamentary precincts and include, successfully, among its electoral candidates in 1983 a suspected, and subsequently convicted, organiser of armed struggle (Negri).

The other central institutions formally entrusted with the defence of Italian democracy – police and *carabinieri*, army and security services – were more clearly polluted. The SIFAR case of 1964 had already suggested the existence of conspiratorial networks linking individuals from the various services, but the left-wing mobilisation of 1968–9 prompted apparently more determined efforts to aggregate the supporters of internal subversion. No fewer than five *coups d'état* were claimed to have reached an advanced stage of planning between 1969 and 1974.[12] Some, like the aborted 'occupation of Rome' by Borghese in 1970, approached the level of comic opera; and their deliberately-leaked details were probably symbolic attempts to make visible to activist outsiders the generic availability for subversion by tiny groups in the police and armed forces. The continuing existence of such networks throughout the 1970s was further suggested by the revelation in 1981 of the membership of the clandestine Masonic Lodge P2 – an aggregate of political, administrative and other élite members with no obvious goals or collective identity but providing a useful focus for indicating less than complete attachment to the framework of the Constitution in the event of a major Communist victory at the polls. More direct linkages with internal violence came with the allegations of the security services' involvement in the seven neo-Fascist bomb massacres between 1969 and 1984, with their 145 deaths and 730 injuries. The results of judicial enquiries leave little doubt that individuals from the services at least gave protection to the actual authors and may have directly participated in the organisation of the crimes. Doubts about the commitment of the armed State bureaucracies to eliminating violent subversion from Left or Right was not confined to politicians and commentators prone to conspiracy theories: in the PCI's 1982 national survey complicity among the

State apparati ran a close second to scandals and injustice as the principal cause of the persistence of terrorism.[13] The belief in the continuing potential for autonomous action in the institutions (police and *carabinieri*) most exposed to left-wing violence was an important factor shaping the responses made by the political élite.

If a rigorous separation between the political community and violence was hard to draw, the distinction between public and private was equally fragile. During the 1970s it was made more problematic from two directions. First, the series of scandals (ANAS, Montedison, Lockheed, Sindona, Calvi) involving the governing parties, especially the DC, provided good reasons to question the existence of a sense of a public interest at the centre. In fact, between 1967 and 1980 the proportion of the electorate doubting the honesty of governments rose from 33 per cent to 85 per cent: 13 per cent declared DC politicians to be dishonest in 1967, 51 per cent in 1976.[14] Second, the boundary between public and private was made a central political issue in the contests over civil rights and feminist issues from the divorce law of 1970 to the referenda confirming the 1978 abortion law in 1981. The unconventional political methods, electoral success and use of the referendum by the revived Radical Party added to the publicity of the conflicts over the priority of individual or collective interests, the identity of the agents entitled to make authoritative definitions of what they were and the extent to which either set of interests was given overriding importance in specific cases by the Constitution. The kidnappings carried out by the Red Brigades focused these general issues most acutely since the government's dilemma to accept or refuse negotiations for the hostages' release posed the specific question of whether its primary obligation was to act as the embodiment of the political community or to defend the life of an individual citizen.

Alongside the relaxation in the classificatory basis of the political community went its decentering, in the double sense of losing both coherence at the centre and some of the links to the periphery. That evolution of political relationships during the 1970s was signalled by the slow decline in the electoral success of the DC which had made the party's centrality to the political order the ideological basis of its self-definition; the increasing difficulty of finding a governing formula, resulting after 1976 in minority governments or governments led by a minority party in the coalition; perception of a rift in consensus between the national and local levels of party organisation; and a decline in the memberships of the major parties and in electoral participation. The drift towards what has been called 'leaderless Bonapartism' (another of the oxymorons traditionally used to describe aspects of the Italian polity) can be divided into three periods – 1970–6, 1977–9, 1980–4 – which parallel the trajectory of the armed community and mark the shifts in the interpretation and management of violence.[15]

In the first period, 1970–6, the DC remained the dominant occupant of the centre, symbolised by its readiness in 1973 to reverse governing alliances from the Centre–Left to the Centre–Right formulae and the exclusion of the PCI. Despite the emergence of political violence, considerable extensions of the right of citizens, in particular *vis-à-vis* the powers of the police, were enacted by Parliament. The liberalising trend was reversed in 1974, the conventional beginning of the so-called 'emergency legislation', in response not to political violence but to the great increase in ordinary crime. The first piece of legislation singling out political violence for specific treatment – the Reale law in 1975 – provoked major conflicts between the governing parties; a compromise bundle of measures was agreed on but declared valid only until the new code of penal procedure was introduced.[16] General anxiety about crime and public order remained far inferior to concern about employment, inflation and welfare reforms in all DOXA public opinion surveys taken between 1970 and 1976.[17]

The unexpected and dramatic electoral success of the PCI in mid-decade was the prelude to the second phase, the period of 'national solidarity' between 1977 and 1979. At the centre the period was characterised by the progressive negotiation of more formal support for a DC minority government to confront the problems of the economy and violence. With the end of the *conventio ad excludendum* against the PCI and Moro's resigned recognition that the era of DC centrality was over ('*il futuro non è piu nelle nostre mani*'), however, the three major participants sought publicly to redefine their political identities. The DC replaced its secretary, carried out the greatest purge of its parliamentarians since 1948 and proclaimed the party's ideological and social 'refoundation';[18] the PCI developed its ambivalent historic compromise strategy alongside the 'Eurocommunist' shifts in economic and foreign policy, redefining itself as a 'party of government and struggle'; and the PSI defenestrated its leadership in 1976, declared the Centre-Left formula extinct and began a search for distinctive ideological and political space. These movements made the ordinary coordinates of government and opposition more uncertain; and for the Left their re-establishment on new terms was made more difficult by the armed community's appropriation of key left-wing symbols and rhetorics of identity to try to legitimate violence.

The years 1977–9 also saw the most coordinated defence of the political community. Party interpretations of violence converged in November 1979 towards agreement to create a single institutional forum, the Parliamentary Commission of Inquiry into the Moro affair, designed both to examine the management of the kidnapping and to provide a general consensual analysis of 'terrorism'. The conclusions were intended to serve as the basis of practical responses as well as to offer a better analytical grasp of the phenomenon.[19] Accompanying the growing consensus came the most focused legislative changes identifying the problem of 'terrorism' and the most coordinated responses to single actions. Joint action was facilitated not just by the least centrifugal formula for government (a minority DC administration for the only extended period between 1970 and 1984) but also by the continuity of personnel in key positions. Only two DC ministers (Cossiga, Rognoni) occupied the post of Minister of the Interior over the entire period 1976–84, the first becoming Prime Minister in 1979–80. Likewise, on the PCI side, a single leader (Pecchioli) maintained the responsibility for the party bureau concerned with political violence. No doubt, too, the abnormally high turnover of both the major parties' parliamentarians in 1976 gave the senior members of the political élite greater authority over their more inexperienced colleagues and therefore greater scope to coordinate actions without strong and divisive pressures towards separate party accountability. Certainly the Moro kidnapping was managed informally, without reference either to Parliament or official party bodies, in a way that was to be impossible in subsequent cases.

The trend towards collaboration at the centre did, however, produce increasing disarticulation with the periphery, especially where violence was greatest. First, the results of the 1975 elections had placed the Left in power in Rome, Milan, Turin, Genoa and Naples, thus introducing a discrepancy between national and local government alliances. Second, the DC–PCI collaboration was very unpopular at local level among the activists from both parties. Only one in five local DC members favoured any kind of collaboration with the PCI, and a clear majority wished the parties to have no formal links at all; similarly in 1978 one in four secretaries of PCI federations indicated the DC as the party most distant from their own, and by

1980 the proportion had doubled to one in two.[20] These local divisions have clear implications, discussed below, for the immediate response to the attack on DC personnel and property at city level. Third, the results of the 1978 referendum on the law ensuring public funding for parties showed the depth of general disaffection with the political centre, in so far as substantial numbers of electors rejected their own parties' directives to support the law and failed only by a narrow margin to secure its abrogation.

The final period, 1980–4, saw the repudiation of the 'national solidarity' alliance despite the lack of any agreed replacement formula. The DC ceded further ground, yielding the prime ministership to the PRI and PSI who acted as minority centres for an increasing aggregation of parties around no clear principle. With the mutual abandonment of DC–PCI collaboration the links between party centres and their peripheries were strengthened, although with the rapid decrease in violence in all major cities the pressure towards local-level joint mobilisation was much diminished. Meanwhile at the centre party interpretations of 'terrorism' began to diverge. Relevant legislative measures were delayed; and the management of the kidnapping episodes in 1980–1 saw increasing public conflict among the parties, some taking independent private initiatives towards the Red Brigades. The clarity of the frontier between political and armed communities, most clearly focused during the Moro affair, began once again to fade, as the primary public interpretive centre itself shifted from the political arena to the courtroom. I shall now consider in more detail the measures adopted to contain and confront political violence in the light of the trajectory of political relations.

AGGREGATING THE POLITICAL COMMUNITY

Defining its enemies

The DC, PCI and PSI began the 1970s with radically different versions of violence. Their disagreements of substance rested also on a contrast in the primacy accorded to one of the two languages, textual and violent, used by left-wing armed groups. The DC gave interpretive privilege to the documentary evidence, which the party treated as containing accurate disambiguations of the meanings of acts of violence. Content and claims were to be read literally, and both acts and texts were identified as the unproblematic product of

Marxism and its encouragement of contestation and class hatred. The activities of the BR and NAP were merely the close relatives of the well-known propensity for coercion and terror in communist systems; they required no special explanation nor any need to make subtle internal distinctions between forms of violence. In the Italian context left-wing violence as the inevitable secretion of Marxism represented the exact counterpart of right-wing violence as the ineluctable accompaniment of Fascism. That conceptualisation of political violence in terms of 'opposed extremisms' suited the DC well. It underlined the party's claim to centrality in a polity portrayed as equally threatened by the degenerate products of both Left and Right, thus extending accountability to their legal political opponents in the PCI and MSI. Doubts about the democratic reliability of the PCI in particular could be reinforced. Even if no direct responsibilities could be attributed to the party, the mere fact of its existence could be blamed for 'objective' encouragement of violence: by the refusal to abjure Leninism the PCI ensured that the armed groups could aspire to winning over the communist rank and file to more radical, faithful, interpretations of shared revolutionary dogmas.

The Left of course took a quite different view, dissociating itself from any responsibility and arguing that the DC's analysis privileged the wrong language. The literal reading of armed groups' texts obliterated the fundamental discriminations between types of violence which provided the real interpretive key. Because clandestine attacks on individuals were foreign to the open, mass and impersonal emphases in the theory and practice of the Left's tradition of violence, the BR could only be right-wing provocateurs, assisted by the security services and tolerated by Christian Democrat governments: Piazza Fontana *insegni*. Once the semantics of violence received proper attention, the texts' left-wing lexicon stood revealed as an artfully deceptive mentioning rather than a genuinely motivated use. Clandestine violence was thus part of a single 'strategy of tension', inaugurated in 1969, designed to halt the working-class advances in the Hot Autumn and to add Italy to the then growing number of South European dictatorships. No distinctive problem of left-wing violence existed.

Realignment of the parties' quite differently-positioned boundaries around 'terrorism' accompanied the convergence on the 'national solidarity' formula. The DC weakened its public commitment to the theory of 'opposed extremisms', acknowledging that neo-Fascism was the greater threat to Italian democracy and that the PCI was an important component of the Republic's defence. Ironically that shift occurred exactly in the period when the public failure and arrest of the early BR membership largely obscured the contemporaneous and less visible formation of the apparatchik milieu. The PCI's first public acknowledgement of the reality of a specific problem of left-wing violence came in late 1977 as a consequence of factors similar to those determining the unions' interpretive shift described in Chapter 3; but it also had a tactical role in the party's general redefinition of its identity and in the self-ascription of its public responsibilities.

The previous identification of all clandestine violence as neo-Fascist had fitted well with the launch of the historic compromise strategy and the rendering acceptable of direct collaboration with the DC. Between 1973 and 1977 the extensive ritual celebrations of the twentieth anniversaries of the events of 1943–7 argued for the revival of the collaboration of Catholics, Communists and Socialists against a re-edition of a single common encircling enemy, Fascism. Once the principle of (at least limited) collaboration had been established by the party accords on the government programme in 1977, the PCI sought more than a merely subaltern role in the struggle against the extreme Right in which, according to its own earlier analysis, the major responsibility had been ascribed to the DC. By acknowledging a genuine enemy to the Left, the party enrolled itself as the specific defender of the left-wing boundary of Italian democracy. The two dominant parties could therefore play equal and complementary roles. The DC would extirpate the potential for right-wing subversion in the State apparati over which it maintained its long-standing ministerial control: the PCI would mobilise its supporters within the social groups courted by the community of armed struggle, especially the working classes, and ensure that the residual sympathy for violence in its own ranks, to be found principally among former partisans, was eliminated.[21] The PSI broadly followed the Communist reconceptualisation, although the party was also tempted by the view that left-wing violence was a product of the conjunction of Catholic upbringing and Communist dogma (*Cattocomunismo*). The use of isolated pieces of biographical and ideological data to depict the bitter fruits of a clandestine version of the historic compromise clearly mobilised fears about the PSI's own fate in a coalition dominated by the PCI and DC. The convergence in party views was actively reflected in their changed stance on the Reale law on public order between its approval by Parliament in 1975 and submission to national referendum in 1978. Whereas in 1975 the PCI had voted against the law and a sizeable segment of the PSI had wished to do so, in 1978 the PCI urged its supporters to vote for the law's retention and the PSI avoided conflict by refusing to offer a clear party directive.[22]

In their substantive analyses of 'terrorism' the three major parties moved towards the identification of a single enemy characterised as an 'armed party' (*partito armato*), unifying the Red Brigades and *Autonomia* in a single attack on the policy of national solidarity.[23] In postulating a common strategic and organisational link behind the apparent differences in types of violence the parties matched an analogous interpretation by the Paduan magistrate, Calogero (see Chapter 5). Their own convergence was thus projected onto a centralisation of their armed enemies, enabling the distinctions between the two communities to be imagined most clearly. The presentation of left-wing violence as an organised political conspiracy had three advantages. First, describing the community of armed struggle in purely organisational terms eliminated the hypothesis that violence might be the direct reflex of economic and social marginality, accrediting the armed groups as representatives of vulnerable strata and inculpating the political élites responsible for distorted development. Second, opposition to a unified armed party could serve as a clear focus for mass mobilisation. As the PCI acknowledged, whatever the true scale of the international connections of Italy's armed groups might turn out to be, any depiction of the problem as extending beyond national boundaries rendered it too vague, distant and powerful to motivate popular mobilisation.[24] In public presentation, therefore, the boundaries of 'terrorism' were influenced by the audience addressed and the practical task at hand. Third, since 'terrorism' was translated into a unified and essentially political object, the party élites were justified in establishing a Parliamentary Commission of Inquiry to formulate a single authoritative version of the causes, objectives and ramifications of the phenomenon. Coherence was therefore imposed on the challenge, and the separate assaults on factory, State apparati and the DC, as well as the property damage and minor acts of sabotage, were linked to a grand design. The establishment of that Commission of Inquiry in November 1979 to deliver a consensual account from the political centre was, however, the last moment of interpretive agreement.

From 1980 onwards the shifts in party relations were accompanied by a dissolution in the consensus over how to define, and how to respond to, 'terrorism'. The victory of the conservative factions at the

DC party congress in February 1980, the PCI's abandonment of the historic compromise strategy in November of the same year and the PSI's attempt to replace the DC as the central governing party demonstrated centrifugal tendencies in the political community analogous to the fragmentation among its antagonists in the community of armed struggle. The DC increasingly emphasised its own role as the primary victim of violence, thus moving away from the view that the policy of national solidarity (which allowed the PCI to claim equal status as a political victim) had been the principal target. The PCI and PSI gave greater attention to the international links, partly in response to the BR actions after 1981 which were themselves intended to show the remaining members' concern for Middle Eastern politics and the peace movement.[25] The parties located the prime movers in opposite directions, however. The PSI looked to Eastern Europe as the clandestine supporter of Italy's apparently indigenous violence, while the PCI sponsored a revival of interest in the continuing role of the conservative forces in the West as active opponents of the claims of the party to a legitimate role in government. In effect the stretching of the boundaries of 'terrorism' beyond Italy corresponded not merely to the greater salience of international issues (for example, the siting of Cruise missiles) in domestic political conflicts but also to the divisions in the community of armed struggle retrospectively revealed by the confessions of former activists after 1980. As the contacts between its leaders and the *Autonomia* intelligentsia were made public, the PSI in particular retreated from the assumption of a single armed organisation directing all violence and including the diffuse attacks on property by the *Autonomia*-oriented groups. Party divergence was clearly signalled by the necessity to prorogue the Parliamentary Commission of Inquiry into the Moro affair four times so that it finally reported in 1983 rather than 1980; by its inability to reach a single consensual account; and by the abandonment of any attempt to achieve the general analysis called for in the Commission's original terms of reference.[26] Once again the parties returned to the disagreements which had marked the earliest phase of violence.

Action at the centre

The task of aggregating the three major components of the political community – the political parties, the State apparati and the population – was in practice largely divided between the DC and the PCI:

the other parties played an insignificant initiating role. At the centre the armed groups' challenge was met by the legislative measures sponsored by the DC but enjoying also the support of the other major parties: in the periphery response belonged primarily to the PCI, with much more dubious general political consensus. The dual pattern of intervention attempted to increase the solidarities among the three primary actors, since one of the goals of the mobilisation sponsored by the PCI in the periphery was to turn the otherwise passive general population into an actor with its own voice.

The major component of the so-called 'emergency legislation' between 1974 and 1980 was directed simultaneously to reassuring the public about the seriousness with which the political élites took violence and to demonstrating specific solidarity with the major category of victims, the police. Emphasising the role of the police was also practically and symbolically essential in order to exclude recourse to the army in preserving public order. Deployment of military units would have appeared to acknowledge a *de facto* state of war – that is, recognition that both armed and political communities were subject to a common and binding set of rules on the conduct of hostilities and that the government and, say, the Red Brigades could be accredited as the equally legitimate representatives of mutually exclusive populations of combatants. No political party could accept such an implied symmetry between the antagonists, especially since it would also confirm the Red Brigades' particular claim to hold sufficient power to transform the rules of domestic political conflict. Frontiers would indeed have become boundaries. Actions which seemed to carry the implications of a military struggle were therefore rejected: the exchange of 'prisoners' through kidnappings was refused, as was the proposal to involve the Red Cross as a mediator to try to secure Moro's release, and even the purely defensive use of soldiers to protect polling stations in the 1979 elections aroused considerable party controversy. Exclusive reliance on the police was the necessary counterpart of the refusal to involve the military.

In pursuit of general reassurance the penalties for possession and theft of firearms and explosives, extortion, armed robbery and kidnapping – whether their motivation was political or not – were considerably increased. In more focused legislation the police were permitted a wider range of circumstances for legitimate recourse to firearms (1975); and their rights to search and detain suspects were steadily extended, initially to cases of apparently unequivocal involvement in a crime already committed (1975), then when individuals refused to state their identities (1978) and finally – most controversially – when they gave reason for the police to believe they were *preparing*, but had not yet *committed*, an illegal act (1980). Police accountability to the magistrature was simultaneously relaxed. Investigations of cases in which the police had used firearms were transferred from junior to senior magistrates, thought to be more sympathetic to police views. When suspects were detained by police, the normal demand for prior authorisation by magistrates was weakened, first, to permit the judiciary to be informed immediately after the detention, then after not more than 24 hours and finally within 48 hours.[27] In 1979, in a further display of solidarity between political parties and State apparati, the penalties for politically motivated attacks on police, prison staff, magistrates and politicians were increased by one-third. Those public gestures were accompanied by specific attempts to strengthen the bonds between political and State élites in defence of the existing order. In a move to eliminate the primary centre for internal subversion the government sent a report on the security services to the magistrature in 1974 demanding investigation, and, on its own initiative, reorganised the entire apparatus in 1977–8 to bring the services directly under the control of the prime minister's office and a special parliamentary committee. Moreover the views of police and *carabinieri* chiefs on the likely repercussions within their forces of political decisions on the handling of violence appear to have been given particular consideration at key moments. The government's refusal to negotiate with the Red Brigades for Moro's release, for example, was strongly influenced by the pressures against any such concession conveyed to the political élite by senior police officers, representing Moro's murdered bodyguards and warning that any sign of apparent indifference to that sacrifice, such as the readiness to ransom Moro notwithstanding the slaughter, would have unpredictable effects among their own men.[28]

So far as can be judged the new laws enjoyed the consensus of the widest audience to which they were addressed. When submitted to referendum in 1978, the Reale law was endorsed by 76.9 per cent of voters, receiving greater support in the more immediately-affected north than the south. Within the north the cities which were the principal scene of political violence actually showed a slightly lower level of approval than the relatively unscathed cities which suggests, as I shall argue on further evidence in Chapter 7, that even among immediate local audiences the activities of armed groups did not in fact provoke a conservative reaction. The so-called 'Cossiga law' (decree law 625/1979, converted into law 15/1980) was supported by the even larger majority of 85.2 per cent.[29] Moreover, the legislation does not seem to have provoked widespread concern about betrayal of the Constitution's guarantees for citizens: asked in 1982 whether the State's strategy of repression had restricted democracy and individual freedom, only one in six Italians claimed that it had.[30]

One question that can be raised is whether the party élites were thought to have gone far enough, rather than too far, in symbolic commitment to the defence of the political community. The slim evidence available suggests that a substantial group among party functionaries and wider publics would have tolerated more drastic responses. In surveys of attitudes conducted in 1981–2, one-half (54 per cent) of PSI delegates to the party congress favoured harsher measures, a surprisingly high figure in a party with a leadership committed to a flexible humanitarian response to violence: 31 per cent of respondents to the PCI's questionnaire supported further legislation while 39 per cent claimed that the existing laws needed to be applied more rigorously.[31] Only one specific measure of greater severity was ever widely discussed – the introduction of the death penalty for 'terrorists', the topic of a popular petition sponsored by the MSI in 1981. The proposal, however, encountered two difficulties. First, although a majority of Italians has regularly declared its approval of the death penalty since abolition, the size of the majority declined significantly from 67 per cent in 1974 to 58 per cent in 1982, precisely during the years of greatest left-wing violence. Furthermore, reintroduction was favoured principally for non-political murders (children, kidnap victims): in any case only one in seven Italians questioned in 1982 believed that it would have any effect in combating political violence.[32] Second, the specific terms of the proposal annulled any chance of its success. For, by embedding the death penalty in the proclamation of a state of war rendering particular areas subject to military law, the MSI automatically conferred the status of legitimate combatants on the armed groups, which was precisely the symbolic recognition which at least the Red Brigades were seeking. No other party could agree to acknowledge, still less legally institutionalise, relations between political and armed communities as civil war: when the MSI bill was presented in Parliament in February 1982, therefore, it was defeated by 292 votes to 21, the opposition extending even to some of the measure's original proponents.

Action in the periphery

Local-level mobilisation against political violence began in 1969, directed against neo-Fascism. It was commonly organised by anti-Fascist committees which constituted a single forum for action by parties, trade unions and other groups, largely stimulated by the Communist-oriented ex-partisans' association, ANPI. With the rise of left-wing violence the committees were institutionalised by local authorities, as in Turin in 1976, and their terms of reference were widened: this was often signalled by a change in name as when the Permanent Anti-Fascist Committee for the Defence of the Republican Order in Milan was altered in May 1978 to the Permanent Anti-Fascist Committee for the Defence of the Republican Order against Terrorism. Their primary task was to emphasise the significance of the Constitution to local populations, reiterate the values, symbols and rhetoric of the Resistance and prevent their appropriation by armed groups. Through public celebrations of key anniversaries, protest demonstrations, seminars and conferences, assemblies in schools and factories and the sponsorship of petitions in support of magistrates and jurors threatened by armed groups, the committees waged an extensive and exhausting ideological campaign against political violence at grass-roots' level.[33]

Strategically the united front presented in the committees served to overcome, or at least to disguise, the persistent conflicts between local levels of different party organisations over the interpretive and practical responses to 'terrorism' and between local and national levels of both major parties. First, the primary immediate victims of violence, the local-level DC organisations, were much less keen to exculpate the PCI from all responsibility than their national leaders appeared to be in their public pronouncements after 1977. Moreover, in contrast to the personnel continuity at the centre, the turnover of local functionaries in the cities most affected by violence was very high, reducing the possibility of informal local consensus. In Turin and Genoa, for example, two in every three section secretaries of the PCI were replaced between 1978 and 1980 which aggravated the disruptions caused by the drafting of experienced party activists into the newly won municipal governments and by the ordinary rotation of party responsibilities.[34] Second, the PCI acknowledged the difficulty of disseminating successfully among militants its own analysis of *left-wing* violence as a distinctive problem. In the party-sponsored national questionnaire of 1982 nearly half (42.6 per cent) of the respondents refused to accept any distinction between Left and Right violence and a further one-quarter (27.6 per cent) claimed that although conclusive proof of identity did not yet exist, evidence of direct collusion was emerging.[35] Third, the views of local and national party leaderships appear to have often been at variance on how to interpret and respond to violence, no doubt partly due to the different pressures and understandings at the two levels. The Turin branch of the PCI was pulled up by its national leaders in 1977 for deviating from the official line; and during the Moro kidnapping, DC debate on the issue was avoided both at local level, where support for negotiations with the Red Brigades to secure Moro's release was greatest, and in Parliament where local representatives could have aired their views publicly.[36] Coupled with the long-standing contrast between the levels of DC and PCI enthusiasms for collective mobilisation, those cross-cutting divisions effectively inhibited the local parties from unifying around positive pre-emptive interventions, rather than simply *ex post facto* protests, against violence. One example was provided by the attempt in early 1979 by the PCI in Turin to encourage direct links between the other two relevant components of the political community, the citizens and the police.

The specific initiative, a questionnaire to be distributed by neighbourhood councils to the entire city population, was the precursor of the union questionnaire at Fiat and other factories. But whereas on the controversial issue of reporting suspicions of individual involvement in violence the unions had interposed themselves as the eventual authors of denunciations to the police, the PCI format guaranteed respondents' anonymity in the direct passage of details to the police and magistrature after preliminary evaluation by an independent committee of guarantors. The objectives were both practical and symbolic: to obtain reliable information and to display direct solidarity between citizens and the representatives of the State. Opponents argued, however, that the proposal was unnecessary and counter-productive. In the first place, article 364 of the penal code already established the citizen's legal *obligation* to report details of crimes against the State (even if only those which carried life imprisonment). In the second place, putting a term as vague and emotive as 'terrorism' into the hands of a population likely to use it idiosyncratically, carelessly or malevolently under a guarantee of anonymity would destroy the local solidarities which were essential to combat violence. And, third, the possibility that any wide support mobilised behind this grass-roots initiative of the PCI could be translated into an enduring political allegiance at their own expense aroused disquiet among political competitors. The parties therefore rapidly divided over whether to adopt the PCI's suggestion, with the DC mostly opposing or abstaining in the neighbourhood councils' debates: 8 of Turin's 23 councils decided to use the questionnaire, 13 modified it to be less contentious and 2 refused to use it at all. In the end 35 pieces of apparently useful information were passed on to the police from the 12 700 questionnaires completed of the *circa* 300 000 distributed. In effect the initiative petered out; and when the PCI organised a national questionnaire in 1981–2, the controversial invitation was abandoned in favour of a request to respondents simply to state whether they had ever witnessed acts of violence and what their reaction had been.[37]

Party dissent over general local measures to confront violence did not cancel forms of limited and individualised solidarity – such as the private meetings of the mayor of Turin with the representatives of every association in the city to persuade them to maintain a visible life-as-normal public presence at the height of left-wing violence, and the passage of a regional law in Lombardy to compensate financially the victims of attacks or their surviving kin.[38] Nevertheless the conflicts among local parties and the disjunctions between centre and periphery in 1977–80 had two important consequences for the dynamics of the relations between armed and political communities. First, they ensured that the activists of armed struggle were not confronted with a univocal rigorous local response against which to unite and in which to find a collective identity. Second, the maximum potential for all-party collective action in the cities where violence was actually taking place and which provided the immediate victims and audiences was inhibited. The emotions and reactions to attacks, which were strongest in those contexts, were not therefore translated into direct pressure on the centre to use its much greater powers and increase the levels of response dramatically. Local victims were not directly re-symbolised as representatives of the national community – thus evading the imposition of a single frame of meaning on all acts of violence.[39]

ISOLATING 'TERRORISM' AND 'TERRORISTS'

'Terrorism' as a legal and administrative category

Accompanying the measures to unify the political community in 1978–80 went the individuation and segregation of its armed enemies, first, by formally incorporating the term 'terrorism' in law and, second, by attempting to mark out its practitioners more clearly. The measures embodying that line of response, however, deliberately ensured the maintenance of distance between the political élite and the armed groups. In each case the centre turned over the actual resources for defining and managing 'terrorism' to other, local, institutions rather than taking over sole responsibility itself. Only as regards the extreme Right did the government itself possess the power to order the dissolution of subversive organisations, for example, and that option was not extended to cover the extreme Left. Due in part to the centre's weakness and in part to deliberate choice, the strategy ensured that no clear and rigid boundary between the political community and its challengers was established. While publicly readable as a sign of weakness, fragmentation according to local management nevertheless made a further contribution to avoiding the establishment of a common focus of identity and antagonism within the community of armed struggle.

Until 1978 the only specific form of political violence which Parliament had acknowledged in law referred to neo-Fascist activities and organisations. The relevant provisions were reinforced in the Reale law largely at the insistence of the PSI and PCI in order to balance the other measures which were clearly intended by their DC sponsors for invocation against the extreme Left. 'Terrorism' did not therefore appear as a legal category until 1978 when, in immediate response to Moro's seizure, a specific crime of kidnapping for terrorist and subversive purposes (article 289-bis) was introduced, with penalties double those for the non-political version. In 1979 an analogous political variant was introduced for criminal associations (article 270-bis), and the motives of 'terrorism' and 'subversion' were made an aggravating circumstance for all crimes. Since they introduced no new type of criminal offence, those measures amounted primarily to a symbolic recognition of a specific, and novel, enemy. At a general level 'terrorism' was left undefined in the laws themselves, its interpretation being deliberately handed over to the local judiciary. Simultaneously, however, innovations were made with regard to regulations covering the key material resources of armed groups, attempting to draw a boundary more sharply around the antagonistic community and influencing relations between the three milieux. The interventions concerned the two sites where their members were known to be physically present – the jails and the wider community.

The policy of visible segregation for enemies of the State – internal exile (*confino*) in a remote village – had been retained after the fall of Fascism in relation to mafia offences and was reintroduced for suspected political subversives by the Reale law in 1975. In 1977 the principle of isolation was extended to the prison system by the initial creation of eleven maximum security jails by ministerial decree, promulgated without an accompanying parliamentary debate. While the immediate cause was the ludicrously high level of prison escapes (515 in 1976 alone) which had included some early Red Brigades' members, the differentiation between maximum security and other prisons was easily converted into a general means of separating members of armed groups from prospective recruits among ordinary criminals.[40] The largely Red Brigade-inspired riots organised against the extremely harsh conditions for inmates (Asinara, 1979) and in concomitance with external attacks against magistrates and police involved in prison administration (the riot at Trani accompanying the kidnapping of D'Urso and the murder of Galvaligi in December 1980) led to the imposition of even more rigid forms of internal and external isolation. The increasingly widespread recourse to article 90 of the 1975 prison reform law, which permitted the suspension of all rights for individual prisoners or sections of jails, virtually separated the roughly eight hundred inmates of maximum security jails from the outside world between 1981 and 1984. The generalised application of a 'terrorist' identity to the prisoners held under those rigorously controlled conditions therefore rested on an administrative innovation providing for non-political local decisions by police and magistrature who held the responsibilities for the classification and de-classification of maximum security prisoners.[41]

Within that normally dispersed population the government deliberately created a communicative centre. Acting on Dalla Chiesa's advice, the Minister of Justice designated Palmi (Calabria) as a maximum security jail, to which the Red Brigades' intelligentsia – and for a brief period some of *Autonomia*'s leaders – were transferred in December 1979.[42] The reunification of its core and fringe members to constitute a single 'university' of armed struggle demarcated the intelligentsia more clearly and made the channels of its influence, hitherto transmitted by individuals in a multitude of not-easily-policed ways across the different maximum security jails, simpler to control. Ironically the strategy of concentration reversed the strength of the boundaries between the intelligentsia milieu and, on one hand, the external affiliates of the Red Brigades' signature and, on the other, the political parties. For direct communicative access became more difficult for BR apparatchiks who resorted to increasingly dramatic symbolic events (the murder of police, jail staff and prison doctors) to display their allegiance to the prisoners in direct antagonism to those categories. But it was made easier for the political parties, especially for parliamentarians, who could use their rights of access to prisons conferred by the 1975 law to make direct – and not merely symbolic – contact with the single visible and apparently authoritative centre of the armed community. As the Radical Party and the DC demonstrated during the D'Urso and Cirillo kidnappings, political interlocutors were enabled to expand the communicative exchanges between armed and political communities.

Apart from innovations to the prison system the political parties took various measures, and proposed others, to isolate the participants in armed struggle by clarifying the legal status of relations in respect of the community's basic organisational resources. The possibility of distinguishing clearly between the levels of commitment of locals and apparatchiks was reduced in two ways. First, by increasing the penalties for detention of weapons and explosives in 1974, 1975 and 1977, the role of merely passive supporter of armed groups, prepared to store and conceal firearms, was made more risky. The costs to individuals who were not themselves activists were aggravated by a second innovation in 1978: the obligation to report immediately all sales and leases of property. By making it very difficult to continue the practice of acquiring leases independently through false names, the apparatchiks became more reliant on 'clean' locals for whom, however, the risks and penalties of classification as active members of particular organisations were also increased. The scope for expressing a *generic* solidarity for armed antagonism in the name of revolutionary values was thereby much reduced: locals who continued to offer support were acknowledging the likelihood of assimilation to a particular signature, as represented in the actions of its full-time activists. By signalling in law an effective levelling of some of the different degrees of commitment to armed struggle and by compelling locals to accept alignment with particular groups or withdraw their support, the measure contributed powerfully to the delineation of sharper boundaries around the armed community and between its different signatures. The effects would have been carried further by the implementation of a proposal in 1979 to introduce a new crime – possession and distribution of documents for terrorist and subversive purposes, carrying a jail sentence of between two and six years.[43]

Had it passed, the measure would have linked the members of the three milieux very tightly and virtually rendered the armed community all but co-extensive with the consumers of its documents. Although possession of the texts for clearly justifiable (for example, academic) purposes was not punishable, considerable pressure would have been placed on newspapers not to reprint them, and the burden of proof would have fallen on individual possessors of 'terrorist' materials to display their innocence rather than on police to demonstrate guilt. Predictably the proposal raised objections in the equivocally-placed mass media as well as among the parties themselves. Although passage through the Senate was achieved, the bill became an early casualty of party divergence after 1980 and was quietly shelved. Thus, although in the period of its own greatest solidarity the political élite contributed to the formation of a jail-based centre for its antagonists, it did not quite reach as far as to make documentary evidence of a relationship to that centre a key unifying principle for identifying membership. The assertions of the existence of a single armed party were not accompanied by specific indication of any single diacritic resource.

Offering exit

Although the identity of 'terrorist' was given increasing legal recognition between 1978 and 1980, at every stage of extension its bearers were provided with a means of exit. Thus in 1978 participants in political kidnappings could earn a substantial reduction in sentence (down from 30 to 8 years in jail) by dissociating themselves from the others and contributing to the victim's release. Again, with the generalisation of 'terrorism' as an aggravating circumstance for all crimes in law 15/1980 the same principle was applied. According to article 4, all former members of armed groups who turned State's evidence to dismantle their organisations were eligible for a reduction of between one-third and one-half of normal sentences. The option of exit was widened still further by law 304/1982, and much later by law 34/1987, both of which provided much more detailed calibration of involvement and benefit.[44] As I suggested in Chapter 2, these measures were efficacious in so far as they exacerbated, rather than caused, the conflicts within the community of armed struggle. Once in place, however, they established the only means for recognising the specificity of politically-motivated crime and permitting a more rapid than normal reintegration of its authors into the political community they had once rejected.

The principles underlying reincorporation were three. First, potential beneficiaries were required to recognise themselves in the identity 'terrorist' by confessing the criminal nature of their activities – jettisoning the argot of armed struggle and acknowledging the State's definitions of criminal behaviour according to the language and classifications of the penal code. In the second place, dissociation from armed struggle had to be total and individual. At the very least personal responsibilities had to be fully confessed, accompanied by explicit rejection of violence as a political method. Third, just as the precise definition of 'terrorism' had been entrusted to the judiciary, so too was the establishment of the criteria and relevant evidence governing assessment of the authenticity and extent of individual dissociation. Interpretation and verification were left to local judicial communities to which the former practitioners of violence had to offer the redescription of their identities.

Suggestions for modes of exit which did not conform to the principles of non-political evaluation or individual dissociation were not acceptable to the political parties. Thus the proposal for a general amnesty, first made in 1979 by *Autonomia*'s intelligentsia and regularly renewed, was rejected unanimously. Since amnesties were political, not judicial, concessions, any such gesture towards the community of armed struggle would have appeared to grant it a formal combatant status, possibly encouraging future recruitment, which was unacceptable for the same reasons as the declaration of a state of war or the symmetrical exchange of political prisoners. Likewise, 'terrorist' and 'subversive' offences were explicitly excluded from the general amnesties of 1981 and 1986.[45] A second option – that a reduction in sentence should be granted to former members of armed groups without demanding at least confession of their own responsibilities or a complete repudiation of their former selves – was first put to Parliament in March 1983 by a heterogeneous group of deputies, mostly from the PR, PSI and Left Independents. No agreement could be reached with the DC or with the PCI, which sponsored their own proposals, since the parties disagreed over the extent of the rupture of past solidarities required from members of the category of potential beneficiaries (*i dissociati*). Hitherto recognition of cases for special treatment had depended precisely on the explicit individual rejection of previous relationships, contributing to the destruction of the armed community itself. To propose a legally-recognised form of withdrawal which tolerated, even encour-aged, maintenance of the solidarities originally underlying organised violence was therefore regarded as unacceptable by the majority of the political élite. Indeed, when agreement among the parties on concessions for the *dissociati* was finally reached in early 1987, the conditions of benefit remained the full confession of individual crimes and a demonstrated distance from the armed community in jail, as well as a formal declaration repudiating violence. Finally, the only other form of accelerated, politically-managed reintegration – a pardon by the President of the Republic on the advice of the Minister of Justice – provoked a furore when its use was revealed for a case in mid-1985. Unlike the other options, a pardon was strictly case-by-case procedure, which suggested the possibility of serious injustices and of political patronage for the better connected affiliates of armed struggle.[46]

In sum the strategy adopted by the political élites over the long *durée* of the challenge was to avoid stating clearly an explicit boundary between their own community and its challengers, to provide resources for State institutions to reach their own substantive local decisions on the precise contours of 'terrorism' and to maintain publicly an asymmetry between the two communities. As a response to the diffuse range of most attacks, the aim was therefore to make the political confrontation entirely notional, to refuse the translation of violence into intelligible forms of political action. But the mainten-ance of that distance was much harder to sustain in the case of highly-focused challenges in the shape of political kidnappings.

MANAGING DIRECT CONFRONTATION

Kidnapping rituals

Between 1972 and 1982 seventeen symbolic kidnappings were carried out by the Red Brigades (15), NAP (1) and the Unità Combattenti Comuniste (1). Only four of those episodes (Sossi, Moro, D'Urso and Cirillo) involved a direct public challenge to the political and judicial communities from which the victims were taken: all were mounted by the BR and prolonged over a period between 34 and 88 days.[47] Each kidnapping served as a vehicle for the concentrated fixing and transformation of meanings and relationships on a terrain most favourable to their organisers. Although in format and basic themes the four cases were simply variants of a single script, their sequence and individual contents were also symbolic markers of the trajectory of relations between and within the armed and political communities. Issues and identities which remained diffuse or poorly articulated or largely hidden were brought into dramatic focus in front of the widest variety of mass audiences possible. All cases received extensive coverage in the media, which relayed details of the acts and utterances of all direct participants as well as secondary commentary and thus provided a major source of information and disinformation for challengers and challenged.[48]

Each kidnapping displayed a highly ritualised structure, reproducing the formal pattern used in many societies for the dangerous moments of contact between the sacred and the profane.[49] The potential sacrificial victim was separated from the ordinary world, incarcerated in a 'people's prison', subjected to a 'proletarian trial', received a 'death sentence' which was temporarily suspended while conditions for his release were set, and finally – with the exception of Moro – returned to the world alive. Each victim's transformation in the world-turned-upside-down of captivity was narrated through between eight and twelve BR communiqués, the published letters to his family or professional colleagues and transcripts of his 'interrogations' and 'confessions'. In each case the victim was depicted as accepting fundamental elements in the Red Brigades' descriptions of political reality and the underlying exploitative dimensions of his role in the judiciary or political system, related through a textually-accomplished conversion leading to resignation or transfer from job, party or professional association. With the basic context of violence backgrounded, the victim was presented as offering confirmation of the BR accusations, the entire episode showing the efficacy of direct challenge. In a society with a strong tradition of attempting to portray and validate contrasting versions of social and political reality in public rituals – especially during the recasting of party identities in the later 1970s – the Red Brigades' kidnappings necessarily attracted widespread attention.

The invariant ritual framework constituted an open structure into which representatives of different social and political categories could be drawn, their identities (re)defined and the translational powers of violence clarified for participants and audiences. By controlling the choice of victim and conditions for release, the Red Brigades could simultaneously address opponents and invite potential allies to transform their spectator's role into active participation. At the limit the boundaries of the ritual itself would be weakened and its formal symbolic components converted into pragmatic elements of future routine interaction. The incorporation of different categories of antagonists into the ritual could therefore be translated into conflict as their contrasting assessments of some of the conditions demanded for the victim's release became visible. The potential for dispute was heightened by giving the victim himself a voice to address public and private figures. In every episode the Red Brigades permitted and published letters from their captive to his family who were thus mobilised as symbols of the victim's ordinary human (explicitly non-political) status. Not only was the display of an overriding general interest in refusing all contact with the bearers of violence threatened by the mobilisation of actors from different sections of the political community: but the very notion of a single public interest on the issue of violence was also placed under direct pressure by the creation of an active speaking position for the claims of private interests. By exploiting the predictable disputes the Red Brigades hoped to provoke a response from their antagonists which would verify their own claims that violence could be an effective method of political conflict and could successfully impose demands on the legitimate representatives of the political community. Acceptance, coerced, as a direct interlocutor in the political domain would thus supply recognition 'from above' for the Red Brigades' claim to identity as the bearers of a collective interest. It would act as a supplement to, or eventually as a substitute for, recognition 'from below', among the groups which the Red Brigades aimed to enrol behind their demands in each kidnapping and which constituted their closest internal audiences.

Various strategies were available to the audiences offered a speech-turn in the ritual. Opponents of violence could refuse to acknowledge the Red Brigades' communications and remain, at least publicly, mere spectators. Alternatively, they could seek to reinterpret the nature of the challenge: the victim could be re-symbolised as a private citizen requiring protection of the State rather than as the (often unwilling) representative of a particular politically significant category; conditions with non-political implications (for example, payment of a ransom rather than the release of 'political prisoners') could be proposed; or other non-political actors could be drawn into the ritual as mediators. Fewer options were available to the potential allies addressed by the kidnappers: declarations for or against the BR attack or the refusal of benefits that it might bring were the only real alternatives. Every ritual episode therefore offered a device for clarifying the relationships within and between the armed and political communities. It rendered visible the assumptions and ambitions, unities and disunities, which were otherwise dispersed through the uncoordinated sequences of exchanges between a range of institutions and armed groups. Their cumulative impact was consonant with the increasing general significance of symbolic struggle in Italian politics during the 1970s.

With hindsight the sequence of four political kidnappings can be seen to mark the three phases in the trajectory of armed struggle: Sossi for the years of Red Brigades' hegemony, 1970–6; Moro for the years of maximum, competitive violence in 1976–9; and D'Urso and Cirillo for the final period of disintegration, 1980–4. The successive episodes traced the progressive loss of political meaning for left-wing violence and was reflected in the progressive reversal in the relative range of audiences incorporated into the ritual from the two antagonistic communities. On one side, the scope of the collective interests which the Red Brigades claimed to be advancing was steadily narrowed by the kind of demands made for the hostage's release. On the other side, the contrasting extension of the range of categories of opponents activated by those same demands worked towards dissolving the sense of any single public interest which might be eventually compromised even by their partial satisfaction. The two trajectories appropriately reached their nadir in the final successful kidnapping (Cirillo) in which one of the then warring BR factions accepted a ransom for the victim through the non-political clandestine mediation of the *camorra* and the security services. The entirely private meaning of the kidnapping ritual, now indistinguishable from the ordinary criminal activities of one of the participants and confined to the political underworld, could hardly have been more obviously displayed. The key aspects of both trajectories can be sketched briefly.

By initiating their political kidnappings with Sossi in April 1974, the Red Brigades aimed to gain the support of the entire extra-parliamentary Left for whom the victim was alleged to be a notoriously unpopular and self-proclaimed antagonist. Their own leading role in armed struggle in that first phase was symbolised in the demand that eight members of a tiny predecessor group (the XXII *ottobre*) be freed in return for the hostage's release. In the second phase, consistent with the group's general objective of recouping its centrality, the choice of Moro in March 1978, the mode of his capture and the conditions for his return reduced the potentially sympathetic audiences effectively to the existing community of armed struggle. The massacre of Moro's police escort was intended to show the 'military' capacity of the BR; and having encouraged the members of minor groups to transfer their allegiance to the most powerful organisation, the Red Brigades' intention to protect its own new affiliates was symbolised in the demand to free thirteen 'political prisoners' five of whom were former members of other groups who had joined the BR in jail. In the third phase the price for D'Urso's release in January 1981 showed a further shrinkage: the demands that the Asinara maximum security prison be closed, that texts authored by BR prison inmates be reprinted in the national press and that the group's leadership in jail express an opinion on whether D'Urso should be freed revealed the now-dominant concern to unify the increasingly fragmented organisation – and to establish its hegemony in prison rather than recruit outsiders. Finally, Cirillo's fate in the summer of 1981 was made to depend on the concession of housing to the very specific, and hardly politically significant, category of earthquake victims around Naples and on a ransom to benefit the single dissident faction responsible for the action.

Since the kidnappings had at least one unequivocal conclusion in the fate of the hostage, they also functioned, unintentionally but inevitably, as clarifying rituals for the Red Brigades themselves. In every case the outcomes provoked or reinforced scissions, revealing the underlying disagreements over appropriate levels and objectives of violence which characterised the community of armed struggle generally. The Sossi episode produced conflict between the apparatchiks and the locals at Fiat and earned the group few new recruits either nationally (Table 2.8) or in Genoa itself where the first indigenous BR aggregation was not formed till more than a year later; the murder of Moro led to the first publicly-motivated secession and to increased estrangement between intelligentsia and apparatchiks; the objectives of the D'Urso kidnapping entrenched the split between its authors and the factory-oriented 'W. Alasia' faction in Milan; and the Cirillo attack led to the definitive severance of relations between the rump of the organisation and the newly-constituted faction based in Rome and Naples which had gone ahead with the kidnapping in defiance of the remaining apparatchiks' explicit veto. Moreover, despite the display of reformist concern for the basic needs of the Neapolitan (sub)proletariat, not a single new recruit in the city was secured by the kidnapping.[50] The attempts to fix the meanings of violence through kidnappings were therefore revelatory of the conflicts as much among participants in armed struggle as among their opponents.

On those opponents' side each successive episode extended the number of active direct participants and in practice increasingly submerged the attempt to demonstrate the Red Brigades' political identity beneath the conflicts among the other actors. In the Sossi kidnapping responses were confined to the magistrature; the dynamics of the Moro case invoked the intervention of the political élite which remained united despite the gesture (barely perceptible outside the professional political community) towards a distinctive position by the PSI; the BR demands for the release of D'Urso saw the separate interventions of the press (publication of BR texts), government (closure of the Asinara prison) and magistrature (concession of provisional liberty to a seriously-ill prisoner as an encouragement for the release of their fellow-magistrate), alongside distinctive involvements of the Socialist and Radical parties; and in the Cirillo kidnapping local DC representatives, agencies concerned with earthquake victims, the two security services (SISMI, SISDE) and the *camorra* all had a hand in attempting to secure the hostage's freedom – although the exchanges were confined to local actors and were suspected, rather than openly acknowledged, during the event itself. Only subsequently did some of the details of the actors and their activities become public.[51]

The combination of narrowed demands, addressed simultaneously to different categories, and more extensive participation changed the public meaning of political violence. In both the Sossi and Moro kidnappings the single condition for release – the symmetrical exchange of the hostage for symbolic 'political prisoners' – was designed to express the claim to equality but absolute opposition between armed and political communities: the murder of Moro's bodyguards and then the captive himself marked the boundary most clearly. In the D'Urso and Cirillo cases, however, the advancing of demands which it was neither unconstitutional nor illegal to concede symbolically dissolved that boundary, accommodating the use of violence within the reformist dimension of ordinary politics. The perennial dispute within the armed community over the role of violence as surrogate or supplement to other conflicts was therefore given a changing ritual resolution: the failure of the Red Brigades to sustain their distinctive national identity provoked the drift into local particularity, undermining the radically oppositional basis of that same identity. As the objectives of BR kidnappings became indistinguishable from the aims of non-violent groups, the group's claims to constitute the centre of a symbolic antagonistic community gave way to the demonstration of the separate factions' peripheral status, not unlike that of the *camorra*, within the community they had formerly aspired to stand outside.

The process of their reincorporation was facilitated by the parallel drift away from centrality among their opponents. The steady retreat from the 'national solidarity' formula was reflected in the management of the kidnappings of 1980–1: the government refused to issue public advice or directives to the other actors involved and was itself divided. The increasing openness of the key symbol of the political community, the Constitution, to revision and interpretation enabled the PSI in particular to use the later kidnapping rituals to assert its own distinctive political identity. Whereas the DC and PCI had used the Sossi and Moro cases to convey publicly their own conviction of the overriding value of the State, the PSI came to insist on the equal importance given by the Constitution to the protection of citizens' lives. The kidnap victims were therefore to be re-symbolised not as representatives of public institutions but as embodiments of a common humanity. Reinterpreting the Red Brigades' challenge in that way permitted the PSI to distinguish its 'humanitarian' responses from the State-centred orientation of the PCI and to attempt to use that distinction to symbolise the distance from its former ally on the Left. In consequence the sense of a political community united around an agreed hierarchy of values and a common centre was diminished, leaving its boundaries uncertain and permeable to the subordinate incorporation of the remnants of the community of armed struggle. The drift away from centrality on both sides, resulting in the impossibility of reaching a consensual retrospective version of 'the problem of terrorism', can be seen especially clearly in the prolonged conflicts over the meaning of the Moro kidnapping.

Moro 1978–84[52]

Moro's kidnapping was a uniquely dramatic event for several reasons: the status and political role of the victim, the massive but unsuccessful mobilisation of police and population, the ambiguous and paradoxical features of the events of its 55-day duration, the massacre of five bodyguards and eventual murder of Moro himself, and the subsequent establishment of a Parliamentary Commission of

Inquiry (CPM) to examine the entire affair and to use it as a magnifying glass to understand left-wing terrorism as a whole. Alongside the emotional impact, the cognitive dimensions of the event and its aftermath must be emphasised. On one side, the Red Brigades sought to validate their claims about the DC's role in international imperialism through the interrogation and confessions of the project's allegedly most authoritative architect. They also aimed to extort acknowledgement of their 'political' status by compelling the representatives of a legitimate political organisation into some form of public, first-person, negotiations for Moro's release, thus transforming the frontier between themselves and the DC into a boundary. For their opponents, the kidnapping was an occasion to demonstrate the pluralistic reality of the distinctions between State, government and party in refusing the BR demands. Subsequent reflection on the events was designed to produce knowledge to combat violence more effectively and to repair the organisational deficiencies in investigation and management which preceded the hostage's murder.

If the entire period from the kidnapping, 16 March 1978, to the conclusion of the parliamentary debate on the CPM's reports, 4 July 1984, is taken as an appropriate unit of analysis, then some further reasons for the event's special status become apparent. First, replicated in the changing interactional structure through which meanings were progressively assigned to Moro's fate was the same drift away from authoritative centres which characterised equally the political and armed communities over the longer period. The orchestration of meanings for the kidnapping provided a microcosm for the processes of identifying the nature of 'terrorism' as a whole. Second, the reconsideration of the events of 16 March–9 May 1978 placed under intensive scrutiny issues of evidence, understanding and response which were otherwise dispersed in time and space. Third, the progressive interpretations by the political parties moved towards a closure based on a reflexive understanding of the relationship between acts and versions of violence and an acknowledgement of the essential ambiguity of violence as a political technique. The form of closure chosen for the Moro kidnapping in 1984 was built on an explicit consensus that the event no longer had any power to disrupt political relations, thus signifying the definitive establishment of a chasm between further events in the political community and the residual world of armed struggle.

The interpretive sequence fell into two clear phases: from March

1978 to March 1979 and from November 1979 to July 1984. The first phase stretched from the day of Moro's capture past two false conclusions – the announcement of his murder in the possibly spurious communiqué no.7 of 18 April and the simulacrum of a public funeral service without a coffin on 13 May – until the approximately simultaneous decision to institute the Parliamentary Commission of Inquiry and publication of the first Red Brigades' analysis of the event, both taking place almost exactly one year after the kidnapping. The second phase was inaugurated by the actual establishment of the CPM in November 1979 after a delay due to the mid-year national elections. Intended as the 'summarising institutional interpreter for the national community' not just of the Moro affair but of 'terrorism' in general, the Commission was given a life of eight months.[53] However, despite the initial stress on the practical urgency of its work, the completion date had to be prorogued four times, so that the conclusions only appeared after the decline of political violence to levels requiring no further preventive legislation. In any case, rather than managing to distil versions of the kidnapping into a single authoritative political account with practical recommendations, the Commission produced one majority and five minority reports: the general enquiry into the phenomenon of political violence was not even attempted. The release of the various reports in June 1983 was timed to maintain the separation of the political inquiry from the contemporaneous judicial investigations. Since the CPM's work had been protected by secrecy, its findings were not made public until after the first-level trial of the BR members responsible for the kidnapping had been concluded in January 1983. Likewise, the parliamentary debate on the reports preceded by several months the reopening of the judicial process in the appeal trial (November 1984–March 1985), the sentences of which were largely confirmed by the Court of Cassation in December 1985. Staggering the public phases of parallel investigations in that way avoided the sense of obvious contrast or confusion between legal and political vocabularies, forms of evidence and assignments of responsibility. The two potentially discrepant sets of accounts were thus kept apart. With Parliament's decision in mid-1984 not to reopen the Commission's inquiries despite alleged obscurities and gaps in establishing even the facts of the case, the second phase in the assignment of political meaning to the kidnapping was effectively concluded.[54]

The interpretive evolution of 1978–84 corresponded to an extension in the range of contributors but a loss of the original members.

During the kidnapping itself control over the public meaning of events was monopolised by three very restricted groups: the Red Brigades, the government and Moro himself. For the Red Brigades, while the attack brought together for the only time apparatchiks from different cities, the action was planned and managed by the four-member 'executive committee' (*comitato esecutivo*) which authored the nine communiqués. Despite the public appearance of group unity, other apparatchiks and locals not directly involved were kept completely in the dark, even in Rome itself, and the consultations over Moro's fate were cursory or non-existent. Since most BR members had not contributed to choosing the target and objectives, they could in any case scarcely decide whether the original aims had been realised.[55] On the government side, once an informal decision to refuse all negotiations with the kidnappers had been taken immediately by the party leaders, management was largely turned over to the inter-ministerial committee on security (CIS) composed equally of senior ministers and police and security chiefs. The ordinary political forums for debate and decision were closed. None of the seven cabinet meetings between 16 March and 9 May dealt with the event at any length; only one parliamentary session devoted to the kidnapping, consisting simply of a minimal report by the government, was held; and the party leaders only met twice as a group. In the DC neither of the party's statutory decision-making bodies (the *direzione* and *consiglio nazionale*) were convened, despite Moro's own appeals and the efforts of his faction members to get them to meet: a representative role was assumed by an *ad hoc* committee of the secretary, deputy secretaries and party leaders in the Chamber and Senate. The third major contributor to the textual exchanges was Moro himself as represented in the signature over the eight letters to his political colleagues which were rendered public by his captors.[56]

Control over the meaning of the kidnapping moved away from that restricted interpretive community from the moment of its conclusion. First, Moro's murder eliminated access to an effectively incorrigible account of the significance of his letters and of his captors' intentions. Second, the members of the Red Brigades' *comitato esecutivo* were unable themselves to produce an extended legitimating account of events and goals. Confirming the milieux-bound distribution of meaning-making resources, they turned the public interpretive role over to the intelligentsia in jail who had actually been excluded from all knowledge of, and involvement in, the kidnapping. The public version of Red Brigades' objectives was therefore distributed after a lengthy delay only in March 1979, at the very time when the intelligentsia were privately accusing the apparatchiks of having actually had no clear aims at all for the attack.[57] The exclusion of the primary BR actors from contributing to the public meaning of their own actions was made definitive by their refusal after arrest to join the ranks of collaborators. Thus the most important political episode of armed struggle has remained unique in so far as no full accounts from either victim or captors have been available to provide authoritative clarification. Third, within the political community the debate was opened up by the government's first report to Parliament in October 1978, made not by the Minister of the Interior at the time of the kidnapping, who had resigned after the murder of Moro, but by his successor who had not been part of the original management committee. The establishment of the CPM formalised the greater range of accredited contributors to the institutional version of the kidnapping since all parliamentary groups provided members. In its turn the Commission broadened the interpretive community still further. Unable to draw on direct insiders, it made use of the judicial testimony of repentant BR activists as well as interrogating on its own account former members of other groups: in most instances, however, their evidence was acknowledged to be grounded on no more than individual interpretation, surmise and hearsay on the key issues.[58] The accumulation of political knowledge of the events was therefore manufactured out of interactions among increasingly peripheral participants to the kidnapping itself. Indeed the shift away from an authoritative centre provided an extended demonstration of the irreducibility of the meaning of violence to the intentions of its users.

Through that shifting communicative structure the most problematic aspects of the kidnapping were examined. Resolving the meaning of the challenge and its wider implications entailed deciding the central, closely-related issues: the objectives of the kidnapping, the identities of the participants and the adequacy of the responses. Which party or policy was the major target, and what short-term goals, if any, had the Red Brigades set themselves for the action? Had the Red Brigades' decisions been determined by other actors, national or international, who might have had a convergent interest in eliminating Moro? Who indeed *was* Moro, either as a political strategist prior to his capture or as the author of deeply ambivalent texts from his 'people's prison'? And, could – or should – the outcome have been avoided? On each of those issues evidence which was either apparent at the time or was subsequently revealed by the Parliamentary Commission and the judicial enquiries was available to license contrasting readings. The ways of dealing with those indeterminate or contradictory elements changed in accordance with the pattern of interpretive interaction. Schematically the parabola which interpretation followed illustrated a shift from the repression of ambiguity to its conversion into contrasting versions and then to the (incomplete) transcendence of conflict and the explicit restoring of undecidability to critical aspects of the affair.

The interpretation of the kidnapping given at the time by the political parties was confirmed by the BR analysis made public in March 1979. As indicated by the date of its occurrence (on the day on which a DC government received a vote of confidence from the PCI for the first time in the Republic's history) and circumstances of its conclusion (the placing of Moro's corpse midway between DC and PCI headquarters in central Rome), the BR objective was portrayed as the destruction of the 'national solidarity' party convergence and the division of the DC. The government's policy of refusal to negotiate with Moro's captors or even to take any action which might appear as an indirect response to their demands was considered unavoidable; and even the party which urged maximum flexibility, the PSI, could make no specific and acceptable alternative proposal. The letters over Moro's signature showing agreement with key aspects of the Red Brigades' analysis of political reality and appearing to urge a negotiated release were regarded as too contaminated by the circumstances of their composition for their putative author to be acknowledged as an independent participant in the ritual. The Red Brigades' text of March 1979 confirmed the identification of the primary target. But, significantly, it did not appear until soon after the first event which could suggest success for the action – the withdrawal of the PCI from the parliamentary majority in early 1979. As in much less important cases, meaning was supplied retrospectively according to the state of relationships among opponents.

By the time of the conclusion of the CPM's enquiries in mid-1983 the interpretive consensus had broken down, as witnessed by the submission of six separate reports. The majority report – signed by the DC, PCI, PSDI and PRI with critical observations from the PdUP and a Left Independent deputy – reiterated the earlier version. It argued that Moro's murder had been decided from the outset and that any attempt to negotiate would therefore have been both useless for the hostage and damaging for community solidarity.

More strongly the majority parties claimed that since the BR appeared to have planned for the kidnapping to last several months the mere suggestion of a possibly less rigid response might itself have been a precipitating factor in the outcome. For even a minimal gesture such as a pardon for a peripheral BR member would have made Red Brigades' intransigence harder to sustain publicly and would have given support to the dissent from the decision to kill Moro which existed among group members. The organisers therefore carried out the murder to avoid both those possibilities: had the original project of an extended kidnapping been adhered to, the majority parties argued, more time and commitment would have given the police forces a greater chance of success in their search for the captive.

The most significant alternative version came in the minority report by the PSI.[59] During the kidnapping the party had sounded out the BR intelligentsia in jail through a sympathetic lawyer but had decided that its members had been excluded from any role in the action. An attempt was therefore made, as the PSI revealed in June 1979, to establish contact with the BR in Rome through intermediaries themselves later incriminated for direct complicity. In default of illumination through the intelligentsia, the PSI relied on the nine communiqués authored by the apparatchiks as its interpretive guide to the affair. Insistence on the validity of the textual evidence to discern BR intentions helped to legitimate the otherwise highly accountable breach of the taboo on contact with suspected participants in armed struggle: it served to confirm the PSI's claim to have been in search of reliable interlocutors with control over the outcome. According to the communiqués, in clear contrast with the March 1979 summary, the major BR objective was the Christian Democrat Party, as indeed it had been since the earliest direct attacks in 1975 which began well before the national solidarity formula was devised: in confirmation of this view, the government of national solidarity hardly received a mention in the nine BR texts. In further dissent the PSI argued that the majority report credited 'terrorism' with exaggerated homogeneity and prevented appreciation of its internal conflicts and unstable decision-making processes. Moreover the outcome of the subsequent political kidnappings of D'Urso and Cirillo, in which more flexible responses had been made and the victims released, confirmed the PSI in its refusal to endorse the necessity and value of the policy of intransigence (*fermezza*) followed in the Moro case. As additional evidence the PSI claimed to discern

1. Terrorists: *Prima Linea* on trial, Turin, May 1981

2. The culmination of the attack on Fiat: murder of C. Ghiglieno, Fiat manager, 21 September 1979

3. Mobilising the working class against violence: PCI deputy, L. Violante, addressing factory workforce, Turin, 1980

5. Turin courtroom 1976: the first Red Brigades trial

7. The solitude of repentance, Turin, 1981

8. The public in court, Turin, 1981

both a specific proposal for a negotiated release and a general justification for the acceptability of all similar solutions in the letters over Moro's signature. Here the party rejected the majority verdict that the letters attributed to Moro were too ambiguous to support any single interpretation, and it made the meaning of the symbol 'Moro' explicitly central to the understanding of the Red Brigades' challenge.

The combination of Moro's condition as a hostage and the content of his letters established an enigma which I have examined elsewhere for the period of the kidnapping itself.[60] Until the parliamentary debate of 1984 Moro's murder and the silence of BR insiders left the manufacture of the 'Moro' of the ritual obscure in contrast to the elucidation of other aspects. Indeed, replicating in miniature the decline of centrality in the political community, Moro himself became a symbol emptied of any clear meaning. The process of semantic evacuation was begun during the kidnapping in order to resolve Moro's anomalous status as the only politician to have acquired, through his kidnapping, an identity and set of relations in both political and armed communities. Different strategies were followed to resolve the classificatory difficulty posed by Moro's simultaneous presence – physical and textual – in the two wholly incommensurable communities and to interpret the content of his messages by reference to their author. The strategy of the DC and PCI, embodied in a weaker form in the majority CPM report, was to deprive Moro of his status in the political community, refusing to respond to his direct invocations and claiming that, since they were contaminated by contact with the BR, his letters had no meaning. The PSI chose the opposite strategy, muted in 1978 but fully developed in its minority CPM report. Rather than designating the victim as polluted and profane, the party accorded him a sacred status as the bearer of an ethical vision superior to the parochial values of both communities and embodying a universal basis for mediation between politics and violence. Moro's own resolution, as contained in his texts, offered a third option – the attempt to de-symbolise himself and thus evade both profane and sacred roles. The letters charted his steady dissociation from any public status: the emphasis on the primacy of his family obligations, his reluctance to assume the presidency of the DC, his rejection of the presence of political colleagues at his funeral and finally, in the perhaps apocryphal *memoriale*, resignation from his party. 'Moro' thus became an empty space at the heart of the kidnapping, from which emanated texts simultaneously insisting on the explicit discussion of violence and its management and containing materials for contrasting answers to the questions they raised.

Each issue questioned the classificatory grid underlying the resistance to violence by the political community which he represented. His acceptance of the crucial Red Brigades' definition of Italian society as in a state of war, symbolised by the acknowledgement of the existence of political prisoners, contravened both the political élite's determination to refuse any such description and his own assertion that there was nothing in common between the Red Brigades' views and his own. The distinction between public and private interests was rendered problematic by his simultaneous insistence that all responses had to be political and that his party negotiate his release in the name of the purely private needs of his own family. The tension between the claims of public and private solidarities – and assumptions implying the primacy of each – was present throughout the letters. The further, related, distinction between the symbolic and the pragmatic was also opened up. Against Moro's acknowledgement of his own status as a political prisoner stood his emphasis on the practical dimension: why should the State collapse because of an exchange of individuals? The assertions offered two contrasting descriptive modes for the event's resolution, the validity of each being undercut by the existence of the other. As the political élite re-examined the features of the consensus against violence which had been deliberately left implicit at the time,[61] so a further identity-questioning paradox was established: Moro, kidnapped as the symbol of unity among the party-political élites and insistent on the continuity of his beliefs despite capture, was transformed into the explicit supporter and symbol of disunity.

The ambivalences thus set in motion, and the evaluations of the event as a whole that they prompted, were dealt with in the CPM by their selective translation into the different party reports. Contradictory elements *within* the event were transformed into conflicts *between* versions. The majority report hung the differences around a polar contrast between closure (*fermezza*) and openness (*trattativa*) to negotiations with armed groups: the PSI rejected that interpretation, arguing that the dilemma of whether to accept or refuse a deal to save Moro's life was present within every participant and citizen rather than dividing them into different camps.[62] The opportunity to weaken the interpretive rigidities was provided by the PCI in mid-1984, publicly formalising the party's increasing divergence from its major co-signatory of the CPM report, the DC. Since the end of the period of national solidarity the DC had presented Moro as a target chosen solely for his internal party role and not as the author of the (temporary) accord with the PCI: the PCI, by contrast, came to favour the interpretations of the attack on Moro which emphasised its aim as direct sabotage of their own advance towards power: more precisely, increasing weight was given to suggestions of foreign intervention in the kidnapping by forces hostile to the party.[63] The PCI therefore demanded the re-opening of the parliamentary inquiries to answer basic but unresolved issues: who in flesh and blood actually planned the kidnapping, conducted the interrogations, collaborated in composing Moro's letters, decided his murder? While concurring on the rejection of the PCI's demand, the five parties of the governing coalition could not agree on one generally acceptable positive version of their own to determine publicly the truth of the affair. The solution adopted was the presentation of three different documents by the several members of the coalition (DC–PRI–PSDI; PSI; PLI) with distinctive emphases in their interpretations of the kidnapping. On the explicit understanding that no political consequences would flow from the debate and its outcome, the separate parts of the three documents were approved by different arrays of parties. Symbolically, therefore, Parliament could be said to have legitimised the acceptability of different accounts, affirming the essential indeterminacy of the facts and recognising that the ambivalences could not be eliminated by interpretation. The power of violence to evade determination by political discourse – the impossibility of definitive translation – was made the basis of closure.

None the less, that very conclusion provoked further versions from inside the Red Brigades. Between 1980 and 1984 the handful of BR members with direct knowledge of the kidnapping had either refused all discussion or offered very generic accounts, arguing that whatever meanings their descriptions could supply would be treated as purely subordinate to the contrasts among political parties. Having originally set their opponents an enigma in the kidnapping, the BR apparatchiks had come to find themselves prisoners of the pre-defined repertoire of meanings associated with different parties. However, the parties' acknowledgement of the event's ambiguities and consensus that they could have no further political effects allowed the Red Brigades' members space to begin to offer their own fuller versions.[64] To do so implied acceptance that the directly political significance of their most dramatic exploit was exhausted and to acknowledge that the event could serve no further role as the meaning-creating justification for continuing armed struggle. The Red Brigades thus accepted that even the authors of the kidnapping no longer had the power to determine its meaning. As well as accepting the general implication of that conclusion, the group joined the political parties in appreciation of the now-uncrossable frontier between violence and politics.

5 The Construction of Judicial Accounts

Since political violence entails illegality, the judiciary always constitutes a major forum for interpretation and response. Attempts to disrupt or disable the legal system have therefore often been a significant part of the strategy of insurgent violence. Symbolically, by showing that their actions cannot be processed through the categories and procedures for assessing ordinary crime, armed groups have hoped to force public recognition of the distinctive status of their methods and to extract an explicit conferral of political meaning for their violence and identities. In addition the frustration of judicial investigations and the exploitation of ambiguous or contradictory features of legal processes can lead not just to pragmatic impunity for the users of violence but also to propaganda advantages deriving from the public demonstration of the State's apparent inability to sanction their activities according to its own rules. In Italy the judiciary paid a high price for that strategy. Between 1974 and 1980 ten magistrates were murdered (two being the responsibility of right-wing groups), three were wounded and three kidnapped; and the magistrates directly involved in investigating political violence were forced into deeply constricting modifications to their working and personal lives by the need for protection. Beyond their role as victims, however, magistrates and judges played a crucial part in both the management of violence and the creation and diffusion of knowledge about it.[1]

In the first place the Italian inquisitorial system of justice gives the investigating magistrates responsibility for directing and monitoring police enquiries and for evaluating evidence and restricting personal freedoms before cases are even brought to court. Individual magistrates could therefore be seen by armed groups as specific antagonists for their accumulated understanding of the world of left-wing violence. The Red Brigades, responsible for five of the eight left-wing murders, considered the investigating magistrates as enemies directly linked to the police and political parties and selected their victims exclusively from that category rather than from among the courtroom judges who might preside over their trials. Second, because of their privileged access to police work and their own investigative role, magistrates were well-placed to provide authoritative public accounts of 'terrorism'. During the worst years of violence some magistrates especially in Turin, spoke regularly at factory assemblies, demonstra tions, seminars and conferences, incarnating the commitment of the judiciary to the elimination of violence and emphasising the need for active solidarity between the State, trade unions and political parties Such activities, offering counter-versions of the meanings of violence of course heightened the armed groups' perception of direct ideologi cal and practical opposition. After 1980 when the detailed results of their enquiries, hitherto covered by secrecy, became public knowl edge, magistrates were regularly interviewed by press and television as experts on armed struggle and interpreters of the latest actions Indeed, in the April 7 case, the number of interviews granted by the magistrate during his enquiries led to accusations that he was deliberately and illegitimately attempting to establish wide support for his controversial conclusions in order to make up for fragile and unconvincing judicial arguments.[2] The often very lengthy judicial accounts of segments of armed struggle have been edited and reprinted commercially and have accredited the magistrature as the semi-official historians of the phenomenon: it was fitting that it should be a local magistrate to offer the first university course on Italian political violence at the Faculty of Political Science in Turin in 1984–5.[3]

In compiling those versions of left-wing violence, their judicial authors have been creative in both the elicitation and interpretation of evidence. For a principal source of data came from the confessions of 'repentant terrorists' provided in the course of interrogations by the magistrates themselves whose own knowledge of the symbols, rhetorics and classifications characteristic of the community of armed struggle was a primary interactional resource in helping to shape the defendants' accounts. Knowing the right questions and decoding answers given in the community's idiolects was a skilled accomplish ment which placed the magistrates (and police) who were already familiar with the political vocabulary of the Left at a considerable advantage over their colleagues. The interpretation of that evidence had then to be finalised for practical use in judicial contexts, governed by legally relevant distinctions and rules of presentation. The magis trates' accounts therefore necessarily embodied a series of decisions on how to constitute the enormously variegated and historically extended phenomena of armed struggle into the appropriate com ponents for judicial evaluation. Apart from the practical difficulties posed by the scale and clandestinity of violence, problems abounded: where the boundaries between legal and illegal subversive actions, verbal and non-verbal, were to be drawn; at what point relations between individuals could be said to constitute a distinct form of illegal association; how individual responsibilities in a collective enterprise were to be fixed; and how far back in time the different projects and organisations of armed struggle could be traced, given the slow formation of the community from its tributaries of different political generations holding contrasting views about the uses of violence.

In providing – inescapably – answers to such questions, the magistrature was faced with two general difficulties. First, the boundary between writing the political history of 'terrorism' and describing the penal responsibilities of 'terrorists' and their organisations was in constant danger of being breached. Contamination of the appropriate judicial criteria by plausible political identifications would threaten to de-legitimate the legal process to the extent that its claim to impartial assessment could be undermined by evident political bias; and, where it was revealed, the armed groups' charges of the institution's effective subordination to party interests could appear to receive confirmation. The second difficulty lay in the coordination of the resolutions of the key issues for interpretation so as to avoid potentially paralysing conflicts among magistrates in different cities or at successive levels of the judicial process. Given the government's refusal, on one hand, to define 'terrorism' and, on the other, to violate the Constitution's prohibition against special tribunals (article 102) by creating a single central judicial body with accompanying decision-making consistency, the interpretive dilemmas had to be worked out within the formal and substantive limits of the existing judicial system supplemented by the specific measures introduced to combat political violence.

Efforts to display external autonomy and internal coherence in the investigations of left-wing violence took place in the shadow of the failures to bring the authors of the most serious right-wing violence to book. The cases of the three bomb massacres between 1969 and 1974 provided stark illustrations of impunity. The Piazza Fontana enquiries remained uncompleted in 1989, after eight separate trials, all assigned to different cities (excluding the city of the massacre itself, Milan) and all varying, annulling or overturning the preceding sentences in fundamental and unpredictable ways. The responsibilities for the 1974 massacre in Brescia were only fixed in 1979 but were regarded as sufficiently implausible to be overturned on appeal in

1982, a decision itself first annulled by the Court of Cassation in 1984 and then revised at the re-trial in 1985. Finally the Italicus massacre, also in 1974, has so far remained unpunished since at the first trial, after nine years of police and magistrates' enquiries, all defendants were acquitted; and later attacks, notably the bomb at Bologna station in 1980 with its 85 dead and 200 wounded, have aroused equally fierce controversy over the investigative failures. Certainly the tiny numbers of right-wing activists, their special concern with single dramatic actions and their desire to hide rather than proclaim their political identities made investigations of their violence objectively more difficult than that of the left-wing groups, quite apart from any deliberate obstruction of magistrates' work by members of the police and security services. None the less the evident failure to identify or to try successfully the alleged authors of the most damaging attacks – a failure attributed to investigative inadequacies rather than the courts' idiosyncrasies – cast generalised doubt on the competence and commitment of police and magistrates.[4]

In examining the magistrates' translations of left-wing violence in this chapter I shall begin by identifying the general sources of political contamination and internal conflicts in the developments in judicial institutions during the 1970s. I shall then consider the factors influencing the evolution of police knowledge of the armed community since it constituted one of the essential data bases for magistrates' accounts; and I shall then turn to the organisation of judicial enquiries, the interpretive consequences of the use of different forms of evidence and the conflicts grounded in those differences. Here the discussion is largely restricted to the pre-trial phase: the courtroom rituals validating the investigating magistrates' versions and reconstructing the identities of former members of armed struggle are treated in the next chapter.

POLITICS AND THE JUDICIARY

The role played by the judiciary in preserving the frontier between political and armed communities must be understood with regard to two related trends in the 1970s: the blurring of the boundary between judicial and political domains and the decline in the judiciary's ideological-institutional cohesion. At the same time as the internal controls over magistrates weakened, the penetration of the institution by external interests increased. At extreme points magistrates were accused of deliberately favouring the continued existence of political violence either because they sympathised with the goals of the armed groups or because the persistence of violence would serve conservative ends. Regardless of the actual evidence for such charges, developments in the judiciary gave them a surface plausibility which rendered the translation of judicial results into political strategies easier and made the achievement of a clearly autonomous, consensual legal version of violence more difficult.

While the formal autonomy of the judiciary from political control had been established by the 1948 Constitution, accompanied by the severing of direct links between the Ministry of Justice and the public prosecutor, the judiciary had remained substantially aligned with broadly conservative political interests until the later 1960s. One of the effects of the 1968–9 movements was to shift the conflicts among its members away from largely internal disputes over career structures, salary levels and authority relations towards fundamental disagreements over the role of the judiciary in a rapidly-changing society. The spectrum of political commitments among magistrates and judges, who were entitled by the Constitution to belong to political parties, became both wider and organisationally better entrenched in the professional association's four major factions (*Magistratura Indipendente, Terzo Potere, Terzo Potere-Impegno Costituzionale and Magistratura Democratica*), representing substantially different views on the proper relationship between the judiciary and political and labour organisations and on the limits to the creative interpretation of the Constitution.[5] Although the dominant position in the National Association of Magistrates (ANM) throughout the decade was held by the most conservative faction, *Magistratura Indipendente*, insistent on the autonomy of the judiciary from all explicit links to political groups, its antagonism to the left-wing *Magistratura Democratica* – sufficiently strong to prevent it accepting MD as a partner in the coalition running the ANM until late 1982 – was not easily translated into control over the direction of judicial decision-making. For between 1966 and 1973 the career structure of the judiciary was reorganised so as to give simple seniority all but exclusive weight in promotion. The importance of competition based on an assessment of the legal merit of a candidate's judicial decisions largely disappeared, so that the power of the senior conservative ranks of the judiciary, especially from the Court of Cassation, to reward formally 'apolitical' judges and to punish those explicitly more sensitive to social and political criteria in their adjudication was vastly reduced.

What the proper interpretation of the law was, whether laws apparently in contrast with the Constitution should be challenged or
ignored, what criteria should be used in making decisions in new
areas of judicial intervention – all became increasingly contentious
issues in an openly divided judiciary. A survey of Milan's lawyers in
1978 indicated that no fewer than 87 per cent believed that the
magistrates' political views influenced their legal decision-making,
not simply in the most obviously controversial area of labour law but
in all criminal proceedings.[6]

Magistrates with too obvious extra-judicial political commitments
were open to sanctions, however, both through the law itself and
through the disciplinary powers of the Higher Judicial Council
(CSM), which was very largely under the control of conservative
judges until the mid-1970s. Several cases showed how accusations of
contiguity with left-wing political violence could be used to try to
define more clearly a set of positive values binding on all judges by
virtue of their profession. Such a basic consensus was envisaged by
the duty of a general 'fidelity and loyalty' (*fedeltà e lealtà*), formally
binding on all public officials including magistrates but without
specification of its scope. In the name of that undefined duty the
Roman magistrate Marrone was stripped of two years' seniority by
the CSM in 1982 (subsequently restored by the Cassation Court
in 1984) for having contributed a preface to a volume highly critical of
the judiciary and offering advice to left-wing activists on how to
thwart its initiatives.[7] Other magistrates were denounced by the
police or fellow-magistrates for suspected involvement in violence. In
1975 a Milan magistrate, De Vincenzo, was accused of links with the
Red Brigades, apparently on no better grounds than the favourable
mention of his name to a kidnapped magistrate by his BR captors: he
was acquitted of the charge. In 1980 a DC senator and former public
prosecutor in Rome denounced ten of his erstwhile colleagues,
including Marrone, for complicity in the subversive activities of the
extra-parliamentary group, *Potere Operaio*. Again the charge came
to nothing, since – after a dispute within the Florence judiciary which
has been assigned the investigation – the ten were acquitted on the
grounds that there was no case for them to answer.

As in the factory context, the accusations by magistrate against
magistrate can perhaps best be compared to charges of witchcraft and
treated as attempts to clarify the shifting boundary between the
judiciary and extreme left-wing politics. For the attack by armed
groups on members of the judiciary raised suspicions about the

possible existence of subversive elements within the institution itself, using their detailed insiders' knowledge to assist the attack. The choice of particular magistrates as targets, the attackers' apparent knowledge of their unpublicised investigative or administrative roles concerning violence, and the revelation of possession of seemingly confidential information – all offered reason for thinking that the relaxation of the boundary between the judiciary and its surrounding social and political order had been exploited to permit the internal encouragement, or even infiltration of active members, of armed struggle. Assurances by ministers that what was often presented as 'confidential information' contained in BR texts was publicly available did little to alter that view.[8] Cases of contact between suspected practitioners of violence and magistrates were sometimes adduced as evidence that the magistrature could not be trusted to oppose violence sufficiently strongly or, more darkly, that some of its members might even be prepared to tolerate attacks as a method of pursuing internal conflicts.[9] Where roles are ill-defined, charges of witchcraft thrive precisely as a means of attempting to demarcate institutional obligations and identities; and it is not hard to see an analogous pattern of role ambiguity and accusations of subversion developing at the borderline between membership of the judiciary and commitment to extra-parliamentary Left politics in Italy after 1970. These ambiguities were accentuated by the accompanying broader changes in relations between political and judicial domains.

The past two decades have seen not merely more explicit political diversity within the judiciary but a shift in the boundaries between the two institutions. The reliable post-war complementarity gave way after 1970 to complicated patterns of conflict and alliance, leading to widespread suspicions of illicit transactions of resources to serve political ends. Expansion in the areas and trials of State intervention and popular participation had brought new activities and old institutions under judicial scrutiny and extended the limits of magistrates' investigative tasks. On one hand, the unravelling of suspect financial dealings and the exploration of the semi-clandestine informal economies often led into the political domain itself and to the incrimination of local and national party functionaries and State personnel. The long list of scandals – ANAS, Italcasse, Montedison, EGAM, ENI, Lockheed, the financial empires of Sindona and Cefis were only the most notorious firms or individuals involved – eventually indicated responsibilities, of different degrees of seriousness, of politicians from most political parties. What from one perspective could be presented as a rigorous application of the law became from a different viewpoint the irresponsible use of magistrates' powers for the political goals of bringing public discredit on representatives of specific parties. On the other hand the weakness of centralised political decision-making left to the judiciary the management of aspects of social and economic conflict normally resolved by legislation and administrative innovation. Magistrates and judges were thus compelled to provide through the legal system solutions to disputes generated by the rapid changes in society and the economy after 1969 for which it was properly the responsibility of Parliament and government to make provision. Carrying out these tasks exposed the judiciary to accusations that its members were attempting to establish new areas of extra-territorial power with no effective forms of accountability either to citizens or other State institutions. No doubt stimulated by judicial investigations of some of their own representatives' activities, the political parties came eventually to propose various new forms of responsibility for the judiciary, whether by creating a more direct parliamentary link to the public prosecutor's office (as suggested by the PSI in 1983) or by strengthening the non-judicial membership of the magistrature's governing body, the CSM, or by making individual magistrates personally liable for recompense to victims of serious judicial errors (as approved in the referenda called for mid-1987).

The management of political violence, *qua* phenomenon of both political and judicial significance, both drew on and focalised the ambiguities in the relationship between the two domains. It also generated public conflicts, exemplifying 'disarticulation', at various levels. Some cases were limited and episodic: on the two occasions when magistrates (Sossi, D'Urso) were kidnapped, different sets of judges took autonomous decisions strongly criticised by the political élite, in the first case to approve the freeing of the 'political prisoners' demanded as the price for Sossi's release, in the second case to permit bail to a seriously-ill member of an armed group in order to influence the Red Brigades to free D'Urso and to try to compensate for the government's refusal of all negotiations. In one limiting case – the trial for the murder of the journalist Walter Tobagi – the dispute between magistrates and politicians provoked a major institutional crisis. Similarly the murders of magistrates often provoked the victims' colleagues into open criticism of the political élite for failing to provide resources sufficiently quickly and on an adequate scale to combat violence. A more enduring level of distrust was reflected in the (unsuccessful) proposal by the PSI in 1983 to establish a parliamentary commission of inquiry to review the judiciary's application of the entire 'emergency legislation' and thus scrutinise critically all relevant levels of its members' activities.

The scope for seriously de-legitimating conflicts between the two domains and for public disorientation deriving from what the PCI, warning the citizens of Turin on the eve of the major Red Brigades' and Front Line trials in 1981 of the disjunction between common-sense and legal meanings of key terms, called 'the abyss between the *coscienza civile* and the law',[10] was however diminished by the sequencing of the major political and legal activity. Public versions of violence were monopolised by the political élite between 1970 and 1980, with their prospectively oriented concerns about the possible consequences of violence: between 1981 and 1985 the judiciary became the constitutive forum for knowledge of 'terrorism', with magistrates and judges taking the role of the primary interpreters of how the by then evident failure of the ambitions for armed struggle had indeed come about. As I noted in Chapter 4 (p. 156) a similar asynchrony, protecting the two institutions from permanent direct comparison and confrontation, characterised the alternation of public debates on the one episode investigated in depth by both politicians and magistrates – the Moro kidnapping. In that particular case alternation may have been deliberate. Over the longer term, how-ever, it was an unintended consequence of the difficulties in the accumulation of police knowledge of left-wing violence on which the accounts of magistrates rested.

THE ORGANISATION OF POLICE ENQUIRIES

The most extensive knowledge about the fragmented community of armed struggle held by any group, not excluding its own members, lay, or should have lain, with the institutions directly charged with repression of its illegal activities – the police forces and the internal security services. To facilitate their investigations, and as part of the display of solidarity with State agencies, the government – having begun the decade by reducing police powers – later restored or extended them and relaxed the police's accountability to the judici-ary. In fact between 1969 and 1974 the right of police to directly interrogate suspects was removed; a suspect's lawyers were granted the right to be present at all interrogations; and wiretapping was placed under formal control of the judiciary who could only authorise it for serious crimes and on whose premises it had to take place. Thus the earliest phase of political violence was actually accompanied by a diminution rather than an increase in the resources for investigation and repression. Only after 1974, initially in response to the increase in ordinary crime, was the trend reversed. In that year, the police right to interrogate suspects for 'summary information' was restored, even though a defence lawyer had to be present. That condition was however waived after 1978 in cases of 'extreme urgency', although the public prosecutor's office had to be informed and the content of the interrogation could not be used as evidence. In 1975 the right to search suspicious persons was conceded and in 1979 was extended to include whole apartment blocks and streets. As mentioned earlier (pp. 137–8), police powers to detain suspects were gradually increased after 1975. The most controversial power, the *fermo di sicurezza*, which could be used before any crime had actually taken place, was generally considered to be dubiously constitutional. It was introduced for one year only and the Minister of the Interior was required to provide Parliament with two-monthly reports on its use. Their evidence suggests that the power was used less widely than was feared and was less effective than was hoped: between mid-December 1979 and mid-June 1980, for example, a total of 606 people were detained under its provisions by the police and *carabinieri* but only one in five cases (128) was regarded as sufficiently well-supported by evidence to be confirmed by a judge. Indeed the measure was regarded as so ineffective that it was allowed to lapse at the end of 1981 after a single prorogation.[11]

No one has claimed that those powers were particularly significant for improving the investigation of clandestine violence. On the darker side, however, the relaxation of direct judicial control over the first crucial hours of police detention did generate accusations that the police were using their increased autonomy to abuse suspects and try to force them to confess. In 1982 the Red Brigades made a series of claims that the police were practising torture – in the best-known case, against its members arrested during the freeing of Dozier. The charges were confirmed by the investigating magistrate and in July 1983 four of the five policemen responsible for Dozier's liberation (the fifth had been elected to Parliament which would not grant his request to strip him of immunity from prosecution) were sentenced to one year's jail. The court's decision was widely heralded as an exemplary demonstration of the State's ability to enforce conformity to its laws even on behalf of victims who themselves deliberately flouted them. However, with far less public clamour, the sentence was overturned in the Appeal Court in March 1984, with the acquittal of all defendants.[12] While isolated cases of ill-treatment may have occurred, the powers granted to the police in the 1970s can hardly be regarded as responsible for introducing violent methods into interrogations; and since the magistrature's investigation of other accusations by BR members ended in their dismissal, there is no evidence of any increase. Certainly in 1982, only 6 per cent of Italians believed that either the police or the investigating magistrates were guilty of systematic violations of individual rights in their repression of political violence.[13] In general, even if substantial positive benefits from their new powers had been enjoyed by police, they would hardly have been adequate to overcome the much more significant negative determinants of the accumulation of knowledge about left-wing violence – the disorganisation of investigations and the cultural estrangement between the police and the community of armed struggle.

Until 1974 no special police agency for the investigation of political violence existed.[14] Its repression fell within the ambit of the ordinary local bureaux of police and *carabinieri*, alongside the acquisition of information by the internal security division attached to the Ministry of the Interior (*Ufficio Affari Riservati*, rebaptised *Servizio Informazioni Generali e Sicurezza Interna* (SIGSI) in 1971) and the secret service (SID) responsible to the Ministry of Defence. In 1974 units specifically dedicated to the investigation of terrorism were established in the periphery in Piedmont and at the centre in the Ministry of the Interior. First, two separate units were set up in Turin to investigate the Red Brigades who had just carried out the 35-day kidnapping of Sossi with impunity. One, under the direction of Dalla Chiesa and with a staff of 40 *carabinieri*, successfully infiltrated the group and, once its specific objective had been achieved, was disbanded and its members returned to other cities. The second unit, created by the police, had barely been established when its director, Santillo, was called to head a new anti-terrorist bureau in the Ministry to replace the SIGSI, too obviously contaminated by the apparent involvement of senior staff in the recent right-wing bomb massacres. The new unit's structure comprised four central divisions (one with operational tasks, three with individual responsibilities for left-wing, right-wing and international terrorism) and thirteen regional nuclei in Italy's major cities which absorbed the existing Turin unit. The new organisation, which employed altogether some 300 staff drawn from the local political offices of the police as well as ordinary personnel, was innovative in its national structure. It overrode the normally fragmented responsibilities of the several police forces, divided both from one another and internally by bureaucratic and investigative barriers as well as traditional rivalries. Such boundaries strongly militated against an adequate supralocal picture of the kind of criminal phenomenon such as the BR signature had begun to indicate in the early 1970s. The unit was successful primarily against right-wing violence, which was regarded as an especially urgent target after the 1974 massacres, and the NAP, due in particular to the contacts of its non-political police agents with the world of ordinary crime in Rome and Naples where the group found support.

Despite those early successes the ineffectiveness of the investigations in the period 1976–8 revealed the progressive loss of police knowledge about the community of armed struggle. One reason lay in the further organisational changes which were made in tandem with the long-awaited reforms of the security services. The law dividing security responsibilities between two new agencies, with internal (SISDE) and external (SISMI) remits, and placing both under the direct control of the Prime Minister's office and a parliamentary committee, was passed in October 1977, to take effect from the following May. However, apparently with a view to outflanking the predictably increasing internal resistance to change, the government acted precipitately in January 1978 to establish the new services and to reorganise the anti-terrorist unit which had been renamed the *Servizio di Sicurezza* (SdS) in 1976. First, in a complicated redistribution of personnel and knowledge, the SdS was dissolved. Half of the central staff of some 115 functionaries and agents, including the entire division concerned with left-wing violence, passed to the new agency for internal security (SISDE). But the staff in its regional nuclei, who had been primarily responsible for gathering the information contained in the now-dispersed archives, passed not to the SISDE itself but either to career positions and cities which had nothing to do with political violence or into the revamped political offices (newly re-christened as the DIGOS) of the local police headquarters, to whose senior officers they were made immediately responsible.[15] Thus, the only staff with a specific knowledge of the individuals and ideologies of armed struggle came to be placed in bureaux where political violence represented just one among many tasks. Equally damagingly, through their incorporation into the local police structure, they lost the direct and boundary-transcending communication with a central agency which had proved so effective in pursuing their geographically mobile armed antagonists. The remaining 58 members of that central bureau who had not been taken on by the SISDE (32 of whom were actually working as bodyguards rather than investigators) formed a new office (UCIGOS) which had neither any archival material on left-wing violence nor any local agents. At the same time the SISDE, in spite of the documentary material and human expertise acquired at the centre, was not provided with any local informants since the entire staff complement of the agency that the SISDE replaced, the SID, had been transferred to the agency now concerned mainly with external security, the SISMI. Even in · 1980 only two-thirds of the total number of employee positions allocated to the SISDE had actually been filled. To complete the organisational chaos, the first director of the SISMI was particularly anxious to remove the taint of subversion and political unreliability from the past and therefore inaugurated his brief period of command by dismissing 370 inherited local informants between May and June 1978.

The reorganisation of 1978 had three, presumably unintended, immediate consequences. First, it deprived the security services and the UCIGOS of all former direct sources of information in Italy's major urban areas. Second, while the SISDE had received from the SdS the primary archival resources of information on left-wing violence, it was accountable not to the judiciary but to Parliament, so that the access to that knowledge passed into a wholly different context of inquiry, sensitive to different pressures. Third, the dissolution of the SdS national anti-terrorist structure destroyed the direct opportunity for a supralocal view of events and changes in the community of armed struggle. Its components were now the bureaucratically separate UCIGOS and DIGOS, resulting in interpretive confinement to local horizons and rendering often incomprehensible signatures or acts of violence whose meaning could only be supplied by a broader informational context. The Moro kidnapping revealed the investigative disarray particularly cruelly. Despite the essentially symbolic recourse to 724 160 roadblocks, the checking of 6 413 713 personal identities and the searching of 3 303 123 vehicles, the police were unable to find Moro, to prevent the wide distribution of his letters by the BR or even to follow up directly relevant pieces of information. The coordination of enquiries among the new agencies was very poor: the committee established for that purpose at the Ministry of the Interior met daily for the first week, every second day thereafter until 3 April (less than halfway through the kidnapping) when it was considered so ineffective that it was dissolved. According to the investigating magistrate, one single functionary in the Rome DIGOS had any knowledge of left-wing violence and he had only the assistance of collaborators who were replaced every six months.[16]

The full revelation of investigative confusion during the kidnapping persuaded the government to institute yet another agency, known informally as the *nucleo interforze*, under Dalla Chiesa in September 1978. The unit was set up with a lifespan of one year and made accountable directly to the Minister of the Interior. Its 230 staff were recruited mostly from the *carabinieri* (180), drawing on the dispersed members of the 1974–5 Turin nucleus, but also from the police (50). Its structure reinstated the principle of a national organisation, permitting as broad an understanding as possible of the connections between apparently isolated local phenomena. Although Dalla Chiesa's appointment was renewed for a further year in August 1979, it was allowed to lapse at the end of the year when he took up the senior *carabinieri* command in northern Italy. His reluctance to continue in the post was at least partly due to the mistrust of such an 'unregulated' agency expressed not only among sections of the political élite but also in the police forces. The establishment of trust was not helped by the failure to send a copy of the government decree listing Dalla Chiesa's powers to the local headquarters of the police, whose senior officers were uncertain of their colleague's authority and whose ordinary agents sometimes refused to accept the credentials of the new unit's local personnel. Opposition also stemmed from Dalla Chiesa's recruitment of some of the most experienced local *carabinieri* and police, depriving their former units of the chance to gain prestige and rewards from successful investigations of political violence.

Despite those initial conflicts, the new anti-terrorist organisation was immediately successful. Dalla Chiesa's previous experience in Turin facilitated collaboration with the local judiciary which, given the salience of the city in left-wing attacks, offered an important investigative advantage. A substantial number of arrests (197 in all) were made in the unit's 16-month existence. At its dissolution the members were either promoted to the SISDE or reabsorbed into their former units where their increased knowledge could be diffused to others. The only subsequent special group to deal with terrorism appears to have been a temporary coordinating committee set up in Verona in 1981 by the Prime Minister specifically to organise the search for the kidnapped US general, Dozier. Apart from the investigative successes, the assignment of particular responsibilities to Dalla Chiesa had one unpredictable consequence. The State's personalisation of its response persuaded some of the earliest arrested and no-longer-convinced apparatchiks of armed struggle to represent Dalla Chiesa as their primary military antagonist with whom they could, honourably, 'negotiate their surrender'. Thus, while they had been unable to establish relations with the dominant actors in the political domain, the repentant full-time activists of violence saw a secondary possibility of 'recognition' from their best-known police opponent, the personification of their milieu's distinctive enemies: both Peci in Turin and Barbone in Milan insisted on making their first confessions to Dalla Chiesa himself.[17]

The implications of the organisational discontinuities in police investigations for the substantive knowledge of left-wing violence were severe. Indeed, the dispersal of human and archival resources was made even more crucially damaging by the absence of any independent centralised data base. Despite the insistent demands made by magistrates, no electronic data bank on left-wing violence existed which might have prevented organisational changes having immediate repercussions on knowledge. The only systematic body of easily recoverable data concerned details of firearms which was of limited investigative use for political crime. A data archive (*Centro Elaborazione Dati*) was formally established at the Ministry of the Interior by the reform of police organisation in 1981 but fundamental issues of rights of contribution and access to the computerised files had still to be resolved in 1984. The linkages between the limited data bases held by police and *carabinieri* were very poor: according to the commanding officer of the CC no interface between the two sources existed in 1980 so that direct reciprocal access to their details was impossible.[18] Information effectively remained buried in local, manually-collated files which, once their contents had been passed on to the magistrature and found insufficient at that time to warrant prosecution, were hard to retrieve and unlikely to contribute to an accurate collective portrait of the community of armed struggle.

On several counts the insufficient attention to left-wing violence and the organisational discontinuities between 1976 and 1978 left the police poorly or misleadingly equipped to chart the crucial period of formation of the stratified community of armed struggle. First, on the cultural dimension, the political and symbolic referents of the increasingly estranged and narrowly bounded world of the armed groups became obscure to police. At the highest level, Dalla Chiesa recorded his sense of the cultural sophistication of the BR apparatchiks' texts and his expectation of finding university professors and economists among their authors. His surprise on meeting the apparatchiks themselves in 1980 indicates the general difficulty of reading the culture of violence accurately from outside.[19] At grass-roots levels of investigative activity it is likely that the domination of the lower ranks of police and *carabinieri* by southern Italians compounded the incomprehensibility of the community's symbols to its investigators. For the public sources of the rhetoric of armed struggle lay in historical and social movements (the Resistance, 1968–9, 1977) and ideological disputes (*operaismo*, the theory of needs) which had been far more significant in the north than the south, particularly in the extent to which they generated new bases for social relations and claims to solidarity. Police recruits from the south were therefore less accustomed to moving easily in the symbolic universe of left-wing political extremism – a cultural disparity which made their understanding of the internal and external boundaries of the armed community and the practical significance of different foci of allegiance and dispute more difficult.[20]

Second, the greatest disarray among investigative agencies coincided with the period in mid-decade when the apparatchiks from the *servizi d'ordine* of the extra-parliamentary groups began to add systematic recourse to violence to their political repertoire. Those activists remained locally visible and retained their police definition as simple 'extremists' since in many cases they continued to participate openly in left-wing demonstrations and protests.[21] No doubt the resulting sense of impunity for their initial ventures on to the terrain of armed struggle encouraged them to continue. No doubt too the long-standing personal relations between core members of armed struggle and the solidarities characteristic of the *servizi d'ordine* made it hard for the police to use the technique of infiltration which had worked so successfully with more disparate membership of the early Red Brigades. Furthermore the youthfulness and neighbourhood concerns of many locals probably made infiltration at the lowest levels equally difficult: the grafting of part-time participation in violence onto existing ties of friendship probably made it easier for the police to form suspicions of individual involvement but harder to obtain direct access and therefore proof. The only three publicly-known cases of infiltration, two leading to the arrests of Peci, Moretti and Fenzi, did not bring results until between 1979 and 1981, although of course there were very likely other cases that have remained concealed.[22] In sum, police organisation and investigative capacities were at their nadir between 1975 and 1978 when the formation of the apparatchik milieu was taking place, both within and between Italy's major cities.

Third, the very success of the first anti-terrorist units in 1974–5 encouraged investigators to make up for their later ignorance by treating the earliest structure of the Red Brigades' organisation as a guide to the nature of all armed groups. But the picture of an overwhelmingly clandestine membership with clear external boundaries and formal internal hierarchies proved to be highly misleading for the understanding of the second phase of armed struggle. Not only did the Red Brigades themselves make much greater use of non-clandestine locals whose allegiance to the signature was rarely complete, but also the more or less transient action-sets emerging from the area of *Autonomia* had very few clandestine members. Paradoxically the deliberate and visible participation in extra-parliamentary politics rendered the members of armed groups more invisible to police than the impeccably anonymous behaviour recommended for them in the formal rules prepared by the groups' founders. Only a very detailed knowledge of individual trajectories and the nuances of text-evidenced identities would have enabled police to track the shifting pattern of involvements accurately and to revise their classifications of 'extremists'; but, for the reasons given above, the detailed information which would have permitted a supralocal grasp of activities was exactly what the police did not have in the mid-1970s. Thus a Turin magistrate could report that the Red Brigades had once again become a mystery for investigators by 1978; Dalla Chiesa could insist in the summer of 1979 on the urgent need to understand *Prima Linea* better; and the magistrate responsible for investigating the *Autonomia* formations in Milan could admit that until the confessions of Barbone in September 1980, he and his colleagues were very largely in the dark about the subjects of their enquiries. The array of organisational and cultural factors hampering the cumulation of police knowledge of the community of armed struggle probably explains its belated repression better than a conspiracy theory – suggesting the deliberate organisation of investigative chaos in order to allow violence to persist as a way of weakening the Left – can do. In fact the police did continue, if slowly, to make arrests throughout the period (the Minister of the Interior reported to Parliament in October 1978 that 325 alleged members of the major left-wing group were in jail). What they lacked was sufficient evidence to keep users of violence in prison or secure their convictions. Furthermore, the difficulties confronting the police were matched by the problems facing the judiciary in directing investigations to produce plausible and legally adequate accounts.

THE JUDICIAL INVESTIGATION OF LEFT-WING VIOLENCE

Italy's judicial processes were widely regarded as inadequate even before the onset of political violence. The delays, inequities and uncertainties associated with the working of the inquisitorial system were already considered sufficiently serious by 1974 to have persuaded Parliament to approve guidelines for a new code of judicial procedures. However, by the time that the government had prepared its revisions in 1978, the level of political violence caused their introduction to be (permanently) deferred. The novelty, scale and duration of armed struggle therefore placed the existing system under great pressure, just as freedoms in work and leisure activities of individual magistrates were constrained by the need for constant police protection and surveillance. Since the inquisitorial system gave magistrates the responsibility for direction of the investigations as well as for decisions at the end of the first phase of enquiries (*istruttoria*), appreciation of the organisational dimension of judicial work on political violence can help to explain both the achievement and the substance of the magistrates' accounts of armed struggle.

The organisation of an interpretive community

The effective role of the judiciary in directing criminal investigations depended on collaboration with the police as well as its own members' commitment. Although article 109 of the Constitution gave the investigating magistrate direct charge of the judicial police (*polizia giudiziaria*), no such autonomous police unit had been created. The members of the police and *carabinieri* assigned to judicial offices tended to be few in number, confined to routine support tasks because of a shortage of auxiliary personnel and to derive little career advancement, and therefore motivation, from their work.[23] Moreover, although under the formal direction of a magistrate, they remained under the bureaucratic authority of their senior local police officer, the *questore*, who was himself not a member of the judicial police and therefore not answerable to the judiciary. In cases of conflict between the two institutions the police authorities were likely to exercise stronger control over the judicial police than the magistrature could. Since clear control over an autonomous investigative resource was thus largely denied to magistrates, their enquiries were powerfully condition by the organisational difficulties of police work itself.

Judicial investigations of political violence were also hampered by internal institutional factors. First, neither the process of recruitment nor the career structure of the Italian magistrature encourages the development of competence in investigating specific types of crime. Most magistrates join young, hold only a law degree without professional experience, receive a very brief apprenticeship and, since 1973, enjoy virtually automatic promotion to the senior ranks.[24] Certainly in the early 1970s they were expected to handle indiscriminately all forms of crime. Indeed those magistrates who were initially assigned to deal with political violence were also expected to maintain equal attention to their other investigative responsibilities, an eclecticism which could reach absurd levels: the Roman public prosecutor assigned to direct the enquiries into the Moro kidnapping was compelled simultaneously to spend time in court on a myriad of trivial cases.[25] Secondly, the volume of criminal proceedings to be dealt with, and the shortage of judges to handle them, rendered still more difficult any single-minded concern with political violence, especially in the cities most affected. In Turin, for example, the total number of criminal cases in the public prosecutor's office increased by 22 per cent (74 862 to 91 023) between 1973 and 1979 while the number of prosecutors remained at 20: the investigating magistrates' offices were slightly favoured since the 15 per cent rise in cases (68 182 to 78 405) was accompanied by a rise in personnel from 15 to 21.[26] In most major centres of political violence the actual complement of magistrates was considerably below the figure officially considered necessary: in Milan in 1984 the formal employment of public prosecutors (43) was inferior to the number requested by the office (50) and far superior to the actual number at work there (33).

The pressures on human resources, stretched by the rise in ordinary and political crime in the 1970s, were further aggravated by the limited level of material assistance to the magistrates investigating violence. No magistrate had access to a computerised data base, at least until 1982 when a system containing information on serious crimes (including political violence) which had reached the trial stage was brought into use in Milan. At a more mundane level, the sharing of offices and secretaries was common. The same Roman magistrate responsible for the Moro investigation had no private external telephone line to his office and was compelled to make confidential calls from a pay-phone in the corridor: all incoming contact was lost in the late afternoon when the switchboard operators went home. On his own description he conducted the enquiries into the most dramatic political crime in the Republic's history with the help largely of his typist. Few resources to improve basic work conditions were made available. The proportion of funds allocated to the administration of justice actually fell from 1.1 per cent of the total budget in 1974 to 0.8 per cent in 1984 and, during the later years of violence, approximately two-thirds of funding was absorbed by the construction and conversion of maximum security jails.[27] Other scarce resources had to be directed into turning sections of judicial offices into fortresses, electronically protected against the threat of attack. Finally, each investigating magistrate traditionally worked in isolation, due partly to the importance given to professional autonomy, partly to the rules of secrecy covering all formal documents until their production in open court, and partly to the ordinary territorial limits of jurisdiction. In practice a magistrate might not know what his next-door neighbour was investigating, let alone colleagues in another city. Those limitations offered formidable initial barriers to the understanding of all forms of organised geographically-extended crime, especially political violence where the ordinary methods of establishing motivation and responsibility for specific illegal acts could not easily be applied.

Magistrates' investigative powers were nevertheless expanded in two directions by government legislative initiatives. On one hand, magistrates were empowered in 1978 to ignore the ordinary rules of secrecy covering inquiries in progress and to communicate their documents and findings with one another as they were made. Informal oral exchanges had certainly occurred earlier: their legality was now assured by law 191/1978 (article 4) which was especially valuable after 1980 in permitting the transcripts of extended confessions to circulate widely. The second direction was very different. Magistrates were increasingly compelled by law to order the arrest and preventive detention, and to refuse the release on bail, of persons for whom they felt sufficient evidence existed for involvement in any politically-motivated crime. In 1975 arrest was made mandatory for all crimes promoting the revival of Fascism: in 1979 it was extended to all acts covered by the 'terrorism and subversion' label and was accompanied by the removal of the magistrate's discretionary power to order the offender's provisional release. Over the same period the length of the maximum legal duration of preventive custody was steadily increased. In 1974 the maximum period between arrest and definitive sentence was increased to between eight months and eight years, depending on the seriousness of the crime; and in 1979, for acts of terrorism in particular, the limits were extended by a further one-third, in theory permitting a defendant to remain in jail for up to ten years and eight months before final sentence was pronounced.[28] That measure survived a challenge to its constitutional legitimacy in 1982 on the grounds that its provisions, which in normal circumstances would have been unacceptable, were justified by the emergency created by public disorder but for only as long as it lasted. But not only did the theoretical possibility of extended pre-trial detention cause concern: so did some actual cases. The central defendants in the April 7 trial, for example, spent between three and four years in prison before the case was finally brought to court.

The April 7 defendants' pre-trial prison careers illustrated a further aspect of the new judicial powers. Individuals arrested on one charge could find that the progressive revelations of repentant terrorists might lead to new arrest warrants, each one bringing forward the initial date from which the period of custody ran and delaying release seemingly indefinitely. Similarly, the increasingly serious retrospective interpretation of left-wing violence accredited by some judicial re-readings of the *anni di piombo*, which I discuss in the final section of this chapter (pp. 200–9), ensured that many former alleged members of armed groups could be kept in prison far beyond either the initial period of preventive detention or the actual completion of their minor sentence in order to await trial on the serious charge of armed insurrection. Probably the most controversial example concerned the Genoan worker and writer Giuliano Naria, arrested in July 1976 on charges of kidnapping, murder and membership of an armed group. Despite having served a five-year sentence for belonging to the BR but having been acquitted in 1983 of the more serious crimes, Naria was kept in jail by fresh charges of participation in the Trani jail revolt and armed insurrection. Notwithstanding serious illness, he was thus denied even the concession of house arrest until August 1985, after sharp public conflict between the judges of different cities and criticism by the political parties.

While Naria's case was exceptional, the combination of mandatory arrest, extended terms for preventive custody and the steady uncovering of further alleged responsibilities about increasingly remote events could generate quite unreasonably long pre-trial detention even for individuals whose renunciation of armed struggle had been publicly recognised by various courts. From one point of view the measures simply granted magistrates more time to complete their investigations in default of the provision of more direct resources to accelerate their work and with regard to the complexity of their object of enquiry. At the same time, by reducing magistrates' discretion to arrest or conditionally release individuals suspected of participation in political violence in the light of the extent of this involvement or particular circumstances, the political élite fixed the judiciary's frontier-defining role more rigidly. Wherever evidence of a 'terrorist' identity could be found – and the evidence required to justify laying charges was less than that for committal to trial which was in turn below that needed for conviction – then the suspect had to be immediately isolated from civil society by mandatory arrest. The magistrates' interpretations of the boundaries of political violence therefore became a key factor in its overall management and gave their authors a primary translational role. By devolving on magistrates the responsibility to make sharp distinctions with increasingly serious practical consequences, the political élite helped to sustain the existence of a frontier between itself and the armed community.

Steps towards establishing an interpretive community to overcome the gaps and conflicts caused by jurisdictional and investigative fragmentation were initiated by the magistrates directly involved. One proposal, informally canvassed among magistrates and politicians, was to allocate all investigations of political violence to one (national) or three (regional) centres which would have exclusive and specialised judicial responsibility. The suggestion was not widely supported, however. Such institutions would have represented too clear a breach in ordinary procedures and would have resembled too closely the special tribunals for political offences of the Fascist period. Both circumstances would have conceded formal recognition of a distinctive political status to armed groups which could be interpreted as uncomfortably close to the legitimacy of the left-wing rebels against Fascism. In default of the institutionalisation of a judicial analogue to Dalla Chiesa's anti-terrorist unit, therefore, the magistrates from the cities primarily affected by violence organised their own informal collaboration, with encouragement – but little substantive assistance – from their governing body, the CSM. In each city, specialised teams of magistrates were created between 1978 and 1981, copying a practice adopted on a smaller scale in Turin in 1976 with regard specifically to investigations into the Red Brigades. The necessity for cooperation was largely stimulated either by clear investigative disaster following from the explicit refusal of collaboration (Rome, after the Moro kidnapping)[29] or by the emergence of evidence requiring more than a single magistrate's energies (in Milan after the discovery of a large cache of armed groups' documents in September 1978) or by the need to follow up wide-ranging confessions as rapidly as possible (in Turin in 1980 following the interrogations of Peci and Sandalo). Groups of increasingly knowledgeable magistrates – some with previous experience of investigating right-wing violence and selected because of it – formed within the various cities' judicial offices, comprising some 7 public prosecutors and investigating magistrates out of a total of 80 in Rome, 10 out of 70 in Milan and 10 out of 40 in Turin. Members included magistrates publicly or privately identified with each of the three major factions (MD, MI, UniCost) of the ANM, so no accusation that the investigation of left-wing violence was the voluntarily-assumed, zealous extension of any single politically-oriented group or policy can be sustained. Indeed only in Turin was there a substantial majority from any single faction, where 7 out of the 10 specialists on political violence were associated with *Magistratura Democratica*. Virtually all left-wing political crime was assigned to members of these groups.

More or less contemporaneously informal meetings were arranged for all magistrates investigating terrorism in the different cities. Sponsored in 1978 by the Milan public prosecutor, Alessandrini, meetings usually included some 20 participants, convened perhaps every two months in the most intensive investigative period between 1979 and 1981. The group had no formally recognised collective identity and did not act publicly as a representative body, although since the Minister of the Interior attended some of its meetings, an informal direct channel for advice and pressure between political and judicial institutions was established. In March 1984, however, 36 of the pool's members sent a confidential formal warning to the government and senior police officers that political violence could not be regarded as over and that the emergency legislation should not be too rapidly and completely dismantled – an action which, when the letter became public, earned them sharp criticism from the extreme Left for assigning themselves the status of a semi-clandestine pressure group.[30] Some of the group's most urgent concerns deriving from the experience of investigating political violence – direct control of the judicial police, establishment of a central data bank – were in fact hardly shared at all by their non-specialist fellow-magistrates.[31]

The main aims of the meetings, however, were not to provide any common judicial version of 'terrorism' addressed to politicians or wider publics, but to exchange information, to reach agreement on the allocation of investigations to particular cities and to build up a consensual understanding and application of judicial categories to the acts and associations of political violence. Coupled with the 1978 lifting of the secrecy rule on the documents accumulated in continuing investigations, the meetings permitted a more inclusive picture of the community of armed struggle than had hitherto been possible through the casual, informal and largely bilateral patterns of access to knowledge outside each magistrate's limited local focus. If the newly-organised interactions could expand the interpretive power to link apparently isolated acts and signatures, the other functions of the meetings sought to close down the judicial effects of that expansion. First, by agreeing informally on how the wide geographical sprawl of organisational activities and individual responsibilities would be divided up for judicial processing among single cities, the magistrates avoided potentially protracted jurisdictional conflicts caused by the mobility of apparatchiks and continuity of crimes and groups. If the evidence of the uncoordinated and largely fragmented inquiries into right-wing bomb massacres can stand as a worst-case comparison, then the delays and unpredictabilities they encountered in securing higher-level decisions on jurisdiction from the Court of Cassation were avoided in the left-wing case. Also, the chance for politically sensitive senior judges in Rome to assign trials to judicial offices believed to be equally responsive to political considerations, should they arise in the course of investigation, was excluded. The 'career' of the Piazza Fontana trials between Milan, Rome, Catanzaro and Bari indicates the juridically arbitrary but politically comprehensible dispersal of investigations which could follow failure to reach agreement among lower-level judges. The specialist magistrates' informal meetings thus served to insulate disagreements from wider interests and to inhibit the translation of narrow legal issues into paralysing public conflicts. In the second place the meetings were a valuable method of promoting consensus on how to describe the phenomena of armed struggle in judicial vocabulary with some consistency. Given the novelty of the crimes and the risks of interpretive disagreements, the task required detailed consideration.

Developing a terminology for left-wing violence

The difficulties of describing the acts and organisations of violence in terms adequate for judicial processing stemmed both from the nature of the categories of the penal code and from the complexity of the community of armed struggle. The most recent detailed legal categorisations of political violence had all been concerned to define rightwing crimes embodying attempts to revive the Fascist movement, introduced and refined between 1945 and 1975. The general definitions of criminal associations under which left-wing groups would fall had not been revised since 1930 and even then the Rocco code had made few changes to its 1889 predecessor. Furthermore, the introduction of 'terrorism' as a legal category in 1978 had not been accompanied by a clear definition of the term and the inclusion of a specific collective crime – 'armed association for the purposes of terrorism and subversion' (article 270-bis) – in the penal code in 1979 relied on the existing formula to identify the nature of an 'association'. However, the organisational nature and activities of armed struggle after 1970 differed profoundly from the models enshrined in the penal code, based on historically superseded types of insurgency.

Very roughly the 1930 code envisaged a subversive group as wholly clandestine, easily demarcated from other political organisations, structured like a military hierarchy and intent on the single unproblematic objective of destroying the State. But the main features of armed struggle in the 1970s were in stark contrast to that picture: rejection where possible of clandestinity, a refusal of any rigorous and formally sanctionable hierarchy among affiliates, the clandestine infiltration of one group by another, the highly permeable boundaries of all groups at local level, the lack of sharp distinctions between the ideologies of the intelligentsia and those of the surrounding society, and the constant pattern of fission and fusion of groups over more than a decade. Both synchronically and diachronically the boundaries around and within the community of armed struggle were extremely unstable. Other legal difficulties arose from the rarity of the recourse to a particular charge: the most obvious example was the offence of armed insurrection against the State (article 284 of the penal code), for which neither a formal description nor the conditions of application had been much elaborated in the existing jurisprudence and mostly remote precedents. Finally, the 1980 and 1982 laws encouraging collaboration by 'repentant terrorists' required exegesis both of the meaning of their formal terminology and of their fit to individual acts of confession. Between the legal code and the novelty of organised political crime, therefore, a large and potentially chaotic interpretive space opened up for judicial readings.

Probably the most important immediate level of judicial determination was to establish an adequate legal description for the organisations of armed struggle. That required a formal list of elements necessary to constitute an 'armed band', to decide on the appropriate definition of its internal structure and to identify the criteria relevant to assessing the contribution of its individual members (article 306). The meetings of magistrates from different cities were devoted particularly to that task. Although it could only be informal, considerable interpretive consensus at that level was in fact reached: disagreements persisted none the less over the character of individual responsibilities for single acts authorised by a group signature and over the appropriate level for a general description of the groups' projects. The most influential definition of an armed band was provided in 1979 by the Milan magistrate Galli who identified four primary attributes: a plurality of affiliates, a single aim, the availability of weapons and the existence of some kind of organisational scheme (not necessarily embodied in a written statute) to which members were oriented. Those features rendered the traditional definition of an armed organisation more flexible. They allowed the judiciary considerable freedom in deciding how broadly or narrowly the group's aim should be fixed (and therefore where the penally-relevant moments of constitution and dissolution of each organisation should be placed). They also relaxed the existing insistence that *all* members of each armed band should *possess* weapons in favour of the condition that at least *one* of their number should merely be able to *obtain* them to carry out the group's projects. The last criterion in particular brought the law much closer to the reality of the fragile patron–client ties through which many *Autonomia* groups did in fact get access to heavier weapons: Galli's success in interpreting article 306 in such a way as to include the unstable formations from the area of *Autonomia* was in fact regarded by their members as sufficiently threatening to lead to his murder in 1980.[32]

The other significant hermeneutic task was to find adequate legal descriptions for the authority structures within the groups so as to calibrate individual responsibilities and the appropriate sanctions. Article 306 in fact indicates no fewer than six potential roles (promoters, founders, organisers, leaders, subsidisers and partici- pants) but, for practical purposes, only the distinction between 'organisers' and 'participants' – crudely, between responsibilities carrying jail sentences of 5 to 12 years and 2 to 8 years respectively – was important. Although one exegetical tradition sought to make the distinction correspond to 'leader' and 'follower', most magistrates adopted a more flexible functional definition which better matched the formally anti-hierarchical nature of most armed groups. No fewer than 13 tasks were considered 'organisational', of which the most important were: control over key resources (weapons, bases, docu- ments), investigating possible targets, taking a leading role in actions, composing the texts claiming these acts, recruiting, and maintaining contacts with other groups. The emphasis on such a wide range of empirical tasks tended to swell the numbers legally classed as 'organisers' in any group at the expense of ordinary participants – in milieu terms, to weaken the distinction between apparatchiks and locals. Thus, as two examples, 90 of the 113 defendants in the 1981 Turin trial of PL as an armed band were characterised as organisers; and the April 7 trial in Rome in 1983–4 included 52 organisers as against only 21 participants. In effect the category of only partially- committed 'local' was much reduced in the legal versions of armed struggle because of the strongly organisational reading of tasks performed as a matter of generic solidarity.[33]

Fixing the limits of an armed band raised a further issue. Given that the single acts of violence were claimed under a collective signature and could be considered as the realisation of each group's programme, how far should everyone who acknowledged allegiance to that signature be regarded as legally responsible for every such act? Could a conspiracy charge (*concorso morale*) be laid against all self-confessed members of a group whether or not they knew of, approved or specifically contributed to a murder, kidnapping or wounding? Resolution of that problem was complicated by the often wide divergence between the formal and substantive patterns of decision-making in armed groups where the rhetoric of 'comparti- mentation' disguised the elements of individual choice, casual selec- tion of targets and sheer chance even from members themselves. In general magistrates favoured a strictly localist solution. Unless there was clear evidence that some extra-local set of members had deliber- ated the specific action, conspiracy charges were extended only as far as the local leaders and organisers of the signature responsible who were operative at the time when the act was committed.

While that narrowing of responsibilities was generally accepted, magistrates in Rome appear to have laid conspiracy charges more widely than elsewhere. An analysis of the arrest warrants against 233 members of armed groups in jail in 1984 indicated that while the charges brought by magistrates in Milan and Turin contained a conspiracy indictment in one case in four (34 ex 133), in Rome the proportion was above one in two (89 ex 165). Similarly, 69 per cent of arrest warrants based on the charge of membership of an armed band carried with them a conspiracy charge in Rome: in Milan and Turin the figure was 33 per cent.[34] Furthermore the suspicion that the Roman judiciary was especially ready to attribute a particularly high degree of ideological homogeneity and collective decision-making to armed groups was reinforced by its controversial handling of a minor group, the *Unità Combattenti Comuniste* (UCC).

The UCC had been active mainly in Rome and Milan between 1976 and 1978, its 28 members being responsible for some 23 acts of violence which included three kidnappings or attempted kidnappings for ransom, one deliberate wounding and three armed robberies. The police investigations led in 1979 to the arrest of several members who – as the first 'repentant terrorists' – gave full details of actions, the extent of individual participation and the group structure. However, despite these extremely individualising accounts, the investigating magistrate incriminated all members of the group for all actions specifically accompanied by documents carrying the UCC signature on the grounds that, penally, the link between membership, explicit assent to the group's programme and realisation of the programme through single actions was rigid. Only in the cases of actions not publicly acknowledged as the UCC's work were the different levels of individual responsibilities assessed. Extremely severe sentences, based on very fragile evidence against the men identified as leaders, and a refusal to apply the law reducing penalties for members who collaborated added to the controversy when the first trial was completed in 1982. However, although an appeal court had reduced the sentences at the same time as it confirmed the validity of the legal grounds for conviction, the Court of Cassation overturned both in 1985. No doubt influenced by the virtual disappearance of left-wing violence, the Court argued that the mere existence of an accompanying text could not be an appropriate diacritic of the extent of penal responsibility and that the extended use of conspiracy charges to support notions of collective responsibility was foreign to Italian juridical traditions. Article 27 of the Constitution and the Court's own past rulings determined that only where specific involvement in an act of violence could be proved were individuals to be held responsible.[35]

Apart from indicating the possible diversity of the Rome judiciary in extending the limits of individual and group responsibility, the UCC case also illustrates the problems for judicial readings of violence represented by two kinds of evidence – written texts and oral confessions. Although the other grounds for public controversy obscured this issue in the UCC trials, the magistrate's decision to override the specific details of responsibilities provided in confessions in favour of responsibilities assigned through the contents of texts represented a particular, and obviously contestable, resolution of conflicts over the status of evidence. Since in applying the grid of judicial classifications the investigating magistrates were compelled to reconstruct historically the trajectories of individuals and groups across a decade of violence, the grounds for interpretive decisions became a central dimension of their entire accounts. The usual links between offender and victim or target in single episodes of ordinary crime (motives of individual gain, personal relations, alibis and so on) were largely irrelevant for organised political crime; and in any case the disorganisation of police enquiries until 1979 ensured the scarcity and weakness of such evidence of that kind as there was. Instead, the judiciary had to rely on the materials contained in confessions and documents as the basis of its versions. Both were controversial; and because they embodied perspectives from distinct milieux, the two sets licensed very different versions of left-wing violence.

THE PERSPECTIVE OF CONFESSIONS

Direct testimonies to the police and magistrature on the community of armed struggle by former members began in 1979: the magistrate Calogero's initially anonymous witnesses in Padua, the UCC members in Rome and an early activist, Carlo Fioroni, from the long-dissolved group *Potere Operaio*, who had been in prison since 1975. In those cases, however, the accounts concerned the (sometimes remote) past, given by men and women who had abandoned any involvement in, or complicity with, violence because of its escalating scale and counter-productive outcomes. The most consequential confessions for the period after 1976 began in 1980 with the arrest and almost immediate collaboration of Peci and Sandalo in Turin, Garigliano and Cristiani in Genoa, Barbone in Milan. The information on their own and others' responsibilities led directly to the arrest of most participants in armed struggle in the north and the seizure of their material resources, especially weapons. Identification prompted further confessions: some were complete, with their authors (the *pentiti*) repudiating armed struggle and their former selves; others (*dissociati*) made at most generic or partial acknowledgement only of their own involvements, refusing to treat the entire past as an error or to betray former comrades. None the less the practice of accepting communication with their former enemies was sufficiently widespread that, for example, even by the time of the first major trials of BR and PL members in Turin in 1981, 69 per cent and 77 per cent respectively of the two groups' defendants had collaborated to some extent with the magistrates.[36] The fullest insiders' accounts on the organisation of violence in Rome, Naples and the Veneto became available during 1982; and by the end of that year the structure and history of armed struggle in every major city and for every important signature had been described in detail by former members. As a result of their judicial significance and wide public exposure through interviews in the mass media, the *pentiti* in particular came to be accredited as the principal interpreters of armed struggle, replacing the intelligentsia as the key mediators of meanings.

The practical effectiveness of the early confessions in identifying the responsibilities and resources of violence stemmed from the specific location in the community of armed struggle of their authors. The activists named above were all full-time apparatchiks, with careers of involvement in organised violence dating from at least the mid-1970s which gave them an extensive knowledge of its evolution. However their direct experiences remained very largely within the confines of single cities. None had reached the most senior apparatchik status except in the case of Peci, although he had been a member of the Red Brigades' 'strategic direction' only for a short period before his arrest; and most were recent or semi-clandestine – but at any rate fringe – members of that particular milieu. Not until well after their descriptions of the organisation of armed struggle had already been provided and validated in court did even partial confessions come from apparatchiks who had had long-standing knowledge of different cities or who had taken a major role in any of the formally national decision-making bodies of any group. Nor did the intelligentsia provide confessions: its members either refused to collaborate or proclaimed themselves innocent of any organisational role in violence. The subordinate status in the apparatchik milieu of the primary collaborators was a significant influence on shaping their accounts of armed struggle, as I shall suggest below. It also indicated a membership niche which was especially likely to generate a wholesale repudiation of armed struggle. For while the core apparatchiks had established a kind of solidarity based on regular meetings and longstanding acquaintance or friendship, their fringe colleagues remained outside that circle and were therefore much more heavily dependent on the psychological and practical support of the locals for the maintenance of their commitment. But after 1979 the participation of locals was sharply reduced as they withdrew the use of violence from their political repertoire, leaving their now fully-committed fringe apparatchik contacts bereft both of the horizontal solidarity of their own milieu and the vertical bonds to ordinary political activity. Unlike the locals they found their whole political identities inextricably bound to violence; and their subordinate role in the apparatchik milieu and its relationships weakened attachment to its evidently increasingly desperate and futile activities. Arrest was a powerful catalyst in forcing appreciation of their isolation and the attractions of positively reconstructing their identities, even without the legal incentives to abjure their pasts.

All magistrates investigating terrorism made full use of the confessions, openly acknowledging particular individuals' contributions as the basis of their own interpretations. Nevertheless, both inside and outside the judicial domain, various kinds of disquiet were expressed about the production and use of confessions as evidence. Inevitably the very fact of collaboration generated hatred among former comrades who had been betrayed and distaste among wider audiences sceptical of the motives of collaborators who until the very moment of arrest had apparently been fully prepared to carry out woundings and murders. A generic suspicion hung over the assertions of the *pentiti*, especially since confessions were rewarded by reductions in sentence: how could anyone capable of believing the ideological fantasies embodied in the texts of armed struggle be relied on to give a fully truthful account of its organisations, avoiding the temptation to settle private scores and knowing that more extensive collaboration entailed larger personal benefits? An *a priori* scepticism, without requiring grounding in evidence of specific falsity, was inevitable. It was reinforced, particularly in accounts of the more remote incidents, by accusations of the absence of independent confirmatory evidence, apart from further confessions. That criticism was, however, vastly exaggerated. Wherever possible, magistrates sought police reports or witnesses' accounts compiled at the time to provide an uncontaminated standard by which to assess confessions; and of course the normal investigative technique of comparing versions given by people isolated from one another and by the same person on different occasions was used extensively. In another direction the nature of the transactions between police, magistrates and the 'repentant terrorists' aroused concern. Some of the fullest confessions had been given first to the police which, especially if they were made while in police custody, initially gave rise to speculation about the nature of possible pressures used to elicit hitherto unthinkable 'betrayals'. Since the official record (*verbali*) of interrogation by magistrates was frequently less a direct transcript than a subsequent reconstruction from notes, omitting the actual questions to which the prisoner was replying, further space for doubt was created. Although the law offered courts the power to concede extenuating circumstances for 'repentant' criminals, investigating magistrates were neither accustomed nor had procedural guidelines to handle formal negotiations with suspects (a law favouring plea bargaining was only introduced in 1981) or to deal with confessions on such a scale with so urgent a need to verify and extend their contents.

Magistrates not directly involved in investigations of violence sometimes laid two specific charges against their colleagues: that the threat of extended preventive detention was being deliberately used to extract confessions from defendants who had the legal right to remain silent; and that illegal, clandestine, negotiations were occurring between certain magistrates and *pentiti* in the construction of confessions. Both charges were made in print in 1981 by members of *Magistratura Democratica*, and both were the subject of disciplinary action by the CSM against their authors. The accusations were defended on the grounds of legitimate criticism (unsuccessfully in the case where the magistrates who had been accused of illegalities were named), and no evidence was produced to substantiate the claims. Commenting on the CSM sentence censuring them, two Milan magistrates offered a single example of a deal: a former affiliate of PL had claimed that he would no longer collaborate with the judiciary since the public prosecutor had broken his promise not to appeal to the Court of Cassation against an appeal court decision acquitting him of membership of PL.[37] The decision not to contest an acquittal verdict by an appeal court was hardly an illegality; and no other cases have been adduced. Magistrates could, however, provide one vital resource to collaborators – assistance in ensuring that they were not returned to a jail where they would be at the mercy of their erstwhile comrades. For between 1980 and 1982 no special prison sections for collaborators had been organised and the conditions for ensuring their physical survival were therefore negotiated between the magistrature, police and Ministry of Justice. Quite commonly, repentant terrorists spent a substantial part of their early detention in police barracks for which a magistrate's consent was required. No doubt minor facilitations in the custodial regime were conceded but no known instances suggest substance to the fear that tacit plea-bargaining between magistrate and defendant might be taking place illicitly in order to swell the confessions with names or episodes that the magistrates wished to inculpate. In any case the investigating magistrates themselves insisted, in accordance with article 6 of law 304/1982, that all confessants' accounts had to be verified in court before any benefits could be granted. With few exceptions collaborators were compelled at least to confirm their pre-trial declarations and to submit to questioning in public. It is more useful, therefore, to examine how the primary reliance on confessions deriving from a structurally-identifiable set of participants worked to validate a particular reading of armed struggle. Given the potential range of classifications to cover the evolution of a decade's armed struggle, the use of *pentiti* provided a specific level of interpretive closure.

As I indicated earlier (p. 194), the particular experiences and knowledge of the earliest collaborators were largely confined to single cities. For example, except for a brief early period in Milan, Peci had remained in Turin as a clandestine BR militant from 1977 to 1980; Sandalo's PL activities were restricted to the same city and Barbone's career was limited to Milan. The single-city focus was of course true *a fortiori* for the locals whose confessions followed the apparatchiks'. Making the accounts of *pentiti* central to judicial readings therefore entailed accepting the limitations of knowledge they embodied. Since none of their authors had been involved in activities beyond their own cities and had no major directive roles, they could offer no clear evidence on links between members of different groups for their primary periods of militancy, between 1975 and 1980, nor could they trace firm connections with the milieux contiguous to the named formations of armed struggle. Acceptance of the scale of their accounts fitted closely with the decision not to have a single judicial centre for investigating and trying political crime, since it localised responsibilities. The same limitations were imposed for the laying of conspiracy charges. The confessions of the fringe apparatchiks established a penally relevant 'centre of contamination' for the responsibilities of others which were made to stretch to the limits of the *pentiti*'s own knowledge. Whatever connections or joint projects there might have been at other levels, especially among the intelligentsia or the earliest apparatchiks, they remained largely irrelevant to the magistrates who based their accounts on the descriptions provided by the early *pentiti*.

Apart from their localising dimension, those descriptions also validated a strongly organisational reading of armed struggle. The translation of what actors claimed to see as generic acts of solidarity with armed struggle into examples of particular organisational allegiances derived its strength from three sources: the position of the early *pentiti*, the timing of their confessions, and the details of the laws rewarding collaboration. First, the fringe apparatchiks did not have sufficient experience at decision-making levels to be able either to appreciate the casual and tenuous nature of bonds behind the formal group charter or to distinguish fact from fantasy in their senior colleagues' claims about the extent and efficiency of group structure. At the same time they were so placed as to picture their direct routine dealings with others in terms of support for specific group projects. Assertions of their firm bonds with 'clients' provided them with status in their own milieu, while the livable quality of their own role was no doubt reinforced by a self-perception simply as locals who had had the courage of their convictions.[38] Exaggeration of the particularity of commitment of members of the local milieu was likely, producing a reading of the complexities of armed struggle in terms simply of specific group loyalties. That reading was of course generally not endorsed by locals who tended to define their own contacts with members of armed groups in open 'communal', rather than narrow 'organisational', terms. Thus Peci was accused, for example, of not understanding the nature of his own BR organisation – of misdescribing its internal division of labour and of giving it a spurious geographical (city) structure.[39] At the level of relations between signatures the same perspective led to the assimilation of minor sets of locals to whatever more enduring group their leading members were affiliated. The neighbourhood-level *ronde* and *squadre* in Turin were assimilated directly to the parent organisation of *Prima Linea* so that casual participants were regarded as members, although carrying reduced responsibilities, of a single armed band. Moreover the judicial definition of an armed band was sufficiently flexible to include as a shared aim merely the conviction that the problems of Italian society could be resolved by violence.[40]

The second important constraint on confessions was contained in the emphasis in the 1980 and 1982 laws on the importance of a confessant's *dissociation* from former comrades and their projects. The need to display as drastic a separation as possible from past relationships in order to earn reductions in sentences reinforced the complementary (re)construction of the *association* to which those relationships belonged. The reading of that association in rigidly structured and hierarchical terms was encouraged by the practical use of confessions to show their authors' divorce from their former selves and lives. Reincorporation in the political community was achieved by suggesting an exaggerated degree of organisational coherence and formality in the now-rejected community of armed struggle. The particular perspective from the apparatchik milieu here matched the legal conditions for the plausibility and efficacy of confessions. Furthermore, since the benefits gained through confession could be withdrawn in the event that deliberate reticence was subsequently revealed (article 10 of law 304/1982), strong incentives to include an exhaustive list of contacts within the organisational schemes existed. Collaborators were under great pressure to extend their revelations as widely as possible, leaving to the investigating magistrates the task of deciding the extent of individual contribution required to warrant the laying of any of the array of criminal charges.[41] At the time of the first confessions in 1980, with levels of violence diminishing but still serious, the investigators themselves were of course urgently concerned to ensure that no one likely to replace the arrested full-time activists remained at large. Since the judicial interpretation of the organiser/participant distinction within armed groups favoured the extension of the organiser category, the eventual allocation of individual responsibilities in penal terms often came to differ markedly from the local actors' own perceptions of their role in armed struggle. The key set of confessions on which most magistrates' accounts were founded tended therefore towards a localisation of the practice and organisation of armed struggles. That the establishment of interpretive closure at local level was in fact a choice, rather than simply a necessity dictated by the nature of armed struggle itself, can be shown by examination of the judicial enquiries where confessions were regarded as forms of evidence subordinate to the texts produced by the various groups.

TEXTUALISING 'TERRORISM'

Matching the importance given by all armed groups to the composition and circulation of texts was the attention given to their conservation. Several bases discovered by the police contained meticulously-ordered archives, containing the documentary production of years of information-gathering and politico-economic analysis. If they could not be stored anywhere with security, the archives were regarded as sufficiently important to be moved around under the direct control of members of the intelligentsia.[42] Leaving aside the accumulations of details on individuals and institutions culled from different sources, the more complex documents used in judicial evidence belonged to different categories. Some were diaries or letters or comments or the rough drafts of texts; others were intended only for internal circulation; and yet others were designed for wider audiences. The enormous prolixity of armed groups left a considerable volume of written traces constituting data from which to reconstruct their boundaries and projects. Technical aspects, such as typewriter derivation or handwriting, provided a means of linking texts to individual responsibility: Marco Barbone, for example, was first betrayed by having addressed by hand the envelopes for documents containing threats to journalists. But their linguistic elements and turns of phrase were also used to identify a controversial history of the evolution of left-wing political violence which transcended what one of its authors called the 'localistic myopia' of other magistrates.[43] Two, initially connected, cases of reliance on documents to reconstruct 'terrorism' beyond the restricted levels of knowledge of the major *pentiti* have been mounted: the use of the charge of armed insurrection against the State, in a highly selective fashion and the identification of a pattern of connections among apparently different kinds of violence proposed by the magistrates responsible for making the prosecution case against some members of *Autonomia*'s intelligentsia. Both instances were controversial even within the particular judicial offices concerned (Rome and Padua) and aroused much public debate further afield. Both also reveal how the conflicts between judicial versions of violence have rested on the credence given to accounts coming from different milieux of armed struggle at different periods.

Armed insurrection against the State

Since by definition a successful armed insurrection ensures that its protagonists will not be subject to a trial for their actions, the charge must necessarily deal with failures. Its use in Italy before 1979 had been rare. Apart from cases involving revolts against Italian colonial rule in Africa, four trials were known to have taken place between 1889 and 1945, with a further four cases after 1948. With the exception of the then most recent instance – the alleged Borghese *coup d'état* of 1970 for which the charge was dismissed by the Assise Court in Rome in 1978 – all previous episodes had concerned either isolated individuals or municipal *jacqueries* of very limited duration and involvement. The jurisprudence concerning the phenomenon was therefore largely undeveloped, with no clear precedents to cover the prolonged and extensive failure of left-wing political violence to achieve its objectives.

Indeed the history of the charge's use against members of armed groups clearly reveals the interpretive uncertainty. In April 1979 the accusation was first formally laid by a Padua magistrate against the *Autonomia* leader Negri, to whom were added a further six defendants in July after responsibility for the investigations had been transferred to Rome. In December of the same year, following the confessions of Fioroni, the charge was extended to cover a small set of former members of the extra-parliamentary Left in Milan, most of whom had been subsequently associated with the broadsheets *Rosso* or *Autonomia*. Only in June 1980 were some members of the Red Brigades – but not the group's original leaders – specifically inculpated and accused of having acted in tandem with Negri and the other defendants. In November 1980 the responsibilities of BR members and *Autonomia*'s leaders were formally separated, suggesting that there had in fact been *two* separate attempts to achieve an insurrection. Finally in February 1982 the Roman magistrate, Amato, issued 269 arrest warrants for armed insurrection, later increased to 426, to cover everyone already convicted, or awaiting trial, for membership of the Red Brigades throughout Italy. Although five years later that case had not yet come to court, the use of the charge had had immediate consequences. Since it carried a maximum sentence of life imprisonment and therefore permitted the longest terms of preventive custody, many former BR activists who had served their full sentences or had become eligible for parole were held in jail because of that single accusation. Most crucially from the translational perspective, because the eventual target of any insurrection was the 'heart of the State' (sc., the seat of government), all proceedings involving the charge were transferred to Rome so that the evolution of the Red Brigades' separate fragments came under judicial scrutiny from a single magistrate for the first time. Actions and activities which had previously been given dispersed local readings could be redescribed and translated onto a national scale by the establishment of a single interpretive site. Evidence and relationships not emphasised within the horizons of a particular city might therefore be attributed a much greater degree of significance once the accusation of armed insurrection brought them under different criteria for interpretation.

Moreover the laying of the charge of armed insurrection actually represented the final stage in an escalating unitary re-reading of left-wing violence by the magistrature. Until 1979 many lesser signatures were penally identified as fragmented 'subversive associations' with no continuing connection to sources of weapons or wider projects; from 1980 onwards several magistrates suggested that those descriptions should be revised (and the members re-tried) on the more serious charge of 'armed band' as the connections between, for example, PL and the *squadre* were indicated in the first confessions; and finally in 1982 the identification of a single project uniting all members of the Red Brigades from 1970 onwards gave at least that group a degree of ideological and organisational homogeneity which had been the ambition rather than the achievement of many older members. The sequence of judicial interpretations and reinterpretations thus followed an analogous course to the evolution of the armed groups' projects themselves – a trajectory beginning with the informal and small-scale, through the formation of the apparatchik milieu, and finally to the attempts of the Red Brigades, *Metropoli* and *Autonomia*'s leaders to create a single project around a central organisation.

The magistrate from the Rome judiciary who supported the applicability of the charge argued that it could be added to the accusation of membership of an armed band because a distinction could be legitimately drawn between merely belonging to a group and active participation in its projects. Levels of single actions did not need to be established as consistently serious since unforeseen external factors could transform apparently minor acts of violence into full-scale successful revolutions: the military insignificance of the Fascist movement in 1922, for example, had been more than compensated by the unanticipated extent of weakness and corruption among State officials. What should count as the principal data were the *intentions* of participants, as discernible in the texts over the group's signature, assumed to represent the explicit ideology of all members. Amato therefore criticised other magistrates for failing to use the charge not just against the Red Brigades but also against *Prima Linea* and, by implication, against any group sufficiently extended in time and space.[44] That 'national' reading was not however shared by most other magistrates from the pool investigating violence. A series of pronouncements in Milan, Turin and Florence in 1981 converged in denying that the charge of armed insurrection could be sustained. They suggested that the actions of even the major groups lacked sufficient coordination and continuity, did not attack directly the major institutions of the State (government, Parliament and the judiciary) and were territorially too narrowly concentrated to constitute a serious attempt at a national insurrection. Furthermore, since the major element in any large-scale revolt was the active participation of the population, the failure of armed groups to win any wide support rendered the charge inapplicable. In sum, neither had an attempted insurrection occurred nor could the groups' actual histories license their members' self-description as plausible potential bearers of any mass uprising.[45]

Magistrates who argued that line took as crucial evidence, not the intentions of some actors but the effects of the armed groups' actions. They placed themselves in the positions taken by their principal witnesses, the former practitioners of violence who now rejected armed struggle and legitimised their collaboration in the name of the failure of their projects. The meanings of armed struggle were therefore regarded as by now clear and fixed – essentially local and fragmented. By contrast, magistrates who supported the invocation of the charge of armed insurrection placed primary interpretive weight on the texts authored by a still publicly unrepentant intelligentsia – in the BR case despite self-confessed involvement, and in the *Autonomia* case because the defendants denied that they had been organisationally involved in any left-wing violence, let alone an armed insurrection. Their texts were largely treated as transparent reflections of the organisation of armed struggle and of the explicit goals of all participants. Their content was given straightforward referential status, ignoring its rhetorical role in seeking to aggregate readers around a particular descriptive vocabulary.

Finally, the evidence of the intelligentsia's texts was precisely the major source of data from which the political interpretations of armed struggle had been built up throughout the 1970s since it was then the only accredited public source of meaning for the acts of violence. The identity of their data base licensed the accusation that the high-level, insurrection-oriented, readings of armed struggle were simply a *continuation* of political readings, illegitimately using the thin camouflage of legal terminology to punish fringe participants very severely and issue a warning to all activists beyond the institutional Left. Such an impression was heightened by the predilection of both Calogero and Amato for much more extensive critical disquisitions on the social origins and political nature of 'terrorism' in their judicial sentences than appeared in those of other magistrates.[46] To that extent the role of the judiciary as an impartial arbiter of the law was threatened with explicitly political contamination. By contrast the readings of armed struggle by the majority of magistrates, based on the evidence of collaborators, represented a major *discontinuity* with earlier political readings since those versions had not been previously available – they could largely escape direct confrontation with political versions. Much of the extended controversy surrounding the April 7 case rested not simply on the attempt to pin direct organisational responsibilities on the intelligentsia but also on the conflicts between the two types of evidence in tracing the evolution of armed struggle.

'Calogero's theorem'

On 7 April 1979 a Paduan magistrate, P. Calogero, signed twelve arrest warrants against some of the better-known leaders of *Autonomia* (notably Negri, Scalzone and Piperno) for constituting the clandestine leadership of the Red Brigades. On the previous day Negri had also been charged by the Roman magistrate Gallucci with having participated directly in the management of Moro's kidnapping. Although between 1979 and the defendants' first appearance in court in 1982 the postulated link with the Red Brigades was formally abandoned, Calogero's initial interpretation of armed struggle as the unilinear evolution of violence directed by a single set of leaders remained the basic feature of his accusations. The hypothesis of systematic connections, at least between *Autonomia* and the Red Brigades, was not new. Calogero's own investigations of local left-wing violence in Padua had actually begun in 1977, resulting then in the acquittal of Negri and several others subsequently arrested in 1979 on the charge of having directed a subversive association; and he had announced the 'working hypothesis' which governed his enquiries as early as May 1978.[47] Nor was the speculation on the connections confined to Calogero alone. A document issuing from the Italian participants in a private conference of magistrates at Cadenabbia in 1978 had already adumbrated the possibility of formal links between the different components of the armed community.[48]

While most attention was focused on connections through recruitment and reciprocal assistance at local level, Calogero undertook to show that behind the apparent diversity and fragmentation of left-wing violence since 1970 lay a single project directed from above by a small group from the milieu of the intelligentsia. He argued that it had begun with the extra-parliamentary group, *Potere Operaio*, which had turned itself into an armed band after a conference in Rome in October 1971. Its clandestine 'military' dimension was the first example of the distinctive characteristic of Italian political violence – an organisational structure with dual legal and illegal levels. The apparent differences of ideology expressed publicly in the legal journals and broadsheets were no more than a camouflage for the unified direction by some of the same contributors of both the clandestine violence of the Red Brigades and *Prima Linea* and the 'spontaneous' lesser violence associated with *Autonomia*. According to Calogero the project initially formulated by some of the leaders of *Potere Operaio* had been subsequently elaborated by the directive body alleged to have organised the apparently very heterogeneous city-based fragments of *Autonomia* after 1973 and accepted by the Red Brigades during the major Fiat strike of the same year. In 1981 he summarised his conclusions as follows:

> the reality which was ignored or rejected was that of the *partito armato*: that is, the existence in our society of a unitary directive group ... working as a centre of planning, organisation and decision-making for 'diffuse' violence and for the attack directed at the major institutions ... For years *Autonomia* and the Red Brigades had joined forces in a dialectical process, united both tactically and strategically, with the aim of promoting civil war and an armed insurrection against the State.[49]

In this analysis the community of armed struggle was dissolved into a single organisation directed from above, datable almost from the first appearance of left-wing violence and tied to one group alone from the extra-parliamentary Left. The extremely variegated types and targets of violence were therefore portrayed as the product of a vertically-organised conspiracy rather than either the outcome of internal and external determinants of the activities of a divided apparatchik milieu or the unpredictable and uncoordinated extension of local-level conflicts. Calogero claimed precisely to have identified the primary conspirators among the intelligentsia.

On his own account his analysis had begun in a comparative reading of the leaflets of armed struggle and Negri's works of political theory. With the help of a mere five police perquisitions, the conclusions he had reached in 1981 rested on two kinds of evidence – the history of *Potere Operaio* recounted by marginal members who had never themselves engaged in violence, and the textual evidence of documents authored by various named segments of *Potere Operaio*, *Autonomia* and the Red Brigades. The oral testimonies provided in the confessions of the insider *pentiti* did not become available until long after Calogero's hypothesis had been formulated. His evidence for the organisation of armed struggle was therefore almost exclusively textual, resting on the appearance in documents of *Autonomia* and the BR of key terms (*basi rosse, stato imperialista delle multinazionali* and many others) and of the contents of innumerable public and private documents indicating justification and support for violence.[50] The existence of the organisation necessary to translate the textual affirmations into the reality of armed struggle was regarded as demonstrated by the alleged consistency between the general targets identified in ideological documents and the actual episodes of violence, rather than by any independent direct proof of the intelligentsia's involvement. By reading the (selection of) documents authored by the defendants largely as literal descriptions, Calogero placed himself in the position of a naive reader, intent on interpreting the phenomenon of armed struggle from the outside as a member of the audiences to which the intelligentsia's claims were directed. While at the time he began his enquiries in 1977, and even at the time of the first arrests in April 1979, that position made use of existing evidence and was not directly in conflict with other available data, it became much harder to sustain after the confessions of 1980.

For the testimonies of the *pentiti* did not confirm, indeed in many cases specifically excluded, any coordination among the various groups in which they had been active. Although the evidence of Fioroni and former members of *Potere Operaio* suggested an interest in violence among some of the group's leaders between 1971 and 1973, and although the testimony of Barbone indicated an involvement of the Milan intelligentsia around *Rosso* in the later 1970s, no indication of continuous coordination among the groups of *autonomi* in different cities, still less between *Autonomia* and the Red Brigades, was forthcoming. Moreover, from the unitary perspective on left-wing violence, to acknowledge the versions furnished by the *pentiti* as the most authoritative descriptions of armed struggle would itself have constituted a serious problem. For the limitations, partialities and local horizons of their accounts entailed just the kind of ideological and organisational discontinuities that the unitary version rejected. Calogero's response was explicitly to claim interpretive priority for texts as the primary source of evidence about the evolution of left-wing violence. His apodictic statements for the overriding value of the documents rested on two assertions: first, that only through the texts could the penally-relevant responsibilities of the intelligentsia be recognised since its members would take little or no part in the actions themselves; and, second, that confessions could never be wholly proof against deliberate alterations of the truth to conceal wider or unsuspected responsibilities. Texts, on the other hand, were beyond revision and their production as armed struggle itself developed generated a fixed and reliable guide to the authorship of the then contemporaneous violence. When the versions contributed by *pentiti* clashed with what could be discovered in the documents, then it was the documents which should be given greater weight.[51] Calogero's unitary account of left-wing violence thus acknowledged the clash between apparatchik and intelligentsia versions of the past: but unlike the other specialist magistrates, he preferred the perspective and sources of the intelligentsia.

Not surprisingly his textual reconstructions encountered wide opposition. The detailed examination of some of his accusations was transferred to Rome which, as the national capital, exercised a claim to jurisdictional competence for charges of armed insurrection; and much of the public controversy over the unitary interpretation was played out there in the trial examined in Chapter 6. The more restricted version of the same hypothesis – the existence of an intelligentsia-driven hierarchical organisation behind the many different signatures of armed groups in Padua itself – remained, however, for local evaluation in the city. There it encountered the opposition of the investigating magistrate, Palombarini, who was obliged to assess Calogero's interpretation and to decide whether the evidence warranted the defendants' committal for trial. The resulting dispute between the public prosecutor and the investigating magistrate accompanied the entire judicial processing of Padua's political violence between 1978 and 1984, leading to public remonstrations, the alternating arrest and release of the major local defendants and lengthy delays in the bringing of the charges to court.

The conflict was neither a simple clash between individual person-
alities nor an opposition between the conceptions of justice characterising different organised groups of magistrates represented by two
of their leading members – Palombarini as the future national
secretary of *Magistratura Democratica* and Calogero as an elected
UniCost member of the CSM. Rather, as Palombarini himself acknowledged, the dispute was global, concerning the entire construction of the case against the defendants.[52] Some divergences arose
over the factual basis of Calogero's argument: Palombarini pointed
out for example, that the genesis of the perfectly open attempt to
organise *Autonomia Operaia* centrally in fact preceded the dissolution of *Potere Operaio* – indeed, as a competing focus of allegiance,
was a *cause* of that dissolution – and could not therefore be seen as its
clandestine outcome. More generally he argued that the necessary
evidence for systematic connections behind the allegedly superficial
fragmentation of *Autonomia* was simply lacking. At most the single
components of that universe, such as the *Collettivi Politici Veneti*,
could be shown to have been armed groups with clandestine structures
and identifiable projects; but no wider links to other signatures could
be adduced. No specifically organisational meaning could therefore
be attached to the occasional meetings of individual members of
Autonomia with affiliates of the Red Brigades or Front Line. Other
conflicts concerned the correct interpretation of the penal code.
Palombarini argued that *Potere Operaio* did not meet the criteria for
legal definition as an 'armed band' or 'subversive association'. If, on
the other hand, Calogero's claim that it did was indeed to be taken
seriously, then *all* known activists should be incriminated, not merely
some of its leaders. In particular, the former influential members in
the Venice region who had given some support to Calogero's
reconstruction could not be treated as 'clean' witnesses to the
involvement of others in violence but should themselves be indicted
as fellow-defendants.

The deepest level of conflict, as both magistrates admitted, was
methodological and concerned the criteria for the interpretation of
evidence. Calogero argued that the acts of violence concurrent with
the appearance of the texts should be described in those texts' own
terms: the intelligentsia's meanings – often rhetorical and hyperbolic
– were to be treated as the basis of accurate descriptions of the
actions' significance. Palombarini asserted that this interpretive procedure generated an unacceptable circularity in the prosecution's
case. For to characterise acts of violence in the terms used by the

intelligentsia was already to define them in terms of their role in a single unified project – a descriptive strategy which entrenched as an interpretive assumption the very connections between the intelligentsia, apparatchiks and locals which required independent proof. Moreover, since Calogero had produced no new empirical evidence, there was no reason to set aside the judicial decisions on *Potere Operaio*'s legal status which had been made in the early 1970s and which had dismissed police claims of its incriminability as a subversive organisation. Only hindsight, exercised with knowledge of the subsequent escalation of violence and of the careers of some of the acts' authors, or deductions from essentially political presuppositions could force a reopening of those earlier readings. The meaning of the use, say, of molotov cocktails in Milan in 1971 could not be allowed, concertina-like, to expand and retract in the light of later developments. In response Calogero insisted that appreciation of the specific dual-level strategy of left-wing violence and its implications for the nature of the intelligentsia's involvements required an imaginative use of the available evidence, the significance of which could indeed only be determined retrospectively once the cover of clandestinity had been breached.

The dispute illustrates the scope for interpretive disagreements once magistrates had been compelled into writing the history of armed struggle to justify their charges against groups and individuals. The validity of the magistrates' choice of legal descriptions for acts and associations, the reliability of confessions and the contrasts between local and national readings of left-wing violence were issues raised during the formally secret pre-trial investigations. Since all judicial versions had to come to court for public scrutiny and evaluation, attention must therefore turn to the organisation and symbolic role of trials as a vital terrain for the ascription of a definitive set of meanings for armed struggle.

6 Staging Political Trials

Between 1978 and 1986 the left-wing political violence of the previous decade was being publicly scrutinised, almost without interruption, in courtrooms throughout Italy. In size and duration these trials eclipsed the normal dimensions of court events with the exception of mafia trials in the south. Between 1981 and 1986 24 first-level trials, each with between 30 and 207 defendants and lasting from two to fifteen months, were begun in ten major cities, accompanied a myriad of lesser cases and followed by briefer appeal proceedings. By the end of 1986, with the exception of the Cirillo kidnapping and the isolated killings of the most recent period, every salient episode and armed formation from the *anni di piombo* had been dealt with in court: in the most significant cases decisions reached at the final level of appeal, the Court of Cassation, had provided judicial closure.[1] Given their scale, content and media attention, the significance of the trials went far beyond their institutional task of acquitting or convicting individuals indicted for specific crimes.

All public legal activity has a strongly ritualised dimension in its very format and theatrical detail; and both were constitutive features of the maxi-trials for 'terrorism'. First, until 1980 most trials were held in modified barracks or in buildings attached to jails: thereafter special courtrooms had to be built for the occasion, often right on the periphery of the city itself, as in Turin, Bergamo and Padua. Both sets of locations provided spatial representations of the exceptional nature of the trials and the separation of defendants and crimes from the surrounding civil society. Most trials saw a vast display of police and *carabinieri* inside and outside the courtroom, adding not only to the drama and the difficulties of access for the general public but also to the cost. Staging the trials was in fact an extremely expensive undertaking, when the costs of construction, police surveillance, protection for participants, allowances for the jurors, witnesses and lawyers nominated by the court and the tying up of local judicial personnel and resources were added up: one estimate put the expense of the initial Moro trial at more than 30 billion lire.

In the second place, the trials were the first, and only, occasion on which many of the primary participants in advancing and resisting armed struggle were brought face-to-face publicly: the representatives of the State and its armed enemies, the public and the 'terrorists', the kin of victims and their aggressors, repentant defectors from violence and the former comrades they had had arrested. These confrontations carried their own dramatic potential, of course, to which the media were extremely attentive. But they also underlined the need to uphold the rules of procedure through which the interactions were managed and which could easily become sources of controversy in their own right. Ensuring that the rules were publicly observed contributed not simply to showing that the State could resist political violence by managing to process it through normal legal channels but also that whatever decisions and meanings were fixed to acts of violence carried the maximum legitimacy that the legal system itself could provide. For many observers and participants, and against widespread expectations, the successful processing increased that legitimacy by showing that at least some State actors were indeed bound by their own rules which could be demonstrated, in unpromising circumstances, to work. The importance of that dimension was enhanced by the direct juxtaposition of two vital trials with the Red Brigades' major ritual kidnappings and their own mimicry of legal terminology. For the third (and finally successful) attempt to try the early BR members in Turin began just a few days before the kidnapping of Moro, and the two events proceeded in parallel throughout the 55 days. Likewise in 1981 the first major collective trials of BR and PL members in Turin, and the earliest in which the chief evidence was provided by the confessions of a former member, were held against the background of four more or less simultaneous kidnappings by the Red Brigades whose victims included that member's brother. While the mere juxtaposition of contrasting applications of the same judicial language could hardly win legitimacy for the BR use, it necessarily focused attention on the State's ability to protect its own terminology and descriptions from external and internal pollution.

The trials' third ritual dimension lay in the actors' concern to establish their political identities. The courtroom became a site for the display and verification of the defendants' attitudes towards their former selves as responsible for the crimes with which they were charged. Actions in court were designed to show continuity or discontinuity with the past, not only positively through assertion of individual identity but also negatively by the establishment of distance from others. Behaviour in the courtroom itself thus constituted an independently effective means of reinforcing or, increasingly commonly, bringing to an end the community of armed struggle by ensuring the public dissolution, ultimately confirmed by the sentences, of former solidarities. Like the rituals of transition analysed by Van Gennep, the trials made up an arena with autonomous power to transform individuals and validate new patterns of affiliation and disaffiliation.[2] Moreover, in so far as the various participants in each trial claimed, or were attributed, representative status for wider collectivities, events in the courtroom took on a symbolic collective dimension of aggregation or disaggregation. By offering a public forum for tracking the interaction of category representatives with one another, each trial generated local patterns of solidarity and estrangement for transmission to wider audiences. The squeezing of collective actors of quite different sizes (the State, armed groups, the lawyering community, the general public) into a micro-arena of direct interaction provided a formidable opportunity for actors to grow or diminish according to the immediate outcome of localised transactions and conflicts and the messages about relative power that they embodied. Such outcomes were only possible when the purely notional confrontations carried by episodic, unsynchronised actions and antagonists remote from one another were converted into real confrontations in a single limited domain. That led to a variety of strategies to alter the rules, admit new allies into the courtroom, deny representative status to other participants – in general to render the boundary around each courtroom either more or less permeable: some of these strategies are illustrated in the specific cases discussed below. In similar fashion the excluded actors with a stake in the outcome could attempt to influence the courtroom interaction from outside – for example, by further violence, passing laws to influence its management, and mobilising the local population to communicate a sense of general solidarity with key participants.

Finally, the decisions reached in the trials created knowledge about armed struggle, in all-but-definitive form for outsiders (including future sociologists). The accounts by former members of armed groups were designed, in different ways, for presentation and validation in court; very extensive details on acts, ambitions and consequences across the entire range of phenomena in the community of armed struggle made up substantial segments of courtroom testimony; and the courts' verdicts established, with little practical possibility for revision except by a higher court, what did indeed happen over a decade and a half of violence. The verdicts were, therefore, doubly performative in most cases: fixing the identity and fate of the single defendants, fixing the meaning of key episodes of political violence for others. In some cities, too, the occasion of a major trial provided a stimulus for the Left to organise, if not exactly a forum for alternative versions of the past, at least a public assembly in which some of the materials and theses not included in that particular judicial event could be discussed; but there can be no doubt that the trials themselves offered far more influential, and usually more realistic, sources of collective self-examination for local political communities.[3]

The court terrain must therefore be analysed as a strategically organised arena for establishing various layers of meaning. The meanings were grounded on the deliberate selection of the particular content to be included in each trial and on the interactions among members of the specific interpretive community responsible for reading that material. Both dimensions must be examined since the wider dissemination of the meanings of armed struggle depended on their local construction. After discussing those organisational issues, I shall illustrate some of the general points in three specific cases: the trial of the early leadership of the Red Brigades in Turin in 1976–8, the so-called *Rosso*-Tobagi trial of *Autonomia*-based groups in Milan in 1983, and the April 7 trial of *Autonomia*'s intelligentsia in Rome in 1983–4. The three examples mark out key points on the trajectory of the judicial interpretations of violence. The Red Brigades trial established, after much uncertainty, that the existing judicial procedures and terminology could be used to translate successfully the acts and actors of a group ready to take extreme measures to prevent their application. It provided the necessary precondition for all subsequent court readings – had the translation failed, or failed to elicit consent to the court verdict and the methods by which it was reached, drastic alterations in penal procedures for handling political violence would very likely have been made. The second instance, the *Rosso*-Tobagi trial, offers a convenient example of the use of, and challenge to, confessions as the basis for the penal-historical reconstruction of armed struggle. Also, through the court's generous interpretation of the 1982 law rewarding collaboration, the political élite was made dramatically aware of the implications for substantive justice in the law's application. More generally the trial showed how meanings could be sealed at the local level and violence interpreted within the horizon of a single city. The third case, the April 7 trial, represented an attempt to translate the accounts already established at local level into the national framework of a single armed party, transcending the apparent fragmentation of types of violence, signatures and aims around which local trials had been built. It also sought to identify the penal responsibilities of the intelligentsia by interpreting its members' (very diverse) contributions to the ideology of armed struggle as organisational directives. The failure of the attempt to make the full set of charges convincing in court matched the earlier failure of competing groups in the community of armed struggle to make violence acceptable as a single national project.

THE ORGANISATION OF COURTROOM ANALYSES

Recontextualising the past

Although the investigating magistrates had divided up the work of enquiries among and within cities, further steps were required to sort out the enormous volume of their results into the appropriate format for single trials in their different jurisdictions. The ordinarily rigid rules on trying obviously-connected offences and individuals together had been relaxed by a 1977 law which provided the judiciary with greater freedom of choice in deciding on the materials for joint or separate consideration in court.[4] Key decisions therefore had to be taken. Would the trials for organisation and membership of an armed band, for example, be dealt with separately from the specific offences committed by the band? Would each signature be treated as a distinct band and given a separate trial? Would all specific acts of violence committed by a group be dealt with together, or would the major offences be considered individually? If the treatment of offences was to be organised on a chronological basis, then where would the divisions be set? These apparently technical decisions had very significant symbolic dimensions since they repositioned and therefore recontextualised the sequence of actions in contrast to how they had occurred at the time. Quite different levels of violence, aims and responsibilities might easily find themselves linked together in a single courtroom, overriding the distinctions which defendants had once thought to be essential in shaping their uses of violence. Collective trials therefore did not simply represent a faithful recapitulation of a past with features perfectly preserved for later dissection: rather, they rewrote the particular segment of the past for which the defendants were called to account. In doing so, they provided a facilitating context for the members of armed groups to see their own pasts differently and in that respect encouraged both the definitive demolition of the solidaristic presuppositions of the community of armed struggle and the reconstruction of its members' identities.

At least some of the decisions on trial content were fixed by contingent factors – the speed of particular enquiries, the timing of the conversion of a well-informed insider, the overlapping membership across different signatures, the need to bring some offences to court before the limits on defendants' preventive detention expired and so on. Indeed the issue of determining trial content did not really arise until 1980, since limited evidence and the refusal of defendants to defend themselves kept most trials short and – once the threat of disruption had been countered – uncontentious. Arrested members of armed groups were usually tried immediately for possession of weapons for which the increased penalties after 1974 guaranteed their detention while wider investigations proceeded. After 1980, however, with several hundred alleged terrorists in jail whose involvement in violence went back at least five years, the problem of selectivity was explicitly posed. In the absence of any single tribunal charged with investigating and judging political violence, the decisions were taken by each autonomous judiciary – a dispersal which necessarily produced somewhat different resolutions of the issues posed by the equally variegated local patterns of groups and actions.

In all cities the local members of Red Brigades were tried as single units, uncontaminated by the presence of defendants with other histories. In most cases *Prima Linea* and its locals received similar treatment. However the question of whether to deal jointly or separately with specific and associational charges was resolved differently by the major judiciaries. In Turin, for example, BR and PL activists were tried first only for their membership of armed bands in 1981 and subsequently, in 1983, for specific offences covering the entire period 1973–80. That division, which was followed in Genoa but not in Rome or Milan, was deliberately made to facilitate the most rapid court appearance possible for alleged participants in organised violence. The magistrates wanted the confessions of Peci and Sandalo to be repeated and verified in court and their authors to be publicly rewarded with light sentences, with the intention of demonstrating to other affiliates of armed struggle that the State would indeed acknowledge collaboration when deciding on sanctions. Associational charges were the quickest to organise since there were few problems either of evidence or of witnesses, given that the majority of defendants explicitly proclaimed their past or present allegiance to the groups. Furthermore the sentences demonstrated that the two groups, especially PL whose looser structure had been harder to characterise formally and whose affiliates often claimed their maximal allegiance only to a local level of structure, could indeed be defined as armed bands, confirming the interpretations given by the investigating magistrates. Validation in court encouraged the use of that interpretation elsewhere: the Milan magistrates investigating the local PL group, for example, simply incorporated the Turin reading into their own documents of accusation.[5]

Members of armed groups, however, argued that the separation of trials on associational and specific charges was deliberately designed to divorce in various ways their actions and aims from the context in which they were conceived. A trial solely for membership of an organisation, it was claimed, necessarily made the group appear a self-contained unity, flattening its trajectory and eliminating the distinctions among members whose degree of support for the different types of violence carrying the group signature had itself been severely discriminatory. Inter-group divergences could also be backgrounded. The decision to stage the two trials of BR and PL simultaneously in adjacent and identical Turin courtrooms seemed to defendants an attempt deliberately to confuse what they saw as basic ideological and organisational distinctions between the two groups. Likewise trials dominated by a long sequence of murders and woundings (the 1983 trial of the Red Brigades in Turin concerned 10 murders and 17 woundings) clearly encouraged a reading of the group's activities on the single linear axis of violence and powerfully inhibited the lateral reintegration of each action in its distinctive context. Furthermore disaggregation of the actions by a single Red Brigades' column into different trials could have a profound influence on their public discussion. For example, the Roman judiciary's decision to include in the Moro trial only those BR actions in Rome up until November 1980 neatly excluded the D'Urso kidnapping in mid-December. Introducing a caesura at that point prevented the simultaneous consideration in court of two kidnappings with contrasting outcomes in which the government had shown different degrees of intransigence towards the Red Brigades and the alignment of the political parties in general had altered. Keeping the two cases judicially apart rendered inadmissible the comparisons which would undoubtedly have led to confrontations. Direct juxtaposition of Moro's murder with D'Urso's release would have suggested that Moro's fate was not fixed from the outset, thus lending support to the claim that the DC had not done enough to save its president – perhaps even deliberately refrained from doing enough, as some of the DC's enemies suggested.

In the case of the armed groups deriving from *Autonomia* the selection of trial content was more complicated since in most cities the numerous formations had been small and short-lived. However the continuity of personnel across different signatures ensured that most judiciaries chose to assess the entire responsibilities of a set of groups in a single trial. In Bergamo in 1982, for example, no fewer than seven separate signatures covering the period 1975–80 were judged together, which put a total of 132 defendants in the dock. The longer the investigations took to come to court, the larger the number of defendants included as a result of later enquiries and the more protracted the trials became: the BR and PL trials in Turin in 1981 lasted 2 months, the first Moro trial in Rome in 1982 9 months and the April 7 trial in 1983 15 months. Obviously such lengthy events acted as major obstacles to the continuing administration of ordinary justice, tying up judges and lawyers as well as keeping some defendants almost permanently in court for two to three years if they were involved in more than one trial. Both the scale and duration of the trials caused serious problems for lawyers which will be examined below. But the strategy of organising inclusive maxi-trials carried one recontextualising effect, influencing the defendants' strategies in court because of what they took to be the likely consequences for interpretations by both immediate and more distant audiences.

For each of the large trials came to be dominated by the single most serious act of violence considered, which lent itself to presentation as the clearest fulfilment of a potential inherent in all less serious actions. The shorthand names by which the trials are generally known show the aggregation clearly. The 'Moro trial' was concentrated all but exclusively on the enigma of the DC president's kidnapping, despite the fact that it also dealt with a further eleven murders (apart from Moro and his bodyguards) and eleven woundings and that the majority (35) of the 56 defendants convicted had actually played no part in the central drama. An analogous case was the equally selectively dubbed '*Rosso*-Tobagi' trial. It was dominated by the murder of Walter Tobagi even though that tragedy was the final act in the seven years of violence considered in court and that all but one of his six murderers (from a total of 164 defendants) played wholly insignificant parts in the very large number of remaining crimes under simultaneous consideration. Both its chronological position and the fact of being the sole case of murder in that trial encouraged the representation of Tobagi's death as the culmination of all preceding violence, as the quasi-natural conclusion of the milieu's projects in which the particular identity of the men responsible could seem almost accidental. The varying recontextualisations of violence entailed in the composition of the specific indictments was an element which could be, and in this case was, challenged. Largely from outside the courtroom the PSI sought to supply a wholly different context for the murder: inside the courtroom defendants on lesser charges rejected contamination by association, insisting that their use of violence had always drawn the line at homicide and that the genesis of Tobagi's murder was tied to the very particular aims of the handful of individuals responsible.[6]

In general terms the confluence of different levels of violence and individual responsibilities in single trials created precisely that relaxation or overturning of boundaries and identities characteristic of the liminal phase of ritual. The overriding of distinctions once believed fundamental by the defendants facilitated their own re-examination of past associations and solidarities and the reconstruction of political identities. Different ways of recounting the past were established as the criteria for defining present individual stances towards the armed and political communities and for asserting conversion to the use of non-violent methods of action. Whereas until 1980 claims to public identity were addressed to the political domain, the subsequent dismantling of that identity was accomplished with reference to the courtroom and the various categories of participants in the judicial process.

Coordinating the participants

Each trial was built around the coordinated interaction of the key personnel: judge, public prosecutor (who had often been a protagonist in the pre-trial investigations), jurors, lawyers, defendants and witnesses. In most trials, too, the representatives of the public institutions under attack and the immediate kin of victims were accorded the right to sue the defendants for damages and could therefore, through their lawyers, play an autonomous role in interrogations and the accumulation of evidence. The formal aspects of the participants' interaction in court were of course governed by the rules of ordinary penal procedure, modified by four measures introduced in 1977–8 specifically to facilitate both the overall management of trials concerned with political violence and the task of the prosecution. The range of grounds for the compulsory invalidation of investigative acts by police and magistrates which had violated procedures was reduced, in effect allowing potentially serious errors at a defendant's expense to be committed without cost; the rules for the selection of jurors were made more flexible in order to weaken the force of attempts to intimidate them; defendants who disrupted proceedings were definitively excluded from the courtroom after a second expulsion for their behaviour; and documents from related investigations (breaching normal rules guaranteeing secrecy for enquiries in progress) could be used as evidence, including the record of 'open-ended interrogations' (*interrogatori liberi*) of defendants elsewhere. That last modification permitted the public prosecutor to introduce into trials accounts given outside the rules covering the production of valid testimony, thus inserting an anomalous further category of participant into the proceedings.[7] Furthermore, apart from their assessments of the magistrates' readings of 'terrorism', the courts were charged with applying the laws of 1980 and 1982 calibrating reductions in sentences and other benefits according to the differential extent of collaboration with the State. For no matter how complete their accounts and their rejection of violence, all self-confessed participants in armed struggle had to appear in court – even when their involvements had been so minor as to earn impunity by the terms of article 1 of law 304/1982 – in order to permit fellow-defendants implicated by confessions the opportunity to challenge their accusers. Within that overall formal framework, therefore, the substantive interactions between the major categories of participants were shaped.

A symbolic model for their relations was embodied in the more or less standard design for the interior of the new courthouses. The most prominent position, at one end of a very long hall, was occupied by the representatives of the State and community: the presiding judge and his deputy were flanked by the jurors and by the public prosecutor and clerk of the court. They were faced directly by rows of lawyers, behind whom were the spaces reserved for journalists, photographers, minor defendants who had been released on bail and finally – a long way from the centre of courtroom activities – the general public. Whereas until 1978 defendants had usually been accommodated on open benches, in the new structures they were placed at right angles to judge and jury in a row of deeply-recessed cages, divided by bullet-proof glass and ringed by police down one side of the courtroom (compare Plates 5 and 6). The spatial positioning of judge and defendants, analogous to the maintenance of a frontier between the communities they represented, virtually eliminated any easily-sustained sense of continuing *direct* confrontation; and since interrogations were conducted directly in front of the judge, the opportunity for others to intervene from distant and obliquely-placed cages was very limited. In cases of serious disruption the microphones and loudspeakers necessary to communicate across such wide distances could be switched off.[8] Just as the courtroom architecture changed during the years of armed struggle, so too did the composition and relations among the three major sets of contributors to determining the public and private meanings of violence: defendants, judges and lawyers.

Until 1980 defendants entered the courtroom either openly proclaiming their membership of an armed group or protesting their innocence. Red Brigades' activists mostly defined themselves as 'political prisoners' and refused to acknowledge the legitimacy of the court to try them, while the members of *Autonomia*-based groups generally pleaded not guilty and defended themselves within the limits of the existing procedures. Before 1979 Front Line affiliates, for example, would not openly acknowledge their group allegiance in court in order to display their rejection of the Red Brigades' call to direct confrontation with the State at all levels. From 1981 onwards, however, the fragmentation of the world of armed struggle, inside and outside prison, was translated into an increasingly wide range of stances on armed struggle, each position corresponding to the defendants' differential acknowledgement of solidarities with former comrades and their interpretations of the past. Table 6.1 shows the distribution of defendants from the major groups in trials between 1981 and 1984 according to whether they insisted on the continuing viability of armed struggle ('political prisoners', colloquially referred to as *gli irriducibili*), protested their innocence or had criticised at least certain aspects of armed struggle ('active dissociates'). In each case the proportion of 'political prisoners', was higher for the Red Brigades than for other groups, testifying to their continuing organisational base in prison and the survival of tiny but still active external nuclei. Also the numbers intent on defending themselves against the charges in court were much larger in the *Autonomia*-based groups than the Red Brigades since the reduced organisation-consciousness among affiliates of Front Line and transient action-sets entailed that locals were especially reluctant to see their generic revolutionary identity collapsed into allegiance to a single signature. For such groups a differentiated set of defence strategies was both possible and plausible.

TABLE 6.1   *Distribution of defendants across courtroom identities in nine trials, 1981–4*

Groups	'Political prisoners'	'Active dissociates'†	Innocent	Not yet arrested*	(Actual number of defendants)
	%	%	%	%	
1. BR					
1981 Turin	57	35	8	–	(72)
1982 Rome	64	19	11	6	(63)
1983 Padua	47	40	–	13	(15)
1984 Milan	67	29	–	4	(114)
2. PL					
1981 Turin	15	48	24	13	(92)
1982 Bergamo	8	46	36	10	(132)
1982 Florence	32	13	39	16	(77)
1983 Brescia	–	59	24	17	(42)
3. FCC, *Rosso*, XXVIII *marzo*					
1983 Milan	23	39	21	17	(150)
4. COCORI					
1983 Milan	14	38	25	23	(79)

* *Latitanti.* None of the *latitanti* in the Red Brigades' trials are recorded as having abandoned armed struggle: in the PL and other trials the numbers of 'dissociates' among *latitanti* varied between 67% and 100%, giving those who rejected armed struggle a clear majority overall.
† Includes defendants who had subsequently retracted their confessions. In the Turin and Bergamo trials of PL the retractors amounted to 30% and 18% respectively of the 'active dissociates' category.
SOURCES
Contro le regole di questo assurdo gioco 1982, 1983. Press reports of the Moro (1982) and W. Alasia (1984) trials.

Use of the court as a site for the renegotiation of identity was essential to the heterogeneous category of 'active dissociates', containing at one extreme those who had simply explicitly declared that they now rejected political violence and, at the other, those who had reinforced their exit by confessing everything they knew on their own and others' involvements. Through the laws of 1980 and 1982, however, the political élite had offered only selective recognition of the possible forms of rupture with the past. The single concession which passed permanently into the penal code was granted by article 4 of law 15/1980, offering a reduction of up to one-half in all sentences and the conversion of a life sentence into no more than 20 years in return for full dissociation from fellow-conspirators and demonstrably effective collaboration with police and magistrature.

Law 304/1982 was more nuanced but applied only to crimes committed prior to 31 January 1982 and on which information was volunteered, after the expiry date of the law had been prorogued once,
before 31 January 1983. According to its terms, full confession could
provide impunity for members of an armed band who had themselves
committed no crime, shown that they had actively severed connections and told the magistrates or the court what they knew about the
group's structure and logistic resources: that clause was directed at
the fringe locals. For more committed locals and apparatchiks who
had participated directly in violence a complete confession regarded
as exceptionally useful by investigators earned a reduction in sentence by two-thirds; less useful but still complete confessions secured a
reduction by one-half; and collaboration restricted to the details of
personal involvement and group structure could ensure diminution
by one-third. The minimal condition for public and concrete acknowledgement that a former member had repudiated the past was his or
her admission that the actions had indeed been 'terrorist' and could
now be recognised as no different from ordinary crimes. The various
options bound together inextricably the intellectual and moral convictions of the meaninglessness of further violence with the achievement of personal advantage through informing on others. Moreover
the specific conditions and scale of benefits raised the further issue of
equitable treatment since they ensured that in some instances the
more deeply involved apparatchiks, whose knowledge of the networks of personal involvements was greatest and who therefore
offered the most valuable collaboration, could serve shorter prison
terms than locals without much useful information to provide. Here
the claims of utility and justice were most obviously in conflict.

For the category of full collaborators (*i pentiti*) whose confessions
had already marked their exclusion from the armed community the
trials represented the public occasion for validating their accounts,
displaying their conversion and conferring dignity on their exit.
Indeed their fate lay very much in the courts' hands since, although
during the parliamentary discussion of the 1982 law the PCI and
PdUP had proposed the inclusion of restrictive empirical definitions
of what would count as 'exceptionally valuable' collaboration, the
government preferred to leave the interpretation up to the local
judiciaries. In addition, for that particular category of collaborators
only, the successful display of unequivocal conversion in court could
earn the further benefit of provisional release from custody at the
close of the first trial. For their former comrades who were in the

egally anomalous position of wishing to abandon armed struggle without acknowledging unconditional allegiance to the State and its demand for retrospective information (*i dissociati*), gaining external recognition of the legitimacy of that stance was much harder. An explicit justification for the critique of armed struggle without abandoning political commitment or accepting to betray erstwhile fellow-participants was first proclaimed in late 1981.[9] But despite attracting growing support and winning the attention of politicians and magistrates no formal legal recognition was accorded until 1987, long after the major trials had been concluded.[10] In court the distinctiveness of the category could be displayed by the use of separate cages: symbolically its members were always placed in cages between the full collaborators, who were closest to the judge, and the 'political prisoners' who were most distant. However, because of their refusal to make full confessions the *dissociati* were largely unable to provide unequivocal evidence of their definitive rejection of violence since they offered few pieces of evidence that could be independently confirmed. Indeed they were vulnerable to the charge that by refusing to provide information to the police on known arms caches and activists' whereabouts, they were deliberately permitting the persistence of the phenomenon to which they nevertheless claimed to be opposed. After 1981, therefore, the trials became a key public site on which to try to sustain both the positive nature of the category *dissociato* and the irreversibility of their own decisions to abandon violence.

The central figure among their audience in each trial was the presiding judge. The day-to-day atmosphere in court was powerfully influenced by his own attitudes (all the judges involved were men) and, notwithstanding the active role played by lay members in Italy's mixed judge–jury system, his legal knowledge was of particular weight in determining both the verdict and sentence.[11] Furthermore his role was enhanced by the considerable experience acquired in a sequence of similar trials. For, like the small set of investigating magistrates, the actual number of judges who presided over the major trials of left-wing violence was restricted, making for a small and cohesive – or at least relatively predictable – judicial interpretive community. In Turin, for example, one judge (Barbaro) handled successively the trials of the Red Brigades in 1978, the *Senza Tregua* group in 1979, the later BR members tried for membership of an armed band in 1981 and many of the same defendants charged with specific acts of violence in 1983: one of his colleagues (Bonu) dealt with both the major trials of Front Line in the city. A similar concentration marked the court phase in other cities. In Milan the judge (Cusumano) who directed one of the earliest trials against an *Autonomia*-based group, the 'Alunni band', in 1980 also handled the *Rosso*-Tobagi case, and a colleague from the Appeal Court (Cassone) managed the trials of the local Red Brigades' column, Feltrinelli's short-lived GAP and one of the small formations of *Autonomia*, the PAC. Finally, in Rome Judge Santiapichi presided over all the most significant trials – the NAP, Moro, April 7 and *Metropoli*. That continuity could have its costs: Santiapichi, for example, was formally challenged (*ricusato*) by defence lawyers in the *Metropoli* trial on the grounds that his opinions on political violence and its practitioners were by then so fully-formed from past experience that he had to be considered biased against certain defendants. But, from the perspective of ensuring the orderly processing of political violence through the courts, the experience of successive trials enabled the judges to deal locally with the disruptive strategies of unrepentant defendants and guide juries through familiarly controversial issues. It also enabled them to acquire a detailed and discriminating knowledge of the different ideological insignia within the community of armed struggle and the signs of individual estrangement from them.

For the judges occupied in some respects a distinctively 'impartial' position between the armed groups and the political élite. On one side, the distinction by the Red Brigades and Front Line between the responsibilities of investigating magistrates and court judges left the latter unscathed, notwithstanding occasional direct threats in court. None of the judges handling Red Brigades' and other group trials were in fact made the objects of attack. On the other side, at least some of the judges who presided over the larger political trials were highly critical of the political élite's initiatives as far as judicial processes were concerned. In Turin Barbaro publicly castigated the government for its general neglect of the judiciary, its *ad hoc* legislative responses of 1977–8 and its failure even to examine any of the issues raised by the BR trial he had conducted the previous year.[12] In the less public domain of an appeal court sentence, the Milan judge Cassone went further, ascribing to politicians direct responsibility for the persistence of political violence and deploring the restrictions imposed by the repentance laws on the court's freedom of judgement to determine individually appropriate sentences, 'stripping [the court] of its most sacred possession, an absolute impartiality with regard to whoever and whatever appears before it'.[13] Such attitudes accompanied a fierce determination to maintain, visibly, the autonomy of the arena they presided over and to resist obvious forms of political pressure. Moreover, the limited participation of the judges assigned to preside over the trials in the major representative bodies of the judiciary, the National Association of Magistrates (ANM) and the Higher Judicial Council (CSM), must have encouraged them to see the maintenance of that autonomy as an essentially local task. Whereas seven of the investigating magistrates were elected to one or more of the directive councils of the ANM in 1981 and 1983 and to the CSM in 1986, only one of the judges (the deputy judge in the Moro and April 7 trials) was even a candidate in those elections.[14] The small number of judges had neither the limited collective identity or public individual authority achieved by the investigating magistrates nor the organisational power to insist that the major official representative institutions within the judiciary translate their dissent from the political management of violence into more serious generalised conflict.

Reinforced by the sense of a closer knowledge of defendants than could be achieved in the more remote understandings among politicians, the insistence on preserving judicial autonomy could lead in different directions. With regard to the particular reduction of discretion imposed by the repentance laws, courts might be tempted, if not wholly to flout, at least to reduce their significance by criticising them openly, by interpreting their provisions very restrictively and by using ordinary articles of the penal code to all but annul the distinction between collaborators and non-collaborators. That direction was taken in two trials in 1982. In the above-mentioned case of the UCC in Rome even unequivocally repentant defendants were given sentences of up to 21 years, very nearly the maximum permissible, even though neither they nor the other members of the group had committed any murders. Likewise in the trial of 132 alleged members of PL and its satellite groups in Bergamo the fully-collaborating defendants were given sentences which quadrupled those sought by the public prosecutor and which fell not far short of the sentences received by the unrepentant 'political prisoners'.[15] As a collective product the sentences, and the sentiments that inspired them, could not be attributed to the presiding judge alone, although of course in so far as they depended on the invocation of rules on extenuating circumstances and the cumulation of responsibilities, the legal expertise of the judge and his deputy was very likely to have been a dominant influence.

Judges might however push in a more positive direction and see themselves as taking a future-oriented active role in national pacification rather than a purely retrospective punitive stance. Instead of attempting to reduce the rewards of collaboration, they sought to extend the number of cases for which *de facto* recognition of dissociation from armed struggle could be granted. By lowering penalties for defendants who confessed their responsibilities and acknowledged the end of armed struggle but who provided neither information on others involved nor a detailed reconstruction of the acts in which they had participated, several courts gradually came to anticipate in practice the political élite's eventual recognition of the *dissociati*. Moreover, where particular aspects of the emergency legislation continued to hinder the exercise of full judicial discretion, constitutional objections on grounds of inequities to similarly-placed defendants could be raised. Thus in December 1983 judges in Genoa attempted to persuade the Constitutional Court to overturn the section of the Cossiga law (15/1980) which, after the lapsing of law 304/1982, continued to prevent courts from applying extenuating circumstances for any 'terrorist' crime. Clause 4 in the same law which empowered courts to grant reductions in sentence only when dissociation was accompanied by practical results for investigations (which were virtually unachievable by 1983 when the police had already discovered almost everything to be discovered) was also challenged by judges. Mostly, however, more relaxed definitions and evidence for dissociation, coupled with the use of the full range of expedients in the penal code, enabled courts to acknowledge forms of exit from armed struggle without extended collaboration. The generous outcome of the Moro appeal trial in 1985 was hailed as a particularly significant public acknowledgement that less than complete repudiation of individual or collective pasts could be considered compatible with an unequivocal rejection of violence.[16] By coming to recognise an intermediate identity between the *irriducibili* and the *pentiti*, judges facilitated the escape route from the category of 'political prisoners' which, as the figures in Table 6.1 indicated, continued to account for a significant proportion of defendants. No doubt their progressive acceptance of the *dissociato* position can also be related to the organisation of the trials. For through the experience of a sequence of prolonged courtroom encounters judges were able to note distinctions among defendants invisible to outsiders and to track the changes in individual attitudes and conduct over the duration of one or more trials. If the investigating magistrates acted as the primary translators of the accounts given by full collaborators, the judges added a specific attention to the meanings of armed struggle as recounted by the defendants who rejected such dramatic conversions but none the less wanted now to refuse violence.

The directly interlocutory role played by judges towards the *dissociati* was facilitated by the much weakened position of the defendants' ordinary legal representatives, the lawyers. As in the case of journalists, the other class of professional mediators between armed struggle and external audiences, the lawyers' Janus-faced work on the frontier between their clients and the State was necessarily burdened with ambiguities. Familiarly intractable problems about where exactly the dividing line passed between offering legitimate assistance to clients and illegal participation in their activities arose for the voluntary defenders of self-proclaimed members of armed groups. Between 1977 and 1981 seven lawyers were indicted not merely for furnishing occasional help to those they represented but for full membership of those same organisations.[17] Most criminal lawyers resisted an involvement which was likely to prove difficult and perhaps dangerous and was unlikely to provide symbolic or material rewards. The lawyers who did accept briefs belonged largely to a restricted group which since at least 1968 had put its technical expertise at the service of left-wing causes, selecting cases and clients according to explicitly political criteria. Precisely because its members rejected a technical approach to lawyering, the increasing use of violence by clients from the extreme Left forced hard reappraisals of the extent of their political sympathies, especially when the murders of a trade unionist such as Rossa and magistrates such as Alessandrini and Galli indicated that the Left in general might become a direct target of attack.[18] The pool of lawyers who made themselves available to cover the array of different stances taken by clients was therefore small and its most active figures remained in constant demand. More than half (25 ex 48) of the lawyers from Milan engaged in the *Rosso*-Tobagi trial, for example, appeared for other defendants in the PL-COCORI trial which immediately followed: 19 of the total of 73 lawyers in the earlier trial (the total includes those from outside Milan) defended simultaneously between two and ten clients each. Clearly, in such prolonged and complex trials the volume of documentation requiring detailed study and the continuity of attendance ideally demanded, especially on behalf of clients unlikely to be able to pay their lawyers full or any fees, placed severe difficulties in the way of an effective court role based on routine defence practices. Any lawyer following the above two cases closely would have been entirely committed, with some breaks, from March 1983 to November 1984. But the practical difficulties presented by the organisation of the judicial processing of left-wing violence, themselves aggravating the emergency legislation's weakening of defence powers through the facilitation of police interrogation and acceptability of some procedural violations, were redoubled by the consequences of the stances adopted by defendants.

Both the traditional mediatory role of lawyers towards magistrates and their own category solidarities were disrupted. The refusal of 'political prisoners' to respond either to the investigating magistrates or in court reduced their defenders' role to fulfilment of the minimal technical tasks. For the opposite reason the lawyers of collaborating defendants found their own legal functions eliminated by their clients' readiness to make full confessions. Indeed their best advice was to encourage the most complete volunteering of information in order to ensure maximum benefits according to the 1980–2 laws, resulting in as apparently unconditional an alignment of themselves with the State as the lawyers of unrepentant defendants seemed publicly to be identified with the community of armed struggle. Availability to defend repentant users of violence was itself explicitly proclaimed as a political action; and nominating a particular defence lawyer after arrest was the most direct way for members of armed groups to indicate whether or not they intended to collaborate.[19] The antagonisms among defendants thus came to be directly reproduced among their lawyers, destroying sometimes long-standing friendships and solidarities, eliminating such informal reciprocal assistance as the (formally illegal) circulation of interrogation transcripts and weakening the capacity of the category to respond collectively to the general reduction in its role and powers. The traditional function of translating clients' understandings and action descriptions into legal categories was largely abrogated in the processing of left-wing violence.

Only the lawyers for the minority category of defendants who protested their innocence were able to take on a regular role, especially if their clients intended to acknowledge having performed certain actions but deny the appropriateness of their characterisation as particular forms of criminal offence. Other lawyers came to see themselves as engaged in defining a new role. In both theory and practice their contribution shifted from sole concern to defend an individual client towards attention to the detailed observance of the rules under which the interaction between defendants and the judiciary took place in both pre-trial and trial phases. Somewhat paradoxically the lawyers of fully-collaborating clients worked to defend the rights of other members of armed struggle named in the confessions – by checking that no unfair questions had been asked, that no more had been made of the response than was warranted and that the transcript of the interrogation conveyed precisely the nature of each individual's involvements.[20] The objective detachment of defence lawyers from exclusive devotion to single clients helped to dismantle the ordinary courtroom diaphragm between defendants and the State. In thus permitting the extension of the modes of direct interaction and reconciliation between representatives of the two communities, the altered role of lawyers also helped to produce a set of local informal guarantors, or scrutineers, of the legality of the achievement of that reconciliation. The unintended recruitment of lawyers into the validation of the rules of the judicial processing of left-wing violence contributed an additional source of legitimacy to the local-level trial management and outcomes. I shall therefore consider three specific trials which not only mark important stages in the determination of the public meanings of armed struggle but also the strategies for creating and resolving particular courtroom conflicts.

CAN 'THE REVOLUTION' BE PUT ON TRIAL? TURIN 1976–8

With the exception of the trial of the evanescent XXII *ottobre* group in Genoa in 1974, the bringing to court of 52 alleged members of the Red Brigades in Turin in 1976 was the first attempt to validate through normal judicial procedures the characterisation of an armed organisation in criminal terms. It was also one of the longest. Shortly after the trial's opening on 17 May 1976, the combined effects of the murder of a judge (Coco), concession of more time to allow lawyers to prepare their defence cases and the incorporation into the same proceedings of the results of parallel enquiries into the Red Brigades' violence in Milan forced its postponement. In April 1977, just prior to the reopening, a prominent lawyer (Croce) associated with the trial was shot: one result was to sabotage the formation of the jury, thus leading to a further postponement. Finally in March 1978 the court reconvened, this time successfully, concluding with the conviction of most defendants on 23 June. As that minimal chronology suggests, the various symbolic and practical outcomes were far from predictable at the time. Only with hindsight was it clear that at its third attempt the trial had in fact secured the boundaries within which future confrontations would be managed, thereby compelling the State's armed antagonists to redefine the meanings that their actions in the courtroom arena could possibly convey.

The *processo-guerriglia* strategy

The Red Brigades' strategy of *processo-guerriglia* was inaugurated at the Turin trial. Although it was only explicitly abandoned in 1983, its eventual failure in Turin in 1978 blunted its subsequent effectiveness, and it was never seriously adopted, or only in isolated and short-lived cases, by other groups. In general, as its name suggests, the strategy can be characterised as the attempt to demolish the boundaries around the legal arena. By a combination of violence outside the court and exploitation of the potential conflicts among their opponents within it, the group sought to realise two objectives: first, to show that the State was powerless either to make the court function at all or, as a subordinate aim, to demonstrate that it was unable to do so without clearly violating its own justice-guaranteeing rules; second, to establish the Red Brigades' political identity, in the double sense of the motivations generating the crimes being judged and of the continuing unity between the arrested intelligentsia and the remaining clandestine apparatchiks.

The particular acts of violence which embodied the strategy for the Turin trial reflected both those internal and external dimensions. The murder of the Genoa magistrate Coco in 1976 saw the completion of the 'Sossi campaign', since he had intervened to block the release of prisoners in exchange for the magistrate kidnapped by several of the Turin defendants. The murder of Croce in 1977 represented the continuation of the conflict inside the courtroom over the nomination and role of defence lawyers. Finally, the 1978 phase of the trial took place against the backdrop of the Moro kidnapping which can be seen as an escalation of the early BR leadership's assault on the DC. Although the connection with the Turin trial has been largely ignored in the exclusive focus on the kidnapping's political meaning, it seems likely that the action was timed to coincide with the reconvening of the trial, which was known well in advance, rather than the parliamentary vote of confidence in the DC government of national solidarity, which was not. The staging of the 'proletarian trial' to which Moro was subjected allowed an interweaving of symbols, meaning and language with the Turin trial which aimed to subvert the judicial system's taken-for-granted terminology and rites by the mere display of an alternative application. It also focused public attention on the defendants and allowed them to be seen – inaccurately – as possible arbiters of Moro's fate.[21]

The external significance of those actions depended on the translation of their effects into the court context. A specific link was provided by the major defendants' decision to revoke the mandate to their lawyers accompanied by an announcement that, since they did not recognise the right of the court to try them, they had no need to defend themselves and would therefore refuse – indeed consider as enemies – any replacement lawyers nominated for them by the court (*difensori d'ufficio*). The strategy was designed explicitly for the 1976 collective trial where the defendants intended to be present in court: it came as a surprise to the lawyers who had hitherto acted for Red Brigades' members in the pre-trial phase as well as in previous court cases for minor individual crimes which they had generally contested only to the extent of refusing to attend.[22] Its symbolic significance – the refusal of any form of mediation between themselves and representatives of the State – corresponded precisely with the refusal to negotiate with the government for Moro's release through any of the neutral agencies proposed (Caritas, the Red Cross, Amnesty International). Here and subsequently, the strategy of revoking the mandate to their chosen defence lawyers was adopted only to cover the courtroom phase of the case. Once the trial had ended, the same lawyers were re-nominated to assist in making an appeal, to be dismissed once again when the trial came back to court. Most of their lawyers seem to have tolerated this strategy, and – since they also acted for the defendants in a range of other judicial investigations apart from the major trial – they continued to have uninterrupted access to their clients in jail.

The combined practices of violence and revocation of defence lawyers threatened to drive a wedge between the representatives of the State (judges, public prosecutors) and the lay members (lawyers, jurors) of the court. First, since according to articles 125–8 of the code of penal procedure all defendants had to have legal representation on pain of the annulment of the entire proceedings, the Red Brigades' refusal to consider themselves defendants and to threaten anyone who took on their defence raised the question of how the State could enrol lawyers to ensure the validity of its own procedures. Second, the murders of Coco and Croce, alongside the general increase of violence in Turin, necessarily affected the recruitment of the public for jury service in the trial. The recourse to violence against individuals and its extension to cover anyone involved in making the trial possible (Croce was the first BR victim outside the group's designated targets of State, factory and DC personnel) could hardly be ignored. Although jurors were not directly threatened by the defendants until the 1978 phase of the trial, severe disruption of their everyday lives and the possibility of physical danger attended active participants in the trial. The problem of enrolling jurors, translatable into a public evaluation of the readiness of the population to support the State against the armed groups, had to be overcome to enable the trial to take place.

Enrolling lawyers and jurors

The judges' immediate response to the Red Brigades' revocation of their lawyers was to follow the law prescribing consultation with the president of the local Bar Council (in the Turin case, Croce) and subsequently direct nomination of suggested replacements. That procedure immediately widened participation to include lawyers who were wholly unsympathetic to the defendants and without professional experience of criminal law, let alone trials for political violence, and who refused to accept nomination.[23] Their refusal provoked a series of conflicts within the local lawyering community and between lawyers and the court judges, which translated the Red Brigades' demands into a series of legal disputes having little to do with political violence. The translation of an issue concerning only a tiny minority of lawyers into a more general conflict was encouraged by the lack of solidary bonds both between lawyers and the judiciary and among lawyers themselves. First, unlike in some other western societies no career path in Italy links the two professions so that no informal networks develop between members of the two categories on that basis. In a survey of Milanese lawyers in 1978, for example, 91 per cent had no dealings with magistrates outside their work and only 17 per cent described their relations as cordial or friendly. One-third of lawyers saw the two categories as explicitly antagonistic rather than collaborators with common interests.[24] Second, among the local community of lawyers, the reluctance of most practitioners to become involved with cases of political violence or to see issues deriving from it as of more general professional concern left isolated those members who did become involved. When in 1976, Croce solicited individual responses on the question whether direct compulsory nomination by the court to defend BR members was acceptable, only 10 per cent of Turin's lawyers replied. The situation was little different in Milan: in 1977 a mere 1 per cent of the city's 3700 lawyers agreed to let their names be put forward by the Bar Council for nomination if necessary.[25] In managing the subsequent conflict, the strategies adopted by Turin's lawyers attempted to widen its scope and to avoid a purely local resolution of the issue: the responses by the judges aimed, in the event successfully, to keep the conflict restricted and thus to contain the powers of violence to exploit existing divisions within and between the relevant institutions.

The Turin lawyers' public reasons for resisting nomination as defence lawyers were various: a general conviction that defendants who wished to should be able either to defend themselves or simply to refuse a lawyer, the impossibility in any trial of employing their professional skills on behalf of clients who rejected and threatened them, the ideological refusal to defend anyone capable of carrying out the kind of actions vaunted by the Red Brigades. The last sentiment was powerfully enhanced after the murder of Croce in 1977 when members of the governing body of the Bar Council announced that they would never defend anyone who had approved of their president's murder. Their efforts, embodied in a series of formal demands between 1976 and 1978, to escape from what many saw as an impossible position took four directions, all of which were essentially designed to extend the dimensions of the conflict beyond the Turin courtroom and to invoke the intervention of external actors. First, the nominated lawyers repeatedly asked that the court transmit the issue of the *difensore d'ufficio* to the Constitutional Court, arguing that the obligation on defendants to have legal representation (introduced by the Fascist 1930 code) contravened both the Constitution and the European Convention on Human Rights to which Italy was a signatory. Second, in late 1976, Croce himself sought to get an explicit judicial recognition of the incompatibility between the defendants and the lawyers imposed on them by denouncing to the public prosecutor in Bologna the (actionable) threats made by the Red Brigades against the specific nominees. Third, he also endeavoured to persuade politicians to debate the draft proposal to alter the law which his Turin colleagues had submitted to them. Finally, the issue was submitted to the national council of the profession in the hope that its members would transform an issue then confined to Turin into a matter for wide discussion and resolution by the government. On each of these different dimensions the conflict could have been widened to incorporate other actors, remote from the immediate pressures of Turin itself and the context in which the issue had arisen.

None of the attempts succeeded. The profession's national council rejected the arguments against obligatory legal representation; the political élite took no action to put the bill on the parliamentary agenda; and the Bologna court, two weeks before Croce's murder, refused to initiate penal proceedings on the grounds that the threats were insufficiently serious. In Turin itself the trial judge refused to transmit the issue to the Constitutional Court, rejected all general proposals for dispensation of the lawyers he had nominated and invoked sanctions against the nominees whose grounds for refusal he considered specious. In 1978 a total of 55 lawyers in fact refused to serve before the necessary group of 20, of very diverse ideological and professional composition, could be finally completed. What united them in accepting, and thus permitted the trial to take place, were local forms of immediate interpersonal solidarity on which, once the attempt to relocate the decision elsewhere had failed, collaboration with the court rested. The general feeling was expressed by one participant as a refusal to stand aside at the expense of a further nominee for whose eventual fate – should the Red Brigades carry out their threats – he would feel morally responsible. Another lawyer, who on the eve of the trial was determined to refuse, changed her mind on the following day as an act of solidarity with a police acquaintance murdered that morning.[26] In the trial itself, unable and unwilling to try to defend their 'clients' in any routine sense, the lawyers declared their intention to act as guarantors of the procedural and substantive legality of the trial.

Although the Red Brigades maintained their strategy in later trials in Turin and elsewhere, no further case of genuine impediment to a trial's taking place occurred. No doubt learning from Turin's experience, the Bar Council in Milan initially obtained informal advice from the various political parties on the names of sympathetic lawyers prepared to be nominated. However, after opposition from members who regarded that method as unduly politicising the issue, the Council drew up a list of lawyers who had already acted in that capacity and who were in fact subsequently regularly nominated by courts. The practice ensured that the number of lawyers involved in the trials was kept restricted, and effectively routinised what might otherwise have been a continually unpredictable response. Together with the enrolment of the other lay category of participant, the jurors, it permitted the State to conduct its judicial rituals locally, fixing the principal limits for the reconsideration of the past.

The composition of an Italian assise court requires six lay members of the public (and up to ten substitutes) to sit alongside the two professional judges and participate in both verdict and sentence. The escalation of violence in Turin in 1976–7 and the murders of Coco and Croce deterred even that small number from accepting to serve. Only four jurors could be found when the court reconvened in May 1977 and the proceedings had to be postponed until 1978. The refusal of the symbolic representatives of the local population to associate themselves with the State threatened the very possibility of holding the trial, as well as portraying the community as uncommitted spectators of a two-cornered contest between the Red Brigades and their political antagonists. In early 1978, therefore, the Regional Anti-Fascist Committee, largely prompted by the PCI, took up the issue of jury representation by circulating a petition demanding that the trial take place and offering through their signatures solidarity to all participants. Thanks to considerable party and union mobilisation, a total of nearly 200 000 signatures was achieved in the ten days before the trial began: ultimately roughly one-third of Turin's population signed.[27] In February 1978, too, the government passed legislation to facilitate the selection of an adequate number of jurors.

Notwithstanding those initiatives, the jury was only formed with great difficulty. It took 143 nominations, which included 134 refusals by men and women who preferred to risk a small fine if their formal reasons for declining were not accepted, before the necessary complement was reached. The general reluctance to participate raised a doubt about the jurors who did accept: might only those who were already convinced of the defendants' guilt and of the need to punish them severely accept selection, thus increasing the likelihood of a sentence wholly disproportionate to these particular defendants' acts of violence or the actual evidence against them and compromising the entire project of processing political violence according to the normal penal code, procedures and equitable punishment? The fear was accentuated by the recontextualisation of the violence being judged: while the specific charges related to the years 1970–4 and included no murders or woundings, the trial was of course taking place in a phase characterised by far more serious violence. The court might therefore be tempted into providing a form of *de facto* recognition for the defendants' claim to be politically responsible for every action, past, present and future, over the Red Brigades' signature; and a harsh sentence might establish a clear symbolic unity between all BR members, jailed or free, as well as provoking conflicts among their opponents over its justice. The mixed judge–jury system, in which decisions are formally unanimous even though they may be taken by majority vote, allows for the judges' own professionally-formed opinions to be overridden by a strong lay consensus.[28]

In the event such fears proved groundless. Following the very liberal conduct of proceedings by the presiding judge, the defendants were given what were regarded as substantially appropriate sentences of between 5 and 14 years' imprisonment, calculated with close regard to the specific evidence incriminating each individual. No concessions were made to the Red Brigades' claim of collective responsibility and no conviction was based on an individual's mere ideological adhesion to the group without further proof.[29] Moreover, whether or not the Turin decision had any particular direct effect, it was indicative of a generally non-punitive stance by courts up until 1980. In at least three other well-known cases – the trials of the members of the *Collettivo autonomo del Policlinico* in Rome in 1978, the *Senza Tregua* group in Turin in 1979 and of the alleged (and later proven) BR affiliates in Genoa in 1980 – the courts opted for conviction on less serious charges than the public prosecutor had argued for or handed down light sentences or acquitted the defendants altogether. Despite the context of increasing violence courts generally showed themselves reluctant to convict on little evidence – which was commonly all the police had available until after 1980. Indeed, it may be that the visible restraint in sentences was a major influence on the widespread public perception that the State's response had been in fact too liberal.[30] Among the participants in armed struggle the court outcomes may have encouraged a feeling of impunity; but they probably also ensured that the claim, made by the Red Brigades in particular, that the State was so remorseless in its indiscriminate repression as to necessitate a wholly clandestine recourse to repeated murders never achieved wide plausibility among other users of violence. The trials did not serve, therefore, to unify the armed community as they might easily have done.

Finally, apart from demonstrating that indeed 'the revolution' could be put on trial and providing examples of enrolment strategies for lawyers and jurors to be followed elsewhere, the successful management by the Turin court compelled the Red Brigades progressively to rewrite their own intentions for the trial. In stating their aims initially as preventing it taking place at all, then as showing that the State would have to violate its own rules to convict members and, finally, claiming that the group's primary objective had in any case been to defend its own political identity, the group progressively retreated towards a purely defensive use of the courtroom, matching the increasing external importance given to displaying identity as a major message in violence after 1978.[31] The concern to use the courtroom as a key arena for the negotiation and renegotiation of defendants' identities was reinforced after 1980 by the juxtaposition of still-convinced practitioners of violence alongside defendants who had come to renounce armed struggle.

CAN CONFESSIONS BE CHALLENGED? MILAN 1983

Typical of such occasions in many respects was the so-called *Rosso*-Tobagi trial in Milan between March and November 1983. Its context was radically altered with respect to the Red Brigades' trial of 1978: violence had dramatically declined so that 'terrorism' was widely regarded as defeated if not yet extinct and the trials were therefore very clearly public inquests on the past. The *Rosso*-Tobagi proceedings were also characteristic of the larger post-1980 trials in so far as several investigations were united for the single discussion, the prosecution case was based largely on confessions and the courtroom performances by a majority of defendants were designed to ratify discontinuities in their identities.

The trial was, however, distinctive in four ways. First, the entire event was dominated, probably more than any other single trial except the Moro case, by a single action – the murder of the Milanese journalist from *Corriere della Sera* and president of the Association of Lombard Journalists, Walter Tobagi, in May 1980. Second, the trial was the first to explore the direct local links between the apparatchiks of armed groups and the intelligentsia associated with *Autonomia*. It was not therefore surprising to find the most important of the three public prosecutors, Spataro, concluding his final speech with praise for Calogero's more general identification of the same link. Third, the maximally reduced sentences on the principal defendants provided almost a limiting case for the application of the laws rewarding collaboration. If any sentence could provide a focus for public opposition, in the name of justice, to the politically-inspired reintegrative strategy for former members of armed groups, the *Rosso*-Tobagi outcome offered a very clear opportunity. Finally, both the investigations and the trial itself were accompanied by a continuing, minority, challenge to the magistrates' reconstructions which were based on the confessions of a key defendant. No such sustained and precisely-directed onslaught on the major form of evidence occurred elsewhere. By publicly scrutinising and eventually validating a detailed and especially salient confession, the *Rosso*-Tobagi trial illustrates the factors which, on one hand, prevented serious challenge within the court to what would normally be considered an unreliable source of judicial proof and, on the other, permitted the particular kind of external challenge that did take place.

Stratified accounts of armed struggle[32]

In handling the principal segment of courtroom activity – the interrogation of the defendants – the presiding judge in the *Rosso*-Tobagi trial was extremely tolerant. In the effort to realise his explicit aim of understanding the world of armed struggle better, he encouraged extended interventions which often strayed far from the particular individual indictments and which were irrelevant by the normal criteria for the permissible scope of courtroom testimonies. In this case as in others a further ambition was detectable – to allow those defendants who had rejected armed struggle to define and develop their new identities to outsiders in public for the first time, and to seek to draw other irreducibly antagonistic defendants into direct verbal interaction and thus provoke a similar change in their views of their enemies and themselves. To have been able to prompt such shifts was regarded with satisfaction: the judge in the Milan appeal trial of PL-COCORI members in 1985–6 stated that the unexpected decision of a hitherto silent and wholly unrepentant defendant to insist on explaining personally the rationale of armed struggle was the finest compliment paid to him in his entire professional career.[33] In the *Rosso*-Tobagi court 95 defendants took advantage of the judge's liberality to take the stand and provide accounts of armed struggle, in 20 cases as full collaborators, 17 admitting their own responsibilities but refusing to discuss others', 23 offering only very general descriptions of armed struggle, with the remaining 35 either asserting their innocence or remaining equivocal in their stances. The potential confusion of conflicting voices and understandings, based on combinations of different experiences, solidarities and resentments over nearly a decade and on strategic options for legal self-defence, was however drastically reduced by the stratification of the three major forms of account given by defendants. Rather than joining interaction to pursue conflicts, their otherwise antagonistic authors were more explicitly concerned with establishing their own identities by way of contrasts, thus facilitating the orderly validation of the descriptions originally provided by the investigating magistrates.

In one respect the versions offered by the full collaborators had already been validated before coming to court. The arrests of other (often self-confessed) participants, the discovery of bases and arms' caches and the decline in violence all testified to the accuracy of their accounts. Indeed, since in accordance with article 10 of law 304/ 1982 deliberate reticence or false testimony would not only deprive them of all benefits of collaboration but increase their normal sentences, the *pentiti* had every incentive to furnish the most accurate account possible, once the decision to confess had been made. Their testimonies mostly consisted of relatively unvarnished descriptions of a string of separate episodes in a format which aimed partly to reproduce as accurately as possible (sometimes even verbatim) their original information-saturated depositions to the investigating magistrates and thus avoid discrepancies encouraging challenge to their veracity, partly to resist being drawn into confrontations with other defendants on fuller and necessarily more controversial contextualisation of actions, and partly to display the completeness of their rejection of violence by a refusal any longer to use the language in which they had once characterised their involvements. The explicitly-proclaimed abyss between the descriptive vocabularies then and now was reinforced in many cases by a shift from the repertoire of solely political motives for their adoption of violence to that of error, contingency and non-political causes. Specific, casual personal events were given significant weight: the death of a parent, a chance meeting with a former comrade, sentimental attachments and so on. Individualising the formation of commitments in such generically comprehensible terms portrayed their authors as subject to the same kind of determinants on action as the ordinary members of the community they were seeking to rejoin. Sheer contingency was often presented as more important in diverting them into the practices of organised violence than the logic of extreme political conviction. As many insisted, and for which they were at pains to find objective signs, their dissent from armed struggle had begun some time before their arrests and forced exclusion. Also, of course, the portrayal of a steadily increasing detachment from armed struggle, depicted as the consequence both of a human revulsion from violence and a recovery of the rational appreciation of its politically disastrous results, reinforced the stated irreversibility of their choice.

The accounts which *dissociati* gave corroborated the complete confessions only at the point of their authors' individual responsibilities. Generic dissociation from violence was not accepted by the public prosecutor or court as a sign of genuine rejection: admission of prior association or of specific involvement in an action was necessary to earn any reduction in sentence. However, by refusing to name fellow-participants, *dissociati* could offer no challenge to the descriptions provided by full collaborators: even to give a variant (false) account in order to undermine the credibility of confessions and revenge themselves on those who had betrayed them to the police would have created the clear impression of breaching their own claims to value former solidarities by refusing to name names. In keeping with the objective of salvaging the ideal components of the past, the versions offered by *dissociati* emphasised the collective local context for specific acts of violence, presenting them primarily as the prolongation of widespread dimensions of conflict. This stance, both in the *Rosso-Tobagi* trial and elsewhere, was not easy to sustain. On one hand the detailed and inescapable convergence of full confessions often rendered the mere confirmation of individual responsibilities redundant as a contribution to public knowledge of armed struggle and closer to simple recognition of the pointlessness of denial rather than a sign of an authentic repudiation of violence. More extended and active forms of self-criticism were demanded, and were increasingly widely acknow-ledged, by courts.[34] On the other hand, encouraged where possible by presiding judges, the unrepentant continuing members of the armed groups also began to offer versions of the past, destroying the diacritic of silence which had separated them from the other categories of defendants and threatening to dissolve the criteria for the distinctive-ness of the *dissociato* position in particular.

Not until 1983 had any self-proclaimed 'political prisoner' accepted a direct and minimally cooperative relationship with the judiciary. Following the example of Red Brigades' members shortly before, several leading activists from Milan's *Autonomia*-based groups used the *Rosso*-Tobagi trial to break with their own previous refusal to partici-pate in the proceedings; they agreed for the first time to offer their own understandings of armed struggle and to respond to some questions.[35] Their accounts were, however, pitched only at a very general level, insisting on the grass-roots legitimation that political violence had enjoyed and linking the phenomenon to the general evolution of the political system. By refusing to discuss either the organisational dimensions of armed struggle or the specific crimes with which the trial was concerned, the authors ensured that no direct conflict with the versions provided by the *pentiti* and *dissociati* could take place. The preservation of a distinctive descriptive repertoire served to demarcate their political identities and reject any rupture with their earlier selves.

The stratification of the three kinds of account of the past reduced the opportunities to contest the prosecution case using alternative accounts by insiders. In most cases the versions did not intersect closely enough to provide material to justify a formal direct confrontation (*confronto*) between defendants over the details of individual involvement and the organisation of actions; and where a dispute over the details of a particular action did occur, both parties had in any case to admit the central, judicially relevant fact of their own involvement in order for their different descriptions to become plausible. Lawyers wishing to defend actively clients who pleaded innocent were mostly compelled to resort to arousing suspicion about the actual genesis of confessions or the genuineness of their authors' repentance, rather than trying to challenge seriously the specific descriptions which incriminated others. Few significant contestations were made or pursued, despite the very large number of defendants and the length of the period (nearly a decade) covering all the incidents dealt with in the trial. The court therefore accepted the versions provided by full collaborators and the prosecution, sealing the meaning of armed struggle at local level. 124 defendants were convicted, 21 acquitted and 5 sent for retrial by a juvenile court. 38 defendants (one-third of those convicted) had their sentences reduced in accordance with the 1980–2 laws, most controversially in the case of two of the group responsible for Tobagi's murder who were sentenced to the very low total of nine years' jail each and were also granted immdiate release from custody pending definitive confirmation of the verdict at appeal or Cassation level. Although the repentance legislation had been applied by the courts since June 1980, in no previous case had a principal defendant obtained direct release after conviction on so serious a charge. At the point in time when other major *pentiti* had been provisionally freed (Sandalo in November 1982, Peci in early 1983), they had been convicted some 18 months previously and then only for membership of an armed band: neither had yet stood trial for single acts of violence and neither was directly responsible for so dramatic an event as Tobagi's murder. Moreover the *Rosso*-Tobagi decision revealed very starkly the different individual fates for near-identical responsibilities produced by confession: the span of sentences received by the six members of the XXVIII *marzo* group ranged from eight-and-a-half to thirty years imprisonment. No other single case illustrated the potential of the laws to produce such marked disparities and raised such doubts over whether justice could properly be said and seen to have been done. Not surprisingly the court's decision renewed the force of the challenge to the central confession, which came not from other defendants or their lawyers but from the immediate kin and the political party of the principal victim.

Challenging a confession

One public with its own very specific interest in political violence consisted of the kin of the victims. In the case of right-wing violence Action Committees had been formed, notably after the massacres of Brescia (1974) and Bologna (1980), to stimulate and, where necessary, contest the work of magistrates which appeared to be inconclusive or worse in the search for justice. On the side of left-wing violence the likeliest cause for concern lay less in the progress of investigations than in the laws rewarding confessions; for they threatened unacceptably low penalties for what, seen from the perspective of the victims and their families, were irrevocable tragedies demanding proper punishment. Indeed, the scanty evidence available suggests that while the majority of Italians acknowledged the need for such measures, although doubting their efficacy, to end armed struggle, disaggregated local figures show that substantial numbers in specific categories regarded the laws as unacceptable.[36]

Not surprisingly, strong opposition to the laws was regularly reported from the victims' kin. But the conversion of those attitudes into collective mobilisation in defence of their specific concerns was inhibited in several ways. First, without any single event like a bomb massacre to unite directly a sufficient number, the heterogeneity of the kin of victims – who were distributed across many occupational categories and social groups – made concrete solidarity difficult.[37] Second, by the time that most of the serious cases came to court in 1983 the 1982 law had already lapsed, leaving the judicial evaluation of the cases produced by the law as the only focus of attention and opposition and rendering pressure on the political élite redundant. Third, the only way for kin to participate in the trial proceedings was by gaining the right as civil plaintiffs (*parte civile*) to contribute to the identification of responsibilities prior to claiming damages. However, the lawyers representing individual families were concerned with different episodes and sets of defendants; and in any case, many families did not wish to seek civil plaintiff status, on the grounds of confidence in the court's ability to ensure justice or reluctance to re-examine publicly their loss or as a sign of having pardoned the aggressors. For the most part, through their lawyers, kin played a supporting role to the public prosecutor, their presence serving especially as a reminder of the enduring effects of what might in court seem remote events, ignored in the exclusive concern with the conversions and new identities of the defendants. In the *Rosso-Tobagi* trial, however, Tobagi's father advanced a version of respon-sibilities which both differed radically from the confession-based account given by the investigating magistrates and was supported by the victim's political party, the PSI.[38] The conflict illustrates how the mounting of serious challenges to confessions required an alliance between interests inside and outside the courtroom – of kin anxious to secure justice and a political party intent on using for its own political purposes the court's power to determine meanings. The escalation of the conflict showed how the basic dispute was rapidly redefined in the course of its translation to successively higher institutional levels. However, the translation of the challenge outside the court's domain through the aggregation of external interests entailed the self-defeating consequence of the disaggregation of the ultimately essential basis of support in the court itself.

Undermining the confession of Barbone, the principal figure in the XXVIII *marzo* group, met the distinct but convergent concerns of both Tobagi's family and the PSI. First, the successful discrediting of Barbone's account would have entailed the loss of benefits for confession, thus ensuring the lengthy jail sentence appropriate, in the eyes of Tobagi's father, to the crime.[39] Second, a demonstration of the falsity of Barbone's version that Tobagi's murder had been planned and executed solely by the six members of his group would leave space for the Socialist version – that the murder had been decided essentially within Tobagi's work context by anti-Socialist groups hostile to his union activities in the world of journalism and especially the conflict-ridden *Corriere della Sera*, shortly to be deeply implicated in the P2 scandal. The tenacity with which the PSI supported that hypothesis without being able to produce any serious supporting evidence has to be set in the context of the party's increasingly severe criticisms of the judiciary, both on general grounds and specifically for its handling of enquiries into left-wing violence. The frequent and well-publicised incrimination of its local administrators provided a background for the PSI's support in 1983 for stricter political accountability for the judiciary; and the judicial interpretation of the party élite's contacts with fringe areas of armed struggle mentioned in Chapter 4 no doubt contributed to the proposal, in the same year, for a parliamentary enquiry into the judiciary's application of the emergency legislation. The reappropriation of Tobagi as the victim of an obscure plot by his political adversaries in one of Italy's most influential newspapers could provide the PSI itself with the status of target of violence, re-establishing the now apparently less secure boundary between the party and armed groups and implying that perhaps the other accusations too were no more than equally baseless attempts to discredit it.[40]

In the courtroom the challenge focused less on the possible internal inconsistencies in Barbone's confession than on its alleged omissions. Making use of a written text to undermine an oral account, the lawyers for Tobagi's family argued that the document claiming responsibility for the murder was too technical and well-informed on the topic of journalism to have been written by any member of the XXVIII *marzo* group. Two of its affiliates, who had made only partial confessions, initially denied that the group had ever had a collective discussion of its themes and that its real authorship and contents might indeed be attributable to an outside source in private contact with Barbone. But the absence of any positive evidence in favour of the PSI's hypothesis caused the court to reject it and to determine that the decision-making processes issuing in violence were confined to interactions within the armed community itself. Thereafter the conflict was pushed outside the courtroom. As the two XXVIII *marzo* members saw their versions serving quite other purposes than the limited ones of casting doubt on the truthfulness of a former comrade responsible for their arrests, they publicly retracted their suggestions of an external inspiration for the attack on Tobagi and thus deprived the PSI account of even residual courtroom support. From 1983 to 1986 the contest moved to steadily more remote national levels. A series of attacks in *L'Avanti* on the integrity of his investigations caused the public prosecutor in the trial to sue three PSI deputies and four party journalists for defamation; their conviction in 1985 provoked the Socialist Prime Minister, Craxi, to reiterate his colleagues' accusations which in turn led to the magistrates' demand that the CSM consider formally this attack on the judiciary; the President of the Republic, Cossiga, in his role as ex-officio President of the CSM, forbade the Council to debate Craxi's assertions on the grounds that according to the Constitution the Prime Minister was accountable only to Parliament; that ban pro-voked the immediate resignations of the magistrates elected to the CSM which were, however, withdrawn after pressure from Cossiga himself.

In effect the attempt by the PSI to resymbolise Tobagi and to suggest that the boundaries around armed struggle were not simply co-terminous with the active membership of the armed groups had provoked what threatened to become a constitutional crisis. But the very process of translating the issue upwards into wider conflicts also ensured that at local level the opportunities for maintaining the dispute were gradually eliminated. The local-level actors who had originally allowed themselves to be enrolled to support the challenge dissociated themselves once it became clear that their own accounts designed to maintain their identities in court were being recontextual-ised as elements in the forum of party rivalries to which they were indifferent. The Tobagi trial shows how the boundary between the institutions of Italian society and direct responsibilities for violence at local level were sealed. The April 7 trial sought to reopen those boundaries in a national direction.

WAS THERE A SINGLE ARMED PARTY? ROME 1983–4

The April 7 trial was the most ambitious attempt in the judicial context to provide a history of armed struggle. The hypothesis that since 1971 a unified project had bound together the apparent differences in signatures and types of violence had been translated into judicial action by the Padua and Rome magistrates with the arrests of April and December 1979. Since the trial itself, finally opening after two false starts on 24 February 1983, was not concluded until 12 June 1984, the still judicially-unverified possibility of a single coordinated armed party provided the backdrop for the progressive determination of local responsibilities in the trials of the early 1980s. Like the failure of the Red Brigades to impose a unity on armed struggle through Moro's kidnapping, the prosecution in the April 7 trial ultimately failed to re-translate local fragmentation into a national-level unity around a single project. On the other side, just as Moro's kidnapping produced the first public scission from the Red Brigades, so the events of the April 7 trial ratified the dispersal of the intelligentsia of armed struggle and of its attempt to provide a positive, strictly political reading for the subversion of the previous decade as a justifiable antagonism not defined by the recourse to violence.

The difficulties for both prosecution and defendants stemmed in part from the context in which their accounts were presented. Given the hypothesis of an all-embracing unity of armed struggle, any judicial verification would necessarily contain a strongly symbolic component, since the number and nature of the relevant defendants, indictments and actions would have to be drastically selective. Equally the actual selection, and the evidence adduced to justify it, constituted, *faute de mieux*, the materials through which the defendants were compelled to make good their claim to be innocent of direct involvement in violence and to an unequivocal and distinctive political identity. The assembling of the case and its management in court help to explain why both prosecution and defence found it impossible to sustain their versions of violence.

Assembling indictments, defendants and evidence

The eventual set of 46 indictments on which 71 defendants were arraigned ranged in seriousness from armed insurrection against the State to the theft of a book of stamps. Twelve defendants were accused of armed insurrection against the State; 40 (including 10 of the 12) of having organised and directed an unnamed armed band between 1971 and 1979, and 27 of participation in the band: 24 defendants also had to answer charges relating to specific offences committed in the period 1973–5. The set of indictments and defendants constituted an extraordinary judicial *bricolage* which pressed at least to the limit, and in some places beyond it, the coherent recontextualisation of the past embodyable in the contents of a single trial.

The original arrest warrants issued in Rome and Padua on 6 and 7 April 1979 postulated a direct link between three groups: *Potere Operaio, Autonomia Operaia Organizzata* and the Red Brigades. Twelve men were accused of having coordinated the actions of all three groups, which were treated unproblematically as unified organisations, and one (Negri) was also charged with direct involvement in the Moro kidnapping and armed insurrection. Over the next two years, prior to the sentence committing the defendants for trial in 1981, the initial version of the structure of the armed community was modified in several ways. First, the organisational dimension in which the defendants were alleged to have participated was made increasingly abstract. The early charges at least linked them to the uncontroversial exemplar of an armed group, the Red Brigades. That was an important tie since neither *Potere Operaio* nor *Autonomia Operaia* had previously been characterised juridically as an armed band although *Autonomia*'s local emanations, which had not been regarded as part of a single nationwide organisation, had sometimes been indicted as subversive associations. However, the link between the defendants and the Red Brigades was quietly dropped in July 1979 and was formally abandoned in November 1980 when the Roman magistrates completed their initial enquiries into the Moro affair. It was replaced, however, by the extension to the original defendants of the charge of armed insurrection directed by a now unnamed organisation (appearing in judicial documents simply with a capitalised O) responsible for having coordinated other, also unnamed, armed bands. No description was given of the nature, structure or continuity of the relationships among its alleged participants that could unequivocally warrant its description as, precisely, an 'organisation'.[41]

The difficulty of delineating a clear armed band was aggravated by the process of selective incorporation into, and exclusion from, the Rome trial of the specific crimes alleged to make manifest the organisation's existence. The particular set of indictments came from only one phase of a three-phase cumulative investigation, each part of which contributed nevertheless to the supporting evidence for the overall hypothesis. The first caesura came with the passage of investigative responsibilities from Padua to Rome, considered the appropriate jurisdiction for the Moro and, subsequently, armed insurrection charges, leaving the local activities of the *Autonomia* component to be investigated in Padua. To Rome also went the documentary evidence supporting the charges. The second phase, beginning in December 1979, rested very largely on the confessions of the former affiliate of *Potere Operaio*, Fioroni, who recounted only the very early years of armed struggle prior to his arrest and had acknowledged his own participation in the most serious single event. His account generated the only specific crimes of which the minority of the defendants were accused: two murders, in the course of a kidnapping and an armed robbery, one attempted kidnapping of an industrialist, one act of industrial sabotage, three (actual or projected but in each instance failed) armed robberies, three thefts and two cases of possession of firearms and explosives. All those offences had been carried out around Milan and Venice between 1973 and 1975: none therefore concerned the period of maximum left-wing violence (in which the group itself was supposed to have maintained its existence) and none could be described as an act of 'terrorism'.[42] The only evidence on the crucial intensive period of left-wing violence between 1976 and 1979 came from the enquiry's third phase – the use of the confessions of the protagonists of the *Rosso*-Tobagi trial, with firsthand accounts of violence in Milan but only hearsay or second-hand evidence for other cities. That evidence concerned only the local set of *Autonomia*'s leaders associated with *Rosso*, whose specific responsibilities in Milan's violence were in fact to be examined in the *Rosso*-Tobagi courtroom, not in the April 7 trial in Rome. In sum, the only acts of violence specifically attributed to the alleged leaders of a putative unified armed party in the trial intended to verify that hypothesis came very largely from one city: no single episodes could be found to cover the other three primary centres of left-wing violence – Rome, Turin and Genoa.

Not surprisingly the heterogeneous array of charges and evidence produced an equally diversified set of defendants. The majority of the twelve men and women accused of armed insurrection were long-term activists of the extra-parliamentary Left, some with a shared militancy going back to the early 1960s, extended in the 1970s in a network of ties whose strength waxed and waned, embodied in their contributions to the journals and broadsheets of *Autonomia*. But alongside the former members of *Potere Operaio* and *Autonomia* stood three self-proclaimed members of separate armed groups (BR, PL, FCC). If the intention behind their inclusion was to symbolise the unity of armed struggle, then their minor status in those organisations did not seriously reinforce the sense of any significant connections. However, rather than these somewhat anomalous presences, a much more significant aspect was the absence, for all or many of the court proceedings, of the central defendants. The three leaders, first of *Potere Operaio*, then of *Autonomia*, had been excluded or excluded themselves. One (Piperno) could not be tried on the charges against him since the extradition agreement with France permitted only in-dictment in connection with the Moro kidnapping; another (Scalzone) had fled to France after release from custody on grounds of ill-health in 1981 and could not be extradited; and the third (Negri), although present at the outset, also escaped to France after his release from jail following election to Parliament as a Radical Party candidate in July 1983.[43] A further three less well-known defendants also found refuge abroad. Among the remainder a particular unity was imposed on a core set of 15 by their having spent four years in preventive detention before the trial began; for the charges of armed insurrection and murder which carried life sentences permitted the maximum period of pre-trial custody, in this case arousing the concern of Amnesty International.[44] That externally-imposed solidarity among the highly articulate minority of defendants largely disguised their heterogeneity and the very uneven weight of evidence against individuals from different positions, geographical and functional, in their milieu. The case that they were called on finally to answer had begun with the intuition of a magistrate in Padua, had been more fully investigated in Rome and had relied very largely for specific evidence on events in Milan. Translated into the materials actually presented in court, the primary evidence extracted from texts and confessions to establish the existence of a single armed party suggested that: in 1971–2 some of PO's leaders had encouraged an amateurish and short-lived interest in obtaining weapons and using molotov cocktails on demonstrations; mostly the same leaders, now associated with *Autonomia*, had sought to finance their political activities by supporting two criminal actions gone very wrong and had had occasional and informal meetings with early Red Brigades' members; and between 1976 and 1979 the specifically Milanese intelligentsia associated with *Autonomia* had offered ideological support and practical coordination of violence by the local apparatchiks. The intrinsic difficulty of clearly confirming or refuting the general hypothesis as supported by so dispersed a set of allegations was aggravated by the events in court.

Failed confrontations

Besides declaring themselves innocent on all charges, the major defendants announced that they intended to use the trial to affirm their own political identities and to challenge the extremely reductive, organisation-focused history of armed struggle that had been written inside and outside the courtroom by the *pentiti*. Their case rested on maintaining a distinction between subversion and terrorism: 'that we have had nothing to do with terrorism is obvious; that we have been subversive is equally obvious. Between these two self-evident assertions our trial will be played out.'[45] They argued that terrorism (then exemplified in the GAP and BR) had emerged ideologically outside the movement of 1968–9 of which *Autonomia* represented both the heir and the barrier against clandestine violence, especially directed against persons. Furthermore, while the prosecution and the *pentiti* emphasised only the conspiratorial *gesellschaft* dimension of armed struggle, the April 7 defendants claimed to be defending the *gemeinschaft* solidarities of extreme Left politics. They argued for the existence in the 1970s of a culture of antagonism to the State which, while it might generically support the potential social and political creativity of violence, could not be reduced simply to the public face of a clandestine organisation. The different armed groups had in fact variously represented either the antithesis or perversion of that culture. Necessarily, therefore, the versions of the beliefs and structure of the antagonistic community provided by the groups' repentant members were in general deformed and false.

However plausible that description of the irreconcilable contrast between essentially apparatchik and intelligentsia perspectives might be, success in sustaining it in court rested on the opportunity to show clearly that the accounts could indeed yield quite different versions of specific issues, that they could be brought into real rather than purely notional confrontation. Likewise, as the separate identities of *pentito, dissociato* and *irriducibile* had been successfully negotiated in the courtroom through the contrast between the kinds of account offered by each category, so the April 7 intelligentsia required a parallel exemplification of evident differences to uphold their own claims to identity. Since, with three minor exceptions, the defendants insisted on their innocence of direct involvement in violence, the difference could not be displayed within their own ranks but had to be found externally. In the event, however, the interactional exchanges which characterised the court proceedings offered very reduced scope for either solidarity or contrast.

Most importantly, the confrontation with the *pentiti* was evaded at key points on both sides. The principal witness for the prosecution, Fioroni, whose testimony was central to the identification of a clandestine level of organisation in the period 1970–5 as well as to the responsibilities for the most damning specific charges, did not appear in court. Investigations by the judge revealed that after leaving prison in February 1982, he had been granted a passport with the direct approval of the Ministry of the Interior and the Roman judiciary, and he did not intend to return from abroad. Despite his absence, however, and contrary to the inspiration behind the repentance laws that accusations had to be sustained publicly in front of the accused, the court agreed to regard his account as admissable evidence.[46] On

the other side, the refusal of Scalzone and Negri to be present
ensured that the detailed testimony concerning the organisation of
violence in Milan for the later 1970s remained uncontested by the two
defendants alleged to have shared the greatest responsibilities. Since
the accusations against many of the other defendants rested substantially on their relationship to the two protagonists, their evasion of
direct confrontation in court was extremely damaging to all. The
general position was worsened by the full validation of the *pentiti*
accounts of Milan's violence in the *Rosso*-Tobagi verdict which was
reached halfway through the April 7 trial. Some of the 47 defendants
accused solely of having organised or belonged to a criminal association were thus placed in the position of being denied the opportunity
both to confront their accusers directly in the pre-court investigation
(at least two had not seen a magistrate since mid-1979) and to
question the principal prosecution witness in court, while finding
their own positions prejudiced by the failure of fellow-defendants to
appear and contest accusations on the very few specific charges
attributed to the alleged organisation.

As a result the courtroom interaction among judge, public prosecutor and the intelligentsia offered no materials for transcending the
conflicts on the details of highly localised issues towards either the
verification of a single coordination of all left-wing political violence
or the rewriting of the place of armed struggle in extreme Left politics
since 1968. Some interrogations were dominated by the defendants'
attempts to convince the judge and jury that the formal identity of
terms used by themselves and by members of armed groups disguised
very different practical referents and could not be translated into any
kind of organisational affinity. Others dealt with the issue of whether
occasional assistance to practitioners of violence by different individual
defendants amounted to confirmation of the existence of organised
relationships. And yet others occasioned flat contradictions over the
often extremely feeble evidence presented by the prosecution.[47] But
the substantial lack of impact that such exchanges made in forming and
modifying the convictions of judge and jury was confirmed by the very
few references to accounts rendered during the courtroom phase in the
1188-page motivation for the verdict and sentence.

Already separated from any continuing involvement with extra-
parliamentary politics by their lengthy detention, the defendants
became increasingly divided amongst themselves in the course of the
trial.[48] In many cases the level of initial solidarity had been largely
residual, based on an already concluded (but still valued) period of

common militancy rather than active collaboration at the time of their arrests – although their defence of the strategy of dissociation among fellow-prisoners gave it a new focus in jail. Under the pressures of unevenly distributed evidence and of the difficulty of communicating a single alternative reading of armed struggle, their solidarity was publicly ruptured in February 1984. A hostile open letter to Negri announced the severing of relationships once his intention not to return to court became clear; the three Milanese defendants most clearly implicated in violence by the evidence of *pentiti* acknowledged their role in a letter to the judge; and the hitherto united set of defence lawyers came to disagree over the appropriate court tactics after their clients' divergences. The end of their solidarity of course worked against any residual chance of successfully asserting a common identity as 'subversives' clearly demarcated from 'terrorists', so that the court's verdict refusing to accept such a distinction was probably anticipated. On the charges of organisation and membership of an armed band and on its particular crimes 55 defendants were therefore found guilty, 14 acquitted and 2 granted immunity from punishment. The 12 defendants charged with armed insurrection were, however, acquitted on grounds of insufficient evidence – a curious verdict since it implied that the insurrection had indeed taken place although these particular individuals could not be unequivocally shown to have participated in it. Further enquiries should therefore have been set in train to identify its real organisers and participants, although the trial of all known Red Brigades' members on the same charge remained to come to court.[49]

If the April 7 trial testified to the failure to re-read the left-wing violence of the 1970s as the product of a single insurrectional strategy, it also both contributed to and ratified the end of the intelligentsia milieu of armed struggle. The definitive loss of collective solidarity paralleled the individualising of reconstructed biographies in the other milieux of the apparatchiks and locals, which had been occurring in the sequence of trials elsewhere. The boundaries of the armed community remained locally-determined with the primacy ascribed to dispersed local meanings, and most of its adherents were progressively reintegrated into Italian society through the decisions of local courts. The disappearance of both BR and *Autonomia* poles of the milieu which had formerly provided the descriptive means to legitimate violence closed the *anni di piombo*. All future legitimations would have to draw on quite different intellectual resources to make the practice of delivering damage thinkable or livable.

7 CUI PRODEST?

The preceding chapters have examined the patterns of enrolment and mobilisation against political violence by its opponents in the institutions of the factory, politics, police forces and the judiciary. Incorporated wherever possible have been the uneven and fragmentary data on the attitudes of different publics to particular aspects of violence and to the immediate institutional responses they evoked, as they were captured in contemporary surveys, questionnaires and referenda. In this concluding chapter I want to focus on some broader consequences not so far treated. I shall examine the translation, on one hand, of views on political violence and, on the other, of organisational innovations to cope with armed struggle into more general patterns of political allegiance and judicial activity; and I shall also consider how the steady rate of conversion towards the repudiation of violence among members of the armed community (from 1983 onwards, with very few exceptions, to be found in jail) has contributed to altering the general relationship between the prison system and society. The specific issues addressed are of three kinds.

In the first place, clandestine left-wing violence in Italy did not provoke a regime collapse such as, say, the Tupamaros caused in Uruguay. But what effects, if any, did it have on the perceived legitimacy of the State and the relations among the political parties? Second, no drastic restrictions of civil or judicial rights occurred on a scale to match the reactions in West Germany or Northern Ireland. But how enduring were the changes in judicial procedures introduced between 1974 and 1982 and to what extent were the investigative and courtroom strategies which had been successful in processing political violence extended to other areas of judicial intervention? Third, the isolation of 'terrorism' had demanded a drastic strengthening of the boundaries between prisons and society. How far was their rapid weakening in the wake of the decline in violence the unintended consequence of the strategy of differential reincorporation of former members of armed struggle into the political community? Such questions point to the necessity to examine as closely as possible the full chain of consequences attributable both to violence itself and to the institutional responses which it elicits in order to understand the phenomenon and its potential more clearly.

THE CONSERVATIVE EFFECTS OF LEFT-WING VIOLENCE?

It is widely stated that in liberal democracies clandestine left-wing violence is not only incapable of achieving its declared objectives of social and political transformation but is also condemned to bring about precisely the opposite consequences – namely, to (re)legitimate the State and prompt a conservative shift in political opinion. As far as its professed aims were concerned, the record of Italian armed struggle is clear: neither its long-term revolutionary goals nor short-term 'disarticulations' were achieved. The only action that could lay claim to more than transient disruptive success was the kidnapping and murder of Moro: the DC lost one of its most experienced leaders, albeit in direct control only of a very small faction in the party, and the PCI was deprived of a sympathetic and attentive interlocutor.[1] Nevertheless it was only Moro's capture itself which convinced the PCI to overcome its anger at the DC's reneging on an apparent agreement over the composition of the new government and to join the parliamentary majority. In any case given the extent of grassroots hostility in both the DC and PCI to their parties' collaboration, the government of national solidarity – and the historic compromise policy – was likely to have been short-lived, even without Moro's murder.[2] Furthermore the escalation of political violence was insufficient in its own right to preserve the formula of national solidarity: the PCI in fact withdrew its active support of the government in January 1979 during the most violent months of the entire decade.

No government, national or local, was brought down by conflicts set off by an act of political violence, not even in the aftermath of the Cirillo kidnapping in which between 1981 and 1985 the steady revelation of details of negotiations with the BR led to several episodes of direct party confrontation.[3] Ironically, the case in which a government came closest to falling was in the wake of an act of international violence, the hijacking of the *Achille Lauro*, which prompted Craxi's (rejected) resignation in October 1985. Furthermore, even at the individual level, politicians who were directly affected by political violence in different ways did not find their careers permanently interrupted. The Minister of the Interior, Cossiga, survived his resignation after the Moro kidnapping to become Prime Minister in the following year; and in 1980 he overcame the attempt to impeach him, for an alleged breach of secrecy concerning a confession made in regard to the son of a colleague, to be subsequently elected Head of State in 1985. That colleague, Donat-Cattin, was himself forced to resign as vice-secretary of the DC as a consequence of the episode but returned to Parliament in 1985 and was appointed Minister of Health in the following year. Similarly although Cirillo had been compelled to give up his public positions after the first official confirmations of the ransom paid on his behalf to the Red Brigades, he had returned to a less visible but none the less public role by 1984. No doubt some of the lesser-known local victims of the Red Brigades' attacks renounced further political activity; but probably in at least as many cases the victims overcame their often severe injuries to maintain their involvements: some indeed attributed a heightening in political commitment precisely to the psychological reactions to their wounding.[4]

If the explicitly disruptive objectives of the armed groups were not achieved, how far was their violence responsible for increasing the levels of consensus enjoyed by the State and by the political parties of the Centre-Right? Tracing such broadly conservative effects is obviously rather difficult. On one hand, it is extremely hard to separate out the independent effects of political violence, and left-wing violence in particular, from the multitude of other issues affecting shifts in political allegiance. On the other hand, answers to counterfactual questions – what would have happened if there had been no political violence? – can be at best highly speculative. Probably no more can be shown than whether political violence appears to have had a *decisive* impact, rather than any impact at all, at national and local levels: what conclusions does the evidence of survey and electoral results license for Italy between 1970 and 1984?

As far as the esteem in which State and government were held, the data indicate that even the most intensive period of violence did not stimulate a general increase in consensus. Although in 1967 identical minorities of Italians (22 per cent) believed that the State functioned reasonably well and that ministers were competent and honest, those figures had plummeted to an again-identical 3 per cent by 1974: by 1980 they had shown only insignificant or no recovery (5 and 3 per cent respectively).[5] Clearly the sharp increase in political violence in the second half of the decade did little in itself to reduce the generalised disaffection towards the State and politicians epitomised in the results of the 1978 referendum on the public financing of political parties. No doubt the perhaps widespread conviction that segments of the State were actively involved in, or at least tolerant of, violence contributed to the failure of violence to re-aggregate explicitly-expressed consensus around the major institutions of the regime.

A similar absence of effects is visible in the electoral performance of Left and Centre-Right parties both at national level and in the cities most affected by violence. Any hopes that the more conservative political groups would draw direct benefit from the prolonged existence of an insecurity-inducing violence were in fact doomed to disappointment. In the national elections for the Chamber of Deputies the combined vote of the DC, PLI and MSI (including the Monarchists) increased very slightly (50.6 per cent to 51.4 per cent) between 1968 and 1972, but the advance was primarily attributable to gains made in the south where almost all the (limited) political violence was the responsibility of the extreme Right. Thereafter it was steadily reduced in each election, falling to 42.6 per cent in 1983. Moreover, the extreme right-wing group, the MSI-DN, which might have been expected to benefit at least in the years dominated by an unequivocally left-wing violence, saw its overall support actually eroded by two-fifths between 1972 and 1979.

Likewise the fears of the Left that violence would necessarily provoke a shift of votes away from its parties, no matter how strongly they accentuated their support for the existing State, were not borne out. The combined vote of the PCI, PSI and the changing smaller formations of the extreme Left (PSIUP, PdUP, PR, Manifesto, DP and others) lost ground between 1968 and 1972, made a major advance in 1976 (reaching 46.6 per cent), followed by a slight decline (to 45 per cent) by 1983 – a trajectory which largely reproduced the performance of its major component, the PCI. Again, the most intense years of left-wing violence did little electoral damage to the Left as a whole: the losses sustained by the PCI between 1976 and 1979 were attributable not to any shift of votes to the parties of the Centre but to former supporters' absentions due to the disappointments provoked either by unrealistically high expectations once the Left had secured power in major cities in 1975 or by the party's abandonment of a serious opposition role in national politics.[6] The phenomenon of electoral abstention, regarded by the Left as a possible consequence of a threatened general retreat from the public domain in the face of violence and likely to be especially damaging to its own support, actually declined during the first phase of violence but showed a rise, 9.1 to 15.9 per cent, between 1976 and 1983. However it is judged to have affected all parties equally and to be at least partly explicable in terms of contingent factors (the reduction of voting age to 18, and the inclusion on the electoral role of emigrants long settled abroad) rather than any direct reactions to violence. In any case abstention appears to have been a geographically-diffuse phenomenon, equally significant in areas which had seen little or nothing of armed struggle.[7]

If any clearly conservative effects of violence on political allegiance did occur, they ought to be most visible in the four cities where the incidence of violence was greatest – effects which unless examined separately might be concealed by the aggregate national figures. However the electoral evidence for Rome, Milan, Turin and Genoa (Table 7.1) in parliamentary and local council elections indicates that, as at national level, the concentration of violence did not damage the Left or aid the Centre-Right.

TABLE 7.1   *Electoral results for the Left and Centre-Right in Rome, Milan, Turin and Genoa 1972–85**

Cities	National				Municipal			
	1972	*1976*	*1979*	*1983*	*1970†*	*1975*	*1980*	*1985*
Rome								
Left	36.4	45.8	49.3	44.6	33.7	44.7	47.2	42.5
Centre-Right	53.8	45.9	46.0	42.2	49.5	45.4	41.3	44.8
Milan								
Left	39.0	45.8	49.9	45.5	37.0	48.9	50.3	48.0
Centre-Right	48.3	41.4	40.7	35.9	43.3	38.7	39.1	35.2
Turin								
Left	40.0	51.7	53.6	50.2	39.4	53.0	55.5	48.2
Centre-Right	45.2	37.8	37.0	33.1	44.9	35.7	35.4	35.1
Genoa								
Left	46.6	55.9	57.0	54.1	47.3	54.9	52.1	52.4
Centre-Right	41.6	36.8	35.8	32.8	37.0	35.4	31.0	33.9

* Elections to Chamber of Deputies for the national figures. The Left consists of the PCI, PSI, PdUP-DP, PR: the Centre-Right, the DC, PLI, MSI-DN. The inclusion of the PSDI and PRI would not alter the general picture.
† Data for 1971 in the case of Rome.
SOURCES
Newspaper reprints of results for each election. J. Ruscoe, *The Italian Communist Party 1976–81* (London: Macmillan, 1982) p. 238, Table 10.3.

The pattern of voting at both national and local level shows that with only insignificant exceptions the Left made steady gains and the Centre-Right equally steady losses in all four cities between 1970 and 1983. The first serious decline in support for the Left occurred in the municipal elections of 1985, well after the acknowledged failure of armed struggle. Whether or not shifts in voting due to the impact of violence were compensated by reverse movements based on other factors, it is clear that the issue of violence alone was not sufficient to provoke any trend at all towards either the main party under attack, the DC, or the Right in general. Only in Rome did the DC itself make a small gain (0.3 per cent) between the national elections of 1976 and 1979, the period in which the assault on the party was largely concentrated. Furthermore the local existence of violence seems to have done little damage to the electoral fortunes of the extreme Left groups and parties closest to the community of armed struggle. While the contamination through armed provocation of their major modes of public protest certainly reduced the attractions of collective mobilisation, it is also true, first, that the political activities of the extreme Left were in organisational and ideological disarray *before* the most intensive years of left-wing violence between 1976 and 1979; and, second, that the electoral fortunes of its changing representatives and cartels, which drew on much wider support than active membership alone, suffered no drastic decline. Indeed in Turin, for example, the combined vote for the PdUP and *Democrazia Proletaria* increased from 1.3 to 1.8 per cent between the municipal elections of 1975 and 1980, and the Radical Party, participating in the national elections of 1976 and 1979, improved its share of the vote from 2.4 to 6.7 per cent. Similar patterns were visible for the extreme Left in the other major cities.

The lack of decisive impact of violence on the electoral support for each party can be seen in a still narrower context, by considering some of the results which closely followed dramatic cases of violence or direct attacks on candidates themselves. The only occasion on which a clear transfer of votes was detectable occurred in the partial provincial and municipal elections held immediately after Moro's murder, which showed a significant sympathy vote for the DC among the 4 million electors.[8] The normal pattern of the absence of any direct consequences was clearly indicated by the 1979 elections in Genoa which were immediately preceded by the wounding of three DC politicians, two of whom were actually candidates for the national and European parliaments. Neither was successful and their party, far from benefiting from any revulsion against the attacks, saw its support eroded from 30.2 to 27.6 per cent.

At national, local and individual candidate levels, therefore, the voting patterns in the four most violent cities confirmed the indications offered by the results of the 1978 and 1981 referenda on two major measures in the emergency legislation. While in all four cities, as in Italy generally, support for the retention of the Reale and

Cossiga laws and of the sentence of life imprisonment was over-whelming, it was nevertheless below the levels both of the national average and of cities elsewhere in the north with a much lower incidence of political violence. Even on so specific an indicator of the reaction to armed struggle the most immediately affected audiences offered a less convinced pronouncement for more rigorous response than more distant publics. Failing to disrupt the patterns of relation-ships among party élites by assault and direct confrontation in the kidnappings, the armed groups also failed to disturb the distribution of support enjoyed by each party through the ballot box. Neither by attraction nor by reaction did the Red Brigades, with their distinctive attention to the political domain, succeed in achieving any clear impact on the Italian political system as a whole or on the position of specific actors within it.

THE JUDICIARY AND THE EMERGENCY

Although no major innovations such as special anti-terrorist tribunals or courts without juries were made to the Italian judicial system, other direct and indirect effects can be charted. The effects were attributable both to the emergence of political violence and to the methods successfully used to combat it, and they contributed to a thoroughgoing debate and redefinition of the place of the judiciary which is far from concluded at the time of writing. As far as the longer-term consequences are concerned, therefore, the balance-sheet can only be provisional.

The most evident consequence of political violence was the block-age of the post-1968 movement towards not merely the extension of individual civil liberties but also to their embodiment in a wholly recast judicial system. Despite the (mainly right-wing) political violence of the period 1969–74, Parliament had approved a frame-work for a new code of judicial procedures in the latter year; but by the time the government had prepared its detailed proposals, the increase in left-wing violence and the difficulties of, so to speak, rebuilding the ship while at sea in a storm caused the suggested changes to be shelved. Within that existing framework the emergency legislation had restricted the discretionary powers of the judiciary in both its investigative and judging functions. First, the gradual subtraction of sole control over the detention of citizens – even if only for short periods and, in the case of the introduction in 1980 of police detention (*fermo di polizia*), as a temporary measure – circumscribed the magistrates' powers. A further limitation was established by the effective abrogation of the right to release from custody anyone charged with a 'terrorist' offence carrying at least a four-year sentence (most relevantly, membership of an armed band), no matter what the magistrate's assessment of the value of detention for a particular individual might be. At the same time of course, from the suspects' point of view, the inability of their inquisitors to do anything but commit them to jail represented an extension of judicial power; and it made the discretion exercised by magistrates over the assessment of evidence potentially justifying arrest a key point of conflict. Second, the determination of sentences was strongly constrained by the laws rewarding the rejection of armed struggle. In effect, while the judiciary was delegated a major role in the management of the frontier between political and armed communities, its general freedom of action was itself constrained by the dual direction of the principal legislation between 1974 and 1982.

In the mid-1980s, once the decline in political violence appeared to be definitive, both trends were reversed. On one hand, in 1984 Parliament renewed its debate on a revised judicial system, reaching agreement in 1987 on the shift from an inquisitorial to a modified adversarial framework to be introduced within two years. On the other hand, most of the recent restrictions on the magistrature's use of discretion lapsed or were abolished. Thus the police powers of temporary detention were not renewed after 1981; and most of the powers to release suspects from preventive custody were restored to magistrates in 1984, for all except the most serious crimes: the special provisions for alleged terrorist offenders were abrogated. As a counterpoint the importance for defendants of an individual magistrate's evaluation of the strength of the evidence to warrant arrest was reduced by the establishment in 1982 of an appeal body, the *Tribunale della Libertà*, with powers to revoke orders to arrest. Also, since law 304/1982 rewarding collaboration had a fixed-term duration (as did the law reducing the penalties for *dissociati* in 1987), the most evident constraints on the courts' sentencing policy were automatically removed. After almost exactly a decade therefore, although the heavier penalties introduced for the most violent crimes and the qualification 'terrorism' to punish all offences more heavily both remained in force, the reform of the judicial system as a whole, shorn of the most significant conditions imposed to meet the challenge of violence, had returned to the political agenda.

Debates on the reform were strongly influenced by the extended informal effects of the judicial management of violence. The evident success of specialisation and team investigations by magistrates provided a model for intervention to repress other forms of organised crime – the drug trade, financial illegalities, the *mafia* and the *camorra*. During the later 1970s, however, investigations into such activities, especially in the north, had been insufficiently resourced because of the overwhelming importance attached to combating political violence; so that the dramatic growth of those crimes in the early 1980s, most visibly in the south, provided a new focus of attention. Between 1980 and 1983 murders attributed to the *mafia*, *camorra* and *'ndrangheta* increased nearly sixfold, from 51 to 287 per year, as competition to control the sectors of the illegal economy in Naples and Palermo escalated into internecine warfare between different factions.[9] In attempting to confront this new emergency, magistrates were offered – for almost the first time – spontaneously volunteered accounts by self-confessed participants in *mafia* and *camorra* activities. The disquiet felt about the judicial use of confessions in the context of political violence was transformed into serious controversy over the legitimacy of extending the status of credible witness to long-serving affiliates of ordinary criminal associations. The judiciary was accused of having developed a generalised faith in all insiders' accounts, learned from the trials of left-wing violence, alongside a diminished concern with the need for supporting evidence. According to such critics, the magistrates had compensated for the ineffectiveness and inadequate techniques of police investigations by altering the nature and extent of evidence required to justify arrests and secure convictions. The combating of political violence had therefore allegedly modified the expectations and values underlying the general administration of justice at the same time as it placed far greater responsibilities in the hands of the magistrates.

Concern about the possible legitimisation of those effects was increased by the informal nature of the extension. Discussions on whether to legislate specific benefits for collaborating *mafiosi* and *camorristi* had not been translated into any parliamentary initiatives since the differences between political and ordinary criminality were regarded as too great to permit directly similar treatment.[10] Collaboration by the former members of armed groups was seen as highly specific in its motivation and effects: crime was simply the means to the realisation of a political project rather than a source of individual rewards to members, so that their publicly-justified withdrawals were directly damaging to the entire basis of criminal activity. In ordinary organised crime the defection of single partici-pants could not have analogous effects in eliminating the socio-economic causes of the phenomenon; and the possibility that accusa-tions against others by self-confessed participants were designed to damage rivals and competing factions and win special treatment for their authors (better custodial conditions, transfer to a favoured jail, protection for kin) could never be discounted. No specific guidelines for evaluating non-political confessions or for sanctioning false or incomplete accounts existed to guide the judicial treatment of the first *mafia* and *camorra* confessions of 1983–4 in the ways provided for political collaborators by the laws of 1980 and 1982. The basic framework remained the ordinary legal provisions for extenuating circumstances and the threat of civil actions promoted by the victims of false accusations, which left considerable space for uncertainty in the management of confessions and their authors at all stages of the judicial process.

No uniform assessment of the judicial handling of such issues can be made since the nature and corroboration of single confessions, and the types of episode to which they referred, were extremely varied. In the case of the *mafia*, most notably the trial of 474 defendants which began in Palermo in 1986, the principal confessions were only offered after the acquisition of other evidence and were scrupulously evalu-ated by the investigating magistrates. By contrast, the incrimination and trials of several hundred alleged affiliates of the Neapolitan *camorra* between 1983 and 1986 rested much more heavily on the often unsubstantiated versions of *pentiti*. In that instance the absence of corroborating proof for the involvement of many defendants allowed the determination of guilt to rest on the overall credibility of the accusers alone and entailed the acceptance or rejection of their accusations *en bloc*. The legal requirement for progressively more rigorous evidence to justify arrest, committal for trial and conviction was undermined by reliance on a single source of proof, and the likelihood of disagreement between courts at different stages of the judicial process was increased. In the particular case of the *camorra*, the validation of confessions at the first-level trial in 1985 was overturned in the following year by the Naples Appeal Court which acquitted 116 of the 191 defendants and reduced the sentences of the remainder. The controversy over the status of confessions raised by the entire investigation would probably not have been so severe, had they not incriminated a popular media personality whose defence was immediately translated into a political issue by the Radical Party.[11]

The acquittal was significant in two ways. First, it was widely read as symbolising the end of the equation between legal truthfulness and post-conversion accounts. The privileged speaking position of the repentant criminal, granted the power to compensate for the absence of other proof, was seriously diminished outside the narrow context of political violence in which the identity had originally been recognised. In fact the Court of Cassation had already begun to overturn decisions of lower courts in the field of organised crime, on the grounds of inadequate or overvalued evidence: ironically the very same section which was widely praised for annulling the controversial convictions of the alleged UCC members in 1985 was equally widely criticised for cancelling or revising other courts' decisions (on episodes of right-wing violence in particular) grounded very largely on confessions or what was now seen as insufficient proof. At that point several senior magistrates intervened publicly to warn against a reverse swing towards the *a priori* rejection of all confessions even as a contributory element in the establishment of legal guilt.[12]

In the second place, the acquittal of defendants who had spent considerable periods in jail and whose arrests could fairly be regarded as too easily ordered underlined the issue of the accountability of the judiciary in the political debate over revisions to the judicial system. The increased scope of the magistrature's interpretive and investigative roles during the years of left-wing violence forced a general reconsideration of the judiciary's relationship, formal and substantial, to political authorities and ordinary citizens. The localisation of the judicial management of violence, and the extension of some of its procedures to other forms of organised crime, tended to diffuse the controversies over questions of boundary definitions more widely than would have been the case in a centralised response, confined to a single tribunal. At the same time the public attention given to the judicial processing of armed struggle provided a focus for more widely-disseminated sources of discontent with the workings of the law: ordinary citizens dissatisfied with its longevity and the uncertainty due in part to the simple number of magistrates who could be involved before a definitive outcome was secured, and politicians resentful of the judiciary's investigation of administrative corruption which concerned the different parties.[13] As a result the close of the 'terrorist emergency' left both the internal and external relationships of the judicial system in need of public redefinition. The problems accompanying the repression of the armed community both high-lighted and exacerbated the scale of the reorganisation.

DETENTION AND RECONCILIATION

Like the projected reorganisation of the judicial system the progressive reform of the prison was a casualty of left-wing violence after 1976. Notwithstanding the violence directed against the institution – one armed group (the NAP) aimed its attack specifically against jails – and the high levels of inmate protest and escape in the early 1970s, a major prison reform law was passed in 1975, which granted inmates formal rights, facilitated temporary exits and introduced new forms of political and judicial surveillance of the institution. Much of the new transparency was lost after 1976 with restrictions on magistrates' powers of intervention, the establishment of maximum security jails, the entrusting of external security to the *carabinieri* and the particular segregation imposed on many political detainees through the use of article 90. The removal of magistrates' discretion in respect of arrest warrants and provisional release on bail for an extended array of crimes ensured that circumstantial evidence was sufficient to motivate the incarceration even of fringe members of the armed community: with the steady prolongation of the maximum terms for pre-trial custody, long periods could be served in jail before a definitive verdict was reached. As a result of the rise in political and ordinary crime throughout the decade the prison population nearly doubled between 1970 (22 117) and 1984 (42 711) and the proportion of inmates awaiting their first trial rose from less than one in two in 1970 to more than two in three in 1982.[14]

The trend towards greater impermeability of the boundary between the prison system and the wider society was reversed in 1984; and, parallel to the changes in the judicial domain, that reversal was the prelude to radical innovations in the role of the penitentiary. First, the limits of preventive detention were considerably reduced in 1984, although for serious crimes they still remained one-third higher than in 1970.[15] Second, in recovering their discretionary powers over the incarceration of suspects, magistrates were also granted wider opportunities to commute imprisonment into house arrest – a measure which symbolically ended the compulsory isolation of all alleged members of armed groups from civil society. Third, also in 1984, the rigid boundaries within the prison system itself were made less sharp:

several maximum security sections were closed and the suspension of ordinary prisoners' rights (by article 90 of the 1975 reform law) was removed for all inmates except those who had murdered in prison.[16] Finally, a new prison reform law in October 1986 weakened the policy of segregation still further. Life imprisonment was effectively abolished, only five years after three in four Italians had voted in a national referendum to retain it; and wider opportunities to leave jail temporarily and to benefit from alternatives to prison were introduced. Indeed by the end of 1987 no fewer than 277 (33%) of the 841 members of the left-wing and right-wing groups still awaiting trial or serving their sentences were under house arrest; and a further 41 (5%) were now permitted to work outside prison during the daytime. The end of the 'terrorist emergency' therefore corresponded to an immediate transformation, rather than a merely conservative re-establishment, of the relations between the prison system and the community. An important practical and symbolic contribution to the redefinition of the boundary was made by the *dissociati* whom the political élite's long-maintained refusal to recognise in law actually provided with a role as the last representatives of the (now repudiated) armed community.

The *dissociati* had built their identity on the possibility of an intermediate position between the political and armed communities: refusal to make a full confession and abjure their pasts maintained their autonomy from the State and its values, acknowledgement of the failure and the errors of armed struggle broke the ideological basis for their former associations. Although, paralleling its hostility to any 'neutral' position except that occupied by the judiciary during the worst years of violence, the political élite was extremely reluctant to grant the stance any general formal recognition, some *de facto* acknowledgement was conceded. Inside the prison system the aggregation of the heterogeneous *dissociati* into distinct sections (*aree omogenee*) was officially encouraged from 1983 onwards, sometimes prompted by direct negotiations between the Ministry of Justice's director of prisons and the leading representatives of the category.[17] The quasi-territorial basis for a common identity, distinct from the political prisoners in the maximum security sections but unable to benefit from the measures of house arrest and provisional release accorded to many *pentiti*, enabled the *dissociati* to develop a new mediatory role beyond the narrow confines of the courtroom.

In doing so, their principal members shifted to new languages to redescribe armed struggle and to legitimate the new relations to which they aspired, thus inaugurating a third stage in the sequence of dominant translations of left-wing violence. The primary vocabulary of the first phase had been political, monopolised by the public, indirect, exchanges between the intelligentsia of the armed community and the political élite. The meanings established in the second phase, from 1980 onwards, had drawn principally on the accounts built up through the interactions of the collaborating apparatchiks and representatives of the judiciary. From among the third set of translators, the *dissociati*, however, emerged two meta-historical characterisations of the past: the language of myth to depict their relations to the State, and the language of Christianity appropriate both to reincorporation into a new form of community and to the attempted public reconciliation of the armed community with its most direct victims. The recourse to the new vocabularies of understanding itself represented a sharp break with both the political and legal terminologies used to handle the rise and decline of armed struggle: it offered a discursive means for the actors to apply symbolic closure and to overcome the estrangement between political and armed communities characteristic of the 1970s.

In practical terms the *dissociati* acted as a prison pressure group to stimulate the external community to dismantle the emergency legislation and to reshape the general relations between prisons and society. As a compact, articulate and politically-oriented group, in many cases with lengthy prison terms ahead, they were better able than ordinary prisoners to address influential outsiders. At the same time they were also concerned to represent what they identified as the general interests of the prison population as well as their own specific case. Since the political élite remained wary of giving official recognition – even retrospectively – to the specificity of political violence and accepting a public dialogue with its former affiliates on their own position, the general proposals received more encouragement and benefited a wider group than the *dissociati* themselves. The successful organisation of a conference inside Rebibbia jail in Rome exemplified that preference. The original suggestion to bring prisoners and outsiders together in jail to discuss aspects of carceral policy was launched by the *dissociati* in August 1983, with a specific focus on the possible modes of exit from the 'terrorist emergency'.[18] However, when the conference did take place in June 1984, under the auspices of the Minister of Justice and in the presence of politicians from all parties, prison administrators and representatives of the intelligentsia, its theme was the broader one of general innovations to prison regimes and the representative of the *dissociati* was only one among the several inmate speakers. Equally their political and cultural interests meant that the *dissociati* were also active in establishing direct contacts with outsiders, breaking down through various forms of interaction the boundary around the prison and facilitating the climate of opinion behind the prison reform of 1986.

One favoured point of contact was the staging of plays to which the public were granted access. A particularly significant choice, which also gave its name to a journal initiated in 1985 by sympathetic former members of the extra-parliamentary Left, was *Antigone*, performed for the first time in Rebibbia as a prelude to the 1984 conference.[19] Sophocles' tragedy was intended to be read in both retrospective and prospective senses. On one hand, the years of armed struggle were depicted as part of the more general movement of extra-parliamentary dissent, based on the search for justice and democracy and with its mass illegalities justified by the discredit and illegitimacy of the Italian State. Although few of the *dissociati* had been directly responsible for murders, most acknowledged their readiness to break the law in pursuit of their political values. Despite the impossibility of allocating neatly or entirely plausibly the roles of Antigone and Creon to the political actors of the 1970s, the figures and themes of the play could be used as a device for claiming a legitimate identity outside the State and for contemplating the past in archetypically human rather than political or legal terms. On the other hand, the central issue in *Antigone* is closure – the possible negotiation of conditions for the burial of the dead and the terms on which violence and its consequences can be comprehended, and therefore deprived of ulterior damage, by all participants through a single acceptable interpretation. The symbolic representation of the transcendence of the divisions between armed and political communities pointed towards the need for both sets of members to invent a formula and framework for reconciliation.[20]

Beside their attention to new relations with the State, a small but particularly visible number of *dissociati* sought to establish links to the Church and to the victims of violence or their kin. Identification of a totalising religious component in their participation in armed struggle generated accounts with several functions. First, they enabled former practitioners of political violence to affirm a continuity with their pre-political selves and the religious activism in which some had been involved: armed struggle could therefore be interpreted as a detour determined principally by a contingent shift in social relations rather than clear ideological rupture.[21] Second, as a non-political community the Church was especially acceptable as an interlocutor to *dissociati* who wished to preserve some of their antagonism to the State but to exhibit a continuity of the idealistic component which had led to their acceptance of violence. Thus weapons might be handed over to ecclesiastical functionaries, as they were in Milan in 1984; the rites of baptism and marriage, sometimes performed by senior prelates, were requested by several couples in jail; and some prison chaplains lent their support to hunger strikes against the deprivations imposed by maximum security regimes. Third, the Church's appeals to the armed community during the kidnappings and funerals of the previous decade had of course been ineffective. But its command of the language of repentance, forgiveness and reconciliation subsequently offered valuable resources for recontextualising as a sign of individual transformation the morally-ambiguous fact of the collaboration demanded by the State. It also provided a vocabulary through which users could act as the representatives of armed struggle in relation to its direct and indirect victims. The often well-publicised sets of exchanges between *dissociati* and the family members of the better-known casualties, including their own direct victims, have represented the final sequence of symbolic interactions to redefine the meanings of past violence.

Public forgiveness for the authors of political murders was inaugurated by the unsolicited initiative of the Bachelet family at the funeral of their father, the vice-president of the Higher Judicial Council killed by the Red Brigades, in February 1980. Thereafter the establishment of direct or indirect contacts, not always successful, between the immediate victims and either the actual authors of the attack or their fellow-members of the armed community increased. Some meetings were maintained as strictly individual and private. Others – such as the encounters in Rebibbia jail between a group of *dissociati* and two victims of Red Brigades' violence in 1985 – were collective discussions of how to orchestrate a general closure of the *anni di piombo*. Partly because of their status and partly because of the importance attributed to public forgiveness by some prominent members of the category, the victims themselves were rapidly converted into symbols of the national community. The lack of drastic political consequences for violence and the possibility of dismantling the emergency legislation raised as a public issue the contrasting irreversibility of damage suffered by private citizens and the response it deserved from the political and judicial institutions. The claims of the public and the private once again became inextricably intertwined in the conflicts over the forms and limits of reconciliation, as the potentially incompatible demands for collective security and individual justice were argued out in different forums.

In the pressure on victims to translate the conflicting sentiments provoked by violence into a single univocal attitude the theme of the necessary indeterminacy of violence recurs. Its specific dimensions in the context of Italian left-wing violence and the responses generated have been examined throughout this book. At the outset lay the conflict within the armed community itself over whether violence was to be used and interpreted primarily as a technique for supplementary use within the existing lines of social conflict or as an immediate creative determinant of a wholly different order. The contrasting readings in the factory and political domains reflected the permanent uncertainty of the intended target and objectives: the Moro affair remained the central symbolic episode precisely because its various aspects forced most clearly a recognition of the impossibility of resolving the interpretive issues into a single consensual version in which the political community could affirm its shared limits. In the judicial domain interpretations divided between local and national readings, each drawing on elements present in the actions, texts and declarations of the members of the different milieux of armed struggle. In each instance the absence of an authoritative interpretive centre permitted continuing oscillation between these contrasting translations of acts of violence into verbal descriptions. Not surprisingly a similar ambivalence was enjoined on the victims themselves once the strategy of individual forgiveness was made a symbol of public reconciliation and the bearer of a univocal set of meanings.

No one has described the tension between the need to find a basis for understanding acts of violence and the knowledge that any clear interpretive resolution must be dangerously simplifying better than the widow of an economist murdered by the Red Brigades in 1985. Reflecting on the reiterated public demand on victims to state publicly whether they pardoned their aggressors and thus to contribute to the closure of the issues raised by political violence, she pointed out that to accept and to refuse to accept a relationship with the author of the damage both carried the risk of a deeper complicity with the ideological presuppositions of violence. In drawing attention to the close links between the cultural basis of armed and political communities in Italy – as others have proposed for terrorism and democracy in general terms[22] – she also comes close to suggesting that the very indeterminacy of violence must be matched by an equal resistance to closure on the part of communities forced into public interpretation of the phenomenon. The appropriate response may be the refusal to confer a single meaning on clandestine violence – a strategy which itself sets up a further paradoxical tension with the demand none the less to act and to secure a better understanding of the shared roots of democracy and violence.

> When these sentiments [forgiveness and justice] become public, when they are claimed – on either side – as the only possible attitude, then we must reflect on their implications while of course maintaining our full respect for those who hold them. The dark side and worrying aspect of the implacable demand for justice is the taste for a vendetta, the desire to annihilate the author of violence, and that means being captured by his own logic . . . [on the other hand] forgiveness responds to the totalising universalism of the terrorist who arrogates to himself the right to destroy the adversary-victim with another universalism, equally totalising, which from a higher place destroys – even if only at a symbolic level – the identity of the adversary-terrorist. Furthermore the implicit message in the strategy of forgiveness [*perdonismo*] is that really what the terrorists have done has not been so terrible, so irrevocable . . . Forgiveness and vendetta are two natural and comprehensible reactions. But they can also be two illustrations of the desire to forget: and it is precisely the forgetting which must be avoided.[23]

Notes and References

1 ITALIAN 'TERRORISM' AS TRANSLATION

1. These figures are taken from M. Galleni (ed.), *Rapporto sul terrorismo* (Milan: Rizzoli, 1981) p. 49, Table 1; R. Murray, 'Political Violence in Northern Ireland 1969–1977', in F. W. Boal and J. N. H. Douglas (eds), *Integration and Division. Geographical Perspectives on the Northern Ireland Problem* (London: Academic Press, 1982) p. 311, Table 12.1; annual reports, *Verfassungsschutzbericht*, for left-wing murders only. I have more to say below on the Italian statistics.

2. The first full-length monograph by a social scientist did not appear until 1986 (G. Galli, *Storia del partito armato 1968–1982* (Milan: Rizzoli, 1986). First-person, mostly experience-licensed rather than research-based accounts by the sociologists Ferrarotti (*Alle radici della violenza* (Milan: Rizzoli, 1979) and Acquaviva (*Guerriglia e guerra rivoluzionaria in Italia* (Milan: Rizzoli, 1979)) had appeared earlier, as had analyses of the representation of 'terrorism' in the mass media by Silj, Morcellini and Grossi.

3. See the survey by A. Schmid, *Political Terrorism* (Amsterdam: SWIDOC, 1983). Schmid actually counts 109 definitions formulated between 1936 and 1981 but adds a baroque 21-line definition of his own.

4. The problems are well discussed for the analogous case of new religious movements, the description of which often relies on defectors' accounts, by J. Beckford, 'Talking of Apostasy, or Telling Tales and "Telling" Tales', in G. N. Gilbert and P. Abell (eds), *Accounts and Action* (Aldershot: Gower, 1983), pp. 77–97.

5. P. Rock, 'Another Common-Sense Conception of Deviancy', *Sociology* vol. 3 (1979), no. 1, pp. 75–88.

6. On 'translation' see the work of M. Callon, 'Struggles and Negotiations to Define What is Problematic and What is Not', in K. D. Knorr, R. Krohn and R. Whitley (eds), *The Social Process of Scientific Investigation* (Dordrecht: Reidel, 1981) vol. IV (1980), pp. 197–219; and 'Some Elements of a Sociology of Translation: Domestication of the Scallops and the Fishermen of St. Brieuc Bay', in J. Law (ed.), *Power, Action and Belief*, Sociological Review Monograph 32 (London: Routledge & Kegan Paul, 1986) pp. 196–233. Although Callon's approach has been developed for the sociology of science, it is clearly itself translatable into other domains of investigation as the articles in Law's volume by Law himself ('On the methods of long-distance control: navigation and the Portuguese route to India') and Latour ('The powers of association') indicate.

7. The figures on violence and attitudes to the political and social systems are taken from G. Guidorossi, *Gli italiani e la politica* (Milan: F. Angeli, 1984) p. 263, Table 38; G. Sani: 'The Political Culture of Italy:

Continuity and Change', in G. Almond and S. Verba (eds), *The Civic Culture Revisited* (Boston: Little, Brown & Co., 1980) p. 308, Table VII.7; p. 312, Table VIII.9. However, in a survey of 5000 citizens carried out by the Faculty of Political Science in Florence in 1980, 8 per cent of respondents were reported to be partially favourable to violence, 1.8 per cent believed it was ineliminable and 0.5 per cent that it was necessary (*La Discussione* (1980), no. 21 (26 May), p. 4).

8. T. Gurr, 'Some Characteristics of Political Terrorism in the 1960s', in M. Stohl (ed.), *The Politics of Terrorism*, 2nd edn (New York: M. Dekker Inc., 1983), pp. 46–7.

9. The data for 1946–77 are taken from G. Viola, *Polizia* (Verona: Bertani, 1977) pp. 217–19. According to figures in Guidorossi, *Gli italiani e la politica*, pp. 225–7, two-thirds of Italians believe that the police should be present and free to intervene 'forcefully and decisively' in demonstrations.

10. Direzione PCI, Sezione Problemi dello Stato Commissione Problemi dello Stato, Federazione Milanese del PCI, *Primo Rapporto sull'Inchiesta di Massa sul Terrorismo* (Milan: May 1982), p. 37.

11. For a general discussion see A. Schmid and J. de Graaf, *Violence as Communication: Insurgent Terrorism and the Western News Media* (London: Sage, 1982).

12. According to a list given in *La Repubblica*, 14 January 1981, 14 papers agreed to publish the Red Brigades' texts while 40 refused. The Press Federation (FNSI) refused to take an explicit line and was hostile to any general code of behaviour. An earlier attempt to secure a news black-out during the kidnapping of Amerio in 1973, proposed by the PCI, had also been a failure.

13. The results of the Demoskopea survey of 400 regular newspaper readers in different cities were published in *Prima Comunicazione* (1981) March, insert, pp. i–xxiv. 46 per cent of respondents accepted the idea of journalists having contact with members of armed groups to secure interviews, although a further 35 per cent claimed that meetings should only be arranged as a stratagem to allow the police to arrest the interviewees.

14. The two journalists, Scialoja and Bultrini, were also temporarily suspended by their professional association and the publication of the results of their actions provoked resignations among senior figures associated with *L'Espresso*: at the time of writing their judicial fate has not been decided. In the case of *Corrispondenza Internazionale* two editors (Fiorillo and Lombardi) were subsequently charged with full membership of the Red Brigades for whom a third editor, Di Giovanni, often acted as a defence lawyer.

15. See the testimonies of Andreotti, then Prime Minister, and the Roman public prosecutor Infelisi to the Parliamentary Commission of Inquiry into the Moro kidnapping (*Commissione Parlamentare d'Inchiesta sulla Strage di Via Fani, sul Sequestro e l'Assassinio di Aldo Moro e sul Terrorismo in Italia* (Rome: Senato della Repubblica, 1983–6), Doc. XXIII, n. 5, vol. 3, p. 150; vol. 7, pp. 124–5. All subsequent references to the published work of the Committee, which runs to 2 volumes of

majority and minority reports (vols 1 & 2), 9 volumes of transcripts of hearings (vols 3–11) and further sets of selected documents, will be made in the abbreviated form of CPM.

16. Ordinance of the Roman *pretura*, 13 January 1981, Judge Aiello, D'Urso vs. Soc. *Corriere della Sera* and others.

17. For one example, see the reference by two BR members (Faranda and Morucci) to their gaining access to one of their own organisation's documents only through the extracts published in *Panorama* (see *Controinformazione* (1979) November, supplement, p. 4).

18. Senator Coco (DC), 10 January 1980. The full debate is cited in P. L. Vigna, *La Finalità di Terrorismo ed Eversione* (Milan: Giuffrè, 1981) pp. 106–262; Coco's definition is at p. 149. Here, as in all subsequent cases, the translation from Italian is my own.

19. Dalla Chiesa's distinctions were given in an interview with E. Biagi on *Rete 4* in March 1981; for Cappuzzo's definition, see his testimony to the CPM, vol. 4, p. 392.

20. These figures have been calculated from the criminal statistics published yearly by the Central Statistics Institute (ISTAT) in the *Annuario Statistico Italiano*. The relative importance of the increases in ordinary and political violence for new laws against crime is considered in Chapter 4.

21. Mary Douglas in particular has stressed the boundary-defining dimension of witchcraft and its general function in a system of social accountability. See the 'Introduction' in M. Douglas (ed.), *Witchcraft Confessions and Accusations* (London: Tavistock, 1970) ASA Monographs in Social Anthropology, vol. 9; M. Douglas, *Evans-Pritchard* (Glasgow: Fontana, 1980).

22. Direzione PCI, Sezione Problemi dello Stato Commissione Problemi dello Stato, Federazione Milanese del PCI, *Primo Rapporto sull'Inchiesta di Massa sul Terrorismo* (1982) p. 37.

23. To my knowledge the rumours, suggestions and evidence for an international dimension add up to this: the possibility of Czech influence (through the visits to Prague in 1974 of a Red Brigades' leader, although the visit is sometimes dated exactly at the time when he was accused of interrogating the kidnapped magistrate Sossi, and later through an alleged cheque for 70 million lire from the Skoda firm to *Autonomia*); two alleged contacts between the Israeli secret services and the Red Brigades in 1972 and 1974; a Bulgarian connection (through the activities of a trade union functionary from the UIL who was the cousin of a BR activist and was suspected of having had specific foreign contacts during the Dozier kidnapping in 1981–2); a Palestinian connection (for the use of training camps and as a source of arms); and European linkages (participation in a joint training camp, organised by ETA, and suspicions that a Paris language school, the Hyperion, was a centre for the direction of continent-wide violence). According to J. Adams (*The Financing of Terror* (Sevenoaks: New English Library, 1986) p. 52), members of the Red Brigades attended 14 out of 28 meetings between representatives of European and Middle Eastern groups between 1970 and 1984, 3 being organised in

Italy itself. There are also wilder pieces of 'evidence', such as the 147-page 'proof' by a former member of the Italian embassy in Moscow that the Red Brigades' communiqués during Moro's kidnapping were actually written by the KGB (CPM, vol. 2, pp. 219–366).

24. A. Ventura: 'Il problema storico del terrorismo italiano', *Rivista storica italiana*, vol. XCII (1980) pp. 125–51.

25. In defining the scope of social science accounts I shall follow G. Pasquino and D. della Porta ('Interpretations of Italian Leftwing Terrorism', paper presented at the IPSA XII World Congress, Rio de Janeiro, August 1982, pp. 13–32) who include interpretations not produced by professional sociologists, some of which might be more narrowly classified as belonging to political science. I shall not deal, however, with the sociological treatments of a favourite topic, the presentation of 'terrorism' in the media, since they do not address the question of violence directly. For the most detailed piece of empirical research in that vein see M. Morcellini and F. Avallone (eds), *Il ruolo dell'informazione in una situazione di emergenza, 16 marzo 1978* (Rome: ERI – Quaderno n. 1, Ufficio Verifica Programmi Trasmessi, 1978).

26. *La Repubblica*, 16 March 1984, p. 4. One Red Brigades leader, Senzani, held university research posts in sociology and several of *Autonomia*'s leaders arrested in 1979 were staff members in the Faculty of Political Science in Padua.

27. See, for example, A. Ventura: 'Le responsabilità degli intellettuali e le radici culturali del terrorismo di sinistra', in C. Ceolin (ed.): *Università, Cultura, Terrorismo* (Milan: F. Angeli, 1984), especially pp. 34–6.

28. So I was told by Marco Barbone in an interview in June 1984. The single piece of contrary evidence I have come across was the explicit adoption of the term '*movimento di guerriglia*' by Martinelli (an activist from Bergamo) who found a justification in S. Acquaviva's *Guerriglia e guerra rivoluzionaria in Italia*. The Red Brigades' reading list for affiliates, published in *Corrispondenza Internazionale* (1980) no. 16/17 (October–December), pp. 289–301, did not include any sociological accounts of Italian violence.

29. The recent work of Franco Ferraresi and others has begun to illuminate the world of right-wing violence for the first time. See F. Ferraresi (ed.), *La destra radicale* (Milan: Feltrinelli, 1984); F. Ferraresi, *The Radical Right in Italy* (Oxford: Polity Press, forthcoming).

30. For the figures on sociology see the Appendix in L. Balbo, G. Chiaretti, and G. Massironi, *L'inferma scienza* (Bologna: Il Mulino, 1975), pp. 266–75.

31. These details are taken from the archives of the CNR's two relevant committees (Economics, Sociology, and Statistics; Political and Legal Sciences). An eighth proposal was submitted but then dropped by its proposers. Another project was financed by the Ministry of Education, and there are likely to have been minor reports at local level, especially sponsored by left-wing town councils to document right-wing violence. Political scientists too paid little attention to the issues: a survey of the discipline's 156 research projects in 1982–3 showed no

project on terrorism, although 6 (4 per cent) dealt with the related topics of conflict, war, violence and youth movements; see (R. Mannheimer, *Repertory of Empirical Researches and Files in Italy* (Milan: Fondazione Feltrinelli, 1983)).

32. CPM, vol. 10, pp. 519–37.

33. P. Calogero, interview in *La Magistratura* (1979) June, nn. 1–3, p. 3. The Turin magistrate Caselli has referred in his general articles on left-wing violence to the writings of his fellow-Turin academics Bonanate and Marletti but has discounted their influence in his judicial interpretations.

34. See the list of sources used by Pasquino and della Porta, 'Interpretations of Italian Leftwing Terrorism', pp. 34–6.

35. For a justifiably severe criticism of the use of evidence by Galli, *Storia*, see the commentary by R. Rossanda in *L'Indice* (1986) no. 9, p. 39.

36. The Bologna papers, presented at the conference *Ricordare e Capire*, in April 1983 have been published in two volumes: G. Pasquino (ed.), *La prova delle armi* (Bologna: Il Mulino, 1984) and D. della Porta (ed.), *Terrorismi in Italia* (Bologna: Il Mulino, 1984).

37. The 'blocked polity' thesis is discussed in the contributions by both editors in D. della Porta and G. Pasquino (eds), *Terrorismo e violenza politica* (Bologna: Il Mulino, 1983). Galli, *Storia*, has provided the most recent and extended version of the hypothesis that conservative forces in cahoots with sections of the security services deliberately permitted the persistence of violence in order to destabilise the Left.

2 THE TRAJECTORY OF ARMED STRUGGLE

1. Thus the terms for murder (*omicidio*) and wounding (*ferimento*) were replaced respectively by *annientamento* ('annihilation') and *invalidamento* ('invaliding/invalidating') or *gambizzazione* ('kneecapping'). No doubt the substitutions provided some psychological distancing necessary for the aggressors to carry out their attacks, as did the assumption of 'battle-names' (*nomi di battaglia*), separating the actors from their real selves, and facilitating the parallel insistence that the victims were symbols, not persons.

2. My use of the term 'milieu' follows the definition by Burns:

> a social system or part of a system through which a person is free to move by virtue of a specific status in it e.g. a factory, a household, an occupation. More particularly the word refers to the boundaries of the social area within which occupancy of a particular status permits movement. Thus in the same hospital a kitchen worker, a physician, a patient are members of differing, though overlapping, milieux.
> (T. Burns, 'The Reference of Conduct in Small Groups', *Human Relations* vol. 8, (1955) p. 469, fn. 3).

As this definition indicates, milieux are not precisely defined, have their own internal hierarchy and status order, and are locally united in specific activities which depend on collaborative participation.

3. E. Durkheim, *The Division of Labour in Society*, 2nd edn (New York: Free Press, 1964) pp. 115–20.
4. 'Facciamo la rivoluzione e poi ce n'andiamo' (see the interview with M. Libardi in *Litterae Communionis*, vol. XI (1984), January, p. 10). The anthology of *Autonomia*'s writings is G. Martignoni and S. Morandini, *Il diritto all'odio* (Verona: Bertani, 1977).
5. Figures from Galleni, *Rapporto sul terrorismo*, p. 118, Table 67. Apart from the four major centres, the cities of Padua, Florence, Brescia, Venice and Bergamo also saw a significant incidence of left-wing violence. The figures in the following paragraph are also derived from tables in Galleni, *Rapporto*, passim.
6. Galleni's figures actually exaggerate the impression of organisational continuity and coverage since actions claimed under the same generic signatures ('armed proletarian communists', 'armed communist squads' etc.) are classified under single headings even though they appeared in very different parts of Italy at quite different times and clearly had no organisational connection. On the other hand some groups which do not appear (e.g. the *Comitati Comunisti Rivoluzionari*: COÇORI) were later charged with having authored variously signed and unsigned actions.
7. O. L. Scalfaro: 'Ordine sicurezza pubblica e forze di polizia nel 1985', *Vita Italiana*, vol. XXXVI (1986), no. 1, pp. 67–8.
8. For LC's figures showing the proportion of women at 26 per cent, which are virtually the only statistics available for any extra-parliamentary Left group in the 1970s, see L. Bobbio, *Lotta Continua* (Rome: Savelli, 1979) p. 149, fn. 46. As in all Italian political organisations the proportion of women in leadership roles was much lower than for the overall membership: in LC it dropped to 10 per cent.
9. *L'Area della Detenzione Politica in Italia*, survey directed by E. D'Arcangelo, Rome, September 1984, Table 5. Many *de facto* couples married in jail, and a few managed also to have children.
10. According to figures provided by the Chief of Police, Coronas, in his testimony to the Moro inquiry (CPM, vol. 4, pp. 58–9). For a retrospective acknowledgement of the place of violence in the extra-parliamentary Left by one of its protagonists, see Bobbio, *Lotta Continua*, pp. 13, 80–1, 89–90, 98–102, 106.
11. M. Galleni, *Rapporto sul terrorismo*, pp. 211–28.
12. A plurality of extreme-Left voices, mostly from *Il Manifesto* and *Lotta Continua*, on aspects and episodes of left-wing violence in 1977–8 can be found in E. Deaglio, L. Menapace and O. Scalzone (eds), *Sulla violenza* (Rome: Savelli, 1978). One episode serving to focus attention on the deliberate use of violence by one extra-parliamentary Left group, *Avanguardia Operaia* (AO), in Milan was the death of a right-wing youth, Ramelli, in 1975: 13 members of AO were arrested ten years later and brought to trial in March 1987. Presumably the contemporary knowledge, or at least suspicion, of the organisation of such episodes helped to inhibit a clear condemnation of violence.
13. The estimate for Milan's extra-parliamentary Left is taken from the local police chief's report, reprinted in T. Barbato, *Il terrorismo in*

Italia (Milan: Bibliografica, 1980) pp. 202–7. Given the difficulty of defining an 'activist', the figures tally fairly closely with other calculations for the major groups (MS, LC, AO). For Italy as a whole *Il Manifesto* was reckoned to have 5960 militants in 1972 (who were so young that, according to one of its leaders, the average age was deliberately pushed up for public consumption (L. Castellina, '*Il Manifesto* and Italian Communism', *New Left Review* (1985) no. 157, p. 29). LC counted *c.* 8000 militants at its congress in 1975 (Bobbio, *Lotta Continua*, p. 148, fn. 46). My calculation of no more than 500 participants in clandestine violence in Milan is based on the number of defendants convicted in the major trials in the city between 1980 and 1984 and takes account of the considerable overlap of the same individuals in different court proceedings.

14. For Red Brigades–*Potere Operaio* meetings see the testimony of an early BR member, Buonavita, cited in G. De Lutiis (ed.), *Attacco allo Stato* (Rome: Napoleone, 1982) p. 137.

15. Published in *Corrispondenza Internazionale* (1980) nn. 16/17. A later extended text was A. Coi, P. Gallinari, F. Piccioni, B. Seghetti, *Politica e rivoluzione* (Milan: G. Maj, 1984).

16. See the editorial in the first issue of *Metropoli*: 'this journal is edited by a group of comrades who, for the most part, have been through 1968, the Hot Autumn, the brief but felicitous experience of *Potere Operaio*, the area of *Autonomia* and its environs', and they referred to 'the intertwining of our discourse with the phenomenon of armed struggle ... the common interest in experimenting on the terrain of illegality' (*Metropoli* vol. 1 (1979) no. 1, pp. 1–2, 33). For some members occasional or one-off publications (*Linea di Condotta*, *Pre-Print*, *Magazzino*) could be included as well as participation in some of *Autonomia*'s broadcasting outlets (e.g. Radio Sherwood in Padua).

17. Editorial statement in *Controinformazione* (1982) no. 22, p. 3, in its own defence against some of its editors' convictions for subversive activities. The journal had had contact with the BR from the outset, had been first incriminated in 1977 and had published 26 issues between 1973 and 1982.

18. *Il Bollettino* began life as a supplement to *Controinformazione*, published a great variety of brief texts mostly authored in jail, and could be bought in extreme-Left bookshops. Between 1981 and 1984 it published 15 issues of up to 75 pages each.

19. See the ten interviews published in *L'Espresso* (16 May 1974; 5 January 1975; 18 June 1978; 23 July 1978; 15 July 1979; 16 March 1980; 20 July 1980; 11 January 1981) and *Panorama* (6 June 1978; 1 October 1979) between 1974 and 1981, as well as the regular commentaries on texts. The interviews with activists were represented by the interviewees precisely as a means of trying to break the interpretive domination of the intelligentsia (see, e.g. *Panorama* 1 October 1979 p. 74).

20. The Red Brigades' particular scheme has been reprinted many times: see, e.g., R. Katz, *Days of Wrath* (London: Granada, 1980) p. 86.

21. Testimony of the head of police, Coronas, in CPM, vol. 4, pp. 68–9,

74, supplemented by my own data for 1980–1. According to police figures, an overall total of 28 949 rifles and pistols were stolen between 1975 and 1979, most by ordinary criminals, although the police were simultaneously able to recover an even larger number. Over the same period 28 automatic weapons, 29 ordinary rifles, 139 pistols and 121 kg. of explosives were discovered in the bases of armed groups. The victims of the five kidnappings were Gargiulo, Moccia, Saronio, Costa and Cirillo: left-wing groups are suspected of responsibility for other cases, besides the known failures.

22.   The evidence of the emergence of the *apparatchik* milieu is taken *inter alia* from the following public sources as well as many judicial documents: for Turin, interviews quoted in C. Stajano, *L'Italia nichilista* (Milan: A. Mondadori, 1982) and S. Genova, *Missione antiterrorismo* (Milan: Sugarco, 1985); for Milan, Libardi in *Litterae Communionis* (1984), vol. XI, January, pp. 9–12 and his contribution to *Contro le regole di questo assurdo gioco* (1982) no. 0, pp. 1–6, M. Barbone, interview in *L'Avvenire*, 9 February 1984, pp. 3–6 and S. Corvisieri *Il mio viaggio nella sinistra* (Rome: L'Espresso, 1979) p. 144; for Rome, the testimony of A. Savasta to the CPM, vol. 9, pp. 265–78.

23.   Figures from Galleni, *Rapporto sul terrorismo*, pp. 211–46.

24.   Calculated from the data in Galleni, *Rapporto sul terrorismo*, Ch. 5.

25.   For evidence of that situation in Rome see CPM, vol. 1, pp. 53–4.

26.   See the interview with 'Claudio' in L. Manconi, *Vivere con il terrorismo* (Milan: A. Mondadori, 1980) pp. 149–68; Peci, *Io, l'infame* (Milan: A. Mondadori, 1983), *passim*.

27.   For evidence on the difficulties of the Red Brigades in Turin to house activists safely and the consequent necessity to refuse offers to become clandestine see Peci, *Io, l'infame*, pp. 74, 99, 124.

28.   On the perceived difference between 'kneecappings' and murders see Peci, *Io, l'infame*, pp. 126–7, 135.

29.   Testimony of General Dalla Chiesa, CPM vol. 4, p. 332. When the content was assembled from external sources (for example, articles or books on the media), the authors were often able to indicate the provenance of almost every phrase. A particularly controversial demonstration was provided by the members of the Milan group, XXVIII *marzo*, responsible for the murder of the journalist, Walter Tobagi, in demonstrating the falsity of the accusations that only better-informed outsiders could have authored the document claiming responsibility (see Chapter 6, below).

30.   Peci, *Io, l'infame*, p. 154. He claims that all BR apparatchiks in Turin were reluctant to write the leaflets and 'left the task to the girls'.

31.   Further details from the depositions at the trial for the murder of the jeweller, P. Torreggiani, are summarised in *La Repubblica*, 26–7 May 1983. The publication of an interview with a clandestine apparatchik from an unnamed group in the Genoa newspaper, *Il Lavoro*, in March 1980, aroused very hostile comments, not only about the fact of publication in itself but also about the seemingly neutral, normalising, presentation of a phenomenon which, it was agreed, ought to be

publicly de-familiarised (see the reprinted interview and comments in Manconi, *Vivere con il terrorismo*, pp. 149–68, 176–82.

32. I am relying in this section primarily on locals' autobiographical accounts given to magistrates. More accessible are the descriptions given in *Contro le regole di questo assurdo gioco* (1982), no. 2, pp. 7–14, as well as the sources in note 22 above.

33. For evidence on the changing composition of school populations, which in the province of Milan increased by 33 per cent between 1969 and 1975 see R. Pasini, 'The Evolution of the Demand for Post-compulsory Education in the Urban Area of Milan: Perspectives and Problems', *European Journal of Education*, vol. 19 (1984), no. 4, pp. 425–36.

34. For the decline in housing occupations and the extension of PCI control into the periphery of Turin after 1975 see S. Hellman, 'A New Style of Governing: Italian Communism and the Dilemmas of Transition in Turin, 1975–1979', *Studies in Political Economy* (1979), vol. 2, pp. 159–97; G. Laganà, M. Pianta and A. Segre: 'Urban Social Movements and Urban Restructuring in Turin, 1969–76', *International Journal of Urban and Regional Research*, vol. 6 (1982), no. 2, pp. 223–45.

35. A map of the distribution of bases (sc., flats, deposits etc. where members, weapons or materials of armed groups were discovered) in Rome is provided by M. Fiasco, 'Roma: la violenza eversiva nel quinquennio 1978–82', in C. Ceolin (ed.), *Università, Cultura, Terrorismo* (Milan: F. Angeli, 1984) pp. 171–2.

36. No precise figures exist for PL, which the signature's variegated local-level structure of *squadre* and *ronde* makes hard to calculate with precision. My estimate is based on the numbers convicted of member-ship of PL and its associated signatures, after allowing for the overlap of the apparatchiks who were indicted in more than one city. No other aggregation sufficiently structured to be called a group had more than 100 members: many had fewer than a dozen.

37. The only other well-known group, notorious more for the identity of its organiser than for the impact of its actions, was the *Gruppi armati proletari* (GAP) associated with Feltrinelli, himself killed attempting to blow up an electricity pylon outside Milan in March 1972. Details of the earliest years of the BR can be found, *inter alia*, in V. Tessandori, *BR. Imputazione: banda armata* (Milan: Garzanti, 1977) and G. Galli, *Storia del partito armato 1968–1982* (Milan: Rizzoli, 1986) Chs 1–5. For the NAP see NAP, *Quaderno n. 1 di Controinformazione* (Milan: 1975).

38. Testimony of Alfredo Buonavita, CPM, vol. 10, p. 602.

39. Testimony of Buonavita, CPM, vol. 10, pp. 576–7.

40. The survey referred to in footnote 9 (*L'Area della Detenzione Politica in Italia*), directed from Rebibbia jail and therefore probably privileg-ing the Roman membership of armed struggle, noted that 18.9 per cent of the sample actually worked for the State or municipal administration (p. 13).

41. Calculated from figures in Galleni, *Rapporto sul terrorismo*, Chs 5 and

6; Direzione PCI, Sezione Problemi dello Stato: 'Attentati e violenze Italia nel 1981'; 'Attentati e violenze in Italia nel 1982'.

42.   See the testimonies of Buonavita (CPM, vol. 10, p. 606) and Antonio Savasta (CPM, vol. 9, pp. 272–7).

43.   According to the Minister of the Interior 158 self-proclaimed members of the BR were in jail in October 1978 (*Atti Parlamentari, Camera dei Deputati*, sessions of 24 October 1978, p. 22 703) rising to 229 – i.e. well over half the then membership – by December 1979 (*L'Espresso*, 24 February 1980, p. 19) and to 364 by November 1981 (*La Repubblica*, 5 January 1982 p. 4). E. Fenzi, in his unpublished *Memoriale* dated 27 September 1982, pp. 17–19, describes the formal BR organisation in prison, created in 1978, as well as exemplifying the full horrors of its power in an account of the truly terrible murder of the former PL activist, Giorgio Soldati, in Cuneo prison. Cases of direct links with locals are instanced at p. 25.

44.   1468 attacks were recorded for the first half of 1979; 371 for the second half: the comparable figures for 1978 were 1998 and 751, and for 1980, 517 and 100 (Galleni, *Rapporto sul terrorismo*, pp. 239–46). These figures are for both left-wing and right-wing violence but there is no doubt that the major drop is attributable to the Left. It is also worth noting that the incidence of violence was always lower in the second half of the year since it included the summer months when, for reasons of security and lack of audience in the holiday-reduced urban populations, very few attacks took place.

45.   This technique had been tried for the first time in the D'Urso kidnapping of December 1980–January 1981 when the intelligentsia in jail were invited to express a view on whether the victim's 'death sentence' should be suspended. The Radical Party's leaders also threw themselves enthusiastically into the public communicative exchange with the *compagni assassini* of the BR: see L. Jannuzzi, E. Capecelatro, F. Rocella, V. Vecellio, *La pelle del D'Urso* (Rome: Radio Radicale Documenti, 1981).

46.   So far as I am aware, the earliest full confessions came in July 1979 from among the members of a minor group, the *Unità Combattenti Comuniste*, which had already dissolved. The milieu location and varying extent of confessions are discussed in Chapter 5.

47.   See the collective document, 'Non è che l'inizio', authored in Palmi jail and inspired by Curcio, distributed in November 1982 and reprinted in *Controinformazione* (1982) December, no. 26, supplement, pp. 11–14. Increasingly unambiguous acknowledgements of failure followed over the next few years. On 21 March 1988, by appearing for the first time as interviewees on state television, three BR leaders in prison (Curcio, Moretti, Balzarani) were able to reach probably the widest possible audience with their assertion that armed struggle was 'definitively concluded'. However the revived political debate whether some form of pardon for terrorists was therefore appropriate was abruptly halted only a few weeks later by a new BR crime – the murder of the DC senator Ruffilli in April 1988.

48.   I have simply counted the list (described as *sicuramente riduttivo*) in *Il*

Bollettino del Coordinamento dei Comitati contro la Repressione (1984) no. 14 (October), pp. 7–9. As in the wider population of the armed community, men (328) outnumber women (116) by three to one in this list. By early 1988 the number of 'political prisoners' had apparently shrunk to 161, out of the 442 left-wing practitioners of violence who were still in jail (*La Repubblica*, 19 January 1988, p. 4).

49. For the figures on the distribution of wanted members of armed groups across Italy and 18 other countries, see the official data cited in *Vita Italiana*, vol. XXXVI (1986), no. 1, p. 68. Apart from simply refusing to acknowledge the receipt of some demands for extradition, the French government turned an especially blind eye to the presence of members of the intelligentsia, even when sentenced to long prison terms (Negri, 30 years; Scalzone, 23 years) for crimes recognised by the French penal code. Although the European Convention for the Suppression of Terrorism had been signed by most governments in 1977, it was not ratified in Italy until February 1986 and remained unratified in France (as of January 1987). In any case its provisions leave loopholes for each government to decide on an *ad hoc* basis what is to count as a 'political' or 'terrorist' crime, in accord with different constitutional guarantees, and it is therefore not an efficacious framework in itself for a common European judicial area (see J. Lodge and D. Freestone, 'The European Community and Terrorism: Political and Legal Aspects' in Y. Alexander and K. Myers (eds), *Terrorism in Europe* (London: Croom Helm, 1982) pp. 79–101).

3 VIOLENCE IN A LOCAL CONTEXT: THE FACTORY

1. A well-known text encouraging sabotage is A. Negri, *Il dominio e il sabotaggio* (Milan: Feltrinelli, 1978). The centrality of the Luddite *rifiuto del lavoro* to the culture of *Autonomia*'s violence is insisted on by A. Ventura, 'Il problema storico del terrorismo italiano', *Rivista storica italiana*, vol. XCII (1980) no. 1, pp. 142–7.
2. The chronological sequence of murders, woundings and kidnappings of personnel affecting the Alfa-Romeo plant at Arese and the Fiat plants at Mirafiori, Rivalta, Chivasso (Lancia) and Sesto Torinese (Frantek), compiled from the data in M. Galleni, *Rapporto sul terrorismo* (Milan: Rizzoli, 1981) *passim*, was:

	1973	1974	1975	1976	1977	1978	1979	1980	1981	Total
Alfa-Romeo	1	–	–	–	1	2	–	1	2	7
Fiat	2	–	2	1	6	3	11	2	–	27

Two employees from the Fiat plant at Frosinone were wounded in 1976 and one murdered in 1978.

3. One estimate put the overall percentage of members of armed groups who were ever members of unions at not more than 5 per cent (P. Feltrin, 'Sindacato e terrorismo', *Prospettiva Sindacale*, vol. xiii (1982) no. 3, p. 168). But the symbolic importance of discovering in 1980 that

one BR member (Alfieri) had managed to reach the executive committee of the Alfa-Romeo council, coupled with the publicity invariably given to the arrest of even a single unionist, belied their quantitative insignificance among the several thousand shopfloor delegates elected between 1970 and 1982 in the factories where the BR could display some presence.

4. The five victims were: Macchiarini (Sit-Siemens), Labate (provincial secretary of the neo-Fascist CISNAL metalworkers in Turin), Mincuzzi (Alfa-Romeo), Amerio (Fiat) and Casabona (Ansaldo).

5. See, for example, communiqué no. 19, 19 June 1978, Turin, reprinted in E. Papa, *Il processo alle Brigate Rosse* (Turin: Giappichelli, 1979) p. 246.

6. Since the armed groups' attacks on managers were often treated as no more than justified responses to Italy's allegedly substantial rate of *omicidi bianchi*, it is worth putting the country's record in a European context. Within the restricted range of comparisons permitted by International Labour Organisation statistics for the period 1969–76, Italy emerges with a consistently better safety record than West Germany, Switzerland and Turkey in the manufacturing sector and as inferior to West Germany, comparable to Switzerland and superior to Turkey in the construction sector (ILO, *Yearbook of Labour Statistics* (ILO: Geneva: 1978), pp. 609–11, Tables 23c, 23d).

7. See, for example, the comments in the dossier for internal use compiled by the UIL at Alfa-Romeo: 'Una cronologia commentata sul terrorismo all'Alfa', dated July–September 1981.

8. The literature on the Hot Autumn and its aftermath is considerable: for recent discussions in English see C. Sabel, *Work and Politics* (Cambridge: Cambridge University Press, 1982) pp. 145–67, and G. Contini, 'Politics, Law and Shopfloor Bargaining in Postwar Italy', in S. Tolliday and J. Zeitlin (eds), *Shopfloor Bargaining and the State* (Cambridge: Cambridge University Press, 1985) pp. 192–218. On the post-1969 *conflittualità permanente* see G. Bognetti, 'Italy', *Comparative Law Yearbook*, vol. 4, 1980, pp. 105–30.

9. S. Hellman, 'Il PCI e l'ambigua eredità dell'autunno caldo a Torino', *Il Mulino*, vol. xxix (1980) no. 268, p. 273.

10. B. Manghi, *Declinare crescendo* (Bologna: Il Mulino, 1977). A useful detailed account of union strategies in the 1970s is P. Lange, G. Ross and M. Vannicelli, *Unions, Change and Crisis: French and Italian Union Strategy and the Political Economy, 1945–80* (London: George Allen and Unwin, 1982), Ch. 2, parts 4 and 5.

11. For some historical data on violent strikes see D. Snyder and W. Kelly, 'Industrial Violence in Italy 1878–1903', *American Journal of Sociology*, vol. 82 (1976) no. 1, pp. 131–62. For contemporary references see the testimonies published in the *Quotidiano dei Lavoratori*, 2–7 November 1977 on workplace violence, and I. Regalia, M. Regini and E. Reyneri: 'Labour Conflicts and Industrial Relations in Italy', in C. Crouch and A. Pizzorno (eds), *The Resurgence of Class Conflict in Western Europe* (London: Macmillan, 1978) vol. 1, at pp. 112, 115. It would of course be quite disingenuous to see this violence solely as

an aggressive workforce tactic and not also as a response to sometimes exceptionally brutal managerial strategies of control – for which, at Fiat, see E. Pugno and S. Garavini, *Gli anni duri alla Fiat* (Turin: Einaudi, 1974).

12. See A. Amin, 'Restructuring in Fiat and the Decentralisation of Production into Southern Italy', in R. Hudson and J. Lewis (eds), *Uneven Development in Southern Europe* (London: Methuen, 1985) p. 178. The figures on strikes in 1979 are taken from *La Repubblica*, 1 July 1986, p. 5.

13. Amin's figures show that whereas in 1973 three-quarters of Fiat automobiles were produced in Italy, by 1979 the proportion was little more than one-half (Amin, 'Restructuring in Fiat and the Decentralisation of Production in Southern Italy', p. 60, Table 7.1); over the same period Fiat's share of the national car market dropped from two-thirds to one-half (ibid., p. 162, Table 7.2). For details of conflict and managerial responses at Alfa-Romeo, see G. Medusa, *L'impresa tra produttività e consenso: il caso Alfa-Romeo* (Milan: Etas Libri, 1983); M. Roccella, 'La composizione dei conflitti di lavoro nella grande impresa: il caso dell'Alfa-Romeo di Arese', *Giornale del diritto di lavoro e di relazioni industriali*, vol. 14 (1982) pp. 251–73.

14. See, for a discussion of this approach, Mary Douglas, 'Introduction', in M. Douglas (ed.), *Witchcraft Confessions and Accusations* (London: Tavistock, 1970) ASA Monographs in Social Anthropology, vol. 9.

15. See Feltrin, 'Sindacato e terrorismo', who discusses the confederations' 'reticence'.

16. On the different traditions of the CGIL and CISL, and especially of their respective metalworker federations FIOM and FIM which were the relevant unions for Fiat and Alfa-Romeo, see Lange *et al.*, *Unions, Change and Crisis*, pp. 114–15.

17. The following details are taken from a dossier dated 3 January 1980, containing texts and commentaries, compiled by the FIM-CISL Provincial Federation in Milan and circulated widely to other branches of the Federation and Confederation.

18. A particularly controversial assertion of a radical difference between *Autonomia* and the BR was made by the Veneto FIM-CISL immediately following the BR murder of a manager from Porto Marghera: see its *Sulla violenza politica nel Veneto*, a 21-page document dated 3 January 1980.

19. P. Feltrin and E. Santi, 'Il terrorismo di sinistra: le interpretazioni', *Progetto*, vol. 2 (1981) pp. 48–55.

20. The term 'symbolic knowledge' and the characterisation of its distinctiveness is taken from D. Sperber, *Rethinking Symbolism* (Cambridge: Cambridge University Press, 1975), Chapter 4.

21. For a reference to this debate in Turin, see the interview with a leading representative of the local PCI, P. Fassino, in G. Pansa, *Storie italiane di violenza e terrorismo* (Bari: Laterza, 1980), p. 147. The PCI, FLM and factory councils also used quotation marks when referring to 'red' terrorism, or 'so-called left-wing terrorism'.

22. As described by a Fiat factory council delegate interviewed in

M. Cavallini (ed), *Terrorismo in fabbrica* (Rome: Editori Riuniti, 1978) p. 42. The earlier activities of Luigi Cavallo who, with management's blessing, had attempted to discredit the Left at Fiat by 'borrowing' its signatures were fresh in the minds of older workers.

23. I have based this section on documents produced by the two sets of factory councils and the contributions to three of the four conferences on terrorism organised by the FLM in Turin in 1979–81, published in the Federation's periodical *Esperienze Sindacali*, vol. 7 (1979) no. 1, vol. 8 (1980) no. 2; and vol. 10 (1987) no. 2.

24. *Esperienze Sindacali*, vol. 8 (1980) no. 2, p. 10.

25. Most of these details have been taken from the descriptions provided by the union and factory council discussants in Cavallini, *Terrorismo in fabbrica, passim.*

26. J. Elster, 'Négation active et négation passive: essai de sociologie ivanienne', *Archives européennes de sociologie*, vol. XXI (1980) no. 2, pp. 239–49; 'Irrational Politics', *London Review of Books*, vol. 2, 21 August–3 September 1980, pp. 11–13.

27. The use of police to investigate the political opinions of workers on behalf of management was notorious: in the 1970s management at both Fiat and Alfa-Romeo was convicted on these practices, which had been outlawed by the Workers' Statute. The difficulties of reaching a common confederal policy were further aggravated by the distinction between the organisational levels recommending suspension (generally the factory council) and those empowered to decree it (the provincial federation of the relevant union). An agreement at the initial level could be dissipated as the issue moved away from the shopfloor.

28. See the *Atti del Convegno Nazionale sul Terrorismo* (Milan: 17 July 1981), published by the Lombardy region branch of the FLM in 1982. No non-union speakers were invited to the earlier internal assembly organised by the Alfa factory council at Arese, 28/29 February 1980. The first occasion on which a Milan magistrate (not himself involved in investigating political violence) spoke at a factory in Sesto San Giovanni appears to have been as late as March 1979. According to the FLM organiser, the meeting was prompted by the desire to show solidarity with the judiciary who had publicly criticised the political élite's handling of violence after the murder of a local public prosecutor, Alessandrini, in January.

29. Direzione PCI, Sezione Problemi dello Stato: Federazione Milanese, Commissione Problemi dello Stato *Primo Rapporto sull' Inchiesta di Massa sul Terrorismo* (Milan: May 1982) p. 48.

30. For the Turin BR apparatchiks' attention to responses at Fiat see Peci, *Io, l'infame*, pp. 136, 139.

31. For Fiat unionisation and PCI figures see R. Gianotti, *Trent'anni di lotte alla Fiat: 1948–1978* (Bari: De Donato, 1979) pp. 217, 238. At Alfa-Romeo the FLM membership in 1975 was only 17.4 per cent (Roccella, 'La composizione dei conflitti di lavoro nella grande impresa', p. 255, Table 5).

32. The figures for the turnover rate (Amin, 'Restructuring in Fiat and the

Decentralisation of Production in Southern Italy', p. 183) and commitment to work (A. Accornero, 'Le idee dell'operaio Fiat su lavoro, sindacato, politica', *Rinascita* (1980) no. 8, 22 February, p. 20) refer to all Fiat plants in Piedmont: it is a safe bet that Mirafiori's rates alone would be higher.

33. A. Accornero, E. Persichella, S. Pizzutilo, C. Sebastiani, 'Primi risultati dell'inchiesta Italsider', *Politica ed Economia*, vol. 11 (1980) no. 4, p. 47, Table 7.

34. Ibid., p. 45, Table 6. The proportion of the two samples giving primary importance to the unions' *lotta democratica di massa* was 16.8 per cent in Taranto, 10.5 per cent in Turin.

35. V Lega FLM, 'Inchiesta sul Terrorismo', supplement to *Il Consiglione* (1980) no. 13, n.p. (table of responses to question 1). The specific division was the body assembly shop (*carrozzeria*).

36. S. Scamuzzi, 'Operai e impiegati Fiat tra vecchi e nuovi radicalismi', *Politica ed Economia*, vol. 13 (1982) no. 6, p. 34.

37. A. Baldissera, 'Alle origini della politica della disuguaglianza nell'Italia degli anni '80: la marcia dei quarantamila', *Quaderni di Sociologia*, vol. XXXI (1984) no. 1, pp. 69–73.

38. On the 'ethnic' divisions in Turin's mobility patterns see N. Negri, 'I nuovi torinesi: immigrazione, mobilità e struttura sociale', in G. Martinotti (ed), *La città difficile* (Milan: F. Angeli, 1982) vol. 5, p. 117. For a comment by an older Fiat worker on the distinction between Piedmontese *capi* and southern unskilled workers see Pansa, *Storie italiane di violenze e terrorismo*, p. 176.

39. Attention was focused on Fiat after an influential reportage of workers' opinions at Mirafiori's gates suggested that the extent of worker solidarity with Casalegno was very low. See the article by G. Pansa (originally published in *La Repubblica*, 18 November 1977) and the response of the Turin trade unions, reprinted in *Una Regione contro il Terrorismo* (Consiglio Regionale del Piemonte, 1979) pp. 106–15.

40. *L'Espresso*, 23 December 1979, no. 51, p. 22. The scale of the unions' organisational effort must be stressed, including frequent meetings in every workshop and 350 general assemblies with interventions by local political figures in Piedmont's factories in 1977–8 alone.

41. For these details see the results published in V *Lega* FLM 'Inchiesta sul Terrorismo', *passim*.

42. Pansa, *Storie italiane di violenze e terrorismo*, pp. 112–33 provides some details on Rossa and the man he denounced, who subsequently committed suicide in jail. Outside the union context, the murder of Rossa – which appears to have been intended as a kneecapping but was transformed into a murder by the individual decision of the principal apparatchik responsible for the attack – generated dramatically negative consequences for the BR. The apparent message, that even members of the Left (Rossa was a PCI activist) could be physically attacked, was reinforced later in the same month by PL's murder of the Milan magistrate Alessandrini. One of Pansa's other interviewees (pp. 208–9) attributes his decision to collaborate with the magistrature in the April 7 inquiry to the shock of Rossa's murder.

43. Peci, *Io, l'infame* p. 57. The *presse* division provided the largest number of victims at Fiat.

44. The following details are taken from G. Ghezzi, *Processo al Sindacato* (Bari: De Donato, 1981); S. Scarponi, 'Licenziamenti Fiat: la vicenda dei 61', *Qualegiustizia* (1981) no. 51, pp. 293–341; L. Mariucci, 'Licenziamento disciplinare di massa e pratiche sleali contro il sindacato: note sul caso Fiat', *Rivista giuridica del lavoro*, vol. II (1980) pp. 421–43; and *Controinformazione* (1979) November, pp. 6–16 and (1980) January, pp. 13–24, 61. The 61 quickly became 60 as one of the suspended workers found another job and played no further part in the conflict, but since the subjects were always referred to as 'the 61', I have followed that practice.

45. Ghezzi, *Processo al Sindacato*, p. 78. Only one in five (21 per cent) respondents interpreted Fiat's action as a deliberate attempt to weaken the union; and even smaller group (13 per cent) saw it as a pretext for getting rid of the most combative defenders of workers' interests.

46. Fiat management later acknowledged the symbolic role of the 61, 'who might just as easily have been 601': see the interview with the firm's managing director, Romiti, in *La Repubblica*, 17 January 1985, p. 7.

47. The details of individual cases for reinstatement which followed showed the FLM to have been entirely justified in refusing blanket protection for the 61. By November 1980 five suits for reinstatement had been won, two lost, and fourteen of the 61 were being investigated for participation in armed struggle (Ghezzi, *Processo al Sindacato*, pp. 140–1). The FLM's courtroom chances had not been improved by the publication of an article by the Communist leader, Amendola, in November 1979 which explicitly linked shopfloor conflict to 'terrorism' and was cited in the judge's verdict: see G. Amendola, 'Interrogativi sul caso Fiat', *Rinascita*, 9 November 1979, no. 43.

48. See Ghezzi, *Processo al Sindacato*, pp. 142–3, quoting F. Mancini and A. Casalegno.

49. For the details of the march used in the following paragraphs I have drawn on the account by Baldissera, 'Alle origini della politica della disuguaglianza nell'Italia degli anni '80'.

50. See for example the interview with the leading figure in the *Coordinamento*, later a PRI member of Parliament, L. Arisio, in *La Repubblica*, 16 October 1980, p. 3.

51. For an analysis of the general tendency, based on the German occupation of Poland during the Second World War, see Jan T. Gross, 'Terror and Obedience: A Society Under Occupation', *Archives européennes de sociologie*, vol. XX (1979) pp. 333–42.

52. Scarponi, 'Licenziamenti Fiat', p. 322: Fiat acknowledged that sending articles to schools was unprecedented. The interview is reprinted in Pansa, *Storie italiane di violenza e terrorismo*, pp. 162–8.

4 MAINTAINING THE POLITICAL FRONTIER

1. See, for example, J. Lodge (ed.), *Terrorism: Challenge to the State* (New York: St Martins Press, 1981).

2. P. Bourdieu, *Essay on the Theory of Practice* (Cambridge: Cambridge University Press, 1977), pp. 12–14.

3. The conceptualisation of the antagonism as a struggle between 'terrorism' and 'the State' is usually symptomatic of a technicist, prescriptive bias which ignores how the political actors who have to make the State work see the issue to which they are devising responses. Even the qualification 'liberal' states is insufficiently discriminatory to understand why particular kinds of response actually do occur. See, *inter alia*, P. Wilkinson, *Terrorism and the Liberal State* (London: Macmillan, 1977); G. Wardlaw, *Political Terrorism* (Cambridge: Cambridge University Press, 1983).

4. ISTAT, 'Statistiche della criminalità, anni 1972–6', *Bollettino mensile di statistica* (1978) no. 24, Supplement, p. 7, Prosp. 1; *Annuario Statistico Italiano* (Rome: ISTAT, 1979) p. 122, Table 112. Robberies with violence and kidnappings were identified as separate statistical categories for the first time in the early 1970s.

5. I have not counted among the political victims the local-level activists, mostly from the youth sections of the MSI and PCI and the extraparliamentary Left who were killed in reciprocal raids. Seven victims belonged to the extreme Right, and fourteen to the Left, between 1970 and 1982.

6. See the BR 'self-interview' of January 1973 reprinted in V. Tessandori, *BR. Imputazione: banda armata* (Milan: Garzanti, 1977) p. 392.

7. See, for example, the testimony of Marco Barbone to the CPM, vol. 8, p. 206.

8. In the kidnapping, and subsequent murder, of Roberto Peci in 1981 one of the kidnappers later indicated that the extent of 'disarticulation' required to secure his release would have been the dismissal of General Dalla Chiesa or the initiation of a formal investigation into the work of the magistrate Caselli: either action would have also lent credence to the 'confession' manufactured for Peci (see the memoir of Roberto Buzzati, quoted in the so-called 'Moro-*ter*' sentence by the investigating magistrate, R. Priore, *Sentenza di rinvio a giudizio di Abatangelo P. e altri*, Tribunale di Roma, 13 August 1984, p. 1277).

9. A succinct summary of the implementation and revaluation of the Constitution is provided by D. Hine, 'Thirty Years of the Italian Republic: Governability and Constitutional Reform', *Parliamentary Affairs*, vol. xxxiv (1981) no. 1, pp. 63–80.

10. Figures on perceptions of party attitudes to violence can be found in G. Guidorossi, *Gli italiani e la politica* (Milan: F. Angeli, 1984) pp. 110–11, Table 3.3. The survey of attitudes towards the MSI is taken from G. Fabris, *Il comportamento politico degli italiani* (Milan: F. Angeli, 1977) p. 91.

11. For details of the entire episode see C. Stajano, *L'Italia nichilista* (Milan: A. Mondadori, 1982) pp. 195–263. Donat-Cattin did not of course know of the affiliation of his interlocutor, Sandalo, to PL. Nevertheless it is revelatory of the lack of distance between the two communities in terms of individual contacts that, having learned unequivocally of his son's participation in armed struggle, Donat-

Cattin should have had no difficulty finding a person known to be close enough to his son to be asked to find him.

12.   A former high-ranking official in the security services, Maletti, made the claim about the *coups* in an interview many years later (*L'Espresso*, 15 March 1981, pp. 35–45). Details of the SIFAR affair can be found in R. Collin, *The De Lorenzo Gambit: The Italian Coup Manqué of 1964* (London: Sage, 1976).

13.   See Direzione PCI, Sezione Problemi dello Stato: Commissione Problemi dello Stato, Federazione Milanese del PCI, *Primo Rapporto sull'Inchiesta di Massa sul Terrorismo* (Milan: May 1982), p. 37. A necessarily somewhat speculative account of Italy's security services can be found in G. De Lutiis, *Storia dei servizi segreti in Italia* (Rome: Editori Riuniti, 1984). Details from magistrates' enquiries into right-wing violence and the involvement of the security services can be found in V. Borraccetti (ed.), *Eversione di destra, terrorismo, stragi* (Milan: F. Angeli, 1986) and G. De Lutiis (ed.), *La strage* (Rome: Editori Riuniti, 1987).

14.   Guidorossi, *Gli italiani e la politica*, pp. 214–15; G. Pasquino, 'Recenti trasformazioni nel sistema di potere della democrazia cristiana' in L. Graziano and S. Tarrow (eds), *La Crisi Italiana* (Turin: Einaudi, 1979), vol. 2, p. 626, Table 28.

15.   The term 'leaderless Bonapartism' was coined by Percy Allum ('The Christian Democrat Regime in Italy: A Form of Bonapartism?', *Current Sociology*, vol. 30 (1982) no. 2, pp. 83–95) commenting on the characterisation of Italy as a centreless society by G. E. Rusconi and S. Scamuzzi ('Italy Today: An Eccentric Society', *Current Sociology*, vol. 29 (1981) no. 1, pp. 1–204). The details on party electoral performance, membership and links to civil society are usefully summarised and discussed in L. Morlino: 'The Changing Relations Between Parties and Society in Italy', *West European Politics*, vol. 7 (1984) no. 4, pp. 45–66.

16.   Agreement on a framework for a new code had been reached the previous year. But since the increase in political and ordinary violence counselled delay in introducing the proposed radical changes from an inquisitorial to an adversarial judicial system, the revision had still not taken place a decade later, leaving the Reale law still in force. An attempt to make some of its penalties still more severe in April 1978 by a so-called Reale-bis law failed because of party conflicts, especially within the DC.

17.   Guidorossi, *Gli italiani e la politica*, pp. 229–30, Table 12. In 1975, for example, the claim that the government's first priority was to improve the state of public order (*ordine pubblico*, 13.6 per cent of respondents) ranked behind not only employment (37.6 per cent) and inflation (36 per cent) but also housing (19.6 per cent) and health reforms (13.9 per cent).

18.   More than one in three (37 per cent) of the DC members of parliament in 1976 had been elected for the first time, lower than the PCI turnover (50 per cent) but substantially higher than the party's previous record (see M. Cotta, 'Il rinnovamento del personale parlamentare democris-

tiano', *Il Mulino*, vol. xxvii (1978) pp. 723–42). One of the symbols of party renewal was the establishment of the *Feste dell'Amicizia* in direct contrast with the PCI's *Feste dell'Unit*.

19. That was made clear by the previous Minister of Justice, Bonifacio, in the Senate debate on the establishment of the Commission (*Atti del Senato della Repubblica*, VII Legislatura, resoconto stenografico, 17 October 1979, p. 1610).

20. Figures for the DC cited in G. Pasquino, 'Il problema delle alleanze', in A. Parisi (ed.), *Democristiani* (Bologna: Il Mulino, 1979) p. 179. For the evidence of the local unpopularity of the PCI's historic compromise strategy among party activists see M. Barbagli and P. Corbetta, 'After the Historic Compromise: A Turning Point for the PCI', *European Journal of Political Research*, vol. 10 (1982), pp. 217, 223.

21. For the PCI's acknowledged shift and admission that its own rank and file with Resistance experience was attracted by violence, see B. Bertini, P. Franchi and U. Spagnoli, *Estremismo, terrorismo, ordine democratico* (Rome: Editori Riuniti, 1978). Party worries about the strength of the Resistance tradition were confirmed in a DOXA survey in late 1977 which showed that PCI members aged 54+ were markedly more sympathetic to greater contact with the clearly violent *Autonomia* groups than the younger age groups (*Bollettino della DOXA*, vol. xxxii (1978) 30–1 January, p. 82, Table 29.2).

22. Although in 1975 the PCI had finally voted against the law, the party had actually supported several of its single clauses. One other party also changed its views: the MSI had voted in favour of the law in 1975 but opposed it in 1978.

23. See, among many sources: for the DC, the articles by P. Jovine in *La Discussione*, February to March 1980, and the testimony of Cossiga to the CPM in May 1980, vol. 3, p. 105; for the PCI, U. Pecchioli in *L'Espresso*, 6 January 1980, pp. 6–7; the strongest detailed assertions from the PSI, which was generally less convinced, were made by A. Ventura, 'Il problema storico del terrorismo italiano', *Rivista storica italiana*, vol. XCII (1980) no. 1, pp. 125–51.

24. PCI, Federazione di Milano, Commissione Problemi dello Stato, *Seminario Terrorismo* (February 1981) p. 7.

25. The kidnapping of the US NATO general, Dozier, in late 1981; the revelation of an alleged link through a UIL functionary, Scricciolo, to Bulgaria; the murder of another US officer involved in the Middle East, Hunt, in 1984; the murder of Conti, a close associate of the PRI Minister of Defence, Spadolini, in 1986.

26. In October 1986, however, Parliament agreed to set up a further, smaller Commission to try to make good its previous failure and to examine in particular the causes and investigations of right-wing massacres.

27. A convenient collection of the relevant legislation passed between 1974 and 1980 is A. Bevere, *Siamo ancora il paese più libero del mondo?* (Milan: La Pietra, 1980). I shall deal with the pragmatic consequences of new police powers for investigations in Chapter 5.

28. See the testimonies to the CPM of Andreotti (vol. 3, pp. 150–1), Cossiga (ibid., pp. 231–2) and General Ferrara of the carabinieri

(vol. 6, pp. 144–5). Andreotti was also approached for reassurance by another major category of State victims, the prison officers (interview in *Epoca*, 13 July 1984, p. 29).

29. Although the parties had issued specific voting directives for the referenda, the extent to which those indications could in fact be flouted was shown by the 1978 referendum on public subsidies for political parties. The approval for the Reale and Cossiga laws was lower in both cases than the electoral support for the parties which declared for their retention; but there seems no reason to doubt that the results indicated wide popular support rather than a mere direct reflex of party allegiance.

30. PCI, *Primo Rapporto*, p. 38.

31. Ibid. For the PSI figures see P. Cayrol and P. Ignazi, 'Cousins ou frères? Attitudes politiques et conceptions du parti chez les militants socialistes francais et italiens', *Revue Francaise de Science Politique*, vol. xxxiii (1983) no. 4, p. 634, Table 1; p. 636, fn. 6.

32. Makno survey reported in *L'Espresso*, 10 January 1982, p. 9. For the figures on general support for the death penalty and the identification of the particular crimes for which it was thought appropriate, see P. Corbetta and A. Parisi, 'Perche più indulgenza verso i terroristi?', *Cattaneo*, vol. iii (1983) no. 2, pp. 21–35.

33. For full details on their work in Piedmont, where several thousand public meetings were organised between 1977 and 1979, see Consiglio Regionale del Piemonte, *Una Regione contro il terrorismo* (Turin: 1979).

34. Mention of the rates of turnover of PCI functionaires is made by Barbagli and Corbetta, 'After the Historic Compromise', p. 239. For statements on the centre/local divergences, see F. Di Giulio and E. Rocco: *Un ministro-ombra si confessa* (Milan: Rizzoli, 1979) pp. 70–1; the interview with P. Fassino in G. Pansa, *Storie italiane di violenze e terrorismo* (Bari: Laterza, 1980) p. 156.

35. PCI, Federazione di Milano, p. 2 n. 24; PCI, *Primo Rapporto*, p. 37, n. 30.

36. For the PCI, Pansa, *Storie italiane di violenze e terrorismo*, pp. 157–8; for the DC local attitudes, see the interrogation of the kidnap victim, Cirillo, published in *Napoli Oggi*, 27 June 1981, pp. 1–2. By way of a regional example, 56 of the 117 DC local sections in the province of Bologna did not even meet between October 1977 and the end of March 1978, i.e. not even during the first phase of Moro's kidnapping (D. Wertman, 'La partecipazione intermittente: gli iscritti e la vita di partito', in Parisi, *Democristiani*, p. 79).

37. Details on the Turin questionnaire and its results are taken from *Nuovasocietà* (1979) nos. 142, 146, 157, 160. One in sixteen (6 per cent) of the national questionnaire's respondents claimed to have known directly of terrorist actions, and half (48 per cent) reported their suspicions to police (PCI, *Primo Rapporto* p. 38). In a Makno survey in 1981 20 per cent said they would always report suspicions to the police, 51 per cent would do so if they could be guaranteed anonymity and 29 per cent were uncertain or would definitely keep silent (*L'Espresso*, 10 January 1982, pp. 6–11).

38. Regional law no. 8, 18 January 1980 which anticipated the national law (466/1980) prompted by the Bologna station bomb massacre. An account of the *anni di piombo* in Turin from the mayor's viewpoint is D. Novelli, *Vivere a Torino* (Rome: Editori Riuniti, 1980): details of his 93 'clandestine' meetings are at p. 28.

39. Cossiga indicated that the strategy of 'selective repression', precisely to avoid unifying the state's opponents, was deliberate government policy (CPM, vol. 3, pp. 207–8).

40. The first five maximum security jails – Favignana, Asinara, Cuneo, Fossombrone and Trani – were ready in July 1977; and specially renovated sections were also added to various existing jails. The text of the decree instituting them and giving the *carabinieri* (under General Dalla Chiesa) specific responsibility for their external surveillance is reprinted in R. Canosa, *Le libertà in Italia* (Turin: Einaudi, 1981) pp. 51–2.

41. The appallingly detailed extent of surveillance can be seen from the decree revoking the generalised application of article 90 to maximum security prisons in 1984, reprinted in *Il Bollettino del Coordinamento dei Comitati contro la Repressione* (1984) no. 15, pp. 4–6. In March 1984 782 prisoners were subject to its regime. For an account of the bureaucratic process of assignment to maximum security status, see the 'interrogation' of D'Urso by the BR (*L'Espresso*, 11 January 1981, pp. 74–90).

42. Testimony of Dalla Chiesa to the CPM, vol. 4, p. 259.

43. Articles 2 and 5, *disegno di legge* no. 601, presented to the Senate by the Prime Minister, 17 December 1979, reprinted in Bevere, *Siamo ancora il paese più libero del mondo?*, pp. 127–35.

44. The details are discussed in Chapter 6, especially pp. 221–2, 301 n. 10. In addition the State offered the major collaborators sums of up to 20 million lire each when they left jail (some refused the money). To permit emigration passports in false names have been issued and in one case at least, a change of name was officially approved. The actual guidelines for rewarding exit once sentences have been served are secret.

45. Other members of the armed community's intelligentsia themselves rejected the idea of an amnesty since it would have given them no opportunity to prove their pleas of innocence in court. The police too were strongly opposed to an amnesty for political crime: see the testimony of Coronas on the effects of the amnesty of 21 May 1970 (CPM, vol. 4, p. 107). Somewhat in contradiction with the government's line, therefore, was the inclusion of the offence of 'subversive association' in the amnesty of 1978. Two opinion polls, taken in late 1987, suggested a continuing strength of public feeling against any generalised pardon for past crimes. According to a DMT-Telemarketing survey of 3000 respondents, only 8% were unequivocally in favour of an amnesty, 44% unequivocally against, and 38% would only accept on condition that it was restricted to those who had not participated in murders or woundings (*L'Espresso*, 31 January 1988, p. 25). A second survey reported that 68% of respondents

opposed any new measures to reduce or cancel sentences passed on terrorists (*Epoca*, 31 January 1988, no. 1947, p. 20).

46.	It was unfortunate that the particular beneficiary, who had already served seven years in jail on by no means the most serious charges, came from a powerful Sicilian family: she was also the ex-wife of a leading member of *Autonomia*'s intelligentsia, himself closely linked to the PSI leadership to which the President conceding the pardon had belonged. For details see *La Repubblica*, 7–10 June 1985. As far as I know, no other pardons for former 'terrorists' have been granted.

47.	The qualification 'symbolic' here is intended to distinguish these cases from the kidnappings carried out solely for ransom and usually unclaimed. Nine of the seventeen cases involved industrial victims (Macchiarini, Mincuzzi, Labate, Amerio, Casabona, D'Ambrosio, Compare, Sandrucci and Taliercio); the remaining four victims comprised the brother of a BR defector (Peci), a local PCI administrator in Naples (Siola), a US general (Dozier) and a magistrate (De Gennaro) whose kidnapping by the NAP in 1975 was too short-lived and too confused to be included in this section's discussion. The kidnappings solely for ransom were indicated in note 21 to Chapter 2, p. 278.

48.	Coverage of the most dramatic case, Moro, was in fact rather uneven among major newspapers (see Table 2D in A. Schmid and J. de Graaf, *Violence as Communication: Insurgent Terrorism and the Western News Media* (London: Sage, 1982, p. 81); and the claims that newspaper sales were a particular beneficiary of sensational treatment are exaggerated. The print run of *La Repubblica*, for example, went up from *c.* 170 000 copies in the days before the Moro kidnapping to 256 000 the day after but had fallen back to normal levels only two days later.

49.	For a more detailed analysis of kidnapping as ritual, see David Moss, 'The Kidnapping and Murder of Aldo Moro', *Archives européennes de sociologie*, vol. xxii (1981) no. 2, pp. 265–95. The other kidnappings discussed below are described in Soccorso Rosso, *Brigate Rosse* (Milan: Feltrinelli, 1976); L. Jannuzzi, E. Capecelatro, F. Rocella, V. Vecellio, *La pelle del D'Urso* (Rome: Radio Radicale, 1981). For the Cirillo case, apart from the press coverage of 1981–4, see the *Relazione del Comitato Parlamentare per i Servizi di Informazione e Sicurezza e per il Segreto di Stato sui Problemi Relativi all'Operato dei Servizi di Informazione e Sicurezza durante il sequestro dell'Assessore Democristiano della Regione Campana, Ciro Cirillo* (Senato della Repubblica, IX Legislatura, Doc. XLVII, n. 1, 10 October 1984).

50.	E. Fenzi, 'Abbozzo di una storia: le b.r.', *Contro le regole di questo assurdo gioco* (1983), Summer, p. 23. In two cases the audience specifically addressed failed to offer whole-hearted support to the BR: the eight members of the XXII *ottobre* refused to show any willingness to be released by making a formal request to the judiciary on their own behalf (G. Guiso in CPM, vol. 6, p. 182), and nine *autonomi* (including Ferrari Bravo, Negri and Vesce) dissociated themselves publicly from the BR-sponsored prison revolt at Trani which accompanied the D'Urso kidnapping.

51. Given the involvement of the *camorra* and security services some details (for example, the knowledge and consent to negotiations of the DC leadership in Rome) will probably never be known. The investigating magistrate acknowledged that his final report was incomplete (*La Repubblica*, 7 November 1986, p. 17) but the repeated calls to set up a Parliamentary Commission of Inquiry have been rejected by the government. Evidence that differences between party attitudes towards the resolution of the Moro kidnapping were scarcely perceived among the Fiat workforce is provided by A. Baldissera, 'Le immagini del terrorismo tra gli operai della Fiat', *Political ed Economia*, vol. 9 (1981) pp. 33–4.

52. The materials published on the Moro case are now considerable. In addition to the eleven volumes of CPM transcripts and final reports, supplemented by the continuing publication of documents used by the Commission, no fewer than 14 of the 57 monographs on left-wing violence known to me deal solely with the kidnapping. In this section I have kept details of the sequence of events, 16 March–9 May 1978, to a minimum. For the event itself the most readable, if highly partisan, account in English is R. Katz, *Days of Wrath* (London: Granada, 1980): some other aspects are dealt with in Moss, 'The Kidnapping and Murder of Aldo Moro', and in R. E. Wagner-Pacifici, *The Moro Morality Play: terrorism as social drama* (Chicago: University of Chicago Press, 1986).

53. CPM, vol. I, p. 1. The terms of reference contained in law no. 597, 23 November 1979 were effectively identical to those approved earlier that year (March 29) by the Internal Affairs Committee of the Chamber.

54. Not completely, however. In May 1986, in response to PCI accusations, the Minister of Justice ordered an administrative enquiry into the alleged manipulation of evidence on the kidnapping in the Rome judiciary: its conclusions, reported as highly critical of the magistrates but excluding any deliberate attempt to mislead, were communicated to the Senate on 12 May 1987.

55. Savasta, a full time BR militant in Rome, learnt of the attack from the television (CPM, vol. 9, p. 291). One member of the *comitato esecutivo*, Azzolini, has since been reported as denying any knowledge of the dissent over Moro's murder in the Roman BR column which subsequently led to a public scission (*La Repubblica*, 18 December 1986, p. 16).

56. Moro is now known to have written at least 38 letters, most of which came to light subsequently and a few of which were never received. They are reprinted in CPM, vol. 2, pp. 91–123. An unsigned, partly incoherent *memoriale* attributed to Moro was discovered in a BR base in Milan in October 1978 (reprinted ibid., pp. 125–75).

57. BR, 'La campagna di primavera', *Controinformazione* (1979) June, no. 15, pp. 83–91. Evidence for its composition in jail came from the only repentant member of the group's early leadership, Buonavita (CPM, vol. 10, p. 594). He also confirmed the exclusion of the intelligentsia from any role in the planning or management of the

kidnapping. For their charge that the 'Executive Committee' did not know what its own goals were, see Fenzi, 'Abbozzo di una storia', p. 17.

58. Nine *pentiti* and one *dissociato* (Morucci) were among the 103 witnesses called by the CPM. The highly selective and largely generic account offered by Morucci, who had participated in the Via Fani massacre and acted as postman and telephonist for the BR communiqués, was the closest the Commission got to an insider's version.

59. CPM, vol. 2, pp. 3–61. The other dissenting reports (MSI–DN, PR, PLI, a Left Independent senator) were based on very specific points of dispute, emphasis or omission rather than fundamental disagreement.

60. Moss, 'The Kidnapping and Murder of Aldo Moro'.

61. See Berlinguer's demand to other parties at the meeting of their representatives on 3 April 1978 not to debate publicly any general issues raised by the kidnapping (summary minute published in *L'Espresso*, 15 October 1978, p. 14).

62. The slim evidence available suggests that the clear majority of the population supported the government's refusal of negotiations: a DOXA survey taken during the kidnapping indicated that three-quarters (77 per cent) of respondents agreed that the government should never negotiate with armed groups and a further 16 per cent, while accepting the possibility of a deal, excluded the possibility of an exchange between the hostage and 'political prisoners' (*L'Espresso*, 23 April 1978, pp. 12–15). After the D'Urso episode when some concessions were made and D'Urso had been released, two-thirds (62 per cent) of respondents were still prepared to refuse negotiations (PCI, *Primo Rapporto*, pp. 37–8).

63. For the divergence of PCI and DC readings of Moro's political identity see the editorials in *L'Unità* and the DC commemorations on the anniversaries of the kidnapping, 1979–85. The PCI has sponsored two studies suggesting decisive foreign intervention: G. Zupo and V. Marini Recchia: *Operazione Moro* (Milan: F. Angeli, 1984) and M. Scarano and M. De Luca: *Il mandarino è marcio* (Rome: Editori Riuniti, 1985).

64. Thus in July 1984, immediately after the conclusion of the parliamentary debate, Morucci and Faranda began to provide a near-complete account, within the limits of their own knowledge. In November 1984 the senior member of the *comitato esecutivo*, Moretti, offered his first, minimal, public comments on the kidnapping (*L'Espresso*, 2 December 1984, pp. 6–11). Much later, in 1987, other representatives of the DC were able to approach the by-then former leading members of the Red Brigades privately to propose full accounts of the remaining obscurities in armed struggle. Even at that late stage other parties voiced suspicions that the DC was preparing to negotiate some form of reduced sentence in return for a finally clarificatory description of the events concerning the party – but at the price of accepting an account which granted the BR authors a retrospective political justification for their recourse to violence.

5 THE CONSTRUCTION OF JUDICIAL ACCOUNTS

1. Because of the differences between Italian and English judicial systems, there are no simple and precise English translations for Italian judicial offices and processes. Since this chapter is concerned with the pre-trial phase of investigations (*istruttoria*) and the following chapter with the trials themselves, I shall distinguish for convenience between 'magistrates' and 'judges'. I shall use 'magistrate' to refer to the *giudice istruttore* and the (*sostituto*) *procuratore della Repubblica*: each has different functions and powers but, in the specific case of political violence, the investigations and accounts were largely collaborative exercises and they can therefore be treated as belonging to a single category. 'Judge' refers to the *giudice* who presides over the trial: a *sostituto procuratore della Repubblica*, usually the person who contributed to the investigations, is of course also present in court as the public prosecutor (*pubblico ministero*).

2. See P. Dusi, 'Il processo "7 Aprile" e la stampa', in Magistratura Democratica (ed.), *La magistratura di fronte al terrorismo e all'eversione di sinistra* (Milan: F. Angeli, 1982) especially pp. 68–9.

3. For substantial extracts from the documents of the April 7 case, see: *Processo all'Autonomia* (n.p.: Lerici, 1979); G. De Lutiis (ed.), *Attacco allo Stato* (Rome: Napoleone, 1982); G. Palombarini, *7 Aprile: il processo e la storia* (Venice: Arsenale Cooperativa Editrice, 1982). C. Stajano, *L'Italia nichilista* (Milan: A Mondadori, 1982) relies heavily on the Turin magistrates' documents in his account of *Prima Linea* in that city.

4. For details of the investigations of right-wing violence see V. Borraccetti (ed.), *Eversione di destra, terrorismo, stragi* (Milan: F. Angeli, 1986). The identification of the major problem as lying in the pre-trial investigation rather than with the court decisions is at p. 17.

5. The four factions belonged to the major professional association (ANM). In 1979 *Terzo Potere* (TP) and *Impegno Costituzionale* (IC) merged to form what is now the single largest group (*Unità per la Costituzione*: UniCost). The following table shows the percentage vote for each faction in the elections to ANM's governing council between 1973 and 1983:

	1973	1975	1977	1980	1983
MI	44.0	42.9	41.1	41.5	36.9
TP	17.6	23.1	19.5	41.1	44.5
IC	25.5	21.1	25.7		
MD	13.3	12.9	13.7	15.7	17.9

6. G. P. Prandstraller, *Avvocati e metropoli* (Milan: F. Angeli, 1981), pp. 69–71.

7. The protracted case against Marrone – whose text had been published in 1975 – is discussed in *Il Foro Italiano* (1983), part III, pp. 416–24. Two further cases of disciplinary proceedings by the CSM against magistrates critical of their profession's handling of political violence are mentioned below, pp. 196, 298 n. 37.

8. As insisted upon by the Minister of Justice, Sarti, during the D'Urso kidnapping (L. Jannuzzi, E. Capecelatro, F. Roccella, V. Vecellio: *La pelle del D'Urso* (Rome: Radio Radicale, 1981) p. 368).

9. A dinner hosted by one Milan magistrate so that a colleague (subsequently murdered) could meet one of *Autonomia*'s leaders caused a brief flurry of interest. In Genoa the son of a local magistrate with power to influence the direction of investigations was alleged to be close to the Red Brigades, a situation which caused the police some concern (CPM, vol. IV, pp. 295–6).

10. *Nuovasocietà* (1981) no. 193 (16 May), p. 31. The issue was entitled 'How to Read a Trial Against Subversion [*eversione*]'. Emphasis was placed on the very different criteria for valid argument and proof in political and legal arenas.

11. Figures from the Minister's reports to Parliament (*La Repubblica*, 20 June 1980, p. 8; 21–2 September 1980, p. 7. 570 of the 606 detentions were made by the *carabinieri* (CC) for whom the confirmation-of-arrest rate (one in five) was very much lower than that of the *Pubblica Sicurezza* (PS) force (one in two).

12. For details see S. Genova, *Missione antiterrorismo* (Milan: Sugarco, 1985). Genova was the police officer (from the DIGOS) directing the operation to free Dozier: he was originally elected to Parliament as a PSDI deputy but subsequently passed to the DC.

13. Direzione PCI, Sezione Problemi dello Stato: Federazione Milanese del PCI, Sezione Problemi dello Stato: *Primo Rapporto sull'Inchiesta di Massa sul Terrorismo* (Milan: May 1982).

14. The details in the following paragraphs are taken from the testimonies of the police and security services chiefs to the CPM (Parlato and Corsini (vol. 3); Coronas, Grassini, Santovito, Dalla Chiesa, Cappuzzo and Santillo (vol. 4); De Francesco, Fariello and Ferrara (vol. 5)). A more accessible account of some aspects, treated over a longer period, is G. De Lutiis, *Storia dei servizi segreti in Italia* (Rome: Editori Riuniti, 1984).

15. See also *L'Espresso*, 18 June 1978, pp. 31–43. Cossiga (CPM, vol. 3, p. 236) reports that former SdS staff were reluctant to join the political offices of their local *questure* because they saw such a move as a career block.

16. CPM, vol. I, p. 36, for details of the volume of checks made by the police between 16 March and 10 May. The magistrate Infelisi's comment on the state of the Rome DIGOS is in CPM, vol. 7, p. 136.

17. Letter of Peci to Dalla Chiesa, reprinted in *L'Espresso* (1980), 28 December 1980, no. 52, pp. 17–19 ('It is with you that I have negotiated my surrender-confession, not with the politicians').

18. CPM, vol. 4, p. 400.

19. CPM, vol. 4, p. 332.

20. This cultural barrier to knowledge is emphasised by Cappuzzo (CPM, vol. 4, pp. 406–8) and, indirectly, by Genova, *Missione antiterrorismo*, Ch. 1.

21. CPM, vol. I, pp. 53–4.

22. For Peci see Dalla Chiesa (CPM, vol. 4, p. 251). The infiltration

leading to the arrest of Red Brigades' members Moretti and Fenzi led to criminal charges and a suspended jail sentence against the police officer responsible. He had organised not merely the planting of bombs to ensure his very fragile agent's credibility with the Red Brigades but also insisted on sharing in the profits from an armed robbery committed separately by the same provocateur. A further infiltration of *Autonomia*-based groups by the CC in Varese and Milan was admitted after the *Rosso*-Tobagi trial but its effectiveness was not revealed. Other double-roles (Senzani as an agent of the SISDE) have occasionally been suggested, without serious evidence or great plausibility.

23. M. Laudi, 'I nuclei di polizia giudiziaria: alcuni rilievi critici sul loro funzionamento e prospettive di rinnovamento', in G. Cotturri and M. Ramat (eds), *Quali garanzie* (Bari: De Donato, 1983), pp. 203–7. For the situation in Rome at the time of the Moro kidnapping see the testimony of the magistrate directly involved, Infelisi (CPM, vol. 7, pp. 128–9).

24. Between 1978 and 1981 18 per cent of the 839 new recruits to the judiciary were aged 23 to 25, and 70 per cent between 25 and 30 years (survey reported in *La Repubblica*, 16–17 September, 1984, p. 7).

25. CPM, vol. 7, p. 150.

26. L. Pepino, 'L'attività e i problemi della giustizia nella lotta al terrorismo', paper presented at the conference *Perchè la barbarie non uccida la democrazia* (Turin: 21–2 March 1980) p. 5.

27. Figures quoted in the survey of the judiciary in *La Repubblica*, 16–17 September 1984, p. 7. Considerable resources were spent on ensuring protection for magistrates, politicians and senior public servants; between 1976 and 1986 the State spent 81 milliard lire on armour-plated cars alone, 68 milliard lire of which went to the Ministry of Justice (*La Repubblica*, 17 October 1986, p. 7, quoting the Minister of the Interior's response to a parliamentary question).

28. Those periods could be further increased if defendants were held deliberately responsible for causing delays or postponements of their trials, as the BR leadership managed to do between 1976 and 1978.

29. CPM, vol. 7, pp. 156, 204–5, 212.

30. See *Il Manifesto*, 26 May 1984, pp. 1, 8.

31. According to a survey of members of the judiciary organised by MI in 1984, only 4.8 per cent of respondents believed that stronger judicial control over the *polizia giudiziaria* was an urgent reform priority and only 2.7 per cent were convinced of the immediate need for centralised data banks (*La Giustizia Chiesta dai Giudici*: Speciale Adnkronos no. 4 (December 1985) p. 15, Table 8.

32. M. Barbone, interview, June 1984. At the trial of *Prima Linea* members in Florence in July 1983, S. Ronconi claimed that Galli had been murdered for having extended the concept 'membership of an armed band' to cover actions previously defined as the less serious offence of mere 'assistance' (*favoreggiamento*) (*La Repubblica*, 29 July 1983, p. 10). Galli's enquiries and conclusions were regarded as so generally penetrating that two different armed groups independently

planned his murder (F. Calvi, *Camarade P38* (Paris: Grasset, 1982) Ch. 10).

33. An extended discussion of the different resolutions of the problems of legal definitions of criminal associations is provided by G. C. Caselli and A. Perduca, 'Terrorismo e reati associativi: problemi e soluzioni giurisprudenziali', *Giurisprudenza italiana*, vol. CXXXIV (1982) Part IV, cols 209–40.

34. *L'Area della Detenzione Politica in Italia*, pp. 24–7. The survey was based on a snowball sample initiated in Rome, numerically privileging the local practitioners of violence. Since arrests and trials in Rome had come considerably later than in Milan and Turin, it may be that the difference in treatment in Rome is only apparent: those initially charged with conspiracy in Milan and Turin and subsequently acquitted of all but a membership offence would have been released from prison by 1984 and could not therefore have fallen into the sample. Furthermore the differences between Rome and cities other than Milan and Turin are not nearly so marked in the case of membership plus conspiracy charges (p. 26). Nevertheless, when taken in conjunction with the following specific case, the research data probably does capture a significantly greater judicial emphasis on collective responsibility in Rome than elsewhere. It could of course also be true that the decision-making processes actually *were* more collective in the Rome cases included in the survey than in those for other cities.

35. Details of the UCC case are taken from sentence no. 1075, pronounced by the First Penal Section of the Court of Cassation, 31 May 1985.

36. *Contro le regole di questo assurdo gioco* (1982) no. 0, p. 9; (1982) Summer, p. 15. Similar proportions are shown for the trials of various groups in Bergamo, Brescia, Florence. A more detailed breakdown is given in Table 6.1 below.

37. Details of the discussion before the CSM's disciplinary committee concerning the accusations made by the Roman magistrate, F. Misiani, can be found in *Il Foro Italiano*, vol. III (1982) p. 513. The better-publicised case against the Milan magistrates R. Canosa and A. Santosuosso, based on an interview in *Il Manifesto*, 30 October 1981, is set out in the sentence of the CSM, 23 March 1984. Their response can be found in the monthly *Alfabeta* (1984) no. 61 (June), p. 37.

38. Peci, *Io, l'infame*, p. 103.

39. See the arguments of the lawyer and Peci's fellow-defendant (acquitted), G. Spazzali, 'Il gioco e le candele', *Controinformazione* (1981) no. 8 (April) pp. 3–4.

40. That broad definition was adopted by the Turin magistrate M. Laudi: see his *Ordinanza di rinvio a giudizio contro Albesano F. e altri*, no. 321/80, Tribunale di Torino, p. 223.

41. Marco Barbone was initially criticised by a fellow collaborator, M. Ferrandi, for having included too many marginal figures (see the unpublished transcript of the *Rosso*-Tobagi trial, Tribunale di Milano, pp. 411–12). Considerable numbers of defendants presented autobiographical accounts of their political trajectories to the examining

magistrates, to stand alongside the formal record of their interrogations. As I shall indicate in Chapter 6, the courtroom could also be used for oral accounts in the same genre.

42. E. Fenzi (*Memoriale*, 27 September 1982, pp. 33–4) reports that his brother-in-law, Senzani, moved around with him two large suitcases containing the entire array of Red Brigades' information and analyses on the prison system.

43. F. Amato, *Ordinanza* no. 995/81, p. 2926.

44. Ibid., p. 2934. Amato also noted that in passing sentence on the alleged leader of the UCC, the judge had suggested that he be incriminated for armed insurrection. Had that happened, even minor groups would have been drawn into the accusation.

45. For relevant extracts from these sentences see L. Pepino, 'Il delitto di insurrezione armata tra mito e realtà', *Questione Giustizia*, vol. I (1982) pp. 647–70. Pepino refers to other juridical discussions of the charge, as well as providing the history of its use on which I have drawn above.

46. See the extracts from both magistrates in G. De Lutiis (ed), *Attacco allo Stato* (Rome: Napoleone, 1982), especially pp. 29–35, 107–14. Amato's *ordinanza-sentenza* contains an extended and inaccurate account of the social origins and motivations of BR members, suggesting that they were equally open to participation in right-wing and left-wing violence and their ultimate destination to the Left was a matter of simple chance (p. 2954).

47. Calogero made it known in an interview to *Panorama*, 23 May 1978, reprinted in Palombarini, *7 Aprile*, pp. 169–71, as well as in a later interview with *Corriere della Sera*, 6 July 1979. He used the same newspaper, on 9 October 1984, to describe how his initial stimulus to investigate Negri had come at his wife's prompting and how he had begun by examining Negri's academic works on political theory (p. 1).

48. See the so-called Carta di Cadenabbia, published in *Critica Sociale* (1979) no. 10, pp. 38–48. Interviews in a subsequent issue of the same journal (no. 14, pp. 24–5) elicited analogous views from two Milan magistrates.

49. *Nuovasocietà* (1981) 13 June, no. 195, p. 9 (translation DM). A succinct extract incorporating this conclusion from his judicial document (*requisitoria*) is contained in De Lutiis, *Attacco allo Stato*, pp. 29–35.

50. Calogero argued, for example, that the simultaneous appearance of the term *stato imperialista delle multinazionali* in a text by the former *Autonomia* leader, Ferrari Bravo, and in a Resolution of the Red Brigades' 'Strategic Direction' in 1975 must indicate direct collusion (De Lutiis, *Attacco allo Stato*, pp. 56–7). The full range of the incriminating terms was displayed in the pre-trial interrogations of Negri and his fellow-defendants (see *Processo all'Autonomia*, *passim*). For the magistrate's benefit Negri's lawyers produced an extended glossary which set out quite different meanings for the most significant terms in their client's ideological production.

51. De Lutiis, *Attacco allo Stato*, pp. 109–10.

52. Interview in *La Repubblica*, 30 October 1981, p. 10. The following

summary of Palombarini's argument is taken from his *sentenza-ordinanza* deposited on 4 September 1981 and reprinted in G. Palombarini, *7 Aprile*. It is worth noticing that while Palombarini reserved his public comments until he had completed his enquiries, Calogero was much more loquacious – permitting himself considerable freedom to criticise Palombarini in interviews.

ن STAGING POLITICAL TRIALS

1. The largest trial of all – 452 BR members indicted for armed insurrection – was finally begun in 1989. Even more gigantic trials for non-political organised crimes were begun in the mid-1980s against *camorristi* in Naples and *mafiosi* in Palermo.

2. For a recent discussion of Van Gennep's approach to ritual, see J. La Fontaine, *Initiation* (Harmondsworth: Penguin, 1985), especially pp. 24–9.

3. Having participated in a debate on Milan's violence in the 1970s, a defendant in the *Rosso*-Tobagi trial (Laura Motta) invited the audience to confront their 'theories' with the reality by attending the court proceedings. Large-scale seminars were organised by the Left and former extra-parliamentary Left in Milan during the *Rosso*-Tobagi trial and in Rome during the April 7 trial in 1983. Milan saw two further collective examinations of the 1970s in 1985 after local magistrates had arrested a dozen former members from one of the *servizi d'ordine* of the group *Avanguardia Operaia* for the murder of Ramelli a decade earlier.

4. Law 534, 8 August 1977, article 2. The law empowered the judiciary to override the normal effects of mutual relevance (*connessione*) in certain cases. One of its side-effects was to threaten to deprive defendants of the benefits in fixing the scale of punishment which normally accrued from dealing on a single occasion with multiple related infractions.

5. See the public prosecutor's *requisitoria* no. 921/80F, pp. 134–5. The Turin magistrate's description itself built on the more formal analysis of an armed band by the Milan magistrate Galli.

6. For some of those defendants' views see *Italia 1983: Prigionieri Processi Progetti* (Rome: Apache, 1983), pp. 15–17. I consider the conflicts in the Tobagi case below.

7. The four measures were contained in laws 534/1977, 74/1978 and 191/1978. The rules on jurors and expulsions were a direct response to the problems raised by the BR trial in Turin.

8. The similar effects of positioning supergrass witnesses in the Diplock courts in Northern Ireland have been noted: see T. Gifford, *Supergrasses: The use of accomplice evidence in Northern Ireland* (London: The Cobden Trust, 1984), pp. 20, 33.

9. The first public defence of the *dissociato* stance is generally credited to a member of PL, Roberto Vitelli, in the Viterbo courtroom and in two articles written for *Il Manifesto* in September 1981. A more elaborate

later defence came in the so-called 'document of the 51', authored by a heterogeneous array of defendants in Rebibbia jail and published in *Il Manifesto*, 30 September 1982 (reprinted in A. Chiaia (ed.), *Il proletariato non si è pentito* (Milan: Giuseppe Maj Editore, 1984, pp. 446–51).

10. The first proposal by parliamentary deputies to reward dissociation without collaboration was made in March 1983 (bill no. 3983, Boato and others) and was revived in the Senate in October of the same year after the elections (bill no. 221, De Martino and others). The government's draft bill, presented to Parliament by the Minister of Justice in December 1984, was eventually passed, after much debate and modification, in February 1987 ('Misure a favore di chi si dissocia dal terrorismo', published in the *Gazzetta Ufficiale*, 21 February 1987, no. 43, pp. 3–6). Its major terms established: 1) Recognition as a *dissociato* required the unequivocal abandonment of all former links to an armed group, admission of all personal responsibilities, behaviour clearly incompatible with any continuing association with armed struggle, and explicit repudiation of violence as a method of political struggle; 2) Eventual beneficiaries included persons, whether presently on trial or previously convicted, who already met those criteria or who, within 30 days of the law's coming into force, informed their public prosecutor that they intended to make the necessary declarations. The law excluded anyone who was charged with massacre (*strage*) or who had already benefited from the repentance laws of 1980 and 1982; 3) The law only covered crimes committed before 31 December 1983; 4) Its provisions converted life imprisonment into a 30-year sentence; sentences for the most serious crimes were reduced by one-quarter, for conspiracy and minor charges alone by one-half and for all others by one-third.

11. Although all deliberations in reaching verdicts must remain secret, the accounts by jurors in the BR 1978 trial (A. Aglietta, *Diario di una giurata popolare al processo delle Brigate Rosse* (Milan: Milano Libri Edizioni, 1979)) and in the Moro appeal trial ('Io, giudice popolare', *Il Manifesto*, 15 March 1985 p. 3) make clear the professional judges' guiding role.

12. See his speech as regional President of the ANM at the ceremonial opening of the judicial year in Turin in January 1979, reprinted in E. Papa, *Il processo alle Brigate Rosse* (Turin, Giappichelli, 1979), pp. 259–63. The point of his accusations will become clear from the discussion of the BR trial below.

13. Sentence no. 30/83, delivered in the Assise Appeal Court of Milan, p. 99. Cassone's comments are worth setting out in full, although of course they cannot be taken as representative of the entire category of judges who dealt with left-wing violence.

> [The legislator], after having ignored for years, or having tolerated for the advantage of politicians in power, the growth of left-wing terrorism and its subterranean links with the Right and with the criminal underworld, aroused himself only when it had gone beyond

every tolerable limit – tolerable, that is, not for the State but for the political élite itself when terrorism began to cut into 'the heart of the State' in which politicians identified themselves. Thereafter came a succession of repressive laws; the removal or weakening of constitutional guarantees; the construction of ever more 'maximally secure', and therefore inhuman, jails; the reduction of the administration of justice to fortresses where the judge is held in suspicion by the new heavily-armed praetorian guards, as well as being subjected to body searches while he sets out to administer justice in the name of the Italian people; the resumption of decrees of the Sacred Inquisition with the immoral and barbarous prize to *delatori* proportionate to the number of human beings that they manage to get thrown into jail.' (pp. 98–9. Translation DM).

14. The successful candidates from the magistrates involved in investigations of left-wing violence were: A. Bernardi, V. Borraccetti, G. Palombarini, G. C. Caselli, P. Calogero, M. Maddalena, E. Paciotti.

15. In the UCC case the sentences were considerably reduced on appeal; and the Bergamo judge felt constrained to defend the court sentence publicly (although generically) in a letter to one of his critics printed in *La Stampa* on 15 September 1982.

16. In this case the anonymous juror, in the interview in *Il Manifesto*, 15 March 1985, p. 3, indicated explicitly that 'it was [the judge] who applied and helped us to apply ... the law as it existed before the appearance of terrorism'.

17. At least two of the seven (Senese, Spazzali, Arnaldi, Lombardi, Fuga, Cappelli, Zezza) have since been acquitted, one committed suicide, two were convicted and two are presently on trial. For one set of views on the difficulties of their role see M. Fini, 'In nome della legge avvocato [sic] alzatevi', *Il Settimanale*, 20 May 1980, pp. 18–21.

18. For an account of these problems, and the acknowledged pressure to de-politicise her own professional work, see B. Guidetti Serra in L. Manconi, *Vivere con il terrorismo* (Milan: A. Mondadori, 1980), pp. 27–34. Her analysis of a lawyer's dilemmas in a particular instance can be found in B. Guidetta Serra, 'Il ruolo dell'avvocato attraverso la cronaca di un processo', *Quaderni Piacentini* (1978) no. 67–8, pp. 49–74; no. 69, pp. 49–68.

19. For the most articulate statement of this position by a defence lawyer see the interview with Marcello Gentili in *La Repubblica*, 28 December 1980. Both he, as defender of Fioroni and Barbone, and the lawyer of Peci were respectively threatened and wounded for their roles.

20. I owe this description to Nerio Diodà. His summary of the general issues involving the defence in the trials of political violence is valuable: 'Valutazioni sulle esperienze di difesa nei "processi politici" ', in G. Cotturri and M. Ramat (eds), *Quali garanzie* (Bari: De Donato, 1983), pp. 100–14. For a specific *cahier de doleances* by a defence lawyer in the *Rosso*-Tobagi trial see the document by A. Medina reproduced in P. Scorti, *Il delitto paga?* (Milan: Sugarco, 1985), pp. 249–53.

21. See the testimony of one of Curcio's lawyers, Guiso, to the CPM (vol. 6, pp. 165–283). One of the defendants has subsequently confirmed their exclusion from any direct involvement in the Moro kidnapping: see A. Franceschini: *Mara, Renato e io* (Milan: A. Mondadori, 1988).
22. Guiso, pp. 209–10.
23. The two different sets of lawyers finally nominated in 1976 and 1978 included very heterogeneous specialists. The Red Brigades' original lawyers asked not to be nominated by the court: no doubt others sympathetic to the extreme Left were not selected in the knowledge that they would offer the same reasons for resisting nomination. The following details are taken from accounts by two defence lawyers nominated in 1978: Papa, *Il processo alle Brigate Rosse*, *passim*, and B. Guidetti Serra: 'Il ruolo dell'avvocato attraverso la cronaca di un processo', no. 67–8, pp. 49–74; no. 69, pp. 49–68.
24. See G. Prandstraller, *Avvocati e metropoli* (Milan: F. Angeli, 1981) Chapter 6.
25. *Eversione, democrazia e rinnovamento dello Stato* (Milan: Teti, 1977), p. 81.
26. Papa, *Il processo alle Brigate Rosse*, p. 115; Serra, in Manconi, *Vivere con il terrorismo*, p. 30.
27. The petition is reproduced in Consiglio regionale del Piemonte, *Una Regione contro il terrorismo* (Turin: 1979), p. 151. An analogous petition had earlier been used in Milan on the occasion of a trial in May 1977.
28. Some commentators saw a conservative bias in the mainly petty-bourgeois and professional class composition of juries in Italy. The actual Turin jury was occupationally heterogeneous: two blue-collar workers, an artisan, a railway employee, three white-collar workers, a housewife, a bank clerk, two insurance agents, a trainee lawyer, the national secretary of the Radical Party (see her account referred to in note 11) and a pensioner.
29. Substantial extracts from the sentence are reproduced in *Quale Giustizia* (1978) nos. 47–8, pp. 6–64. Papa, Aglietta and representatives of *Magistratura Democratica* – among many others – agreed that the handling of the courtroom interaction and the arguments motivating the sentence offered the defendants every guarantee that the legal system provided.
30. In the PCI's 1981–2 survey, in reply to a question on the actions of police and magistrature against terrorism, the largest single group of respondents (38 per cent) claimed that the State had been too permissive – a response consistent with the already-noted sizeable reservoir of support for harsher sanctions (see Direzione PCI, Sezione Problemi dello Stato: Federazione Milanese del PCI, Commissione Problemi dello Stato, *Primo Rapporto sull'Inchiesta di Massa sul Terrorismo* (Milan: May 1982), p. 38).
31. For the BR revisions of their own, and their opponents', alleged aims, see the documents reprinted in Papa, *Il Processo alle Brigate Rosse*, *passim*; their final assessment is at pp. 235–56.
32. The following details are taken from the transcript of the trial. In

building up the characteristics of the different types of account I have also drawn on the statements, depositions and autobiographical documents of defendants in other trials in Milan. All trials relying on confessions showed a similar pattern of accounting strategies.

33. See the article 'Quel processo così sofferto' (*La Repubblica*, 11 March 1987, p. 8) by the President of the 3rd Section of the Milan Appeal Court, Luigi Giucciardi. His assessment of the effect of the trial, which had just been annulled on purely technical grounds by the Court of Cassation (preceding an identical decision annulling the sentences on PL members by the Appeal Court in Turin) was that its successful encouragement of dialogue with former enemies had recovered for civil society at least 100 defendants.

34. For some empirical examples (public appeals to desert from armed groups, interviews proclaiming individual defection) from Genoa and Turin see L. Saraceni, 'Ancora sulla dissociazione dal terrorismo', *Questione Giustizia*, vol. II (1983) no. 4, pp. 769–802.

35. Notably the somewhat enigmatic Corrado Alunni, one of the very few clandestine apparatchiks of *Autonomia*, who had maintained his earlier links to the Red Brigades. According to one hypothesis, he had acted as a long-standing double agent for the BR in other Milanese groups.

36. Direzione PCI, Sezione Problemi dello Stato: Federazione Milanese del PCI: Commissione Problemi dello Stato, *Primo Rapporto sull'Inchiesta di Massa sul Terrorismo*, pp. 37, 46. 59 per cent of the overall national sample was unequivocally in favour of the repentance legislation: but 31 per cent of blue-collar workers and 38 per cent of shopkeepers and artisans in Milan considered the provisions inadmissable. For the results of later public opinion polls on the issue of reductions in sentences for terrorists, see Chapter 4 note 45 p. 291–92.

37. An Association for the Victims of Terrorism was formed, headed by a local DC politician in Turin, M. Puddu wounded by the Red Brigades in 1978. According to Puddu, few of its members had received financial compensation from the State by 1987, although by law 466/1980 grants of tax-exempt 100 million lire were available to victims. For discussion of the limitations on eligibility among victims (at least 80 per cent invalidity required) and the refusal of the government to extend the coverage of law 466 (already retrospective to 1 January 1973) see the correspondence between another DC victim and the Minister of the Interior reprinted in A. Iosa, *Ad un passo della morte: un 'gambizzato' dalle b.r. racconta* (Milan: Quaderno n. 7 del Circolo C. Perini, 1982) pp. 38–42.

38. The only analogous case of active kin-based contestation of confessions was the Moro appeal trial. Two of the lawyers representing the families of Moro's bodyguards and associated with the PCI contested the accounts given by the semi-repentant BR members Morucci and Faranda. One (Zupo) co-authored a book on the kidnapping which argued that the affair was orchestrated from abroad, directed against the PCI (see G. Zupo and V. Marini Recchia, *Operazione Moro* (Milan: F. Angeli, 1984)).

39. The motivations of Tobagi's father are clearly indicated in an interview with him in 1982, reprinted in Scorti, *Il delitto paga?* pp. 219–23. The book, published under the auspices of the PSI on the eve of the appeal trial, sets out the party's case.

40. In a Milan party broadsheet the PSI compared its two martyrs to violence: Matteotti and Tobagi (*Il Garofano Rosso*, June 1983, no. 5, p. 4).

41. Despite the formal separation between the April 7 defendants and the Red Brigades, an informal connection was cultivated after 1980. Several *Autonomia* leaders were incriminated for active participation in the Trani jail riot organised by the BR in late 1980; one (Piperno) was subsequently incriminated for involvement in Moro's kidnapping and murder; and – on a more obviously symbolic plane – the Roman judiciary initially intended to celebrate the Moro and April 7 trials in the same courtroom in alternate weeks.

42. One of the deaths was particularly tragic, although hardly terroristic: the manslaughter of a wealthy left-wing militant (Saronio) during a kidnapping by his fellow-activists to finance their work, the ransom being demanded from his family even after his death. The peculiar horror of this episode made it the charge above all others on which the defendants alleged to have been involved protested their innocence and sought to distance themselves from Fioroni who had confessed his own role.

43. In September 1983 Parliament voted, first, to waive Negri's immunity from prosecution and, second, to permit his re-arrest – which could not be carried out, however, since his extradition was refused by the French authorities. Negri was soon to be disowned by the party that had secured his election, and his interviews given to Italian press and television earned him little public sympathy.

44. See *Amnesty International Newsletter*, vol. xiii (1983) no. 8 (August) pp. 4–5. It ought to be said that the concern voiced also by the Italian intelligentsia was not widely shared outside it: in a survey taken after Negri's escape two-thirds (62.9 per cent) of respondents were in favour of his immediate return to jail despite the long period already served: fewer than one in five (18 per cent) thought that he was entitled to some form of alternative detention such as house arrest (*L'Espresso*, 9 October 1983, p. 24).

45. 'Do You Remember Revolution?, *Il Manifesto*, 20–2 February 1983. Their broad arguments were outlined most succinctly in that article but had earlier been diffused to various audiences through *Alfabeta*, *Metropoli* and the broadsheet *setteaprile* as well as through collective letters addressed to a wider public (for a good example see *La Repubblica*, 9 November 1982, p. 6).

46. It refused, on the other hand, to consider a last-minute letter from his former lawyer, Gentili, who asserted that, without wishing to betray the confidentiality of his relationship with the client whom he had publicly disowned precisely for refusing to confirm his evidence in court, Fioroni's original description of responsibilities for Saronio's kidnapping and death could not have withstood questioning. Even if it

had not, however, Fioroni's evidence on the other charges was not thereby directly weakened, although of course his general credibility was put at risk.

47. For two particularly bizarre sets of prolonged interrogations (bizarre because of the distance between the evidence contested and the accusations of armed insurrection against the State) see the transcripts of the interrogations of Ferrari Bravo, reprinted in *Adierre* (Venice: Com 2, 1983) and Vesce, reprinted in *4 anni, 6 mesi* ... (Venice: Com 2, 1983).

48. Negri had explicitly dissociated himself from the remnants of *Autonomia* in 1981 (see Chiaia, *Il proletariato non si è pentito*, pp. 445–6). Some defendants who had been freed before the trial began participated in public meetings with residual members of the extreme Left, such as were held in the Libreria Claudiana in Milan in early 1984. However the major topics were repentance, dissociation and the possibility of a generalised amnesty rather than any revival of direct political commitment.

49. The eventual outcome of the localised Calogero–Palombarini dispute over the intelligentsia's role in the allegedly centralised organisation of *Autonomia* in Padua favoured Palombarini's version. Notwithstanding the heavy penalties demanded by Calogero as public prosecutor, six of the same April 7 defendants were acquitted by the Padua court in January 1986 on all charges of direct logistical and organisational involvement in local armed groups.

7   CUI PRODEST?

1. Some years later it was revealed that Moro had had two secret and apparently influential meetings with the PCI secretary, Berlinguer, shortly before his kidnapping; see the account given by L. Barca in *Enrico Berlinguer* (Rome: L'Unità, 1985).

2. See the analysis by Barbagli and Corbetta, 'After the Historic Compromise: A Turning Point for the PCI', *European Journal of Political Research*, vol. 10 (1986) pp. 213–39. The evidence on the PCI's reluctance to vote for the Andreotti government in March 1978 and the decisive impact of Moro's kidnapping comes from F. Di Giulio and E. Rocco, *Un ministro–ombra si confessa* (Milan: Rizzoli, 1979) pp. 65–6.

3. The issues included: the alleged role of the President of the DC in ransom negotiations; his connections with leading figures in the *camorra*; reticence on the part of the victim in his accounts to the investigating magistrate; and false accusations by the PCI against senior Neapolitan DC politicians for involvement in the negotiations.

4. See the comments of the former president of the Committee for Small Business and subsequent chairman of the Turin city transport department, Ravaioli, who was wounded by the Red Brigades in 1978 (*La Repubblica*, 21 September 1985, p. 9). De Carolis and Tedeschi (Milan), Castellano and Peschiera (Genoa) and Fiori (Rome) were among the other political victims who continued their careers.

5. G. Guidorossi *Gli italiani e la politica* (Milan: F. Angeli, 1984) pp. 214–15, Table 4.
6. P. Corbetta and H. Schadee, 'Le caratteristiche sociali e politiche dell'astensionismo elettorale in Italia', *Il Politico*, vol. XLVII (1982) no. 4, pp. 671, 673.
7. Ibid., *passim*. Abstention here includes failure to vote at all and the consignment of invalid ballot papers.
8. The DC gained nearly 5 per cent, alongside an even greater loss (9 per cent) for the PCI. However, in two of the major centres, Pavia and Viterbo, the temporary nature of this shift was shown by the losses sustained by the DC in the subsequent elections in 1983.
9. Figures from the *Annuario Statistico Italiano* (Rome: ISTAT, 1983) p. 134, Table 129; *ASI* (Rome: ISTAT, 1984) p. 118, Table 121. The best-known victims were General Dalla Chiesa, murdered with his wife in Palermo in September 1982, and the PCI deputy, Pio La Torre.
10. An opportunity to offer reduced sentences in exchange for collaboration, had the political élite decided to make the extension, could have been provided by the major legal measure introduced to combat the mafia more effectively, the La Torre law 646/1982.
11. The defendant, Tortora, was elected a European MP in 1984 and subsequently became president of his party. At the first trial he was sentenced to ten years' imprisonment but was acquitted on appeal.
12. See, for example, the arguments of the Attorney-General in Rome (M. Boschi, 'Dal pentitismo all'antipentitismo', *La Repubblica*, 4 October 1986, p. 8).
13. In 1986 the Radical Party found no difficulty, therefore, in collecting sufficient signatures to launch three referenda on the accountability of magistrates, the abolition of the standing Parliamentary Committee to verify (and frequently block) charges against members and the system of election of political and professional candidates to the CSM.
14. Figures on the prison population and its composition, as at 31 December each year, have been taken from the *Annuario Statistico Italiano*. The trajectory for the entire period shows a steady annual increase, punctuated only by short-lived falls after the amnesties of 1978 and 1981.
15. By law 398/1984, with effect from November 1985 for terrorist offences, the overall maximum term for preventive detention was fixed at six years, with specification also of the sub-maxima for each phase of the investigation from arrest to irrevocable sentence. As a result many prisoners had to be released as the legal limits of their detention were reached. In the cases of annulment of lower courts' sentences by the Court of Cassation (Chapter 6, n. 33, p. 304) release of at least minor defendants was virtually assured. According to the Minister of Justice, 7999 men and women had to be released in 1986 (*La Repubblica*, 22 April 1987, p. 15). In November 1986 the limits for the phase prior to the first verdict were extended by one-third for serious crimes, including political violence, although the cumulative total remained unchanged: the extension was introduced specifically to prevent the

release of the defendants in the *mafia* maxi-trial in Palermo before its conclusion.

16. The text of the ministerial circular no. 3068/5518, 31 October 1984, abolishing the use of article 90 and containing a detailed description of the surveillance techniques to remain in force, is reprinted in *Il Bollettino del Coordinamento dei Comitati contro la Repressione* (1984) no. 15, pp. 4–6.

17. Official encouragement to prison management to create 'homogeneous areas' was contained in the Ministry circular of 3 September 1983, reprinted in A. Chiaia (ed.), *Il proletariato non si è pentito* (Milan: G. Maj, 1984) pp. 268–72. Details of the negotiations between Amato and Franceschini (ex-BR) to create one in Novara prison in mid-1984 are contained in the letters reprinted in *Il Bollettino del Coordinamento dei Comitati contro la Repressione* (1984) no. 14, p. 12.

18. See the document 'Per il convegno a Rebibbia', dated August 1983 and signed by 40 members of the *area omogenea*, reprinted in D. Repetto (ed.): *Il clandestino è finito?* (Rome: AdnKronos Libri, 1984) pp. 78–83.

19. It has since been performed elsewhere. Use of *Antigone* to portray the issues behind armed struggle (recently by R. Rossanda, 'Introduzione', *Antigone* trans. L. Biondetti (Milan: Feltrinelli, 1988)) has been very controversial. It is strongly opposed by one of the BR's victims, Carlo Castellano, in 'Caro papà perché le BR hanno ucciso Ruffilli?', *La Repubblica*, 12 May 1988, pp. 1, 4. Other plays have also been staged: in December 1986 a group of female prisoners, mostly former members of PL, organised an evening in a Turin theatre for which they were released from jail for a few hours.

20. One deliberately innovative act of reconciliation with the State was taken by a group of Milan *dissociati* in November 1984: they indicated to the public prosecutor in their trial, Spataro, where the weapons which they had left buried could be found.

21. See, for example, M. Libardi in *Litterae Communionis*, vol. XI (1984) no. 1, p. 9. As the example of Libardi indicates, the use of religious discourse was by no means confined to *dissociati*. However its adoption by influential *dissociati* in jail (e.g., Vitelli, Funaro, Franceschini) gave them a more significant effect in weakening the prison–society boundary. For an example of their positions see the special insert 'Anni di piombo e coscienza cristiana', *Com-Nuovi Tempi* (1983) n. 32 (October 9) pp. 7–18.

22. N. O'Sullivan: 'Terrorism, Ideology and Democracy', in N. O'Sullivan (ed.), *Terrorism, Ideology and Revolution* (Brighton: Wheatsheaf Books, 1986) pp. 3–26.

23. Carole Beebe Tarantelli, 'Io, vedova delle BR, vi dico ...', *La Repubblica*, 1 February 1986, pp. 1–2 (translation DM). She explores similar themes at greater length in 'Io, Ezio e i terroristi', *Antigone* (1986) no. 1, pp. 3–5.

Index